HISTORY OF THE DARJEELING DISTRICT

HISTORY OF THE DARJEELING DISTRICT

ME. C. DOZEY

GYAN

Published by

Gyan Publishing House
5, Ansari Road
Daryaganj, New Delhi-110002
Phone: 011-47034999, 9811692060
E-mail: books@gyanbooks.com

Distribution Network
gyanbooks.com
India, USA, Canada, UK, Australia

ISBN: 978-93-7169-879-5 (PB)

First Published, 1835

2nd Impression 2025

Printed at: Gyan Press, Delhi.

HISTORY OF THE DARJEELING DISTRICT
Author: E. C. DOZEY

KINCHENJUNGA AT SUNSET.

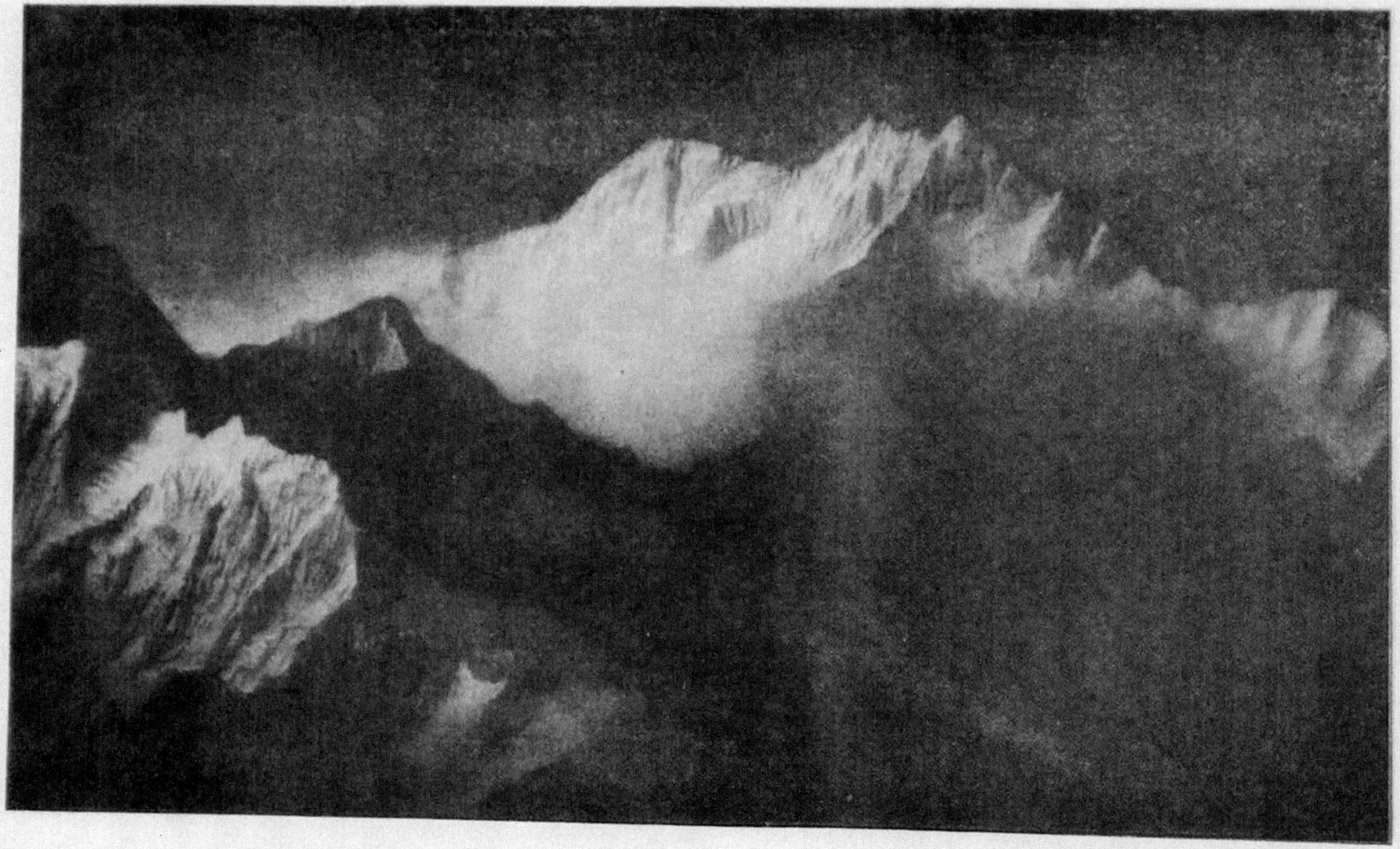

'Tis good to see the virgin snows
No man has ever trod,
The Saints alone, around His throne,
May walk the heights of God.

A CONCISE HISTORY OF THE DARJEELING DISTRICT SINCE 1835

WITH

A COMPLETE ITINERARY OF TOURS IN SIKKIM AND THE DISTRICT

E. C. DOZEY

Illustrated by 1 coloured and 20 half-tone Plates

"Just the cheering clasp of a friendly hand,
Just a word from one who can understand :
And we finish the task we long had planned."

TO

SADIE

TO WHOSE SOUND CRITICISM

AND KINDLY ENCOURAGEMENT

THIS WORK

OWES THE QUALITIES

FOR WHICH

IT WAS CHIEFLY COMMENDED

PREFACE

"A chiel's amang ye takin' notes,
And, faith, he'll prent 'em".—*Burns.*

The manner in which the first edition was received both by the public and the press has been gratifying in the extreme.

My thanks are due to the press, whose kindly attitude has encouraged the issue of this revised and enlarged edition, as the first had apparently, and to some extent however small, met a decided want. Thus encouraged, every work on the subject to be found in private as well as public libraries in Darjeeling, Calcutta and even the British Museum has, during the past five years, been referred to in order that each event and project which had contributed to the growth and prosperity of Darjeeling should find a place in this record. At the same time I have not been insensible to shortcomings in certain directions, sometimes in the form of errors that had escaped detection, often due to printer's pie, and accordingly an effort has herein been made to present to the reader a clean and accurate history of the district.

In many passages of the book material changes have been made ; much fresh material has been added especially in connection with the following :—The Tea Industry ; Tours in and around the district ; our relations with the State of Sikkim ;* while facts, figures and distances between the several stages in the Itinerary of Tours, which were taken from official records, have been so closely scrutinised as to preclude the possibility of errors occurring in this edition. The tourist may, therefore, safely depend upon the accuracy of the data now furnished.

The sum of these alterations and corrections will, it is hoped, be regarded as such an improvement of this work as will make it more worthy of the attention it received. The most of these changes have been made of my own motion ; but for some of them the reader is indebted to the late Dr. F. Kenay of 'West Point' whose knowledge of the 'Early History' of the district was unique.

Finally, the title and sub-title have been slightly modified, as neither succinctly set forth the full scope of the work.

E. C. DOZEY.

CALCUTTA

The 20th April, 1922.

---

*"*Sikkim & Bhutan*" by J. C. White (the first Political Officer of those States) ; and the Introduction to the *Sikkim Gazetteer* by H. H. Risley.

HINTS TO VISITORS.

E. B. Railway.

"He will sure take the hint from the picture I draw."—*Smollett.*

1. During the months of April and May, and again in September and October there is always a rush for Darjeeling. To secure a good seat on the *right* of the coach, so as to be away from the rays of the afternoon sun, be at the station at least half an hour before scheduled time.

2. But if there is any heavy luggage to book be at Sealdah even earlier ; and if possible, have your ticket purchased and the booking done during the forenoon.

3. The bedding, which accompanies you, is taken charge of by the through-guard, who will hand you a coupon in return, which must be surrendered at Santahar when changing into the night train.

4. Always have your night berth booked before undertaking the journey.

5. If four of a party travel together in the first, or second class, a compartment can be reserved for their exclusive use.

6. Ladies should always be provided with dust cloaks which will be needed shortly after leaving Sealdah, as the dust raised from the track smothers one.

7. From October to March a change to warmer garments while approaching Siliguri is necessary ; great-coats and wraps should be always handy so as to guard against the sudden and extreme changes of temperature experienced during the ascent to Darjeeling. From May to October a waterproof and an umbrella should form part of the tourist's outfit.

Invalids.

8. An invalid chair at Sealdah, Santahar and Siliguri, as also an invalid first class carriage on the hill section, can be arranged for at either terminus by giving 24 hours' notice to the respective Station Masters.

D. H. Railway.

9. Binoculars and cameras should always be handy or else much of the beauty of the panoramic views will be lost, especially on the hill section.

10. At Siliguri the traveller is only allowed 40 minutes in which to partake of *Chota hazree,* and to book his bedding. The following procedure should therefore be adopted :—As quickly as possible a seat on the *left* of a carriage in the toy-train should be acquired and the light luggage booked (for only handbags and wraps are allowed in the compartment on this line) before the refreshment room is entered. After the disposal of this meal if there is still a few minutes to spare, and the morning be clear, a fairly good view of the snowy range, which is 96 miles away, may be had from the south end of the platform.

Coupons.

11. Messrs. Thos. Cook & Sons' coupons are accepted at face value at all recognised hotels, while the Alliance Bank of Simla, Darjeeling Branch, is always prepared at a small charge to accept cheques on banks in Calcutta and other chief towns.

12. Beware of touts, and so-called 'guides'.

Mountain-Sickness.

The reason for recommending a seat on the *left* of a carriage is threefold :—1st. It is shielded from the early rays of the sun which at best of seasons are far from pleasant ; 2nd. It affords frequent views of the plains throughout the journey ; and 3rd. Prevents giddiness from which not a few suffer, due to the ever shifting scenes of the hillside which are forced on the vision when seated to the right of the carriage. Further, experiments conducted on Mt. Blanc (15,780′) have conclusively proved that ordinarily rarefied air has a marked effect on both the muscular and nervous systems owing to a diminution of the atmospheric pressure by which the blood is unable to extract a sufficiency of oxygen, and so brings about an increase both in the pulse and respiration, which induces many to feel faint. And if to these are added the disadvantages of a bad seat it follows that the effects are accentuated.

Remedies.

Asperine, or phenacetin, with brandy taken in small doses, it is claimed, affords relief, if it does not cure. Chlorate of potash taken in 10 grain doses in a wine-glass of water, repeated every two or three hours, if necessary, proved efficacious in the ascent of the Karakorum range, and was subsequently employed in Sir Douglas Forsyth's Mission to Yarkund in 1873-74 by the surgeon to the expedition who testifies "to its value in mitigating the distressing symptoms produced by a continued deprivation of the natural quantity of oxygen in the atmosphere. The large proportion of oxygen contained in the salt probably supplies the blood what in these regions it fails to derive from the air, and thus restores through the stomach what the lungs lose. Whatever the explanation of its action, however, there is no doubt of its efficacy in relieving the dreadful nausea and headache produced by the circulation of an inefficiently oxygenated blood"—so says Edward Whymper in his account of *"The Great Andes of the Equator"*.

For those who believe in homœopathy the following prescriptions may be followed with decided advantage as there is a marked similarity between sea-, and mountain-sickness:—

Coculus, 6th potency two drops, or globules taken during the journey and whenever the tendency to vomiting recurs.

Ipecacuanha—200th potency taken a day before journey and in case of those who suffer inordinately, a drop again before entraining.

DARJEELING, PAST AND PRESENT

PRESS NOTICES ON FIRST EDITION.

Capital of 18-5-17 :—"Mr. E. C. Dozey, who is not unknown in local journalism, has brought out a book on Darjeeling, which is something of a history, something of a guide, and pleasantly encyclopedic. His style is gossipy and his method instructive. The price of the book is Rs. 3/8, for which you get plenty of information and many attractive pictures."

The Englishman of 24-5-17 :—"Though this work may not originally have been intended for a *guide-book*, it is, nevertheless, *one and an excellent one too. Replete with information* of the kind that is most useful to the *Traveller and Visitor* to Darjeeling and its vicinity, it also contains chapters on Industries, Flora and Fauna, Shikar and reminiscences of the author who is a well-known personality in the district. Its list of tours and description of Kurseong, Kalimpong and Siliguri make interesting reading...........It will, by its fund of useful hints and information it contains, amply repay the purchaser; indeed, the book is one which all intending a trip, brief or prolonged, to the Queen of Hill Stations should be in possession of."

The Empire of 28-4-17.—"There are books which do all that is required of them in the "guiding" line without being blatantly of the guidebook type, and such an one is Mr. Dozey's work. In it one can get all the information needed about Darjeeling, Kurseong and other hill stations in the district with such notes upon their various activities, institutions, and industries *as to form a veritable compendium. But Mr. Dozey is most interesting when he comes to the subject of Pic-nics and Tours*, and here he is really at home for he has travelled widely on business affairs in the foothills of the great Himalayas."

The Darjeeling Advertiser of 1-5-17.—"Since the days the "Himalayan Art Journals" were written by the late Sir Joseph Hooker, several books and guides of Darjeeling have appeared. But the *literature* on Darjeeling *has certainly been enriched* by the publication of Darjeeling, Past and Present, which as its name implies contains a very interesting account of the past and present history of the district. Mr. Dozey being an old resident writes from personal knowledge and from records the collection of which must have entailed considerable trouble and study. He writes in an easy and descriptive style".

"To those who would learn all about Darjeeling, and to the *excursionist the work will supply systematised information under every conceivable head.*"

The Statesman of 16-6-17.—"This work has the great merit of being written by an old resident who knows every stick and stone in the neighbourhood, and who *has also the art of writing in an entertaining manner*. There is no subject in which Mr. Dozey does not take a lively interest. He tells you all about Old Darjeeling; describes the various hill people; and gives an account of trips out of Darjeeling. *In fact, Mr. Dozey has compiled a chatty guide which may well be found to be a more interesting companion on the journey to Darjeeling than much* recent *fiction.*"

PREFACE.

(1st Edition).

My little book, I send thee forth today
  Upon a sea of criticism, thy way,
Upon its voiceful waves, I'll watch, and if
  Thou'rt treated hardly, like many a tiny skiff
That has been launched, and lost, on other seas,
  I shall be pained; for thou art dear to me.

The materials which form the basis of this work were contributed, during the intervals of business, as *leaders* and articles to the defunct 'Darjeeling Times', and to the Press in general. Since then the writer has striven to obtain and place on record complete data under each head, and especially in connection with the several projects and industries which have contributed materially toward the growth and prosperity of Darjeeling, lest these in the march of events be as—"Ships That Pass In The Night."

The portions appertaining to the 'Early History' of Darjeeling were culled from 'The Darjeeling Gazetteer*', 'The Statistical Account of Bengal'* and 'The Hand Book of Darjeeling',* and amplified by the reminiscences of a few of the oldest residents in the district, to one of whom has been given the privilege of serenely looking back over the span allotted to man.

Chapters III to VI, Part I, to which are appended a Map of the Town, a Street Directory, and a List of the Principal Buildings, should enable the tourist and new-comer to find their way about without the aid of so-called 'guides' (Indians) who often as not prove more a bane than a boon: Parts II to IV are devoted respectively to the special features of Kurseong, Kalimpong and Siliguri; to the Itinerary and Sketch Map of Tours which should prove useful to tourists in their excursions in the

---

*By Mr. L. S. S. O'Malley, I.C.S., Dr. W. W. Hunter, I.C.S., and Capt. J. G. Hathorn, R.A., respectively.

District of Darjeeling and Sikkim ; and to the several Railway projects, sanctioned during the past two years and in the course of construction, by which the resources of Northern Bengal will be tapped.

In all works of an historical nature, criticisms will arise. In the few instances in which these occur—notably the article on the 'food problem' and its corollary 'an adequate fodder supply' on which the writer has had the temerity to advance solutions as, although the matter received the earnest attention of both the Forest Department and the Local Government, no practical solution was arrived at owing to these two moot questions not being fully understood, or considered by those at whose hands a solution was sought—the underlying motive has been the welfare of the populace, for the price of food products has been ever on the upward curve thereby bearing with undue hardship on the masses who under present conditions are barely able to eke out an existence. If the suggested solutions prove adequate, the powers-that-be should give immediate effect to them ; if inadequate, it is hoped that other and abler pens will thresh these problems threadbare until correct solutions have been arrived at.

The writer is obliged to Messrs. Johnston & Hoffmann of Calcutta, and Messrs. J. Burlington-Smith and M. Sain of Darjeeling, the last especially, for kind permission to reproduce their photographs (duly acknowledged on each) which illustrate this work.

Finally, it was the desire of the Author to produce a work worthy of Darjeeling : how far the effort has succeeded is left to the Reader to determine.

E. C. DOZEY.

DARJEELING,
The 28th June, 1916.

IN THE PRESS

FOREST LIFE IN INDIA

Being

Reminiscences of the Author

During Eight Years spent

IN THE FOREST

In connection with

His Timber Business.

CONTENTS.

Hints to Visitors.

DARJEELING.

PART I.

PART II.

KURSEONG.

PART III.

PART IV.

RAILWAYS.

APPENDICES.

ILLUSTRATIONS.

ADDENDA & CORRIGENDA.

ADDENDA.

1. Add to last footnote on page 2—

In return the Government of India has donated 10 lakhs per annum to this State for the material help given in the war. In 1920, we had 10 Gurkha regiments of 2 battalions each numbering 18,000 men.

2. Insert as a fresh sentence after "plant", line 7, para 2, page 16—

A little beyond the Panchanai bridge starts the confines of that notorious tract far-known as 'The Deadly Terai'. No spot in India, which is famed for its settings in antithesis and climax, can compare with this region, the mere mention of which conjures up from the nebulous past the shades of the greatest Saint that ever lived, and that also of the sorriest of Sinners that ever breathed the breath of life. It has given us the Gautama Budda, who was born in Kapalivastu in the Nepal Terai, and, strange to say, that ogre of execrable memory, the Nanna Sahib, the author of the Massacre at Cawnpore, who found no fitter asylum and a last resting place for his remains than these fever-, and mist-haunted tracts.

3. After "pine" in 1st footnote on page 18 add (*Pandamus Ultilissimus*).

4. Insert an asterisk after "Gurkha" in line 1, para 2, page 39, and add as footnote—

'Gurkha' does not mean a race but simply the followers of the King of Gurkha, which was in the centre of the Kingdom of Nepal.

5. Insert an asterisk after "panchayet", line 8, page 47, and add as a footnote—

Megasthenes, the Greek historian, who resided at the Court of Chandragupta (the grandfather of Asoka of Buddist fame) tells us that this system of self-government was inaugurated by that enlightened monarch in the year 325 B.C.

6. After "Mission Fields", page 73 insert an asterisk, and add as a footnote—See Appendix II—On Religions.

7. Insert a bracket after Rs. 6,600 in line 8, page 75.

8. After "Buddist Monasteries", page 76 insert an asterisk, and add See Appendix II A—On Buddism.

9. Insert "called" before 'Geylukpa' in line 2, para 2, page 80.

10. For the last 2 lines on page 183 read—of land at Seebpore covering 270 acres formed the nucleus of the Royal Botanic Garden, Calcutta. In the centre of this garden is the Kydd monument, a white marble Grecian urn with figures round it on a tall plinth surrounded by a circular base.

11. **After "spot", line 7, page 257, insert, Riang.**

CORRIGENDA.

1. For '2nd' in last line on page 23 ... Read, and.
2. ,, 'electroclier' last line on page 28 ... ,, electriclier.
3. ,, 'extend' in 2nd last line para. 1 page 38 ,, extended.
4. ,, 'track' line 4, para. 2, page 62 ... ,, trek.
5. Transfer 'in The Light of Asia' from line 4 to after Edwin Arnold in line 6, page 77.
6. For '18th' in line 13, page 79 Read 8th.
7. ,, 'Appendix II' in footnote on page 93 ... ,, Appendix IV.
8. ,, 'were', line 3. para. 4, page 96 ... ,, was.
9. ,, 'devasted' in 3rd last line, page 137 ... ,, devastated
10. ,, 'who' in 2nd last line, page 143 .. ,, which.
11. ,, 'consecreted' in line 6, page 148 ... ,, consecrated.
12. ,, 'lip-up' line 6, page 155 .. ,, tip-up.
13. ,, 'track', line 13, page 188 ... ,, tract.
14. ,, 'Appendix II' in footnote on page 206 ... ,, Appendix IV.
15. ,, 'Purest' in line 3, page 262 ... ,, pure.
16. ,, 'Jangri' in line 5, page 265 ... ,, Jongri.
17. ,, 'the' line 2, para. 2, page 271 ... ,, to.
18. ,, 'covered', line 1, para. 2, page 273 ... ,, covers.
19. ,, 'slight', line 9, para. 2, page 311 ... ,, slightest.
20. ,, second sentence, para. 1, page 319 read

The road here suddenly ascends a steep gravelly hill, and opens out on a short flat, or spur, from which the Himalayas rise abruptly clothed with forest from the very base. The little bungalow of Pankabari, my immediate destination, nestled in the woods crowning a lateral knoll, above which to the east and west, as far as the eye could see, were range after range of wooded mountains 6,000 to 8,000 feet high.

PLATE I.

THE QUEEN OF HILL STATIONS.

DARJEELING

CHAPTER I.

Foreword.

In these strenuous days when the struggle for existence shackles men to their desks, or keeps them tied to counters in the sweltering heat of the plains, the very mention of Darjeeling recalls memories of the last but too short week-end during which as much of pleasure as was possible was pressed into it. And yet that word 'pleasure' conveys so much and sometimes so little, according to the idiosyncracy of the individual, for some take their pleasures as they *come*: others *seek* them. The following data have accordingly been collated in order to afford the latter an opportunity of making their next visit, or it may be the first, to this Queen of Hill Stations interesting.

The majority of pleasure seekers, and even tourists take the toy-train to be a means to an end, while to the former Darjeeling stands for all that helps drive away cankering care evanescent though the respite be! Few, however, know of the circumstances under which this Sanitarium passed into our hands; or of the discomforts endured by tourists who undertook the journey between the years 1855 and 1877, which then cost fully Rs. 300/- as well as absorbed the best part of a fortnight,* but which is now accomplished in nineteen short hours; or that two routes (constructed at a great expenditure of money and the loss of many a life claimed by the deadly Terai through which the road from Siliguri to Pankabarie—just below Kurseong—wended its way) were adopted one after the other to be abandoned in turn for the last which now completely links Calcutta to Darjeeling, a distance of 386 miles, by railway.

*See Appendix I.

History.

History—I will answer you by quoting what I have read, somewhere or other, in Dionysius Halicarnassensis."—*Bolingbrooke.*

Prior to the year 1816 the whole of the territory known as British Sikkim belonged to Nepal, which had won it by conquest from the Sikkimese. Owing to a disagreement over the frontier policy of the Gurkhas, war* was declared towards the close of 1813 by the British, and two campaigns followed in the second of which they were defeated by General Ochterlony.† By a treaty‡ signed at Segoulie at the end of 1816 the Nepalese ceded the 4,000 square miles of territory referred to above, which in turn by a treaty signed at Titalya on February 10th, 1817, was handed over to the Rajah of Sikkim with the apparent object of hedging in Nepal with the kingdom of an ally, and preventing all possibility of further aggrandisement by the Gurkhas.

In 1828 Lt.-General (then Captain) G. A. Lloyd and Mr. J. W. Grant, I.C.S., the Commercial Resident at Maldah, after

---

*Strange to say, the necessary funds to prosecute this war to a successful issue were supplied by Arjunji Nathji of Surat; but to what extent has never transpired. For these services he was given a *khilat* by the Government 'for the joy of the capture of Nepal'. Not to be outdone, and in order to commemorate the honour conferred on him, he built a temple named Shri Balaji at a cost of 3 *lakhs* of rupees, and endowed it with the entire revenues of the village of Shewni , which had been granted to him in perpetuity by the Gaikwar. It is sad to relate that the descendants of this man, who was at one time the Rothschild of India, are starving at the present day in Surat.

†The Ochterlony Monument, which stands on the *maidan* (green) in Calcutta, recalls the achievements of this general who in conquering this race of warriors sowed the seeds of an everlasting friendship between Thomas Atkins and the Gurkha; and, indeed, between the two *rajs* as shewn below. From the gallery at the summit of this column, which is 165 feet from base to cupola, an excellent bird's-eye-view of the town of Calcutta may be had. Admission to it is granted by the Commissioner of Police.

‡By the same treaty, the Nepal Durbar ceded certain territories which have furnished us with sites for the principal hill stations in India:— Almorah (5,510′), Mussoorie (6,600′), Naini Tal (6,407′) and Simla (7,075′).

On the outbreak of the great war (1914) this State furnished two contingents numbering 13,950 men, at the same time refilling the gaps in the 38 battalions of the Gurkha Rifles by drafts of 8,000 men to keep them up to normal strength, *i.e.*, 30,400 of all ranks. Finally, it voluntarily contributed no less than 10 *lakhs* in cash, as well as furnished supplies, such as cardamomum and spices for Indian troops. Truly a great record for a State so small as Nepal!

settling the internal factions between the Nepal and Sikkim States, found their way into Chungtong (Plate XIX) to the west of Darjeeling, and were much impressed with the possibilities of the station as a sanitarium. The year following the former officer visited Darjeeling to be followed shortly after by Mr. Grant and Capt. J. D. Herbert, the then Deputy Surveyor General, Bengal, who likewise reported favourably on the situation of the hill of Darjeeling. The Court of Directors of the East India Company accordingly directed that Lt.-General Lloyd be deputed to start negotiations with the Sikkim Raj for a cession of the hill either for an equivalent in money or land. This transfer was successfully accomplished on February 1st, 1835, through the personal influence and efforts of Lt.-General Lloyd with Sikkimputti, the aged Rajah, who handed over a strip of hill territory, 24 miles long and about 5 to 6 miles wide, stretching from the northern frontier of the district to Pankabarie in the plains, which in its trend included the villages of Darjeeling and Kurseong, "as a mark of friendship for the Governor-General (Lord William Bentinck) for the establishment of a Sanitarium for the invalid servants of the East India Company". In return the Raja received an allowance of Rs. 3,000/-, which was subsequently raised to Rs. 6,000/- per annum. This exchange, however, considered at that time from a financial point of view was entirely in favour of the giver as the revenue derived from the hill never exceeded Rs. 20/- the year.

The year following we find Lt.-General Lloyd, who was appointed Local Agent, and Asst: Surgeon A. Chapman engaged in exploring the land and the trend of the country. In 1839 the appointment of Local Agent was abolished and Dr. Arthur D. Campbell, a member of the Indian Medical Service, and the Asst: Resident at the Court of Nepal, was appointed the first Superintendent, a post which he held for twenty-two years. The same year Lieut: Napier of the Royal Engineers (subsequently Lord Napier of Magdala) was deputed to lay out the town and construct a hill road which would connect at Siliguri with the Grand Trunk Road, measuring 126 miles, which had been started from Karagola Ghat opposite Sahibgunge on the

East Indian Railway, spanned five large rivers, and eventually completed in 1866 at a cost of Rs. 14,68,000/-.

The trace of the Calcutta Road to the east of the hill on which the Jalapahar Cantonment stands was completed in January, 1838, by Lt.-General Lloyd.

In a short time the town boasted of a drive 16 miles long, of a broad road named after the Governor-General, Lord Auckland, while the alignment of a road, since known as the old Military Road, measuring 40 miles, was started in 1839 and completed in 1842 at an expenditure of Rs. 8,00,000/-. The trace of this road may still be seen from Pankabarie in the Terai winding its way up to and past Kurseong, having no less than 300 bridges to cross, where it ascends to Down Hill to the east of that station, and continues on its course along the spurs until it reaches Senchal when it descends suddenly to Jorebungalow near Ghum, from where it gradually rises and worms round the east of the hill until the Chowrasta is reached. This road unfortunately proved unsuitable* for the cart traffic owing to its steep gradients, and as it was also found incapable of meeting the expanding requirements of the district, sanction was accordingly obtained in 1861 for the construction of the Cart Road,† from Siliguri to Darjeeling, 25 feet in width, which cost about £6,000 per mile. It is on this highway chiefly that the Darjeeling Himalayan Railway works its way in and out of the several spurs slowly but surely creeping up the hillside to its terminus at Darjeeling.

These peaceful avocations were suspended for a time only. In November, 1849, Sir (Dr.) Joseph D. Hooker and Dr. Campbell while travelling in Sikkim, with the permission of

*P. G. Hamerton (Author and Artist) in *'Round My House'* comments upon the same sad state of affairs :—"In the West Highlands where there are few narrow roads laid out by the military who had imperfect ideas of what is convenient to a civil population, I well remember making an excursion into Argyleshire and being compelled to send the carriage back because the roads were so bad that they turned out to be useless."

†The alignment of this road was entrusted to Mr. Dewar (an Anglo-Indian) of the Survey Department. For this work the Government not only named one of the roads in Kurseong after him, but also allotted him a piece of land measuring 14 acres in Sepoydura, midway between that station and Toong, on which he erected a cottage after retirement. This building was eventually purchased by the Belgian Order and demolished to make way for the 'Retreat' to which its Priests to this day resort every week-end.

both the *Rajs*, were treacherously arrested and imprisoned. Under the orders of Namgoway, the brother-in-law of the aged Rajah, and Dewan of the State, Dr. Campbell was subjected to severe indignities. He was bound hand and foot, knocked down, kicked and buffeted, and finally had his head forcibly bent over his chest with the apparent object of causing a dislocation of the cervical bones and death. This failing in its object, he was cast into a room measuring only 12 × 4 feet in which he was confined until December, 24th. Sir Joseph Hooker was placed under surveillance only, and not permitted to communicate with Dr. Campbell. As no protest on the part of the British Government could obtain their speedy release, a punitive expedition was forced over the borders in February, 1850, the *contretemps* ending in the withdrawal of the allowance as well as the annexation of the *whole of the district of Darjeeling* which covers an area of 640 square miles. Thus did the district of Darjeeling pass into our possession, and that too without a shot being fired! This acquisitive power of the British was predicted by George Thomas, the Irish Adventurer* (who had carved out for himself a Principality at Hirriana in the Panjab, and was thus the first Britisher to set foot in the Panjab, and not Lord Lake, the conqueror of the Lion of the Panjab, as tradition has it) at an interview with Lord Wellesley at Lucknow in 1802 who, when shewn the new Map of India, swept his hand athwart it and said:—"All this ought to be red." The great Ranjit Singh†, Ruler of the Panjab, some 40 years later also exclaimed, when shewn a similar map in which British possessions were coloured red:—"Close it up, as all will soon be red." And if all is not red, this much is certain—the influence of red pervades all in this the land of our adoption.

"Spread it then,
And let it circulate through ev'ry vein
Of all your empire; that where Britain's power
Is felt, mankind may feel her mercy too."

---

*"*European Military-Adventurers of Hindustan.*"—by Herbert Compton: T. Fisher-Unwin.

†The Hon'ble Emily Eden (sister of Lord Auckland the then Governor-General of India) in one of her letters describes this wonderful man as "looking exactly like an old mouse, with grey whiskers and one eye only."

Towards the close of the year 1860 Dr. Campbell represented to Government that for sometime past the Sikkimese had been violating the chief articles of the treaty signed at Titalya, and was accordingly instructed to proceed in person with a detachment of the Corps of Sebundy Sappers, consisting of 207 rank and file, into Sikkim and take formal possession of a portion of Sikkim Giry to the north of the Ramman and the west of the Great Rangneet river. On November 1st of that year the expeditionary force numbering 160 only under the command of Cap. Murray, assisted by Lieut. Beavan and Sergt. Jones, occupied the village of Rinchipong,* about 40 miles from Darjeeling. The force proved quite inadequate for such an undertaking and was in consequence forced to beat a hasty retreat with an uncivilized and exultant enemy pressing hard on the rear guard, until it had repassed in safety the old fort of Darwa Garat and had recrossed the Rangneet by the cane bridge into British territory. A reign of terror ensued in Darjeeling for some days thereafter; "the guards were called in, the ladies huddled into one house, while the men stood on the defensive, to the great amusement of the Sikkim officials at Tumlong, whose insolent bearing to us increased proportionately." The Government then awoke, as it usually does, to a correct sense of the magnitude of the undertaking and accordingly moved troops from near and far to restore our damaged prestige. Lt.-Col. Gawler of H. M's 73rd. Foot was appointed to command the invading force,† which consisted of 2,600 rifles, two mountain batteries and a detachment of artillery. The Rangneet was crossed on February 2nd, 1861, and the enemy who numbered over 800 strong was surrounded and badly beaten at Namchi. Tumlong, the then capital of Sikkim, was entered by the British on March 9th, and a final treaty signed on the 28th. idem by the Rajah (80 years old) who was compelled to abdicate in favour of his son, Sikeong Kuzoo Sikkimputti, expel the obnoxious Namgoway, as well as pay an indemnity of seven thousand rupees.

---

*See No. 23, Plate XIII.

†Sir Ashley Eden accompanied the expedition as Envoy.

For our further political relations with this State see—State of Sikkim, Part III.

The Daling Sub-division, of which Kalimpong is the head-quarters, and which is bounded on the east and west, respectively, by the Jaldakha* and Tista rivers, together with the Bengal (and Assam) Duars† were annexed from Bhutan on November 11th, 1865, and included in the district of Darjeeling, thereby increasing the area from 640 to 1164 square miles.

Communications.

Up to the close of 1854 it required some leisure, a heavy purse, and any amount of stamina, for the visitor to Darjeeling had to choose between the following modes of transit:—

The Road Journey.

To plod the entire distance of 401 miles along dusty trunk-roads in the plains portion and rest at the close of each stage in tents or the conveyance hired, be it gharry or palki, for in those days dak bungalows were not ready to hand ; or, if one of the more fortunate ones, to put up through the influence of friends in common at the residence of officials, or planters (indigo) living along the route.

The River Journey.

"Silent it moves, majestically slow,
Like ebbing Nile or Ganges in its flow."

To embark in a frail craft (having a more fragile dinghee—boat—in tow for the servants and luggage) from Chandpal Ghat, Calcutta, for a journey of at least a week up the Ganges during which progress was necessarily slow and dependent upon favour-

---

*'The hidden river', so called because (like the Mahanadi) it flows for a part of its course under porous gravel and detritus.

†These Duars, or doors of Bhutan are eighteen in number. Of these eleven open into Bengal, and seven into Assam. The Bengal Duars are located at Dalimkote, Mynaguri, Chamurchi, Luckee, Buxa, Bhulka, Bara, Goomar, Reepoo, Cherung and Bhag or Chota Bignee. The term 'Duars' which properly should be applied to the mountain gorges or passes alone has been extended to the plains with which they communicate.

able winds, as the force of the flood tide in the higher reaches of the river causes but a slack-water; or oftener on the staying power of the crew who either bent to the oar, or painfully dragged the boat upstream by a tow-line (*gooning*) until Karagola Ghat was reached. That is, the river journey covered 270, the plains road 142, and the hill section 40 miles.

The E. I. Railway.

The march of progress may be gauged by the following:—From February 3rd, 1855, when the line was opened for traffic as far as Raneegunge, a distance of 120 miles from Calcutta, the river-journey kept diminishing as the terminus of the line was ever extending northward. In October, 1859, we find that it had been advanced to Rajmahal; while early in the following year Sahibgunge, which is 219 miles from Howrah and the terminus of the visitor to Darjeeling, was reached. From this station to Karagola Ghat, on the opposite bank of the river, a five-hour river-crossing had to be accomplished before proceeding by hackery cart to Dingra Ghat, and from there by one of the following modes of transit:—Gharry* or palki-dak, pony or cart, to the foot of the hills past Purneah, Kissengunge and Titalya (where there is still to be seen the ruins of the foundations of the barracks which once accommodated the troops on their way to, or from Darjeeling, and the cemetery wherein lies many a brave heart, a victim to the deadly Terai fever); and thereafter a tedious journey of 56 miles through the Terai and over the hill road *via* Pankabarie, Kurseong, Dow Hill, Senchal and Jorebungalow (Plate XIX) when the traveller landed tired and worn out at the Chowrasta, Darjeeling.

The E. B. Railway.†

The first train steamed out of the Sealdah platform for its then terminus—Ranaghat—on September 29th, 1862. Within

*Dr. (Sir) J. D. Hooker paid as much as Rs. 240/- for his gharry-dak from Karagola Ghat to Siliguri.

†These details were very kindly supplied by Mr. J. Coates, Agent, E. B. Railway, as no data were available either in the 'Darjeeling Gazetteer,' or in Hunter's 'Statistical Account of Bengal.' The completion of this line from Sealdah to Kushtea took a little under 3 years.

a month and a half, that is, by November 15th, the line passed through Poradah Junction (a little to the south of Damukdea Ghat) on its way to Kushtea.

In 1869 the cart road from Darjeeling to Siliguri was completed.

On August 28th, 1877, the Northern Bengal State Railway,* was opened for traffic between Atrai (a few miles to the north-east of Sara Ghat) and Jalpaiguri.

It will thus be seen that by the completion of the E. I. R. line as far as Sahibgunge the river-journey had ceased to exist as far back as 1860, and that between the years 1869 and the half of 1877 the traveller had the option of either proceeding by rail to Sahibgunge then by road to Siliguri, and finally by tonga as far as Toong only; or by the E. B. Railway to Poradah, then a short march to Bhairamara, and from Sara, on the opposite bank of the river, along a trunk road of about the same length as when travelling by the E. I. R. route. In the latter half of 1877 the road journey only covered the distance between Poradah Junction and Atrai from which place the traveller entrained for Jalpaiguri.

On December 8th, 1883, the E. B. Railway was extended from Poradah Junction to the Ghat, since known as Damukdea, and so the one at Bhairamara was abandoned.

Through Communications.

The 19th of January, 1878, however, ushered in a new era for the break in the metre-gauge line between Poradah and Atrai was linked up *via* Bhairamara, and formally opened for traffic by the late Sir Ashley Eden, Lieut.-Governor of Bengal, thus establishing through communication between Sealdah and Jalpaiguri (and extended to Siliguri on June 10th, 1878); while a contract was placed with Messrs. Tom Mitchell and Rumsey of Calcutta for the construction of the tramway to Darjeeling.

---

*This line, now the E. B. Railway, which was first called the Northern Bengal State Railway, was surveyed in 1871-72. By the end of March, 1873, its whole length of 204 miles was staked out; so that it took just a little over 5 years to complete.

At the close of the year following the E. I. Railway workshops at Jamalpore undertook the building of engines for this line, the first being named the "Tiny." At this period the tramline worked up a zig-zag from Gyabarie to Giddapahar* (between the Mahanady and Kurseong stations, and did not worm 5 miles round the spur as at present), and as the gradient was severe it followed that only very light vehicles were run on the line. The 'Tiny' was first brought into use on the occasion of the visit of Lord Lytton†, the Viceroy, in March, 1880, and proved incapable of dragging the extra baggage which such a visit entailed, and so an army of coolies was immediately impressed into service to assist this mite with large hawsers to drag its precious freight to the 18th-mile terminus. From this point the Viceroy rode into Kurseong and put up at the Clarendon Hotel, which was built by Mr. James White (one of the pioneers of the tea industry in Assam who was induced to settle in this district owing to its healthier climate) shortly after he had laid out the Singel Tea Estate in 1862. Bar the small annexe added by the present owner, the original building has stood the ravages of time and has ever since catered for the wants of visitors to Kurseong.

Shortly after this visit the steam tramway was extended to Toong, from which station the traveller either rode in, or drove in a tonga to Darjeeling until July 4th, 1881, when the line was pushed on to the terminus and its designation changed to that of—'The Darjeeling Himalayan Railway.'

---

*The Vultures' Rock.

†Darjeeling was visited by Lord Lansdowne in 1895. As this station is at its best during the winter, Lord and Lady Curzon and family spent a week at 'The Shrubbery' in January, 1903. On the return journey the late, and first Lady Curzon trollied right down to Sukna.

CHAPTER II.

The Journey.

"Not all roads lead to Rome—only that you have begun to travel."
—*R. L. Stevenson.*

Sealdah to Siliguri—335 Miles.

Those who now have occasion to travel to Darjeeling will appreciate the efforts of the Eastern Bengal Railway in trying to provide for the comforts and convenience of its passengers. These attempts have materialised in the provision of new and extremely well-fitted carriages, replete with every comfort; indeed, the consensus of expert opinion has classed them as the most luxuriously fitted coaches in India. The Darjeeling Mail train which is 650 feet in length, weighing 361 tons, and built at an expenditure of Rs. 2,45,000/- is the fastest train in India doing 50 miles an hour from start to finish. It is made up of nine bogie carriages, each 68 feet in length, which were built in the workshops at Kanchrapara, and is capable of accommodating 59 first-class, 63 second-class, 104 intermediate and 158 third-class passengers ; total 384.

Composition and fittings of the Darjeeling Mail.

The comfort of the passengers has been the primary consideration as evinced by the numerous devices which, though small in themselves but when taken collectively, contribute not a little to our creature comforts. The bathroom, on the down journey especially, will be appreciated as in addition to the usual shower-bath it is provided with a spray-bath from jets along its walls. The electric fans are also now placed over the heads of the diners instead of the centre of the table thereby adding to the pleasures of the meal. Another convenience is the electric cigar-lighter which will save the loss of temper and keep the atmosphere from turning 'blue,' a condition which did not prevail prior to the introduction of this patent device. The train is lit throughout by electricity, its lavatories are provided with paper towels (in rolls), while the basins are fitted with receptacles containing liquid soap. The guard's and luggage vans, and the dining saloon are furnished with fire-extinguishers, while an alarm communication is attached to each compartment.

The mail train leaves Sealdah Station at 4-42 p.m. Standard time (i.e., 5-6 p.m. Local time) for Santahar where a transhipment is at present necessary at 9-15 o'clock to the metre-gauge line, and arrives at Siliguri at 6 a.m. the following morning. The hours of arrival and departure are subject to frequent changes necessitating a reference to the official Time Table obtainable at the bookstall at Sealdah, and other stations.

Shortly after leaving Sealdah the canal which encircles Calcutta is crossed by the Balliaghatta bridge, and then the train rushes on at an average speed of 50 miles an hour through boundless fields, dotted here and there with clumps of fruit trees, feathery bamboo topes; and such palms!—cocoanut, date, fan, and areca—which fringe the borders of each village perched on hillock, or high ground, until Siliguri is reached when the scenery suddenly undergoes a complete change, dense forests, deep ravines and sharp curves replacing the monotony of the landscape of the plains which throughout Bengal presents the same aspect.

Dinner is served in the dining-car, while early morning tea may be had at Jalpaiguri at 5 a.m., Siliguri being reached an hour later.

The Hardinge Bridge.*

A photogravure and short account of this bridge are given in order that the traveller may have some idea of the magnitude of this project.

Structure of Bridge—1st. The piers are on well-foundations the tops being 3 feet above the lowest water-level. In plan, the masonry is 55 × 29

*The longest bridges in the world are :—(1) The Tay Bridge in Scotland (2 miles, 73 yards); (2) the Ohio Bridge in the U. States (2 miles); (3) the Victoria Bridge in Canada (1 mile, 1320 yards); (4) the Forth Bridge in Scotland (1 mile, 245 yards); (5) the Brooklin Bridge in the U. States) 1 mile, 245 yards); (6) the "longest bridge in the world is that which was completed on the 2nd April, 1905, and crossed the Zambezi, being the most important link in the Cape to Cairo railway; and (7) the

PLATE II.

THE HARDINGE BRIDGE.

This bridge, which has 15 spans measuring 350 feet, 6 of 75 feet and 2 of 10 feet each, and is 5,900 feet long from abutment to abutment, or 1 & ⅛th miles, was formally opened to traffic on March 4th, 1915, by Lord Hardinge, Governor-General of India, and earned Mr. (Sir) R. R. Gales, the Engineer-in-Chief, a Knighthood as well as a seat on the Railway Board.

ft. with semi-circular ends and straight sides. The main piers are carried on wells sunk by dredging to a depth of 160 feet below the lowest water-level, being the deepest foundations of their kind in the world.

2nd. The wells contain about 15,300 tons of masonry and an average of 355 tons of steel work.

3rd. More than 38,860,000 cb. ft. of stone was utilised in the construction of 1 and 2; while 170,000 barrels of cement were used upon the works.

4th. The girders are 52 feet deep and weight about 1,250 tons per span, while the total weight of the steel work of the girders is nearly 21,000 tons; and each span erected and painted was estimated to cost 600,000 rupees.

5th. Each well contains 50,000 field rivets, which together with those in the spans and pierheads make up a total of 1,700,000 rivets.

6th. There is a clear headway above highest water-level of 40 feet, and 71 feet above lowest water-level. At high flood-level 2,500,000 cb. ft. of water will pass under the bridge every second.

7th. Earthwork—The approaches, which together with the bridge is 15 miles long, consumed 160,000,000 cb. ft. of earth, while 38,000,000 cb. ft. were used in training works.

8th. Labour—In February, 1912, no less than 24,000 labourers were employed on this bridge.

9th. Cost—On the bridge proper Rs. 391 lakhs, on approaches Rs. 84 lakhs; total Rs. 475 lakhs. The final charge, however, was estimated to be well within 400 lakhs.

10th. It occupied just 5 years from the time the preliminary surveys were made to the date of the opening for traffic.

On the other hand, the linking of the line from Bhairamara Station *via* Paksey and Issurdhy (a terminus of the Serajgunge line) to Santahar was done at convenience by the staff of the Eastern Bengal Railway, and yet complaints were frequent regarding the want of proper accommodation, and even the want of adequate shelter for the passenger traffic which was compelled to tranship at the last station in all weathers.

New York Bridge (1½ miles) will be the largest structure in the world for it will have two decks, the lower 150 feet above water level, which will carry 14 railway lines, 2 broad roads and 2 foot-paths. The cost of the undertaking is estimated at £40,000,000.

A Retrospect.

The public desired the change (but see Part IV), and yet as the project neared completion it was felt that every girder added to the structure drew the days of Sara Ghat to a close. Although the bridge was expected in some directions to add to our comforts yet the thoughts of other days would arise and take us back to the time when the Sara-Bhairamara ferry-system was established so far back as January, 19th, 1878, and dinner enjoyed on the deck of the "Osprey," or later still on the "Porpoise," and of the chota hazrees partaken of in the early mornings long before the sun had risen to make the day uncomfortable thereby reminding us of those compelled to sojourn in the sweltering heat of the plains.

On December, 8th. 1883, the Eastern Bengal Railway was extended from Poradah Junction to the Ghat, now known as Damukhdea, and so the one at Bhairamara was abandoned. Ever since the ferry has plied regularly between Sara and Damukhdea but not between the same ghats as owing to the continual changes in the course of the Ganges and the shifting banks of the stream, the landing stages have been from time to time removed from place to place. In fact, up to the present day (end of 1914) no permanent ghat exists at Damukhdea, while that at Sara was constructed as late as 1889. As these banks were changing both in depth and position, a system of flat-landings was devised, with which we have been so familiar. That is, we have seen Sara as it has been for the past twenty-five years but shall lose sight of it in the near future as the new line will run *via* Paksey and Issurdhy to Santahar thereby ensuring a permanent station which will materially reduce the working expenses of the line as the ferry-system swallowed up no less than 300,000 rupees in its maintenance annually.

Siliguri to Darjeeling—51 Miles.

Interest is necessarily aroused in the wee, toy-train with its two-feet gauge and its miniature locomotives, built by Messrs. Sharpe, Stewart & Co. of Glasgow, which are capable of drawing for a short distance a 50-ton load up a gradient of 1 in every 15

PLATE III.

ELGIN (RHEINSTEIN) VILLA.

THE MAHANADY BRIDGE.

SADIE VILLA.

feet. The speed of this little train is limited to 10 miles an hour on the hill section as a safe-guard against accidents especially on the down journey. The new bogie cars are all that could be desired, and run with little or no oscillation thereby materially adding to the comfort of its passengers. A special coach with a settee on springs can be attached at short notice for the convenience of invalids.

This line which owes its inception to the late Sir Ashley Eden and Sir Franklin Prestage, the first manager of the Darjeeling Himalayan Railway, cost about Rs. 52,000/-; or £3,500, (at the current rate of exchange) the mile ; the road on which it is laid was constructed at an expenditure of Rs. 90,000/-, or £6,000, the mile. This road has been handed over by the Government in the Public Works Department to the Railway authorities to provide for its prompt and adequate repairs, as well as to ensure the communications being kept open even during the rains when slips of no mean dimensions are not infrequent.

The Deadly Terai.

1. See Plate XIX—The D. H. Railway and Its Extensions.

2. The Mileage of the railway is marked in red on little, oval discs attached to iron stanchions throughout the route, while that of the Cart Road is painted in black.

3. Figures within brackets, which denote altitude above sea level, are the latest aneroid readings by the Public Works Department.

4. The D. H. Railway passes over 550 culverts and small bridges which are numbered serially on little tombstone shaped pieces of wood.

Just as the train steams out of the Siliguri platform (392′) at 7 a.m. the new extension to the Tista Valley, 29 miles long, will be seen to the right of the 'Siliguri Road Station', wending its way north-east across the plains to enter the Terai from which it emerges at Sivoke (500′) to worm its way 100 feet above the level of the Tista river until it reaches its terminus—Kalimpong Road Station, 2 miles from the Tista Bridge.

After a run of 5 minutes the Mahanady bridge, which is about 700 feet long, is reached (Plate III).

The Mahanady river is a mighty torrent in the rains, but in the dry months it contracts to a quarter of its size and is only some two feet deep. At this period, and about three miles up its course, it disappears* for about a mile during which it works its way under the sands.

At the third mile is Panchanai Junction, one of the termini of the Kissengunge line, which is 66 miles in length. Here, on the right, may be seen the first tea nursery with its seedlings, shaded by thatched coverings, to be subsequently planted out 3 feet apart and in parallel rows facing east and west in order to obtain the maximum amount of light and heat so necessary for the well-being of the plant. From this station to Sukna, where the actual ascent starts (Plate IV), the line on either side is fringed with magnificent, stately trees, such as the Shorea Robusta (*sal*), Dillenea pentagyna, Bhutea frondosa, Terminalia Tomentosa (*Pakasaj*) and Savannah, several species of palms, and creepers. At the 6½-mile, and on the right of the line is the Mohourgong Tea Estate surrounded by elephant grass, tangled undergrowth and cane-brake, the haunt of the tiger, panther, elephant, buffalo, bison and deer.

Sukna (the dry spot) is at the 7⅛th-mile. At this station in the winter of 1900 the staff was held up one bright morning by a tiger which had spent the early hours lying on the cool, cemented surface facing the booking office. Needless to say that its days were numbered, for a Nimrod happened to be at the Forest bungalow, and at the earnest solicitations of the staff came across and despatched it. Again, early in February, 1915, the rumble of the incoming train awoke a tiger which had been asleep under the first railway culvert just out of the station limit, which in its mad rush out knocked over an Indian wayfarer who just managed to crawl into the station shaking like an aspen leaf where he was surrounded by enquirers travelling in that mail. Once again was master stripes seen by the writer at 5 minutes to 1 p.m. in March following just opposite the Forest bungalow calmly eyeing two fat kine

Sukna (533')

*The Bashkos river in Asia Minor runs for several miles in a subterranean channel under the hills before reappearing again.

PLATE IV.

TRAIN RUNNING THROUGH THE TERAI.

which were grazing on the flat facing the building. As the visit was so unusual he got away before a *bead* could be drawn on him. On another occasion a herd of wild elephants caused a little flutter among the station staff, and also compelled the driver of a train to back right into Sukna, as they were far from disposed to yield up the line on which they were meandering at will. Once again, and as late as 1916, Oakley, a driver of the line, came across a tusker and two females at the 10th-mile while taking down the evening passenger train. To drive them off the line he blew the whistle, which so irritated the male that it tore up the mile-post and was about to charge the train when a bright thought flashed across the mind of the driver, *viz.*, to blow off as much steam as possible from the blow-off cocks of the engine. The hissing sound was enough for the lot for they scampered down the hillside faster than one would ever imagine such monsters could move.

A little to the north-east of Sukna are the Forest bungalows where during the winter months the students of the Forest School at Kurseong encamp for practical training in sylviculture, road-aligning and bridge-making.

From this point onwards on one side of the line, ferns, stagmoss and linchen may be gathered by stretching out the hand; while on the other are deep ravines and gaping chasms, which at some spots are so precipitous as to be named 'sensation points'. During the rains fleecy, white mists rise out of these ravines and are made resplendent by the rays of the sun which seldom penetrate the valleys.

The Ascent.

Abreast of these buildings the train starts winding its way in and out of the lower spurs gradually but surely creeping up the hillside. At the 11½-mile is the first *loop*, while at the 12th-mile the train steams into Rungtong, which nestles in a curve of the hill. The second *loop* is at the 14½-mile, a spot which has earned quite a notoriety as being the sanctuary for panthers, for here on the left of line is the trap constructed by the P. W. I. (of the line) in which over 60 panthers have been trapped and

Rungtong (1404')

shot, while on two occasions two at a time have been caught. At the 15½-mile is the third *loop* (Plate V), after passing which the train spins through Choonbaty (the lime kiln, where on the right will be seen the old dak bungalow in use in the days of the tonga service as the halting place for lunch) before the first *reverse* is zigzagged over at the 17½-mile. The origin of these reverses, according to tradition, is ascribed to the wit of the wife of the engineer entrusted with the trace. Having got so far it appeared to him that the trace was at fault and that a fresh survey would have to be made. But here 'the help meet for man' stepped in and solved the difficulty by suggesting that as in tight corners in dancing reversing was permitted, why should not a reverse similarly here overcome the difficulty? To resume.

Choonbaty (2000′)

From this reverse the train starts climbing its way to Tindharia* (the three ridges) which is reached at 9-18 a.m. where a halt of 5 minutes is allowed for light refreshments. To the east of the station stand the workshops of the three connected lines—the D. H. Railway, the Kissengunge and Tista Valley lines. A little beyond this station is the second *reverse* and the fourth *loop*. This *loop* gives a fair idea of the ingenuity displayed in their construction. A large amount of work was done at this point to form the sharp curve of the loop, which is only 58 feet in radius

Tindharia (2748′)

The third *reverse* at the 23¼-mile has to be passed before Gyabarie (the cowshed) is reached. Darjeeling is now just another 27¼-miles away. A little beyond Gyabarie is the fourth and last *reverse*, then the Pagla Jhora, or mad torrent, which in the rains is a very pretty cascade, but a bane to the railway for it is reputed to have cost fully a *lakh* of rupees to revet.†

Gyabarie (3416′)

---

*Facing the refreshment room is a splendid specimen of the screw-pine, the leaves of which are worked up into the famous Panama hats.

†The Pagla Jhora in July, 1890, washed away nearly 800 feet of the road and line, and also the whole hillside fully for 500 feet on the upper road. Indeed, so great was the destruction that it was seriously contemplated deflecting the line and carrying it round the hill at this spot.

PLATE V.

THE DOUBLE LOOP.

The next run lands us at the Mahanady Station, which takes its name from the river it overlooks, and which is 27 miles from Siliguri. From this station right on to Kurseong excellent views of the plains are obtained, as also of the three rivers, the Balasan,* the Mahanady† and the Tista,‡ which bathed in sunlight look like three narrow, silvery ribbons. The Sukna road appears like a long straight line at the end of which tiny, white dots indicate the houses in Siliguri.

Mahanady (4120′)

Kurseong (Plate X) is at the next halt, where a substantial breakfast at 10-19 a.m., awaits the arrival of the traveller whose appetite has by this time received a keen edge owing to the bracing air. This town is only 20 miles away from Darjeeling, and contains a number of European Schools, and itinerant vendors ready *to do* the unwary tourist with Brummagem ware to which they take their solemn affidavit that these have but lately arrived from sacred Tibet. It is here that we first see the true inhabitants of the hills. Good-humoured,

---

* The Balasan rises in the spurs below Lepcha Jagat (where there is a Forest bungalow to be seen from Darjeeling to the south of the Station) and flows past Panighatta in the Terai, where it is spanned by a suspension bridge.

† The Mahanady river rises near Mahaldiram east of Kurseong and after flowing eastward suddenly turns and passes to the north of the town of Siliguri. Four miles below, and to the west of that town, it receives the waters of the Balasan, the combined volume eventually forming a tributary of the Ganges.

‡The Tista rises on the further side of the Himalayas in lake Chalamu, which lies to the north of the Donkia Pass and is 17,500 feet above sea-level and 74 miles to the north-east of Darjeeling and is augmented by the streams which rise in the Thangu (44), Yeumthang (42) and Donkya La ranges (41) Plate XIII. After receiving the combined waters of the Ramman, the little and great Rangneet rivers it debouches through the gorge at Tista Bridge, takes a southerly course as far as Sivoke, where it emerges into the plains, to proceed further south through Jalpaiguri until it meets the great Brahmaputra river at Fulcherry Ghat, or Tista Mukh (mouth). The combined waters flow on to Goalundo where the Padmah, an effluent of the Ganges, merges into it and forms the mighty Megna (sky-blue river) from the midstream of which the stately firs over 50 feet in height, which line its banks, look like ordinary pins thus giving one a fair idea of its width (60 miles across) and of the volume of water it discharges into the Bay of Bengal. The network of rivulets between this river and the Hooghly, which constitutes the deltaic region, covers no less than 32,000 sq. miles.

happy-go-lucky, healthy and strong are the little hill people, who have broad faces, straight, black hair, drawn eyes and ruddy cheeks. They wear a short smock made of some dark, warm material fastened at the waist by a belt, while a non-descript felt hat jauntily covers the head. They do all the work of the tea gardens and towns for the climate does not suit the man from the plains, and so few Mahomedans and Hindus are seen in the district. And now with the advent of a new race comes also a new religion—Buddism—which takes outward expression in little paper flags and large cloth banners on which are stamped stereotyped prayers which waft in the wind fastened to poles or strings until blown away from their attachments, which is considered a good omen in that their prayers have reached heaven to be answered shortly.

Kurseong (4864′)

The old Pankabarie Road joins the Cart Road at the bazar. Across the valley and to the west are the mountains of Nepal and the frontier Fort of Elam, which is held by Nepalese troops ; to the south will be seen the wide belt of forest called—'The Deadly Terai.'

Sixteen miles away and to the south-west is Mirik (5000′).

The Clarendon, and Sorabjee's Hotels cater for those who desire breaking journey at Kurseong.

Another run of 20 minutes and the train halts at Toong (where the Toon tree thrives). Midway between this station and Sonada is the Brewery located in the old barracks in which troops on their way to, and from Darjeeling rested for the night. Peach, apple and pear trees are to be seen for the first time on the little holdings attached to each hamlet ; but the fruit never matures owing to the excessive rainfall, and are in consequence harvested when only three-quarter ripe. From this point onward the line is mainly built on the Cart Road.

Toong (5656′)

At the 41½-mile the bazar and station of Sonada (the abode of bears) is reached. It is just 10 miles to the south of Darjeeling. In the early *seventies* there were but two houses in this station. The first was to the immediate north of the water-tank and formed one of the chain of rest-houses built by the Burdwan Raj, but which has since been converted into the summer residence of the members of the Italian Mission of Khrisnagar ; the second, a little beyond and to the right of the line, (now the central structure) was 'The Traveller's Rest-House' built by John White in 1870, but now materially altered and renamed 'Ardgowan.'

Sonada (6588′)

Tourists desirous of visiting the Cinchona plantations at Mongpu (5200′) alight here and wend their way uphill to Serail (5600′). Sonada and its environs are called 'Pacheem' by the hill people ; some use the term to solely denote Hope Town, which is 2 miles below and to the south-west of the station.

Hope Town.

"Hope never comes that comes to all."—*Paradise Lost.*

In the days when Major Lindsay, R. E., was Manager of the E. B. Railway the intention of the authorities was to extend the line, which then reached Jalpaiguri only, not to Siliguri as at present, but to Adlapore in the Terai and from thence run a narrow gauge railway to Panighatta and up the valley (and below Hope Town) to Darjeeling. This village was built in anticipation of the line passing through, or below it; hence its name—'Hope Town.'

The Hope Town scheme was started in 1856 by Messrs. Fred. Brine (who once owned the plot on which Government House, Darjeeling, stands), the Executive Officer of South Hidgelee, near Diamond Harbour, and E. D'Cruz of the Financial Secretary's Office, Calcutta. The other pioneers were:—Mrs. Henrietta Colebrooke Taylor (widow of Col. Taylor), Dr. Roberts of Raneegunge, Capt. Mitchell of the Ordnance Department, Fort William, Messrs. Deare (of Monghyr), Rundle, Waters, the Rev. Mr. Greenfield (of Purneah), and Conductor Vaughan.

Hope Town consists of a few English cottages in the centre of which is St. John's Church built in 1868 by Mr. Ted. Brown of 'Sungma', Nagri Spur (whose descendants still own this garden), in behalf of Mr. John Stalkartt,* who resigned indigo for tea in the year 1864 when he purchased a small cottage and an extensive tract of land from Mr. Fred. Brine on which he laid out the 'Oaks Tea Estate,' which is still owned by his heirs. 'Chota Ringtam' which he purchased subsequently has been swamped in the cluster of gardens in that locality which was bought by a syndicate.

From Sonada to Ghum the line works in and out through heavy forest, chiefly oak, which clothes the hillsides.

The next station is Ghum. Its temperature is invariably more than 5° lower than that of Darjeeling, and between 10° to 15° below that of Sonada due to a break in the Sewalik, or lower range of hills which skirt the Himalayas, through which the wind sweeps and condenses the moist air of Ghum into a chilly, clinging mist which pervades everything. Convalescents should, therefore, have their great-coats handy, if these have not already been requisitioned at Kurseong, or Toong.

Ghum (7407′)

Ghum (the gable-shaped village) is the highway to the following places:—The road to the east, known as the Peshok Road, ends at Tista Bridge on the way to Kalimpong lately much in evidence owing to the Colonial Homes (like those founded by the great George Muller at Bristol, on the inspection of which the Chinese Ambassador exclaimed—"If anything has shaken my materialism it is these homes") brought into being by the exertions of the Rev. Dr. J. A. Graham, D.D., C.I.E. These Homes have cared for and launched into useful spheres of life hundreds of European and Anglo-Indian youths of both sexes. A diversion at 'the 6th-Mile' along the Peshok Road has been made to the Takdah (Hum) cantonments where a battalion of Gurkha troops is quartered. To the south-east lies the Catchment Area and reservoirs which supply Darjeeling with water, while beyond is Tiger Hill (8,515′) from which on a clear day, which may be counted on the finger tips of ones' hands, a view of Mount Everest

---

*It may be of interest here to record that a branch of this family established the Ropeworks at Goossery, near Calcutta, which is still the leading business in that line.

(29,141′)* may be had—the lot of the happy few! Here, also, are the Golf Links located at Senchal (8,163′) laid out on the flat, once the grounds of the first cantonment established for European troops. To the west, and only 3½ miles away, is the famous Ghum Rock which stands at a heavy list over the road and fully 95 feet high. Its summit is flat, and on it many a pic-nic party is held; and from which a good view of the plains as well as of the Nepal frontier may be had. Tradition states that from here when the land was under the sway of the Nepalese criminals were hurled down. To the immediate left of the station is the first Buddist monastery, while above and facing Ghum are the cantonments of Katapahar and Jalapahar, in the order in which they stand, in which detachments of British troops are quartered during the summer. From here the line descends, and after passing the fifth and last *loop*, Darjeeling, (6,812′) which is 4 miles away, is reached.

Katapahar (7886′)
Jalapahar (7701′)

The Gradient.

The gradient from Siliguri to Sukna is 1 in every 281 feet; throughout the remainder of the journey it is 1 in every 30 feet, while that between Ghum and Darjeeling, which when 'compensated for curvature,' works out to as much as 1 in every 16. In accordance with a scheme of some magnitude now in hand (1919), which gives the approach to Darjeeling quite a battlemented appearance the fifth and last *loop* at Batasia will reduce the gradient to 1 in every 22½ feet.

It was the intention of the Railway Authorities to remove 8 out of the remaining 10 level-crossings immediately after this *loop* was completed (at a cost of Rs. 125,000/-), but further work was deferred, at the request of the signatories to the Memorial to H. E. the Governor on the subject of level-crossings, in favour of the removal of 18 other crossings near

*A jagged line of snow connects the two highest mountain peaks—Everest and Kinchenjunga. The line of peaks is not so much a chain as the advanced portions of a vast table-land called Tibet, forming an immense country to the north of India. See Part III, Chapter IV, To Gyantse—2nd the Beyond, *et sequor*.

Sonada to be resumed again when this improvement is effected, as this is the most congested part of the whole Cart Road, and the neck of the bottle for the three roads converging at Ghum, *viz.*, from Sonada, Sukiapukri (on the high-road to Nepal), and Takdah, which connects with Tista Bridge on the one hand and Riang in the Tista Valley on the other. Had this scheme been carried out in its entirety the permit system under which motors are now run would have been done away with between Darjeeling and Ghum, but as matters stand it will remain in force for sometime to come.

The Panorama.

About midway between the two stations a grand panoramic view of the Queen of Hill Stations (Plate I) bursts into view with no more befitting back-ground than the Snowy range* of which the chief peaks from left to right are :—Janu, or Masked Rainbow Hues (25,300′) ; Kabru or the Horn of Protection (24,015′) ; Kinchenjunga, or the Five Peaks (28,145′) ; and Pandim, or the King's Minister (22,020′). Owing to the immensity of this range it leaves an impression on the mind that it could be easily reached by a day's march, whereas, being fully 35 miles away as the crow flies, it would take the best part of a fortnight to arrive at its base *via* Phalut, which is the extreme north-west point of the British boundary in the Singalila range.

Darjeeling.

On arrival at Darjeeling the men mount ponies, and the ladies and children get into dandies and rickshaws (provided by the Railway Company at a small charge) which carry them away to the several hotels and boarding establishments, to be followed shortly after by female porters who bear their burdens on the back supported by straps fastened to the forehead, or

---

*The respective positions of the four chief peaks are marked on the Sketch Map of Tours—Plate XIII.

shoulders when the weight is excessive.* The dandy is a chair with a well in front, not unlike that of the carriages in the plains, which rises to the level of the seat, and is carried by four stalwart men, usually Bhutias, who place the horizontal cross-poles by which the dandy is supported on their shoulders and swing off with their fares up and down hill at a jog-trot, looking extremely well pleased if the occupants shew the slightest sign of nervousness.

The Return Journey.

To ensure a sleeping-berth especially, a seat should be booked a day or two before on both the hill and plains railways.

Week-end visitors naturally desire continuing on in the delightful climate of Darjeeling until the very last moment, and accordingly travel by the down mail which now leaves at 2-10 p.m. Standard time. The mail steams into Siliguri at 8 o'clock giving the traveller a full hour in which to change into lighter garments as well as dine before stepping into the E. B. Railway coach for Santahar, where (at present) a transhipment to the broad-gauge takes place at 4-56 a.m., Calcutta being reached at 10-41.

Family parties, however, would probably find it more convenient to leave Darjeeling by the 9-38 a.m. passenger train, which arrives at Siliguri at 3-33 p.m. (oftener 4 p.m. and sometimes even later) by which they have 5 hours in which to feed and attend to children, as also the necessary heavy baggage prior to proceeding on by the mail at 9 p.m.; whereas a continuance of the journey by passenger, which leaves that station at 4-35, entails a rush, then dinner at Parbatipore at 9 o'clock, and finally a transhipment at Santahar at the most inconvenient hour of 2-45 a.m.

Dinner may be had at Siliguri between 7 and 7-30 p.m.,

---

*As an instance of the extraordinary carrying capabilities of these hillmen the following is recorded. A Bhutia navy in 1912 was seen by the writer carrying a bale of cloth weighing 4 mds. 8 srs. from the railway goods shed to Commercial Row on a very rainy day when a slip meant dislocation of the neck and instantaneous death. The bale was duly delivered at destination.

before the Darjeeling Mail arrives at 8, by giving the Manager of the Refreshment Room due notice on arrival.

Line Motors.

The following project has been formulated and will very shortly materialise.

In order to shorten the time spent on both journeys, as well as to give the traveller a better scenic view of the mountain ranges, Mr. R. B. Addiss, the Enterprising Manager of the D. H. Railway, has called for quotations from Home for the supply of motors which will run on the present lines and land passengers at either terminus quicker than by the mail train. Leaving Siliguri a little before the train starts, passengers, it is expected, will be landed at Darjeeling about 11 a.m.; and also enable them to leave about 4 p.m. in order to entrain into the E. B. Railway on scheduled time.

Motor Service.

It is now possible for people travelling to Darjeeling to cut off seven hours on the there-and-back journey by utilising a new motor service operating between Siliguri and Darjeeling.

Mr. A. Stephen, of the Grand Hotel, Calcutta, meets passengers on arrival of the mail train at Siliguri at six o'clock in the morning. Then follows a 3½ hours' glide through the most charming scenery. In many places the motor road—the going is wonderfully good all the way—shoots off from alongside the rail track, thus allowing travellers a chance of peeps at many glorious and little-known valleys.

The up journey takes only about half-an-hour longer than the down. The mail train leaves at 2-10 p.m. daily. It is possible to leave Mount Everest Hotel at 3-30 p.m. and arrive at Siliguri at 6-30 p.m. an hour and a half before the train, so enabling one to change into the waiting train for Calcutta, pack away luggage and lounge over the excellent dinner provided at the railway refreshment buffet on the station, long before the inevitable rush which commences when the hill train arrives.

The new motor service includes free carriage of luggage and servants. The fares are exceedingly reasonable.

CHAPTER III.

Hotels and Boarding Establishments.

"'Shall I not take mine ease at mine inn?"—*Shakespeare.*

As the scheduled time of arrival of the mail is 12-53 p.m. Standard time, the traveller gets in a little before luncheon to which ample justice is done. Of hotels there are many to choose from, while of boarding houses there are a dozen to suit the purse of all.

Woodlands to the right rear of the station platform is but a walk of 5 minutes; Drum Druid, Rockville (the Grand) and Bellevue are reached through the Mackenzie Road, the main artery of the town, which joins the Auckland and Post Office Roads and Commercial Row at the foot of the Darjeeling (Planters') Club; the Central Hotel and Central House are located on Mount Pleasant Road; while the last and by far the most imposing is Hotel Mount Everest (Plate VI) a palatial building standing on the Auckland Road. The shortest way to this hotel is by the Banstead Road to the immediate east of the Station House.

The Evolution of Hotels.

The evolution of hotels in Darjeeling began in 1839, when 'The Darjeeling Family Hotel,' which contained but 12 rooms, was followed by 'Wilson's Hotel' which was established (by the proprietor of the hotel of the same name in Calcutta, now known as 'The Great Eastern Hotel') in a two-storied house containing 18 rooms. A large one-storied building of the same name (Castleton, in which the District Engineer's Office is now located) now stands on the same spot on Hooker Road. Then Woodlands* came into being, to be followed shortly after by

---

*No details *re* accommodation at Woodlands and its two sister institutions—Drum Druid and Rockville—could be obtained although the manageress was referred to on two separate occasions.

Drum Druid,* Rockville, Bellevue, and the Central Hotel, which can accommodate 40 boarders and is situated at the junction of the Post Office and Mount Pleasant Roads; the transition eventually evolving 'Hotel Mount Everest.'

This hotel, which was completed on the 12th October, 1915, was the scene of a fashionable gathering the evening following when a dinner was given by the proprietor, Mr. A. Stephen, to commemorate the opening of this up-to-date hotel built on the latest principles adopted in all continental hotels. To say that this palatial structure is unique is but to repeat a truism, for it is unsurpassed by any building of a similar nature in the East.

The hotel which commands a view of over 100 miles of the snowy range, and stands well above the town on the Auckland Road, was designed by Mr. Stephen Wilkinson, the architect. At present the building consists of a central block, with a north or right wing attached thereto, and contains 120 rooms furnished with all appliances which go toward making life comfortable. But when the existing annex is domolished and the left wing added the number of dwelling rooms will be increased to 170. On the ground floor is a large lounge, which is 85 × 50 feet, luxuriously fitted up with arm chairs upholstered in dark green leather and small tables arranged on a highly polished wooden floor which is covered with handsome rugs. From the east of this hall the ascent to the dining room above is made by the grand staircase, which is one of the features of this building being 16 feet in width until midway when it branches off to right and left. The dining hall has a rich panelled plaster ceiling, while from the centre of each panel hangs an electroclier of

*Drum Druid was owned by Mr. John Lord, *quondam* editor-proprietor of 'The Darjeeling Times.' At his death the hotel passed into the hands of Mr. Piperno Boscolo, and finally, on the demise of the latter, into that of Mrs. Herlihy. The following may also be recorded here : —Boscolo being a shrewd man of business obtained a lease from the Cooch Behar Raj of a part of the hilltop immediately above and to the north of the old bandstand on the Chowrasta at a peppercorn rent, which at his demise passed into the hands of the Oakley family, and from it to that of the Bank of Bengal, which, after starting excavation work with the object of erecting a building in keeping with its prestige, suddenly stopped work, leaving an unsightly mixture of stones and sand where once stood graceful trees and foliage plants. It is understood that this site was lately bought in by the Cooch Behar Raj for 1¼ *lakhs* of rupees.

PLATE VI.

HOTEL MOUNT EVEREST.

beautiful design; the walls are panelled up to a height of 7 feet in highly polished wood which gives the room a pleasing and warm effect. Four fire-places serve to heat the room, while four concealed passages behind curved and mirrored sideboards enable the servants in attendance to appear as if by magic.

Seated round such a table one can truly say with 'Punch' :—

"How good to sit at twilight's close
In a warm Inn and feel
That marvellous smell caress the nose
With promise of a meal!
How good when bell for breakfast rings
To pause, while tripping down,
And snuff and snuff till Fancy brings
All Arcady to Town."

This building already possesses a most imposing frontage, but when the scheme has been given full effect to and the left wing added, Darjeeling might well be proud of possessing one of the grandest and most up-to-date hotels in the Orient.

LIST OF HOTELS, &c.

Darjeeling.

Hotels.

Name.	Location.	Manager.
Bellevue	Commercial Row	Mrs. Kelly
Garrets (Central House)	Mount Pleasant Road	Manager
Central Hotel	Post Office Road	Mr. Daroga
Drum Druid	Commercial Row	Mr. Mahoney
L. J. Vado, Ltd.	Ditto	Manager
Hotel Mount Everest	Auckland Road	Manager
Park Hotel	Meadow Bank Road	Ditto
Rockville (The Grand)	Harman's Road	Mr. Mahoney
Woodlands	Off Cart Road	Ditto

Boarding Houses.

Ada Villa	Observatory Hill	Mrs. C. T. Kirby
Alice Villa	Mount Pleasant Road	Manager
Annandale	Cart Road	Mrs. Carter
Beechwood House	Mackenzie Road	Mrs. I. Stuart
Caroline Villa	Kutchery Road	Manager
El Esparanza	Ditto	Mrs. Sells
Fern Cottage	Post Office Road	Mrs. Rowe
Havelock House	Auckland Road	Mrs. Black
La Roche	Kutchery Road	Miss Billon
May Cottage	Lloyd's Road	Miss De Souza
Moss Bank	Cart Road	Mr. A. J. Stanton
The Labyrinth	Auckland Road	Manager
	Ghum.	
Balaclava Hotel	Old Military Road	Manager
	Kurseong.	
Clarendon Hotel	Cart Road	Mr. H. H. Pell
Sorabjee's Hotel	Ditto	Manager
Wood Hill	Club Road	Mrs. Hasell

Places of interest and business in Darjeeling may easily be traced by means of the attached Map and the following

Street Directory.

DARJEELING.

Ashley Road
French Hat Shop
Dr. Cautley's Dental Surgery

Auckland Road
Glen Eden Laboratory
Sligo Hall (Cooch Behar Residence)
The Manse
Union Church

Birch Hill Road
Diocesan Girls' School

Government House.

Brynguine Road
Lowis Jubilee Sanitarium

*Calcutta Road**
Lodge Mount Everest

*There is a Ladies' Cloak and a Gentlemen's waiting-room situated on the left of the Calcutta Road, a few yards to the south of the old Bandstand on the Chowrasta.

Street Directory—(Contd.)

*Cart Road**
Armed Police Barracks
Eden Sanitarium
Queen's Hill Girls' School

Commercial Row
Benmore
Boseck & Co. (Jewellers)
Burlington-Smith (Photographer)
Frank Ross & Co. (Chemists)
Hall & Anderson (Drapers)
Mitchel & Co. (Tailors)
Mrs. Ottewill's Millinery Establishment
Senchal Dairy Farm Depot
Smith Stanistreet & Co. (Chemists)
Whiteaway Laidlaw Ltd. (Drapers)

Convent Road
Loreto Convent

Dispensary Road
Victoria Hospital

Harman's Road
The Maharani Girls' School
The Parsonage (C. E.)

Hooker Road
Castleton

Jalapahar Road
Contonments
Kenmuir Point
St. Paul's School

Lebong Road
Contonments
Cemetery—Old & New
Kutchery
Presbytery (R. C.)
Race Course
St. Joseph's College

Lochnagar Road
Lloyd Botanic Garden
Loreto Convent
R. C. Chapel

Mackenzie Road
J. Freer & Co. (Furniture, &c.)
Hingun & Sons (Tailors)
Municipal Office
Post & Telegraph Office
Sadie Villas†
Sain, M. (Photographer)
The Rink Theatre
Town Hall

---

*In 1839 a Corps of Sebundy Sapers (local militia) was raised with the intention of employing it chiefly in making and keeping the hill roads in repair, and incidentally for the defence of the Station and District of Darjeeling. Its strength was as follows :—

1	Commandant*	2	Jemadars	180	Sepoys
2	Sergeants*	2	Havildars	1	Drummer
1	Corporal*	10	Naiks	2	Khalasis
2	Subadars	2	Buglers	2	Bhistis.
			*Europeans		

For some unexplained reason this corps was placed under the direction of the civil authorities.

†Renamed—Dulce Domum, Kali Villa and Wayside.

Street Directory—(Contd.)

Mackintosh Road

Colinton (Cooch Behar residence)

Girivilash (Digapatia residence)

Mall, or Chowrasta

Alliance Bank of Simla

F. H. Hathaway & Co.

Gymkhana Club

J. F. Madan's Stores

Natural History Museum

Post Office—Branch

Secretariat Buildings

Southfield

St. Andrew's Church (C. E.)

The Park

Volunteer Headquarters

Old Post & Telegraph Road

Chapleton

J. F. Madan

Prestage Road

St. Columba's Church (Scots)

Mission House (Scots)

Rangneet Road (east of Mall)

Dr. Smith Bros. (Dental Surgeon)

Monastery—Buddist

Bhutia Busti

Ging

GHUM.

Buddist Monastery

Senchal Dairy Farm.

Early Rising.

"The eye sees what it brings the power to see".—*Thos. Carlyle.*

The morning following arrival and a little before sunrise, the visitor if he is an early riser may

> 'Thus improve the pleasures of the day,
> While tasteless mortals sleep their time away';

and have his first, grand view of the highest mountains on the face of the earth which are covered by perennial snow up to the 16,000 feet level during summer, and up to the 13,000 feet level in winter. Doubtless pictures and photographs (Plate XVI) have made this scene familiar; but the true majesty and grandeur of these mountains are evanescent and cannot be reproduced and fixed however subtle the hand of the artist be. Accordingly, it can only be fully appreciated by watching the glow of the morning creep softly over these jagged peaks and observing the deli-

PLATE—VII.

MAP OF THE
TOWN OF DARJEELING.

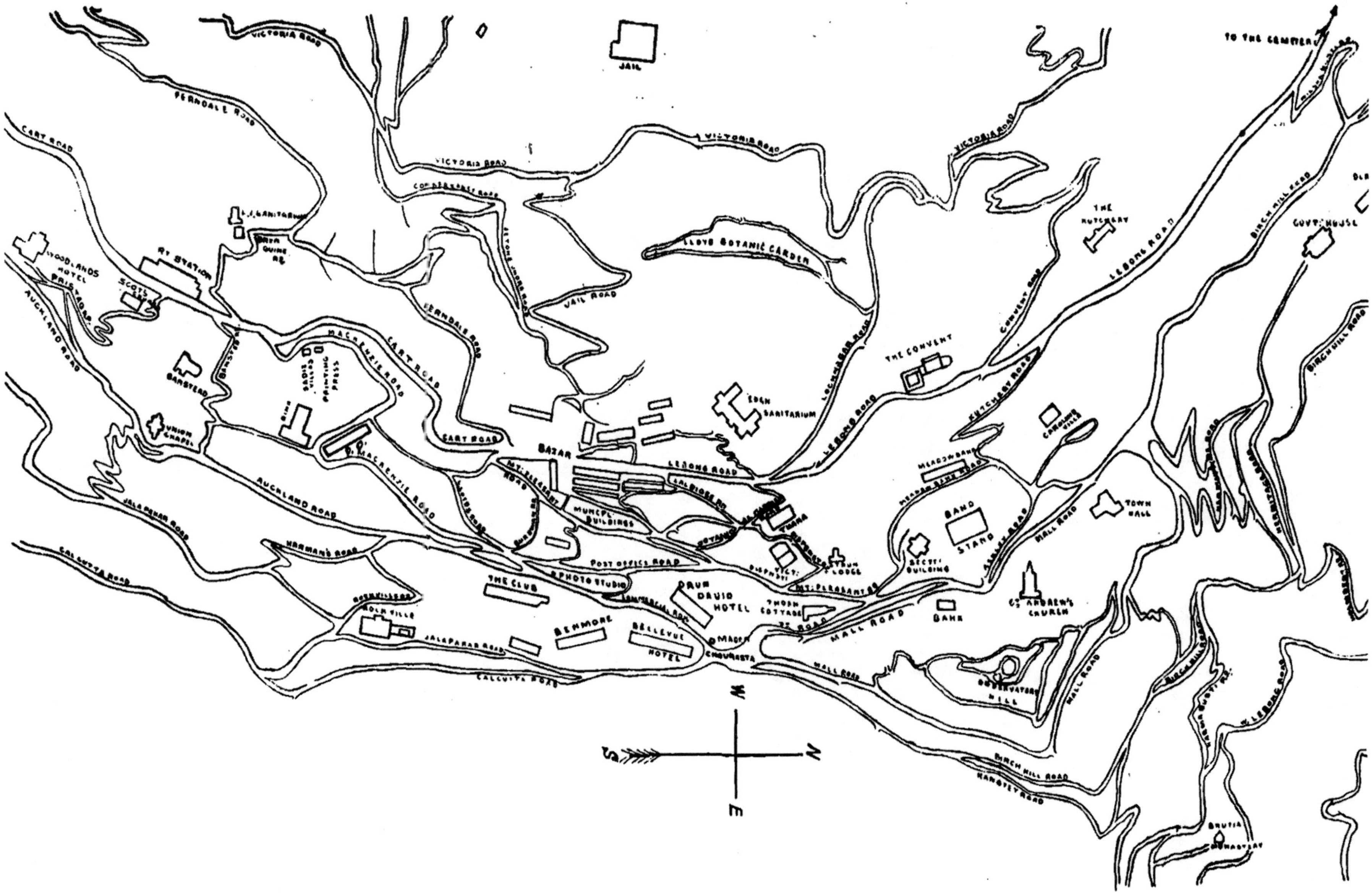

cate, variegated tints that the snows and clouds, which hover over them, assume against a background of azure blue. These glorious views last but a short half-hour, seldom longer ; but all day long the scene lingers in the memory, to possibly be reawakened at sunset. A double rainbow* reflected on the hovering clouds is a rare sight; rarer still is a double rainbow seen in the valley; while of all the grandest sights is a view of the snows during a storm. On two occasions only during the past twenty years has the last been the lot of the happy few. The whole firmament was covered over with dark, heavy-laden clouds, which, while deluging the town, had a large triangular rift just over the snowy range through which the peaks shone with the dazzling, scintillating light of a mirror ; indeed, so bright was the reflection that it pained the eye to gaze at it for any length of

---

*For those who wish to *see* and appreciate the next bow the following is reproduced.

A bow is—"A cloud of mist, that smitten by the sun, varies its rainbow hues"—*Wordsworth.* Frequently there are two bows, one above the other, when the lower of the two is always the brighter. As the lower is produced by the rays of the sun (or moon) falling on the *upper* surface of the raindrops, which are refracted and thrown upon the inner surface of the back of the drops and so bent towards the earth where it reaches the eye of the observer, whose back is toward the source of light. In the upper bow, the rays first take the *under* surface of the drops, and go inversely through the same process of refraction &c. ; and so we have the colours in the two bows inverted, *i.e.*

In the upper bow we get from above below :—Red, orange, yellow, green, blue, indigo and violet.

In the lower we have—Violet, indigo, blue, green, yellow, orange and red.

And, again, when the sun (or moon) rising or setting is paralleled to the horizon, we have two complete semicircular bows ; and as it rises higher and higher, the smaller do these circles appear until the lower disappears when it reaches an altitude of 42 & 1-3°, while the upper ceases to exist when an altitude of 54 & 1-3° is attained.

Finally, as the eye of the observer is the apex of a cone of rays of light, and the circular bow the base itself, it follows that we can only see the upper half of the bow. Such conditions exist only when looking at, or *up* to the bow ; when looking *down*, however, on a bow, as from the summit of a mountain, the whole circular base is seen, *i.e.*, the bow appears a circle. A close observer will also have remarked that the rain drops can only be seen falling from the inner or lower bow.

The above illustrates what Carlyle means when he asserts that "knowledge is power," which enables the eye to *see* and appreciate the wondrous beauties of creation : the want of which causes Blackie to exclaim—"It is astonishing how much we go about with our eyes open and yet see nothing! This is because the organ of Vision, like other organs, requires careful training."

time—a marked contrast to the usual dull, dead white of the snows.

Spell-bound before such a range the visitor passes the hours, and when the mists and clouds cover the snows in a shroud one can always enjoy the rich and varied vegetation, which changes according to the season, and especially so in summer when the hillsides are aflame with the blossoms of the rhododendron and sweet-scented magnolia. To those given to botany a visit to the Botanic Garden and Birch Hill Park would well repay the outing.

After a day so spent, the observer should be able to say with Horace :—

"Happy he, and he alone,
Who, master of himself, can say,
To-day, at least hath been my own,
For I have clearly lived to-day :
Then let to-morrow's clouds arise,
Or purer suns o'erspread the cheerfull skies";

or—

"To me the meanest flower that blows can give,
Thoughts that do often lie too deep for tears."

Communications.

District Roads.

There are 533 miles of roads in the district. Of these 37 only are under the control of the Municipality, 51 constituting the Cart Road have been handed over to the D. H. Railway to maintain, while the remainder is under the charge of the P. W. D. and the District Board which allocates funds to the managers of the tea estates for the upkeep of the roads leading to, and through their plantations.

The Tista Valley Road, which connects Siliguri with Rungpu on the borders of Sikkim and is 46½ miles in length, was completed shortly after the district was annexed in 1850. It was materially widened and improved in 1888 by the Madras Sappers for the expedition commanded by Genl. Graham in order to enable him to push on the punitive force with which he hurled back the Tibetans who had invaded Sikkim, as well as brought the latter State under better control.

The Siliguri-Naxalbarie Road—Prior to 1895 pedestrians had to ford the Balasan river, which is fully 200 yards wide, to enable them to attend the weekly market (*hât*) held at Matigora. This was accomplished in the following primitive but risky manner. The coolies attached to the several gardens located in this locality used to collect on either bank on their way to, or from this mart, then join hands with a strong leader and wade into the shallow but swift current in a long line which kept bobbing up and down during the process of water-treading as they lost their foothold to land fully half a mile from the point at which they entered the river.

Bridges.

The Balasan.—The mortality from such crossings assumed gigantic proportions until the Government during the tenure of Sir Chas. Elliott was at last moved on a protest from the Planter's Association to take up the question of the speedy construction of bridges over these mountain-streams. In 1895-96 a frail wooden structure was rushed up on piles by the P. W. D. across this river, with the result that it lasted only 5 years. In August, 1910, when a fairly heavy rainfall occurred, the western portion of this bridge was washed away thus causing a complete interruption to all traffic for the balance of that season. It was replaced by the present wooden bridge, which being over 300 yards in length claims to be the longest structure of its kind in Bengal.

In 1915, a stone-bridge was thrown across this stream by the Railway Authorities. Apparently in this instance again due allowance was not made for the scour caused by the stream when in flood and so the pierheads at both ends collapsed thus causing a dislocation of traffic on the Kissengunge-Matigora Line.

The Panighatta suspension bridge was completed in 1901. From off this bridge a fairly good view is obtained both of the mountain gorge above, and the plains below.

Three other bridges which were thrown across this stream in 1902 are located at Ambutia, Namsu and Avongrove, respectively. And when the following project materialises, *viz.*, connecting Garidura and Tong Song by a cart road, motorists may dash out for a spin from Siliguri (or the opposite end) along the Matigora road, then along picturesque lanes which sinuate through partial forest tracts until they reach the last stage from where exceedingly pretty views of the Balasan and its rugged banks may be had.

The Tista bridge was suspended across this river shortly after the Dalingkote or Kalimpong Sub-division was annexed from Bhutan in 1865. Being over 300 feet in length it sways under the tread of passengers, as well as at each strong gust of wind.

The Mahanady bridge formed a part of the scheme entrusted to Lt. Napier when Darjeeling was first acquired by us. It was slightly widened (but still too narrow for the expanding requirements of the district) and strengthened when the D. H. Railway came into being in 1880-81.

CHAPTER IV.

DARJEELING.

Physical Aspects.

The district of Darjeeling lies between 26°-53′ and 27°-13′ north latitude, and between 87°-59′ and 88°-53′ east longitude; that is, 35 × 18 miles in length and breadth, respectively. Its area is 1,164 square miles of which 445 square miles are under reserved forests; and its population according to the last census (1911) amounted to 265,500* souls of which 135,000 were Nepalese and other hill tribes, while only 2,808 were Europeans. The density *per* square mile, eliminating the area under forests, works out to 370 persons. The town of Darjeeling, the administrative headquarters of the district, which is situated in 27°-3′ north latitude and 88°-16′ east longitude, covers an area of 4.85 square miles, and has a population of 24,579 souls.

Darjeeling, according to 'The Gazetteer,' derives its name from the Buddist monastery, which once stood on Observatory Hill (7,163′) just above the Chowrasta or Mall, called 'Dorge' and 'Ling,'† the place where the precious stone emblematic of the thunderbolt of Indra (the god) rested. The latter part of the derivation in the light of the following appears to be laboured in the extreme.

In 1835 when this strip of territory was gifted by the Raja of Sikkim, the village of Darjeeling consisted of a monastery on Observatory Hill around which clustered a few huts with a

*Few people unconnected with the district know that the Terai is included in it, and consequently are under the impression that the above statistics apply to the mountainous portion popularly spoken of as 'Darjeeling.' Thrown into divisions the population stands thus:—The Siliguri, or plains sub-division has a population of 72,246 souls, that of Kurseong, a part of which is sub-mountane, numbers 41,207; while Kalimpong and the Sadar divisions have 49,320 and 102,577, respectively = 265,550.

†The Trident, or Trisula of the Hindus, is symbolical of the Trinity.

population of about 100 souls, from whom a revenue of Rs. 20/- *per annum* was assessable. At this period the material and spiritual welfare of the inhabitants was the care of the Llama, or priest in charge of the monastery, named Dorge, who was responsible to the Durbar of Sikkim for the collection and transmission of the revenue from this village, which was borne on the *Touzi* (Land Revenue) ledger under the heading 'Dorge-Ling,' or village governed by Dorge—a name by which it was known at the time, and which for the want of a better appellation was subsequently extend to the whole district when annexed by us in 1850.

Boundaries.

"Thou hast set them their bounds, which they shall not pass;
Neither turn again to cover the earth."—*Psalms.*

The configuration of the district resembles roughly an inverted wedge with its base resting on Sikkim; its sides pressing in between the buffer States of Nepal and Bhutan, while its apex, which projects into Bengal, separates Purneah and Jalpaiguri. On the east the Jaldakha river separates Darjeeling from Bhutan, on the north (commencing from the west) the Raman, the Little and Great Rangneet rivers, and the Tista and the Rongli intervene between it and Sikkim, while on the west the Singalila range and the Mechi river demarcate the boundary of Nepal.

Lakes.

There are, according to the late Sir W. W. Hunter, two lakes in the district. One is situated about 6 miles south-west of Hope Town; the other, called Ramtal, adjoining a little stream named the Ramthi *nadi*, a few miles to the east of the Tista. This lake measures 550 × 200 yards.

The Town.

The town of Darjeeling nestles on a ridge which starts at Ghum and varies in height from 6,500 to 7,886 feet above sea-level. The ridge may be likened to the letter **Y**, the base resting at Katapahar and Jalapahar while the two arms diverge from the Mall, one dipping suddenly to the north-east and ending in the Lebong spur, the other running north-west (on which Birch Hill stands) passes the St. Joseph's College and finally ends in the valley near the Takvar Tea Estate.

The People.

"And what the people but a herd confused,
A miscellaneous rabble."—*Milton.*

While the dominant race is Nepalese and accounts for half the population, the other half is made up of Bhutias, Lepchas, Tibetans, Mechis, Rajbansis and a heterogeneous lot, such as Santhals, Chota-Nagpuris, Hindus, Mahomedans, Peshwaris, Afghans, Kashmiris, Jews, Chetties, etc., attracted to the district by its climate and trade, as well as by the high wages obtaining in the tea gardens, cinchona plantations and other industries.

As the Nepalese (Gurkhas) have been so much in evidence during the present war the following details will doubtless interest a large circle of readers, and especially the military with whom they have fraternised on the 'Western front.'

In Bengal and, indeed, in every province of India, while the dialect spoken differs in different localities, yet it is understood all over a very much wider area. Not so in Nepal where the population is neither homogeneous with one religion, one language, one set of manners and customs, nor the same habits of life and thought. It is, therefore, an ordinary occurrence to find an inhabitant of Nepal unable to understand a single syllable of the conversation of his next door neighbour. Thus, the Limboo, whose home lies between the Mechi and Arun rivers in Eastern Nepal, has a different dialect from that of the Jimdar, or Karatis, who inhabit the trans-Arun region. So also have the Newars (clerks), the Mangars (soldier class), the Gurungs (shepherds), the Yakhas, the Sunwars (goldsmiths), the Tamangs (Nepalese × Bhutias), etc., each a separate dialect, a separate form of worship, and separate manners and customs.

To bridge these differences of dialect that of the Chettris, called Khas-Kuras, forms the *lingua franca* of the whole of Nepal.

Apart from these dividing lines, the close observer will be able to differentiate the several classes and clans by their physiognomy, which falls under three main headings:—

A-type. The long nosed, big-eyed, and tall in stature:—The Brahmans; 2. Thakuri; 3. Chettry; 4. Newar; 5. Kami; 6. Sarki, and 7. Damae.

B-type. Intermediate between A & C:—The Mangar; 2. Gurung; 3. Tamangs.

C-type. Flat-nosed, small and oblique-eyed, and small in stature:— 1. The Limboo; 2. Jimdar, and 3. the Yakha.

The Newars are the most intelligent in class A; though type B, as a body, is less intelligent than A, it is more enterprising and hardier but a thoroughly improvident lot; while C, which is in every way inferior to both A and B, is the hardiest and with a more martial spirit.

According to their social scale these people are divided into the following classes:—Khambas, Murmirs, Limbus, Yakhas, Jimdars, Damae, Sarki and Jharti. Of the remainder in Darjeeling "the Kamis, who are blacksmiths and goldsmiths, number 9,800 souls ; the Damae, or tailor, total 4,600 ; the Sarki, who work in leather, aggregate 1,800 ; and the Jharti, who once were slaves, closes the list with 3,450*." The next in order of importance is the barber, who is also the village surgeon and physician. These five castes, together with the *mōchi* and *dhobi* are so low in the social scale that they may not enter the courtyards of the temples, and are also required to step off the road on the approach of a member of the higher castes, especially the Brahmin, in case their shadow should fall on him necessitating thereby many ablutions and penances.

The religion of these people is Buddism, which is strongly tinctured with Brahmanical rites.

In order to discourage emigration the Nepalese Durbar has placed a ban on women leaving the country on any pretext whatever.

---

*'The Darjeeling Gazetteer'.

The Bhutias include Sikkimies, Sharpa, Dhrukpa and Tibetan-Bhutias. These people are a cross-breed between the Tibetan, who settled in Sikkim, and the aborigines of that land, the Lepcha. They number about 10,000 souls.

The Tibetan hails from the closed land of mysteries; while the Lepcha once possessed all the hill territory of Sikkim and Darjeeling including the Daling Sub-division. They are born naturalists, and have separate names for nearly every bird, plant, orchid and butterfly to be found in these regions. They have a written language, but, strange to say, no history either of themselves or others. Their original habitat extended for over 120 miles along the southern face of the Himalayas from the river Kossee in Nepal on the west to about 50 miles due east of river Tista. There are two clans, the Kamba and Rongpa; the former though now practically the same as the latter originally migrated into Sikkim from over the Himalayas fully 300 years ago. This race is short in stature, seldom taping over 5 feet in height. The Maharaja of Sikkim is a Kamba. At first his office carried no priestly powers; but now he is acknowledged as the high priest of Buddism in Sikkim.

The Mechis inhabit the Terai tract extending from the Brahmaputra to the Kossee river, which is 20 miles to the west of the river Mechi, thereby roughly covering an area of 250 × 15 miles. They claim to hail from the Bhutan Duars, and have no written language.

The Rajbansis, or Koches, are to be found throughout the foot of the Terai. This is an aboriginal race which once ruled over an extensive tract in the Terai, but have now spread over the whole of the Baikantapur Raj, which extends from Siliguri right down to Jalpaiguri, and have also migrated as far as Cooch Behar on the one hand, and Goalpara, in Assam, on the other. Their womenfolk dress in bright colours very much after the style of the Sonthali the *sari*, or skirt, being fastened beneath the arms and extending as far down as the knees only.

The Bhutias in Darjeeling live as a body in Bhutia Busty, or village, situated to the north-east of the hill: here at times may be seen absurd and grotesque dances in which the participants wear masks representing the animals to be found in the district, and also fanciful dragons, etc.

The one given in February, the Tibetan New Year, excells all others, and is the occasion for much feasting and a continuous round of pleasures to which the officials and leading Europeans in the station are invited. These 'devil dances' are a leading feature of Lamaism, and consist of a series of most violent exercises in which sword-swinging forms no little part. The costumes worn are composed of the most elaborate of Chinese silks over which bright coloured sashes are plaided, while the rich headgear is invariably surmounted with a peacock's feather, which apparently has some occult meaning not divulged to the uninitiated, for we see their soldiers armed with bows and arrows and obsolete weapons of sorts have such feathers stuck in their cane helmets—doubtless a talisman of some sort. These weird dances which are stepped to the tune of most distracting strains call for no little physical effort which completely exhaust the performers, who seemingly only get revived after heavy potations of a country-distilled liquor called *kudo*, brewed from the seed of the millet, are indulged in.

The hill tribes as a class are exceedingly lighthearted, generous to a fault, fond of pleasure in any form, law-abiding,* excitable, and aggressive to a degree when their *amour propre* is touched, which often as not is resented at the point of the short-sword—the *kukri*.

The Caste System.

"Hereditary bondsmen! know ye not
Who would be free, themselves must strike the blow?"—*Byron*.

The village is the unit of all constitutional Government, and its members may by ability rise to the highest appointments in the gift of the State. Not so in the East, where the accident of birth relegates the individual for life to the trade or occupa-

*And no wonder when this trait its characteristically expressed in one of their commonest of proverbs—"There is no answer to an order; there is no medicine for death."

tion of his father in which he may try to excel, but which on no account must he attempt to over-ride by means of education. Such a system when left to itself necessarily produced a phlegmatic temperament, which brought about a certain amount of contentment, and he *then* ascribed the evils, if any, attending his condition in life to the unerring laws of *Karma* or *Kismet*, *i.e.*, fate.

The uplifting of the masses is apparently a prerogative of the missionaries, and so we find Carey in 1800 busy at Serampore (near Calcutta) teaching the first batch of pupils the three R's. Thirteen years later the Western Indian Mission came into being, to be followed by a host of similar institutions which sprang up all over the country. But the credit of placing higher education within the reach of the masses goes to the great David Hare, whose statute stands in the grounds of the institution started by him, and now known as the Presidency College, Calcutta, where youths can obtain a collegiate education run on lines similar to those at Home for the nominal sum of Rs. 120 per annum. Beside the above, we have the Scotch and Oxford Missions turning out fully qualified graduates annually in alarming numbers, and thus ever adding to the ranks of the 'Unemployed'.

What phenomenal results have followed the efforts of these well-meaning teachers, and what a harvest of disaffection and even sedition is being reaped from these sewings! In 1800, pupils, who were satisfied with their lot, had to be collected with persuasion: in 1911, when the last census was taken, there were 10,18,931 males and 1,02,981 females declared as 'literate in English' throughout India and covering all classes, creeds and castes, for whom it was not possible for the Government to find employment as pointed out by Sir Madava Rao in his presidential address to the students of the Madras University:—"at the present day the cultivator, the weaver, the trader, the soldier, the artisan, the Brahmins, and perhaps even the barber, one and all, are fired with the desire to train their sons for Government employment or other sedentary intellectual employment; and in this desire have quite overlooked the fact that such people so far as food, clothing and shelter are concerned are *consumers* and not *producers ;* while those who depend for their livelihood on a salary drawn out of the taxes cannot add to the wealth or the prosperity of the country." Such being the case the educated men, instead of merely seeking to enter the public service, or become lawyers, should largely give themselves to the improvement of Agriculture and development of Manufactures.

And what the result of hankering after intellectual employment? In 1904 there were 400,000 candidates, whose ranks were daily receiving accessions, in quest of employment, and thoroughly dissatisfied with their social status. Yet with these irrefutable data staring it in the face the Government continues its policy of placing cheap* education within the reach of the masses, and thus by continuing to disseminate knowledge awakes its twin sister discontent, and in its wake raises that hydra-headed monster—sedition—among the lower orders especially, as they are unable to get suitable employment outside their original spheres in life, which by that very education has become irksome and distasteful ; that is, a *môchi* (cobbler) or *dhobi* (washerman) who is a plucked 'B.A.' despises his late calling while starving in quest of a clerkship. He *now* nurses his disappointment by hating the Government that gave him an education which has from his present stand-point turned out more a bane than a boon. In days gone by, when he remained unlettered, he ascribed all his ills to *Karma.*

It will be admitted that in the above short enquiry, the fact has been established that in the effort of the masses to over-ride the disabilities of the social scheme and so break through the hitherto iron-bound shackles of the Caste System discontent and sedition, in place of the calm placidity that reigned throughout the land before education was carried to the very door of the nation, have arisen and are now hand in hand stumping the country. And so it requires no special seer to predict that the new nationalist spirit—the handmaiden of knowledge—will in a short time accomplish that which social and religious reformers

---

*At the Presidency College, Calcutta, the cost per student is Rs. 360/- towards which the benign Government contributes no less than Rs. 230/-. In other Indian colleges the charge is about Rs. 100/- less. Indian female education being still in the initial stage the expenditure rises as high as Rs. 533/-, the State paying practically the whole amount.

have failed doing ever since the time ot Budda. There have been many revolts against the caste system in India, but all have failed, because each revolt meant little more than the formation of a new caste, until the advent of Budda, some 2,300 years ago, who taught the *equality of all men* as the fundamental principle in the new creed of Nirvannah which he preached, and which is now known as Buddism. And had it not been for the schisms that followed shortly after his death it is certain that the Brahmins (and there are none so astute and alive to their own interests and power) together with the whole caste system would have been relegated to oblivion. The fact, however, unfortunately remains that they succeeded in regaining lost ground and in fastening fresh and galling shackles on the lower orders of the Hindu Hierarchy.

Education has awakened the whole nation as a body, and the new Nationalist Spirit which is now the dominant force in the country is leading men to ask whether a national life on a caste basis can ever be possible. Is caste consistent with democracy? Hitherto caste has been able to accommodate itself to pressure put upon it from outside and yet to preserve itself alive. Will it do so again? Will it survive Parliamentary government as it has survived railways, waterworks and the Universities?

India must advance economically if she is to maintain a place among the nations ; and economic progress means the rise of innumerable occupations to which caste cannot accommodate itself with sufficient rapidity. The forces operative against caste, therefore, are widespread, they are inseparably bound up with the progress of the country, and they spring from within and are not imposed from without. Whether caste will still survive, in ways that are at present unforeseen, is one of the questions which only time can answer.

Marriage Rites.

"Hanging and wiving goes by destiny."—*Merchant of Venice.*

The essential features of these rites as practised generally among hillfolk of this district will be lightly touched upon.

No age limit is fixed, for marriage between infants, and

adults are equally in favour among all hill races ; while intermarriage between the different castes is practised to a limited extent. Widow remarriage on the other hand while prevalent to a certain degree among the Nepalese and Bhutias is a recognised institution among the Lepchas.

Astrology plays an important part in determining the auspicious hour in which the groom, preceded by a band of minstrels, and followed by a host of friends and admirers all mounted on ponies (for the first time in their lives) which have been supplied by the bridegroom, who ever after is the bondservant of the obliging Kayah (money-lender), calls at the house of the bride-elect who sits decorated and veiled in the courtyard which has been festooned in bright colours and shaded with the delicate shoots of the maling bamboo awaiting the advent of her future lord and master. On arrival the groom is met by a priest who chants *mantras* (incantations), after which much feasting accompanied by heavy potations of country liquor is indulged in to a late hour of the morning.

Among the Bhutias and Lepchas the rite usually extends over two stages. The first, in which the groom is required to live in the same house as his *mother-in-law* ! for a period which may extend to two years, or more, until *she* is satisfied as to his docility before he may start a home for himself. Sometimes a further stage is insisted upon, *viz.*, he is called upon to pay *rit*, or the market-value of his wife (as is practised to this day among the Arabs), before he may strike out for himself. When such sanction is accorded the usual cavalcade is formed, as when he first visited his bride-elect ; but on the return journey the wife, after being heavily veiled, is slung hammockwise in a sheet the ends of which are attached to a long bamboo pole and carried behind the husband, the two being followed by a motley crowd mounted on steeds and a host of urchins and the curious, who disperse only after they have enjoyed the groom's hospitality along with the invited guests. Therefore, the greater such a crowd the happier the groom ! for it gives him spontaneously a status in his circle as being a man of means, for which he pays during the remainder of his life, being the bondsman of the obliging shylock, who swindles him at every turn.

The custom among the Nepalese varies as much as the many castes and sects into which this race is divided. The Brahmins or priests, and the Chettris or soldiers, are married by a Brahmin priest who reads the ritual from the *Vedas*, the sacred book of the Hindus, to be followed by a feast to which all and sundry are invited. The lower orders, however, dispense with the services of a priest and are pronounced man and wife by a *panchayat* (assembly of five people)—an institution peculiar to India, which gave to every caste the elements of self-government, or, as Elphinston (the ablest Governor that ever controlled the affairs of the Bombay Presidency), ingeniously hath it, "gave to the people justice when they could not get it elsewhere."

The Nepalese have the distinction of indulging in two forms of marriage. In the first, the bride is wooed and won with the consent of her parents or guardians ; while in the second she is first abducted and thereafter married with the consent of her people. The first procedure corresponds to the Brahma form of marriage according to Hindu Law, while the second is known as *Churia-bia* (marriage by stealth), and corresponds to the Gandharva form of the same law.

Enticement and divorce are common occurrences, the delinquent being mulcted with the cost of the *rit*, and all incidental expenses incurred for the wedding by the aggrieved husband.

Polygamy is very prevalent among all grades of Nepalese ; while polyandry is peculiar to Tibet alone.

Servants and Wages.

As the climate of these altitudes does not suit the man from plains, almost all the domestic work is carried on by Paharies, Bhutias and Lepchas, who having an innate apathy for water must be carefully watched if clean work is desired. Some, however, make exceedingly desirable servants being neat, clean and smart in appearance ; but these are generally sought after by the managers of hotels and boarding establishments who pay rather high wages for such servitude.

Kits (table-servant) may be had from Rs. 12/- to 16/-; Khansamas (cooks) from 16/- to 30/-; Ayahs from 12/- to 20/-;

Masalchis from 4¾/- to 8¾/-; Sweepers (whole time) from 8/- to 12/-; Bearers from 12/- to 16/-; Grooms 10/- to 15/- and Bistis (water-carriers) from 1/- to 3/- per mensem.

This fraternity is exceedingly proud of certificates when presenting them for inspection: oftener they belong to a *bhai* who has hired them for the occasion. It were best, therefore, if the selection of servants were left to resident friends in the stations along the D. H. Railway, or to the managers of the different hotels and boarding houses.

Darjeeling—Past & Present.

"And oft a retrospect delights the mind"—*Dante*.

Darjeeling in 1835 was but a collection of about 20 huts with a population of 100 souls. In 1840 the town consisted of the Kutchery (located in the building now in occupation by the Gymkhana Club) and about 30 other buildings of the meanest description; and the following residences which had some pretensions to respectability:—Mount Pleasant, the residence of Lt.-General Lloyd; One Tree House, since known as Beechwood, which was occupied by Dr. Campbell, and thereafter by Lord Ulick Browne, quondam Commissioner, Jalpaiguri Division; another named "Bryanstone"* after Brain Houghton Hodgson, in which Sir Joseph Hooker lived in 1848, but now the seat of the Rector of St. Paul's School: also the original St. Andrew's Church at which the Chaplain of Berhampore officiated occasionally. By the end of 1845 Darjeeling put forward some real pretensions to respectability, for in 'The Darjeeling Guide' of that period we find mention made of the following buildings:—Rockvile, described as the largest house in the station; Lloyd's Bank, which stood on the plot since converted into The Pleasaunce; Oak Lodge, Vernon Lodge, Cheveremont, Woodlands,

*"This building was first named 'Herbert Hill' after Sir Herbert Maddock (whom Hodgson succeeded as Resident at the Court of Nepal in 1833) who had built it as a residence for himself, and from whom Hodgson bought it in 1847. It was located in a narrow clearing of majestic forest that then clothed the mountains of (British) Sikkim on every side, and crept up to the walls of the *few* houses of which the station consisted."—*Life of Brian Houghton Hodgson* by Sir W. W. Hunter.

in which Capt. Bishop, who commanded the troops, lived ; the Dell, now the Dale, in which Dr. Griffiths the then Civil Surgeon resided ; Colinton, now the summer residence of the Maharaja of Cooch Behar ; the Glen and Salt Hill. The hotels of this period numbered two only ;—'The Darjeeling Family Hotel,' and another, 'Castleton,' owned by Mr. Wilson, the proprietor of Wilson's Hotel, Calcutta, now 'The Great Eastern,' but still known as 'Wilson's' by the Indian jehu of that city.

According to 'The Hand Book of Darjeeling,' published in 1863, (and now materially added to) there were about 70 houses in the station of which the buildings of note only will be inserted in the tabular statement below. As the plan of the ridge on which the town stands may be likened to the letter Y, it would be well to keep to this arrangement and start from the base, which rests at Senchal and Katapahar, and work downwards and forwards in parallel rows :—

SENCHAL.	CANTONMENTS.	1ST PARALLEL.	2ND PARALLEL.	3RD PARALLEL.	4TH PARALLEL.
Officers' Mess Balaclava Hotel	Church (R.C.) Convalescent Depôt Artillery Quarters Hospital	Bryanstone Oak Lodge Chevremont Colinton Vernon Lodge	Starts' Cottage Neible's Cottage Ence Cottage Woodlands Banstead Belombre Bryguine Site Railway Station	Beechwood House. Holburn House Bazar Lt. Whish's Cottage Jail	Rockville Exchange Hall Chapleton Victoria Terrace Bhutia School Post Office

5TH PARALLEL.	6TH PARALLEL.	7TH PARALLEL.	8TH PARALLEL.	9TH PARALLEL.
Drum Druid Dale Duka's Delight Alice Villa Thorn Cottage Dispensary Sapper Lines Rosamond Hill O'Donoghne's Cottage	St. Andrew's Church Dharbanga House Mount Pleasant Lloyd's Bank Sunny Bank Convent Lochnagar Gallows, The	Kutchery Mall Side Hadham Lodge Meadow Bank Maples	The Green Halcyon House	Castleton Dak Bungalow Happy Valley Cemetery

It would probably interest not a few readers if we attempted to rehabilitate some of these tenements, and accordingly the following account is given:—

Senchal.

Although this spot was abandoned as a cantonment in 1867 yet we find the officers clinging to their quarters and commodious mess. Balaclava, as its name implies, was started by Nicholson (one of the famous six hundred who took part in that ever memorable charge) who lead the guard-of-honour when Lord Roberts visited this station. Needless to add that the two heroes shook hands on this occasion. Having made his pile (for who did not in those days?), he sold out to Hirlihy of the municipality, the management devolving on his able wife who a short while after was induced by the syndicate, which had purchased both the Woodlands and the Drum Druid Hotels, to take them over on the hire-purchase system, in which she was materially aided by John White, whose liberality has been commented upon elsewhere.

Jalapahar.

From Salt Hill Road (opposite the Union Chapel) to the Depot at Jalapahar, which was circumscribed up to the close of 1870, the whole of the hillside was covered by such dense forest and heavy undergrowth of maling bamboo that tigers abounded therein, one of which as late as 1880 killed a grass-cutter on the spot on which 'Bagmarie' stands (*i.e.*, the place where a tiger had killed) on Auckland Road.

About the year 1840 the occurrence of a fire, which swept the hillside, from Salt Hill right up to the spot on which the Depot now stands, of every vistage of vegetation, gave Jalapahar, the 'burnt hill', its name.

As the Convalescent Depot was erected in 1848 we may be sure that the St. Francis' Church (R. C., now the St. Joseph's) which was cruciform in shape and of lath and plaster, came into being about the same time to minister to the spiritual wants of the invalid soldiers. It was rebuilt in 1880: its old doors and windows now form part of the cottage attached to 'West Point'. St. Luke's (C. E.), on which now hangs the same bell which once tolled the worshippers to the original St. Andrew's Church, was built as late as 1885.

The gunners of the artillery were located in two small cottages named 'The Eagle's Nest', which on being gutted by fire in 1871 gave place to the commodious barracks erected at Katapahar.

Darjeeling.

In the first parallel we get Bryanstone, of which full details have been given ; then Colinton, next Vernon Lodge in occupation by Major Harman of the Trigonometrical Survey of India founded by Col. Sir George Everest.

The first three in the next row are closely associated with the pioneer missionaries, for Start, Neible and Wernicke are well-known. In Ence Cottage Mrs. Wernicke started a miscellaneous depot and dairy farm ; Woodlands, then a two-storied structure, was owned by Assistant Surgeon Collins, and occupied by the Bishop of Calcutta. In 1872 this building passed into the possession of Roberts, an ex-army sergeant, who being an accomplished musician improvised a band which discoursed music at the balls and public functions held at Dunn's Assembly Rooms—The Green—which was demolished subsequently to form the lawn and tennis court attached to Halcyon House. In 1870 we find this versatile man installed both as manager of the 'Delaram Tea Estate', and proprietor of the Clarendon Hotel at Kurseong. The latter venture proving lucrative he moved on with the advance of the *line*, bought Woodlands, built the three-storied Annexe attached thereto and bought the Drum Druid Hotel also ; all of which to this day are spoken of by the populace as 'Roberts' Hotels'. In Banstead we see installed Dr. Schilich, the first Conservator of Forests, and subsequently Prof. of Forestry in Cooper's Hill. On his vacating, it was taken over by the Scot's Mission and is now its permanent habitation. Brynguine (subsequently the site of the Lowis Jubilee Sanitarium) with its extensive grounds, in which there was a large pool, accommodated the school for Young Ladies started by Miss White; while Belombre (next to the Station House) has ever since its construction been occupied by the family of Lt.-Col. Crommelin, R.E., who built the last three houses.

The first in the next row is Beechwood House, whose successive occupants have already been given. Then comes Holburn House (now in Lloyd's Road) built and occupied by John White. A small bazar composed of tinroofed shanties catered for the wants of the inhabitants on the same spot on which now stand clean three-storied concrete structures rushed up by G. P. Robertson, the Engineer to the Municipality. Immediately below this site is the cottage in which Lt. Whish was murdered by a fanatic in 1857, and which on subsequently being enlarged accommodates the Superintendent of the Jail. The next is the Jail.

In the fourth parallel, and highest on the ridge, stands Rockville in which a Young Ladies Institution was conducted by a Miss Wight ; below it was the Exchange Hall (now the site of Hall & Anderson on Commercial Row) in which services were held for a good many years after the spire of St. Andrew's Church had collapsed in 1867; then comes Chapleton, on the Post Office Road, in which those of the Baptist persuasion met for divine service under the pastorage of Mr. J. C. Page, until the Union Chapel was erected on the Auckland Road in 1869 by Mr. T. Kenay, the Engineer. In Victoria Terrace, Mount Pleasant Road (occupied now by Robert & Co. and Master's Curio Shop), Conductor Spencer Robinson managed the Carrying Co. and Tonga Service started by Lloyd, the banker. To the north of the Bazar and just below the Eden Sanitarium stands the same house which was once the Post Office; but now in occupation by the Police Sadar Office. Above it (now the site of the Sanitarium) was the cottage built by Dr. O'Donoghue, which in turn became the Bhutia Boarding School, and the residence of the House Surgeon of the Sanitarium.

Starting from the Chow in the next parallel we come across the Dale and Duka's Delight (after Duka, a Swiss, the Civil Surgeon)—then Alice Villa built by Dr. O'Donoghue, and

Thorn Cottage both of which were occupied in succession by the Planters' Club prior to its transfer to its present site in Commercial Row. Rosamond Hill, now the San, next comes prominently into view for on it were located Rosamond House, the Cottage built by O'Donoghue, and the Sappers' Arsenal, which was placed at the base of the hill and at the junction of the Cart and Lochnagar Roads. All three buildings were struck by lightning early one Sunday morning in 1876 which entirely consumed the first and caused the third to explode killing the entire guard, and so produced such a panic that the neighbourhood was deserted for days thereafter. To the south of the Dispensary were the Sapper Lines now occupied by the local police.

In the sixth parallel Darbhanga House to the south of St. Andrew's Church gave place lately to Southfield ; while just below was 'Mount Pleasant' the residence of Lt.-Genl. Lloyd, the discoverer of Darjeeling (since converted into The Pleasaunce). On the ground floor of this building, and facing the road, Dr. O'Brien started 'The Darjeeling News' in 1873 ; the first floor was set apart for the bank, while to the north of the building was a pretty cottage in which the Manager, Mr. A. B. L. Webb, lived. The original Sunny Bank (now the Park Hotel) seemed fated to be utilised as a school for we find that it sheltered the Boys' School started by the Capuchin Fathers before the Jesuits took it over for the St. Joseph's Seminary, which eventually worked its way to North Point as the St. Joseph's College. The Convent now invites our particular attention as it is not only one of the oldest buildings in the station but also the pioneer in matters of education (See diagram 3, Plate VIII). In the foreground stood the orphanage, the ground floor of the main building was the chapel ; the half of the first floor on the left was the vestry while facing it was the office ; the second contained the cloisters of the novitiates ; the connecting wing was reserved for the dormitories of the pupils and the cubicles of the nuns ; while the block in the background was set apart for instructional purposes. Pretty Lochnagar with its orchards and well-laid out grounds is no more, for it gradually succumbed to the erosion which even now threatens the existence of the new Kutchery, and the main buildings of the Happy Valley Tea Estate which since 1879 have been already once removed bodily to a higher level. Lochnagar will, however, be always remembered as the residence of the Rev. Mr. Macfarlane, who in 1870 started a school in that building for the uplifting both mentally and spiritually of the indigenous population.

The spirit of decorum seems to have been as dead in Darjeeling as it was in Calcutta for a good number of years, for we find the Gallows had been erected on an open spot in the Botanic Garden and on the plot on which a small cottage acted as museum until Lord Carmichel gave Darjeeling a building to the west of the Park worthy of the name of Museum.

In the next line the original Kutchery (now the Amusement Club) has elsewhere been mentioned at length, and so we turn to Mall Side in which Martin, the contractor, started a millinery establishment, and which for a number of years thereafter was eagerly sought after by similar firms in Calcutta which desired opening out branches in this station, the forlorn hope, as usual, being led by Whiteaway Laidlaw, Ltd. In 1870, Meadow Bank was a boarding establishment owned by Mrs. Crofton, sister-in-law to Doyle, who ran the Drum Druid Hotel and owned the Bloomfield Estate (now the site of the Armed Police Barracks) which to this day is called 'Dally-Kaman' by the paharies. Meadow Bank was eventually bought by the Government and handed over to the Board of Revenue. The Maples has always been connected in the minds of the old residents with the Wine Stores started by John White, as prior to his venture people had to shift as best they could for such viands.

'The Green' has already been referred to, and so we pass on to the next parallel containing Wilson's Busti Road (now Hooker Road) in which there were a few cottages chief among which was Castleton (alias Wilson's Hotel) a two-storied structure (which was levelled by an earthquake) in which Mrs. Dupin conducted a girls' school where they obtained a *finish* in every conceivable subject including French—as per advertisements of the period. Lower down was Happy Valley Tea Estate laid out by Hart (brother to the Collector of Customs, China ; and who married one of the daughters of Capt. Keble, our local poet) and the late Mr. Paul, I.C.S., quondam Dy. Commissioner, Darjeeling.

The Lebong Spur.

On the way down to the Ging Monastery we come across the two bungalows of the late Genl. Mannering (an Anglo-Indian) who compiled the only standard Lepcha Dictionary and Grammar published under authority. Between these buildings and the present parade ground stood the Rev. Mr. Page's bungalow, while on the flat was a large tank to the north of which stood the spacious stables of Mr. J. W. Grant (who accompanied Lloyd to Darjeeling in 1828) which lodged his stud of 25 racers and English hacks; a little further down (and on the spot on which the Orderly Room now stands) was a two-storied building in which lived Grant's son, a planter, until the whole spur was acquired by the Military authorities for the erection of the barracks at Lebong in the year 1888 after the conclusion of the Sikkim Expedition. A little lower down was the cottage of Lloyd the banker, which was used as the Mess until suitable accommodation was assigned to it in the general scheme. Further down hill was the home of the *great* Mandelli, who converted a large bungalow in his grounds into a museum which in a short time attracted universal recognition.

The Horse-Shoe.

In the horse-shoe nestling between the Lebong and Takvar spurs stands 'Hillside', in which the Dalai Llama lived when he sought the protection of the British Government when harried over the borders of Tibet by the Chinese in 1910. To the west of this building stood 'The Shrubbery', as Government House was then called, which successively passed through the hands of Edward Hepper, Brine of Hope Town reputation, Sir Thomas E. Turton, then Barnes (by which name it was known for years) until it was purchased by the Cooch Behar Raj, to be handed over in turn in the year 1877 to the Government by the late Maharaja of Cooch Behar. Just behind and to the north of this building stands 'Snowy View' which temporarily sheltered the pupils of the Loreto Convent until a permanent abode was erected to the north of the Eden Sanitarium by Judge Longhnan and two other gentlemen in 1846.

The Takvar Spur.

About a mile below the Cart Road Treutler's Farm and tea garden nestled in the hollow of the spur; and about the same distance lower down was the Takvar Tea Estate superintended by Capt. J. Masson, late proprietor of the River View Estate, which adjoined it, and of 'Clear Point,' on the site of which Girivilash was subsequently erected by the Digapatia Rajah.

Growth of Town.

From a very early period the population shewed a marked tendency to increase owing to the security afforded life and property under the British flag, as also to the even-handed justice meted out by Dr. Campbell, for we are told that many flocked to this station from the plains, while hundreds were drawn over the borders in search of employ. In 1872 the town contained 3,000 inhabitants, which at the end of the next 20 years had quadrupled itself. In 1901 no less than 17,000 were resident in the town of Darjeeling, which during the summer months rose to 24,000 owing to the influx of visitors which follow the movements of the Government. The last census taken in 1911 shewed that the urban population had risen to 24,579, and that of the district to 2,65,500, of which only 2,808 were Europeans. The cause of this rapid expansion was due to three factors:—Darjeeling is the summer seat of the Local Government as also the Sanitarium of both Bengal and Burma, thus drawing many from both places in search of health, while the tea industry, which by this time had practically spread over all the hillsides, employed thousands of operatives.

It is not generally known that only 22 years ago (1896) the Mall was reached by the Tonga, and Auckland Roads, or from the railway station by one of two narrow paths—Banstead and

Lloyd's Roads ;—and also that Beechwood Estate, which was covered by forest, contained a solitary house, Beechwood. At that time this estate formed a part of the Judge property ; but it was subsequently bought by Mr. Carl Forstmann, who bid over the heads of the City Fathers who desired acquiring it for a park. The year following Mr. R. T. Greer, C.I.E., I.C.S., under the provisions of the Land Acquisition Act, acquired the land on which Mackenzie Road was constructed at a cost of Rs. 65,000 (exclusive of the actual cost of making the road) thus giving full scope to the new proprietor to open out the estate. Darjeeling is indebted to this energetic and popular Deputy Commissioner for the following also :—The widening of the Chowrasta and the erection thereon of the Old Bandstand, and the electric installation, both of which were completed in the years 1896-97, respectively.

The town has during the past few years grown apace both in regard to the number of its new houses as well as the replacement of unsightly structures by others more in keeping with the architectural design of adjacent residential buildings. The first in order of such improvements is Hotel Mount Everest, followed closely by Southfield, the next the ferro-concrete structure ('Rainbow') built for Mr. P. L. Roy, Bar-at-Law, on the vacant plot to the north of Carmichael Court in which the members of His Excellency's band are quartered. Hadham Lodge and Warwick House have likewise given place to Durly and Eden Chines, Ivanhoe, Kenilworth and Westward Ho ! Then followed the Natural History Museum, to the south of the Secretariat Buildings, a three-storied, concrete structure containing 20 spacious rooms. 'Lavendar Lane,' which connects the Mackenzie and Lloyd's Roads, has been taken over by the Municipality from the proprietors of the Beechwood Estate, railed in, widened and duly lighted, thereby affording the public an opportunity of easy access at all hours to the bazar ; while the last item in this programme is the acquisition of the plots on which dilapidated huts now stand in the vicinity of Mary Ville and Moss Bank, and others to the north of the Station House on the Cart Road. Many of the roads have also been widened, the last being the Auckland Road, just above the Town Hall, in which blasting had to be resorted to ; and accordingly the residents of the houses in its immediate vicinity were warned to vacate their premises during certain hours of the morning when these operations were in progress. Apparently one of these charges was either too large, or not sufficiently imbedded in the rock for large pieces were sent flying about the neighbourhood one of which caused some damage to the kitchen of 'Rhododendron Villa' while another made a large hole in the east wall of that building.

The town now contains 351 houses (as against 70 only in 1870) and with some shew of truth boasts of a few excellent villas, the properties of Indian noblemen and Europeans, such as Colinton, the summer resort of the Maharaja of Cooch Behar ; Girivilash, owned by the Raja of Digapatia ; Bagmarie, the property of N. C. Bose, the attorney ; Terpsithia Estate, purchased by the late Sir Chas. Paul, Advocate-General of Bengal ; Elgin (Rheinstein) Villa (See Plate III.) built by Carl Forstman ; Sadie Villas (since renamed by respective owners—Kali Villa, Wayside and Dulce Domum) constructed by E. C. Dozey ; Singamari House erected by A. A. Price ; Southfield, the residence of Sir R. N. Mukherjee ; and Rose Bank, the summer seat of the Maharajadhiraj of Burdwan.

Chief Public Buildings.

The following is a list of the chief public buildings and places of interest in the Darjeeling district, and the dates on which they came into being :—

1765—Buddist Monastery (ruins on Observatory Hill.)
1843—St. Andrew's Church—C. E. (rebuilt in 1882 and added to in 1897)
,, —Bryanstone at St. Paul's School.
1847—Loreto Convent (rebuilt in 1892 and added to in 1915)
1848—Jalapahar Convalescent Depot.
1851—Hindu Mandir
1852-62—Jumma Masjid
1864—St. Paul's School, Jalapahar
1865—Old Cemetery
,, —The Jail
1867—Jalapahar and Katapahar Cantonments

1868—The Darjeeling (Planters') Club
,, —The Convent Cemetery
1869—Union Chapel
1870—Charitable Dispensary
1874—Bhutia Boarding School
1876—Buddist Monastery, Ghum
1877—Birch Hill Park
1878—Lloyd Botanic Garden
1879—The Shrubbery, now Government House
,, —Victoria Boys' School (Kurseong)
,, —Buddist Monastery, Bhutia Busty
,, —St. Joseph's Church (R. C.), Jalapahar
1880—Brahma Mandir
1883—Eden Sanitarium
1887—Lowis Jubilee Sanitarium
1888—St. Joseph's College, North Point
,, —Lebong Cantonments (enlarged 1909)
1889—St. Mary's Training College (Kurseong)
,, —St. Luke's (C. E.), Jalapahar
1890—St. Helen's Convent (Kurseong)
1891—Railway Station
1892—Lodge Mount Everest
1893—Church of the Immaculate Conception (R. C.)
1894—St. Columba's Church (Scots)
1895—Queen's Hill Girls' School
1896—Buddist Monastery, Ging
,, —Old Bandstand
1897—New Kutchery
1898—Secretariat Buildings
,, —Dow Hill Girls' School (Kurseong)
1899—The Visitor Press
1900—Rink Theatre
,, —Colonial Homes (Kalimpong)
1903—Victoria Hospital
1904—Diocesan Girls' High School
1905—Golf Links
1906—F. H. Hathaway & Co.
1907—The Goethals' Memorial School (Kurseong)

,, —Hindu Public Hall

,, —The Parsee Cemetery (enlarged in 1910)

1908—Maharani Girls' School

1909—Pleasaunce

,, —New Cemetery

1910—Takdah Cantonments

,, —Terraces in Market Square

1912—Lodge Lebong

1913—Chinese Club

1914—Annexes to Government House

,, —Hospital of His Excellency's Staff

,, —Small-pox Hospital

1915—Natural History Museum

,, —Hotel Mount Everest

,, —Southfield

,, —Bloomfield Barracks

1921—Town Hall

The Food and Fodder Problems.*

It would appear that the authorities have for sometime past been so engrossed in giving its urban population of 24,579 souls residential quarters, an increase in the electric lighting scheme, and a third recreation ground that its inner wants have been quite forgotten, *viz.*, a better and more regular supply of market produce.

---

*Contributed to *'The Darjeeling Times'* on *7th April, 1912.* "The restrictions to grazing grounds which are steadily taking place in these hills is proving not merely a hardship to native cattle owners but to the public indirectly. The Forest Department for several years past oblivious of local conditions the consequence of its policy, has been trying to *force* the gowala (cowherd) to stall-feed his cattle on the European method—ignoring the fact that hill cattle do not thrive on such a system—and with this object have laid down a policy of slowly but steadily restricting the grazing grounds, in spite of frequent protests from milkmen and cattle owners"—*The Darjeeling Advertiser* of the 30th May, 1916. See also editorial in its issue of the 13th June, 1916.

Darjeeling, however, is not alone in the demand for larger grazing areas. The All-India Cow Conference passed a resolution in December, 1917, "that, in consequence of the fact that the want of pasture grounds has been partly responsible for the high rate of mortality among bullocks, cows and calves and the consequent scarcity in the supply of milk and milk products, this Conference recommends that the Government will be pleased to take immediate steps by necessary legislation or otherwise to provide adequate pasture grounds".

For some years past Darjeeling has suffered from a scarcity in both the meat and milk supply; and more so during the 'season'. A solution to the first has still to be found; the export of vegetables and market produce† either restricted or stopped ; while the milk supply problem has been solved by the versatile *gowala* in his own inimical way—'arf and arf'.

The scarcity in the meat supply has in a great measure been brought about by the further curtailment of the areas thrown open to grazing in the several blocks of the Darjeeling Division thereby compelling cowherds to track over the borders into Sikkim and Nepal. The whole question, therefore, of an adequate fodder supply will herein be considered as, although the matter received the earnest attention of both the Forest Department and the Local Government, no practical solution was arrived at owing to the factors which govern this moot question not being fully understood, or considered by those at whose hands a solution was sought.

The forest blocks in and around Darjeeling for the past few years have been so drawn upon for the fuel-supply that a closure of large tracts against all grazing has been forced upon

---

†"Market Rates" shewing the prices for each class of fruit, vegetable, meat, &c., are published weekly in *'The Darjeeling Advertiser'*. The following is a list of the chief comestibles offered for sale here :—*Fruits*—Apples, cocoanuts, guavas, jack-fruit, leechees, lemons, mangoes, oranges, papayas, peaches, pine-apples, plantains and plums; also all fruits from the plains and Afghanistan, which are imported. *Vegetables*—Beans, beetroot, brinjals, cabbages, carrots, cauliflowers, celery, cucumber, leeks, lettuce, melons (water and marsh) mint, parsnip, peas, potatoes (ordinary and sweet) pumpkins, rhubarb, sugar-cane, tomatces (ordinary and tree) turnips, thyme and yams; also all varieties grown in the plains and neighbouring valleys where the heat is tropical.

The following excerpt from "The Hand Book of Darjeeling" would prove interesting to residents especially, and make them long for the return of such 'good old times':

Mutton was sold at 1/12 to 3/- the quarter; *beef* 'at moderate prices'; *fowls* at 3 to 5 per rupee; *Masheer fish* from the Rangneet at 4 annas a seer (our supplies are at present obtained from Sara Ghat stored in ice at 1/4 per seer); *potatoes* at 2/ the maund (now at 4/); *vegetables* were dear and only obtainable from Treutler's Farm and the Jail (which still does the major portion of the supply); *pigeons* at 3 to 4 annas each; *pork* and *ham* were excellent, the latter being sold at eight annas a pound; half-grown *geese* at one rupee each, half-grown *ducks* at 4 to 5 per rupee (they are now 1/4 each); *eggs* at 3 for an anna; *milk*, Great Scot ! at 12 to 20 quarts per rupee (now 4 seers per rupee); *butter* at annas twelve per lb.; and one lb. loaves of *bread*, baked by Schow, the Danish baker, at 7 per rupee.

the authorities with the result that kine have either to be stall-fed (a rare thing for the *gowala* to indulge in, indeed, it is doubtful if he could devote the necessary time to it) or allowed to starve, thereby affecting the yield of milk and its price which is still on the upward grade owing to the quartering of the Gurkha Battalion at Hum whose diet is chiefly composed of milk and its adjuncts. To overcome the shortage in the area open to grazing the authorities have for the past few years cast about for a solution of the fodder problem and with this end in view planted out 40 acres of land at Posambing (near Ghum) with *dub* grass. This trial from its very inception was bound to end in failure for the habits of this grass were not understood by those entrusted with the experiment. And it seems to those acquainted with agriculture that the experiments and subsequent achievements of the Allahabad Fodder Farm should have been well known to Forest Officials in general who from time to time are intimately concerned with the formation of forest villages and their upkeep.

Such being the case the next attempt at a solution of the difficulty, *viz.*, the erection in certain blocks of bathans or byres—was also far from satisfactory, for it did not appeal to the Indian who being conservative did not take kindly to the innovation and the more so owing to the levy of a nominal rent for the use of the paddock, and accordingly he migrated with his cattle over the borders into Sikkim chiefly where grazing is not restricted. It now devolves on the writer to indicate wherein both schemes failed, as also to suggest the only lines on which an adequate fodder supply could be raised and maintained in the areas thrown open to grazing.

It is an axiom in grass-farming, as in agriculture, that a thorough knowledge of the various soils which are found in India as also the nature of the several fodder grasses, are of the utmost importance. Likewise, if growth and expansion are desired, a sufficiency of food and water are essential for the well-being of the corp. Apparently all these conditions were either ignored or overlooked for an examination of the plot at Posambing shewed at a glance that although it had an exceeding heavy gradient yet it was not divided off into small plots by *bunds* (ridges) in order to retain the entire rainfall, which when thus held up not only gradually percolates through the soil carrying with it certain elements from the atmosphere but also the necessary food products (manure) to the roots of the crop. Failure was, therefore, courted at the outset.

The next attempt, *viz.*, the erection of byres, would have fairly met the requirements of the case to a limited extent had certain conditions been observed, that is, those byres would have maintained a greater number of cattle than they do under the present system of partial stall-feeding. But in the laying out of these paddocks we again find an absolute disregard of the very grievances that the Forest Department have against the admission of cattle into its areas, *viz.*, the damage done to all growth by trampling, for experience has established the fact that cattle munch 10 *per cent.*, and destroy 90 *per cent.* of any field or common over which they graze. Such being the case it was expected that the same measures would have been adopted as was done by the Australian farmer who was not slow to recognise and obviate this difficulty, *i.e.*, he divided and sub-divided his fields into plots just large enough to furnish his herd with sufficient fodder until the other plots closed to grazing had fully recovered. Acting on this principle of rotation it was found that 53 acres sown with *Paspalum Dilatatum* (which was lately tried in Tirhoot with some measure of success) carried no less than 63 head of cattle. Taking these figures as a basis of calculation we find that the plot at Posambing would have yielded sufficient fodder for 47 kine. Similarly, the exact quantity of land necessary for pasturing a given number of cattle in this district is a matter of simple arithmetic, and as the numbers—7551* in the Darjeeling Division—are far from excessive it must be admitted that the necessary acreage could, and should be set apart in terms of the Grazing Rules published in 1884 by which "*one half* of the area under forest is open to grazing, while *10 acres* of the area is allowed for each head of cattle." In contravention of the above Ruling we find that the Government of Bengal in its covering letter to the Forest Administration Report of 1912-13 agreed to

*According to the Cattle Census of 1912.

the further curtailment of the present and apparently inadequate area in the following terms:—"The question of reservation of grazing lands for the milk supply of Darjeeling has been further examined, and in view of the extension of the practice of stall-feeding it has been found possible to reduce the area in the Darjeeling Division from 13,000 to 8,000 acres"*, which doubtless was based on paragraphs 41 and 62 of the report in question, from which we learn that "the number of cows now grazing in the forests, compared with the number grazed in 1904-05† is less" and also that "the number of stall-fed cows at the close of the year had risen to 61"—out of the 7,551 cattle which supply the wants of an urban population of 24,579! It, therefore, follows that the greater the constriction of the area the less the number of cattle which can be supported on it, the surplus being forced to treck over the borders: consequently, the converse of the proposition adopted should be considered and given effect to, *viz.*, to increase the area in terms of the Ruling cited, or, as predicted in 'The Darjeeling Gazetteer', the day is not far distant 'when the population will have to import its milk supply from the plains'.

It may be contended that the fodder supply of the town falls more under the purview of the Municipality than of the Forest Department, and the writer is disposed to agree with this view, for "ever since 1866 the Municipality has retained possession of the 622 acres originally intended for grazing grounds". It, therefore, devolves on the Government to insist on this area being thrown open to grazing, or have it transferred to the control of the Forest Department to be utilised for the purpose for which it was originally ear-marked. Such an area, however, would support only a fraction of the number of cattle in this division, and so it behoves Government (whose first consideration ought to be the welfare of the people rather than bring about an

---

*That is, a little over *one* acre only has been allowed for each head of cattle instead of the *ten* allotted by the Grazing Rules.

†Surely more recent figures ought to be available! However this may be, it follows that the numbers must necessarily decrease in proportion to the curtailments as they advance. Indeed, the present quotation but proves the converse of the proposition the Forest Department has been at such pains to establish.

increase of revenue by resuming this plot under the provisions of the Forest Act) to place a sufficient acreage at the disposal of either department, which together with the above 622 acres of land would yield the requisite amount of fodder for the support and well-being of the 7,551 cattle in the Darjeeling Division. It, therefore, follows that until this desideratum takes place so long will our kine be ill-fed, thereby affecting the yield of milk; and, what is of greater moment, if the difficulty experienced is not speedily removed, the *gowala* will either go over to the Military authorities at Hum in appreciable numbers, or, worse still, migrate over the borders, thereby accentuating the present scarcity in the supply of meat and milk.

In May, 1916, the meat scarcity had assumed such alarming proportions that the Market Superintendent was deputed to proceed to Calcutta with a view to arrange, if possible, for the supply from that city. And yet while a remedy lies at our very doors, these make-shifts are being resorted to, to the detriment of the consumer.

Having disposed of the land and paddock questions, all that is now left is to name the chief fodder grasses which if planted out would fully meet all the demands made upon them. The *Paspalum Dilitatum* in addition to being a large yielder of successive crops possesses exceptional vitality, for it throws out a mass of roots (thus incidentally acting as a surface binder and so would prevent all erosion of our hillsides, another question which has for sometime past been engaging the attention of the Government) which penetrates the soil to a depth of 12 inches or more, thereby rendering it immune to the attack of frost: indeed, when the sugarcane had been entirely blighted this grass was just shewing signs of attack. Planted in drills 18 inches by 6 inches apart it yields no less than 50 tons to the acre. The *Parba*, or thatching grass, which is so well known in Allahabad, Chota-Nagpur and the Sonthal Perganas, should be given a chance, for its value as a fodder plant is known to the Indian Cavalry who entirely feed their chargers on it.

Finally, the daily export of market produce, which is neither restricted nor stopped, and which during the past 5 years has assumed scandalous proportions thereby raising the price of all articles over 50 *per cent* on that which obtained but a short while back, is calling for legislation. It accordingly follows that for want of suitable legislation on the one hand, and a correct solution of the grazing problem on the other, the ratepayer may truly be said to exist between the devil and the deep sea.

Biography.

"I can trace back the time to a far distant date,
When my forefathers toil'd in these fields ;
And the gardens I now own on the *Sircar's estate*
Are the same that my grandfather till'd."—*Anon.*

As missionaries invariably accompany, or follow the *flag* we find them installed, with a few other settlers, as the first pioneers ; and also their descendants not only the oldest residents but also in the ranks of the fortunate ones who came in for the major portion of the loaves and fishes in the shape of land which a benign Government was granting with a lavish hand to attract squatters. It would, therefore, be well to give here a short account of these families lest the following in the march of events be as—'Ships that pass in the night.'

There landed at Bankipore in 1838, when the voyage to India was round by the Cape, and occupied fully six months, the following Prussians of the Gosner Mission :—Wernicke and his bride, Stoelke, Truetler and Brundine, who in 1841 were invited to Darjeeling by the Rev. Mr. Start to join in his efforts to convert the people as also to establish industries, the lot being worked on the Moravian system of self-support. The journey from Karagola Ghat to Takvar covered a period of two months, as the impedimenta included tents which were pitched and struck daily ; while that from Pankabarie, which is only some 7 miles below Kurseong, to the Lepcha hut, in which they were lodged on arrival, took 3 days as they were carried on chairs to which two bamboo poles were attached. Withal these hardships and inconveniences the party held together until the retirement of Start, when each one struck out for himself. Truetler started a farm on a site just a little below the St. Joseph's College where he did so well that he also shortly after returned to his native land; Stoelke laid out the Steinthal (Peace Valley) tea garden, while Wernicke built 'Volkrow' on the site on which the Jail now stands. In exchange for this piece of land the Government gave him an extensive plot (little dreaming at the time of the potentialities of the district) bounded by the following—The Cart Road on the west, the Tonga Road on the north, and the Auckland Road on the east—and on which he built 'Gloven' in which his widow lived without a break for 70 years. As there were no builders and contractors in those days he struck out in this direction, built the old market-place and throve, for within a short space of time many buildings were rushed up on this estate.

Start, Truetler, Schultz, and Cumley (also John White) have passed away without giving hostages to fortune ; while Judge, Kenay, Keane, Mandelli, O'Donoghue, Power, Rosamond, Stoelke and Wernicks are still well-represented in the district.

JUDGE, GUSTAVUS, SEPTIMUS—died at the age of 73 after having spent more than 50 years in Darjeeling. He was one of the pioneers in the tea industry, and founder of the Judge Property which was bounded as follows:—The Auckland Road on the east, the Lloyd and Ferndale Roads on the north, and by Banstead and Brynguine Roads on the south, and a second plot which was enclosed by a vertical line extending from Annandale, on the Cart Road to the south of the station, right down to the valley on the one hand, and the ravine, which is the boundary of the Burdwan Raj at Kakjhora further south, on the other.

The first strip covered a very large area, indeed, including the Upper and Lower Beechwood, the Cart Road being the dividing line. The former, which contained but one house—Beechwood—buried in dense forest, was purchased for a *lakh* and thirty thousand rupees by Carl Forstmann, who built all the houses along the Auckland and the Mackenzie Roads, which now form the Beechwood Estate, Ltd.

The heirs of Judge now possess:—

A—Houses, 1st. Strip—Lower Beechwood on which now stands the 5 Beechwood cottages, the Albion and Trio cottages, North View, and the shops and dwellings in 'Judge Bazar' on the Cart Road : 2nd

Strip—Rockwood, and the cottages and huts below, and to the south of Moss Bank.

B—Gardens—They practically own the whole of the Rangli-Rangliot Tea Estate, to the south-east of the Hum Cantonments and overlooking the Tista Valley; and the Aria Tea Co. Ltd., Darjeeling.

KENAY, THOMAS—was appointed Garrison Engineer at Jalapahar in 1864.

From 1835, when we acquired the villages of Darjeeling and Kurseong to 1864, Darjeeling was apparently quite satisfied with its water-supply (which at best was most questionable) from the following sources:—

A—The Convent obtained its drinking water from a masonry well to the immediate north of its music cubicles.

B—The Town, commencing from the Cemetery end, was supplied from the following springs at

1. Castleton, on Hooker Road.
2. Struan Lodge, at the junction of the dispensary and Mount Pleasant Roads, and
3. Lal Digi (red tank which took its name from the enclosing brick-walls) situated between the Musjid and the Dispensary; while
4. Those living along the Auckland Road, and further south, depended upon the springs at Glen Eden and West Point.

Shortly after Kenay's appointment as Garrison Engineer he was offered, and accepted the post of Engineer to the Municipality; and proved by the improvements inaugurated by him that the selection was a happy one.

His attention was necessarily drawn from the beginning of his tenure to the impurity of the water-supply, and with a view to improve it set about building the reservoirs at Senchal, erecting cisterns at St. Paul's School and Rockville, and laying conduits, and 13 miles of piping through which the town is now supplied with pure water. Among other improvements effected by him are:—

1. The erection of the barracks at Jalapahar and Katapahar.
2. The rebuilding of the old barracks at Jalapahar in 1871.
3. The erection of the Union Chapel in 1869.
4. The re-roofing of the St. Andrew's Church in 1873.

5. The building of the St. Joseph's Church in 1880 at Jalapahar, and
6. The construction of Sligo Hall and the two Auckland Villas for the Cooch Behar Raj.

He left three sons—Dr. F. Kenay ; Mr. J. J. Kenay, late A. T. S. D. H. Railway ; and Mr. J. Kenay of the Maharanee Tea Estate, Toong—and the following properties :—

Assyline Villa, Shannon Lodge, Charlemont, Fir Grove, West Point (all of which are to the south of the town) and the buildings in Commercial Row in which Mitchell & Co. Hall & Anderson Ltd., and Frank Ross & Co. are located.

KEANE, MAJOR—laid out the Maharanee Tea Estate, Toong, and subsequently acquired Avongrove, Sonada ; and left them to his two sons, J. P. and R. Keane, respectively. The widow of the former married Mr. J. Kenay ; while on the demise of the latter son, Avongrove passed into the possession of a later generation.

MANDELLI, WILLIAM—Ornithologist—was the son of Count Bastel-Nuovo, an ancient Maltese family. On joining the forces of Garibaldi he fell out with his family and ever after adopted the maternal name of Mandelli. He formed a unit in the force sent by that General to S. America, and as that project ended in a fiasco, and rather than face the jibes of his family, he worked his way to India where his attainments soon attracted the attention of the leading scientists, including the famous Dr. Jerdon.

While Superintendent of the Land Mortgage Bank's gardens, which on the one hand covered the whole of the east slope of the Lebong Spur and on the other extended up to Dewai Pani (mineral springs) he found the time to devote to his pet hobby and established in a short time a museum containing specimens of the fauna of the district so unique that it attracted world wide reputation ; and after his demise drew purchasers from England, and even Europe. Some of the specimens, notably a very rare snow-pheasant, named *Ornithocus Mandelli* after him, were bought by the 'Crystal Palace' where they are to be seen to this day.

He once owned Mandelli Gunge on which the following shops now stand in Commercial Row-The Senchal Dairy Farm,

J. Burlington-Smith, Mitchell & Co., Hall & Andersan, Ltd., Frank Ross & Co., Ottewill's Millinery Establishment, Whiteaway Laidlaw. Ltd., J. Boseck & Co., Smith-Stanistreet, and York Villa on the Post Office Road.

He left three daughters who still reside in the station.

O'DONOGHUE, DR. JAMES—who was the first doctor appointed (under the fiat that went forth on the return to Calcutta of Dr. Hutchinson, who was deputed by the Government in 1871 to analyse and report upon the water-supply of Darjeeling) to attend to the assistants of the Terai gardens owned by Lloyd, the banker, left all his property to his brother, whose heirs now own the Pattabong, North View and Thealand gardens.

POWER, MORRIS—had been directly and indirectly connected with the district for over 40 years, and its history. In 1864 he accompanied the Trades' Mission to Bhutan under the direction of Sir Ashley Eden which culminated in the war with that State, and the subsequent annexation of the Daling Sub-division of which Kalimpong is now the headquarters. We next meet him installed as Vice Chairman of the Municipality, an appointment which he held for 17 years prior to his retirement from the public service. He left an only son, a Captain in the army, and three daughters to whom the following properties have been bequeathed:—

Ashley Dale, Commercial Building, Emerald Bank, Kilfane Lodge, Mall Side, Myrtle Lodge, and Verbena Villa.

STOELKE left an only daughter whose two sons (Sinclairs) are now the managing-proprietors of the Steinthal and Rishi Hat gardens.

WERNICKE was succeeded by his sons Andrew and Frederic. The former started as an assistant at Takvar, while the latter joined Capt. Jerdon at Soom: the two subsequently combined and laid out Lingia, Toomsong, Marybong and Gumba tea gardens, the last two being purchased by the late Sir Robert Laidlaw. So profitable was the culture of tea in those days that they quickly acquired Salt Hill (which subsequently was bought by N. C. Bose, the solicitor) and the following properties:—

A. Houses—(1) Clover Cot, Fox How, Holmdene, Midwood, Orchid Lee, Willowdale, and Pekoetip, Stepaside and the 5 Mall Villas (the last seven of which in 1916 passed into the possession of an Indian Syndicate).

(2) Armadale, Carlton Villa, Castleton Cottage, Gloven, Maud's Cot, Muriel Cot and Perleberg.

B. Gardens—Bannockburn, Glenburn, Lingia, Pandam and Toomsong.

WHITE, JOHN—of Her Majesty's 6th. Foot, who landed as a private at Senchal in 1860, built 'The Traveller's Rest' at Sonada in 1870, and the cluster of buildings (with the exception of Ashley Dale, Mall Side, the Chines, and Caroline Villa) just below the Amusement Club ; as well as left his widow a considerable fortune after having during his lifetime donated large sums of money to charities and public institutions, such as the Eden Sanitarium and the Colonial Homes at Kalimpong.

MACKINTOSH of the Panjab Educational Service laid out the Minchu garden (which was subsequently acquired by the Wernickes), and built Thorn Cottage and Sunny Bank, on the site on which the Park Hotel now stands ; and other properties along the road named after him. These, like his descendants, have passed away, and his name would have been forgotten had it not been for 'Mackintosh Road'.

ROSAMOND, the Inspector of Police, left an only son and two daughters. On retiring from service he started a general business including a bakery which proved a veritable gold mine for in the space of a short time he acquired a part of the hill to the south of, and overlooking the Mall on which the following houses were built :—Alma Cottage, Auckland House, Auckland Cottage, Campbell Cottage, Carbery House, the site on which Messrs. Whiteaway, Laidlaw Ltd. have erected their spacious premises and the adjoining building in which Smith, Stanistreet & Co. is located, and York Villa, below these buildings and on the Post Office Road.

CHAPTER V.

BUILDINGS AND PLACES OF NOTE.

Mission Fields.

It would probably interest not a few readers if a brief account of the early efforts in the Mission field were recorded prior to enumerating the principal places of worship, and other data connected therewith.

As early as 1841, that is, only six years after we had acquired Darjeeling, the Rev. Mr. William Start visited the station and started work among the Lepchas at Takvar (below the St. Joseph's College) on the Moravian system of self-support. In 1842 among those drawn to this field of work were Messrs. Treutler, Stoelke, Wernicke, Brundine and the Rev. Mr. C. G. Neible. The Rev. Mr. Schultze joined for a year only (1842), while Mr. Cumley was connected with it from 1848 to 1852. Between these missionaries a Nepalese and Lepcha dictionary was compiled, while Genesis, part of the Exodus and the Gospels of Matthew, Mark and John were translated into Lepcha. Luke and the Acts of the Apostles were translated into Nepalese. The first three on the retirement in 1843 of Mr. Start through old age, left for other and more lucrative occupations, and their descendants are now the oldest planters in the district; but the Rev. Mr. Neible continued labouring in the vineyard until his death, which occurred on October 9th, 1865. About this period the Baptist Mission was represented by Mr. C. J. Page. On June 10th, 1870, the Rev. Mr. Macfarlane of the Scottish Mission started work in Darjeeling which owing to indifferent health he was forced to resign to other hands in favour of a residence in Kalimpong, where he died in 1887 after having done much for that station.

The Roman Catholics followed close on the heels of the Moravian missionaries, for we find that Mother M. Teresa Mons assisted by Sister Gabriel had started the Loreto Convent on October 10th, 1846, at 'Snowy View' to the north of Birch Hill, which at the close of the same year was transferred to its present site. Then came Father Accursius who after labouring for many a year was buried in the grounds of the Convent in 1885. Mother Mons was buried in Lucknow on November 21st, 1886. This mission through the untiring efforts of its Jesuit Fathers has left its mark both in Sikkim and Darjeeling, and claims more converts than all the other missions put together.

In the early sixties the Non-conformists began to increase in numbers and it was accordingly found necessary to build a place of worship for its adherents—The Union Chapel.

The Scandinavian Mission since 1892 attends to the spiritual wants of the population of Jorebungalow, as well as the Bhutias in the Market Square of Darjeeling.

Another mission (medical) under the guidance of Mr. and Mrs. J. W. I. Wright was established in 1896 at Sukiapuri in the valley seven miles beyond Ghum and on the road to the Nepal frontier. It affords relief annually to over 10,000 patients.

CHURCHES.

St. Andrew's Church.*

The foundation stone of this church was laid on St Andrew's day, November 30th, 1843, and the erection of the edifice was the care of Capt. Bishop, who commanded the troops of the station. It could accommodate a congregation of 150 persons, and cost Rs. 9,000/-. The first divine service was held in October, 1844, the arrangement at that period for the conduct of worship being—the Chaplain of Berhampore officiated for six weeks during each of the two half seasons. It had no clock tower like the present building, and the congregation was seriously informed by the benign Government that as it could not afford a clock, the attendants would have to content themselves with a sun-dial, the gift of a generous visitor !†

---

*See Plate VIII.

†The Altar of the present edifice was presented by the late Mr. John White, of H. M.'s 6th Foot who had spent fifty-two 'Xmases in Darjeeling. His other contributions were :—An X-ray apparatus, as also a sum of Rs. 25,000/- to the Eden Sanitarium, and Rs. 20,000/- to the Colonial Homes at Kalimpong.

The spire which was struck by lightning in September, 1867, collapsed and so all services were suspended as the shock had rendered the building unsafe. In May, 1879, the Corner Stone of the new edifice, erected on the old site, was laid by Bishop Milman ; but it was not completed until just three years after. The first peals of the organ were heard on Easter Day, April 1st, 1877 ; the clock tower (with its bells which chime the hours and cost Rs. 6,600/- was built in 1883 while the north and south transepts, with porches, were added in 1897. Along the walls of the interior of the church are inlaid mural tablets to the memory of some of the oldest residents and settlers, chief among them being Lt.-General Lloyd, the discoverer of Darjeeling. (See also Chapter XII).

Its hours of divine workship are:—Sundays, 8 and 11 a.m. and again 3 and 6 p.m. Holy Communion is celebrated at 7-30 a.m. on Thursdays; Matin is said daily at 8-15 a.m; Evensong on Wednesdays and Fridays at 6 p.m.

St. Columba's Church. (Scots).

This place of worship, just above and to the east of the Station House, was built in May 1894 by the Church of Scotland Mission. Its services are held at noon each Sunday and again at 6 p.m., which in the winter months is changed to 5-30 p.m. The sacrament of the Lord's Supper is celebrated at the close of the midday service on the last Sunday of each month.

Church of the Immaculate Conception.

The Church of the Immaculate Conception was built in 1893 on the site of the old Loreto Chapel by the Rev. Bro. Rotsaert, S. J. who also designed the St. Joseph's College, North Point. It can accommodate a congregation of 300, and has some beautiful Bavarian statuary presented by the parish. Its hours of divine worship are:—Sundays, first Mass at 7 a.m., socond at 9 a.m., Benediction at 5-30 p.m. Week days, Mass at 7-30 a.m. The building is attached to the Loreto Convent, which is just beyond the Eden Sanitarium and below the Cart Road.

This church was built in 1869 on the Auckland Road.

Protestants who are not communicants of the above mentioned churches attend its services which are held on Sundays at 11 a.m., and again at 5 p.m., and on Wednesdays at 5 p.m. Sunday School is held at 3-45 p.m. The sacrament of the Lord's Supper is celebrated at noon on the first Sunday of the month.

Union Chapel.

Buddist Monasteries.

The Budda, who was born at (now) Bhulia in Oudh about the year 500 B. C., and died 420 B. C., at Kasia, a town about 80 miles to the east of his birth-place (Kapilavastu), started his ministry at Benares ; but as he was accredited with having obtained the 'pure light' at Budh-Gaya, a temple 175 feet high was erected at that place in 150 A. D. and dedicated to his memory. Vain thought ! for it may with truth be said of him :—

"I made my life my monument".

All that the Occident knows of the doctrines of Budda has been acquired from the translations of the Northern Volumes (Kanjur) made by the Tibetans (whose king Srong Tsan Gampo deputed his minister Thuni Sambhota about the year 632 A. D. to visit the Buddist monasteries in India) which in turn were translated by that indefatigable scholar and traveller Alexander Csomo de Korosi (who lies buried in the cemetery in Darjeeling) ; from the translations of the Sanskrit volumes made at the expense and under the personal supervision of Brian Houghton Hodgson, the Resident at the Court of Nepal ; and from the translations of the Pali documents by Sir Monier Monier-Williams, K.C.S.I., &c.

Buddism, which was evolved by Prince Siddartha Gautama about the beginning of the 6th century B. C., is a philosophical system in which self-conquest and universal charity are the leading tenets ; and of which the following were its ten commandments :—

1. Kill not any living thing ; 2. Steal not ; 3. Commit no adultery ; 4. Lie not ; 5. Eat no food except at stated hours ; 6. Meet frequently in prayer ; 7. Use no wreaths, ornaments or perfumes ; 8. Use no high

or broad bed, but only a mat on the ground ; 9. Abstain from dancing, singing, music, and worldly spectacles ; and 10. Own no gold or silver in 'The Light Of Asia'—
of any kind, and accept none.—injunctions which have been exquisitely rounded off by Edwin Arnold

"The five Rules of Budda for Householders—

1. Kill not for pity's sake, and lest ye slay
The meanest thing upon its upward way.
2. Give freely and receive, but take from none
By force or greed or fraud, what is his own.
3. Bear not false witness, slander not nor lie
Truth is the speech of inward purity.
4. Shun drugs and drinks that work the wit abuse
Clear minds, clean bodies, need no *Soma* juice (wine).
5. Touch not thy neighbour's wife, nor commit
Sins of the flesh, unlawful and unfit."

In accordance with the 6th. mandate we find its followers, like those of Mahomed, meet five times a day for worship :—

1st. At daybreak.
2nd. At 9 a.m., when the heat of the rays of the sun begin to be felt. During this ritual tea is served out three times.
3rd. At noon, when the first meal of the day is partaken of, and which consists of meat in all its forms, cereals and tea ; fish and fowl being prohibited.
4th. At 3 p.m., when tea is again partaken of three times.
5th. At vespers at 7 p.m., when after liberal potations of tea the monks retire for contemplation to their cells :—

while in terms of the 10th and last, the order of monks most revered are the Bhikshus, or those who exist by begging, having 'no script or purse, nor thought of the morrow.' The similarity of the last injunction is marked, indeed, in the two religions one of which was promulgated about 550 B. C., and the other in A. D. 33, by The Christ.

The simplicity of Buddhism when compared with Brahmanism, the then existing religion of India, soon attracted many devotees, the chief being the king Asoka who propagated it by sending missions to various countries* thereby leading to the ultimate separation of the Buddist system into the two great divisions of Northern (Maha-yana) and Southern (Hina-yana). Indeed, this was inevitable when Kanishka the Indo-Scythian king of Kashmir, who came from the north and reigned about the year 75 A. D., and extended his dominion to Gujarat, Sindh and even Mathura, became a convert. We, accordingly, find Kanishka representing the Northern system and Asoka the Southern ; and also that while *Sanskrit* was the medium by which these doctrines were expounded in the north, *Pali* was the basis of instruction in the South.

All Buddist now arrange themselves under the two chief banners:—the Maha-yana or northern wheel, whose cult is followed by the people of Japan, Manchuria, Mongolia, China, Tibet, Bhutan, Sikkim and India, notably at Budh-Gaya, a district in the province of Behar ; and the Hinayana, or southern wheel, which claims the populations of Ceylon, Burma and Siam as its adherents: so that the followers of the two sects number 450,000,000, or half the total population of the world according to the latest religious census. Necessarily, a third system soon sprang into being, named Madhayana-Yana, which was a compromise between the two, with a few adherents in each of the countries mentioned.

Buddism was originally a brotherhood, for its founder, who was wise and very far-seeing and opposed to all ecclesiastical organisations, enjoined his followers a little before his 'translation'—"To hold fast to the Law ; and to look not to any but yourselves as a refuge."

Soon after his death the prelate of each monastery became supreme and exercised powers which brought about an elective system culminating in the evolution of the Dalai Llama as the spiritual leader of Buddism.

*Fa-hein, the Buddistic Baedeker, tells us that about the year 400 B. C., 100 years after Budda's doctrines were promulgated, there were fully 500 Sangharamas or monasteries in the Frontier Provinces to the north of Peshwar. This region, which was once Buddistic in faith and adjacent to Afghanistan, is now populated by fanatical mahomedans whose sword and crescent are ever ready for any religious war—*Jehad*—against the infidel be he Christian, or of any other persuasion.

This religion was introduced into Bhutan about 350 years ago, where its spiritual leader is called the Dharamaraja ; and into Sikkim about a century earlier where the following monasteries were established in the order given: Pamionchi, Tassiding, Changachelling, Raklang, Tumlong, Chumbi, and those in Darjeeling (which prior to 1835 formed a part of Sikkim).

Brahmanism and Buddism being contiguous, it followed that there was no dividing line in their tenets, nay, rather, the one merged into the other as permanently and as softly as the shades of two different colours in juxtaposition run into each other and blend, until the more virile gradually assumed an ascendancy over the other. So Buddism was gradually supplanted by Vishnuism and Shivaism until by the end of the 18th century the former had very nearly ceased to exist in India*; indeed, its very temples had been taken over by the Vishnuites, for we find that at Puri, where Jagannath is enshrined, this temple was originally dedicated to Budda.

Darjeeling Monastery.

The Darjeeling monastery, which once stood on Observatory Hill, was built in 1765, or 156 years ago, as a branch of the Phodang Monastery of Sikkim. It was looted and sacked by the Nepalese in 1815, leaving only a small shrine called Mahakal on the site which once marked its location. What remained of it was transferred in 1860-61 to the flat to the north-east of St. Andrew's Church, and in 1878-79 was finally removed to Bhutia Busty, where it still exists. On the way to it by the Rangneet Road and about 300 yards below the Chowrasta stands a pure white *Chorten*, or relic-tomb, which like the majority of ritualistic symbols of the East conveys a hidden truth. The central prong of the trident pointing upward, at the head of the column, represents 'ether'; the lateral ones running into each other and forming a crescent 'air'; the shaft, 'fire', the sphere, 'water', while the solid, square base stands for the 'earth'.

The Llamas who have successively held charge over this institution are:—Kachang incarnate llama, 2. Ponlop Sos Sang, 3. Ponlop Yamku, 4. Dorlop Nimadhuba, 5. Kachang incarnate

*Buddism had been once the religion of India for a period of a thousand years.

llama, 6. Ladak Amji, the last being a Ladaki who obtained the seal from the Kamrapa who had no power to extend his authority beyond Tibet, and although acknowledged by the Maharaja of Sikkim is yet looked upon unfavourably by the Buddists as a class.

Ging Monastery. The Ging (4,000′) monastery, which is three miles to the north of the town, is reached by the Rangneet Road to the east of the Mall. It was originally situated below the village of Ging but was demolished under certain political differences after 1860-61. When these differences were settled in 1879, after the Sikkim trouble, by the late Sir Ashley Eden, a thatched structure was erected on the present site, which in 1896-98 was rebuilt in stone through the exertions of the present high priest, Lodio Llama, to which, be it added, no contributions were received from the Pomionghi body. It belongs to the Red-sect called Lhachun-pa. These sects are commonly spoken of by the colour of the caps they wear: hence the red-sect, the yellow-sect &c. According to A. H. Savage Landor, the Tibetan Explorer, who was cruelly tortured in 1897 and then ejected from that land, there are two other inferior orders of llamas called Julinba, who wear white and black caps. These are craftsmen who work at painting, printing, pottery &c. besides making themselves useful in the capacity of cooks, water-carriers, shepherds &c. to the inmates of the several monasteris in Tibet.

Ghum Monastery. The Ghum monastery was founded in 1875 by Llama Sherabgyatsa, one of the Yellow-sect Geylukpa, and was intended primarily as a place for political meetings more than as a monastery. It receives a grant of Rs. 60/- *per mensem* from the Government, is managed by a secretary and a committee, and has some fifty monks in residence. On the 27th March, 1918, this monastery was the centre of much interest for some 5,000 people visited it on that day to witness the unveiling and consecration of an image of Champa or Maitraya, the Coming (5th) Budda. This huge image, which is over 15 feet in height, was constructed under the personal supervision of Trome Gishay Rimpoche, an eminent Llama of Chumbi. The construction proceeded almost day and night until the image was completed in the course of a single month, and cost some 25,000 rupees. The lower portion is made of clay within which are located 16 volumes of the sacred commandments of Budda printed in Tibet from blocks. It is alleged that the interior of the image is full of precious stones, emblems and other costly articles, while the surface is made of a composition of clay and pounded gold and valuable stones, such as rubies and turquoise ; while on the forehead is set a jewel glittering like a diamond and said to be a cat's-eye of priceless value.

The Maha-yana.*

The northern Buddists, who are also called Thechhen, establshed themselves in Tibet in 747 A. D.

The northern wheel is divided into :—

Up to 1030 there was no split in the camp and the old school was known then, and even now as Nyingmapa.

Yellow Sect-Yelungpa 1040 A. D., and Kadampa 1030 A. D.

Red Sect-Kargyupa	1030	,,	Dikungpa 1140 A. D., and Talungypa 1190.
-Changduk	1170	,,	Barduk 1205 ,, ,, Looduk 1210.
Rarmapa	1150	,,	
-Sakyapa	1060	,,	Ngorpa 1425 ,, ,, Jenangpa 1275.
-Orgyonpa	1500	,,	
-Mindolingpa	1500	,,	
-Ngadakpa	1500	,,	
-Kartokpa	1460	,,	
-Lhachunpa	1700	,,	

The Hindu Mandir.†

According to tradition handed down from member to member of the family of the present high priest, Ambic Misser, the original temple was erected some 89 years ago on the same spot on which the present building stands. It certainly existed before the year 1830 when the first Marwari firm, named Samboo

---

*These details were supplied by Mr. K. Shempa, Honorary Secretary of the Northern United Buddist Association.

†See Plate VIII.

Ram & Chunilall was established in the market-place, and like the green bay-tree is flourishing to this day. The present structure which is certainly one of the oldest buildings in Darjeeling was in existence, but without its enclosing walls, in the year 1851, as proved by Col. Sherwill's map. It was erected by Rangit Singh, an ex-army Subadar employed in the local Police Force, and endowed with a sum of Rs. 3,400/- in the 6 per cents.

There are five separate little buildings containing the following gods:—

Radha-Krishna, known also as			Lukshmi-Jaganath
Mahadeo-Parbati	,,	,, ,,	Siva-Kali
Ganesh	...	...	The elephant-headed god
Mahabir	...	...	The monkey god
Tulsi	...	...	The tree god

See Appendix III—On Hinduism.

The Brahma Mandir.

The Brahmo or Theistic church which is affiliated to the Sadharan Somaj of Calcutta, (and faces the Government Printing Press on the Cart Road) was consecrated on the 1st Baisak (15th April) 1880. The building can accommodate a congregation of 100 persons at its services which are held every Sunday morning at 8-30 a.m. in Bengalee, and occasionally in English. These services are conducted by members of the Sadharan, the New Dispensation, the Adi Somaj, and even Unitarian churches. The building was erected through the untiring efforts of Messrs. Troylokonath Chakravarty (the then Head Master of the Government Bhutia Boarding School) and Moti Lal Haldar.

The Mosques.

The mahomedans assert that their musjid at Laldigi (red tank), which originally was a small building erected on the edge of this tank, dates as far back as 1786, and in proof of their claim refer to the invasion of China by their co-religionists about that period. It appears that on the return journey to India a moulvie

PLATE VIII.

ST. ANDREW'S CHURCH.

HINDU MANDIR.

ORIGINAL CONVENT.

PRESENT BUILDING.

worked his way back through Tibet and Sikkim and took up his abode at Laldigi, which is now a flat to the east of the Victoria Hospital. However this may be, the following facts are on record. The present Jamma Musjid was erected by Naser Ali Khan, Daroga Salamat Ali, Munshee Tarikulla and other mahomedans most of whom were Government servants. This building, which is situated below and to the west of the Central Hotel, came into being between the years 1851 and 1862, as it does not appear in Col. Sherwill's map published in the prior year, but finds a place in the official map published in 1862.

The Chota (small) Musjid in Butcher Busty below the Cart Road and near the Railway Station, was erected some years later.

The Anjuman Islamia (governing body) was established in December, 1909, since when it has taken charge of the Jumma and Chota Musjids, rebuilt the former at an expenditure of Rs. 13,000/-, and established schools for boys and girls which now number 44 and 34 respectively on their rolls. A Musafir Khana has been built for the reception of travellers of any caste or creed, and furnishes them with a shelter free of charge for a period of three days. This body also arbitrates both in civil and criminal cases among the followers of its creed. The income of these mosques is derived from shops situated on musjid land which fetches a rental of Rs. 65/- p.m., a grant-in-aid of Rs. 32/- from the Government, and an allowance of Rs. 20/- p.m. from the Municipality.

The followers of Mahomed range themselves under two banners, and are known as Sunnis or Hunfis, and Shiahs. The latter being in the minority are not represented at all in this town.

Masonic Lodges.

"We meet as shadows in the land of dreams,
Which speak not but in signs."—

St. Ronan's Well.

An older lodge of the same name, No. 1525, E. C., existed for a period of three years only (1884-86) without much furthering the cause of freemasonry in the hills. One of its founders, and the first Master, was Mr. Andrew Holmes who was re-elected the year following to fill the chair. The next year it faded away. It was resuscitated again as No. 2439 E.C. on the 18th May, 1892, and opened with 14 members on its rolls who met at 'The Himalayan Club' for more than three years in the building on the Cart Road now in occupation by the Government Printing Press. As its situation was found inconvenient and the accommodation unsuitable, Sir Chas. Elliott, the Lieut-Governor, was approached on the subject with the result that the site on which the lodge stands at present was made over to the freemasons. The building was erected by raising a Debenture Loan of Rs. 12,000/-, bearing interest at 6 per cent. repayable in ten years. The loan was paid off during the incumbency of Mr. P. N. Mukerjee (I.G. of Registration), who was off and on Secretary and Treasurer during the years 1893-97, so that the building now belongs to the Lodge.

Lodge Mount Everest.

Of the nine founders, including the late Maharaja of Cooch Behar, father of the present ruler, two only are still with us— Mr. T. N. Partridge of Darjeeling, and Mr. H. F. Brown of Ghum. Its members meet in the lodge, which is at the junction of the Mall and the Calcutta Road, on the last Saturday of the month at 9 p.m. during the season ; in the winter months the meetings are held at Jalpaiguri.

Lodge Lebong which was founded in 1912 is situated in that Cantonment.

Government House.

The site on which Government House stands was granted to Mr. Edward Hepper about the year 1840. It then passed into the possession successively of Brine and Martin, the contractor, from whom Sir Thos. E. Turton bought it and built 'Solitaire' on it. This property finally passed from 'Barnes' Estate into the hands of the late Maharaja of Cooch Behar (father of the present ruler), and during his minority was purchased by the Government, on October, 31st, 1877. Additions and alterations were made to it to adapt it for the residence of the Lieut.-Governor of Bengal; and it was renamed 'The Shrubbery'. It was first occupied in the summer of 1880. Subsequently, the porch and

PLATE IX.

GOVERNMENT HOUSE.

tower were added by Sir Ashley Eden, to whom Darjeeling is so much indebted! The grounds were artistically laid out in 1878 under the direction of Sir George King of the Royal Botanic Garden, Calcutta. The Durbar Hall, in which all State functions are held, was built during the tenure of Sir C. Elliott. On the left of the walk the residence of the Private Secretary and the Guest House are seen on the way to the main building, a stately structure in keeping with the status of the Head of the Province. To the west of the Government House is the residence of the Staff Officers, while at the back is the Durbar Hall, and the recreation ground, 160 × 100 yards, on which all sporting fixtures, including Gymkhanas take place.

The Governor's residence is one of the prettiest places in India, glorious views of the mountain range being obtainable from the grounds where primroses and blue-bells grow on velvety lawns, and gardens that are filled with roses, carnation, geraniums and violets.

Round the Governor and his Staff revolve the Government set, which, with the distinguished visitors, make up 'society' in Darjeeling.

In April, 1914, quite a host of workmen were engaged pushing on the completion of the buildings for the Staff, and members of His Excellency's band. The appearance of the approach to Government House was improved, while the interior underwent such changes that it is doubtful if the prior occupants could recognise it as "The Shrubbery."

At the entrance and to the left of the gate, a Visitor's Book is maintained in which those entitled to entree to Government House indite their names against subsequent invitations to State and other functions.

The following was the account of the last State Ball:—Two hundred and fifty guests attended the state ball given last night. Long before the appointed hour rickshaws were busy landing their occupants at the porch, who then passed into the hall between two gilded elephants, the Burmese emblem of power, from whose trunks hung bright, fretted lamps. The white Ball room, which was picked with decorations in red, formed a background of great beauty to the dancers whose sombre evening dress was relieved by the gay and gorgeous uniforms of His Excellency's Staff and Military Officers. At midnight the dancers passed through banks of scarlet runners, thrown into relief by trusses of eucharis lilies whose dazzling whiteness contrasted with the deep red of the roses, to the supper room from the walls and ceiling of which for the nonce a vine laden with bunshes of grapes hung from trellis-work, while 17 tables shone with candelabra and silverware. Dancing was resumed after supper and continued till 3 a.m.

The Kutchery.*

The first courts were held in the building at present in occupation by the Gymkhana Club and continued doing so until the year 1878 ; the sittings next took place in the premises since handed over to the Government Printing Press on the Cart Road ; and finally a permanent habitation was allotted to them below the Lebong Road a little past the Convent.

A part of the new structure was burnt down on January, 1st, 1896, and with it the major portion of the records of the contained offices. The burnt portions were rebuilt, and added to materially for the accommodation of the Sessions Court, that of two Deputy Magistrates, and the Subordinate Judge as well as the following offices :—Forest, Police, Income Tax, Excise, that of the Deputy Commissioner, and the Treasury.

The courts sadly needed a Bar Library, which was eventually supplied by the public and litigants. The library was formally opened on July, 22nd, 1914, by the late Mr. Nichol, Sessions Judge, after a short but facetious speech in which he referred to the legal profession as one ordinarily looked upon as a necessary evil, which, however, was belied by the fact that funds towards the erection of the building for this library were mainly contributed by the clients of the Bar who shewed their appreciation

---

*Originally built for the accommodation of Indian visitors, then converted into a butcher's shop, and subsequently into the Town Hall prior to its being used as the Kutchery and Treasury—"*Darjeeling, the Sanitarium of Bengal* by R. D. O'Brien, M.B., 1883.

of the help received in a very substantial manner, indeed, thus disproving the libel on an honourable body of practitioners.

The library has three rooms one of which has been set apart for the use of literate litigants, as presumably 'the waiting room' attached to the courts is anything but a comfortable place to wait in, in that the furniture is scanty indeed.

The Bengal Secretariat Building.

This three-storied building which locates the following offices and was erected in 1898 can be seen from the west of the old bandstand on the Chow :—

Floors.	Offices.
Ground.	Chief Secretary to Government.
	Under Secretary, Political and Appointment Departments.
	Secretary, Revenue and General Departments.
	Under Secretary, ditto.
	Office of the Political and Appointment Departments.
	Secretariat Library.
First.	Secretary, P. W. Department.
	Under Secretary, ditto.
	Consulting Architect to Government
	and following offices :—P. W. D., General, and Revenue Departments.
Second.	Secretary, Financial and Municipal Departments.
	Under Secretary, ditto.
	and following offices :—Financial, Municipal, and Accounts.

Carlton House and Struan Lodge.

Carlton House on Mount Pleasant Road, alongside the Pleasaunce, contains the following offices :—The Inspector General of Civil Hospitals, and the Inspector General of Registration. On the same road, and a little lower down, is Struan Lodge in which the Engineer to the Municipality holds his office. The Municipal Office is just below the Eden Sanitarium, and to the north of the Market Square ; but will adjoin the Town Hall on the Mackenzie Road from 1921.

The Darjeeling Club.

The Planters' Club which was founded in 1868 was first located in 'Thorn Cottage,' then 'Alice Villa' and finally in the present building which is above and to the east of Commercial Row. It was converted in 1908 into a Limited Liability Co. and styled "The Darjeeling Club, Ltd." Officers attached to the several services and planters are *ipso facto* entitled to membership ; others if properly vouched for are readily admitted as members. There are four billiard tables, a large and well-appointed reading room and library in the upper floor immediately above the dining room ; there are stables for member's horses as also a three-storied concrete structure erected to the east of the main building for the accommodation of servants.

The fees are :—Entrance fee Rs. 70/-.
Annual subscription Rs. 12/-.
For temporary members Rs. 16/- per month.
Army and Navy Officers of and above the rank of 1st. Lieutenant Rs. 10/-; below that rank Rs. 5/- per month.

The Post and Telegraph Offices

are now located on the Mackenzie Road to the north of the Rink Theatre.

The Jail.

In a small cottage which once stood to the north of the Jail, which was erected in 1865, lived Lt. Whish, who was murdered in that solitary building by a mahomedan fanatic in 1857. It was subsequently enlarged to accommodate the Superintendent of the Jail.

The first jail was necessarily a small one. The present structure which stands on 116 acres of land consists of a number of buildings enclosed within a high brick wall and contains the following accommodation ;—There are 11 cells, the barracks can receive 119 convicts, while a separate building is set apart for the reception of 4 European delinquents (which, happily, has seldom been occupied) and 9 under-trial prisoners.

Its bakery supplies the troops and the public with bread ; while its chief industries are oil-pressing, bamboo and cane-work, carpentry and boot-making.

The Hindu Public Hall.

This building which is a two-storied, stone structure located in Chandmari, the Indian portion of the Town and below the Market Square, contains a spacious hall in which public meetings of the Hindu Community are held. The "Kassiswari Darjeeling Library" and Reading Club are located in it. A brief account of the vicissitudes through which this building has passed would probably be of interest to Indian readers, and accordingly the following brief summary is given.

About the year 1890 the late Mr. M. N. Banerjee, quondam Government Pleader, and subsequent Secretary of the Hall, convened meetings with a view to obtain funds wherewith to erect a public building for the exclusive use of Indians, and with this project ever before him approached many a leading Ruler and influential Indian. The first to respond to such a call and donate a sum of Rs. 1,000/-, as a nucleus, was *the* late Maharaja of Cooch Behar, after whom the hall has been named—"The Nripendra Narayan Hall". With this sum a small building was constructed in 1891 for religious purposes. Subsequent efforts produced a total donation of Rs. 40,000/- with which a suitable structure was erected on the site on which the present building stands. This hall, which unfortunately was not insured, was burnt down on April 29th, 1906. It was again mainly through the untiring efforts of Mr. Banerjee that funds were once more forthcoming, as also building materials, with which the present structure was erected. The foundation stone was laid by Sir Andrew Fraser, Lieut.-Governor of Bengal, on October 16th, 1907, and the building completed as it now stands early in the year following. It can accommodate 2,000 souls, has a large and well-equipped stage, besides contains the Library and Reading room referred to above.

The fortunes of this hall have ever since the demise of Mr. Banerjee been watched by his sons successively, who as secretaries have guided it successfully through many a financial crisis.

The Market Square.

Those who have not visited this station since 1900 will not be able to recognise this locality which has been transformed by the late Mr. G. P. Robertson, Engineer to the Municipality (who during his short tenure did so much for Darjeeling) from a collection of filthy, tin-roofed shanties of variegated hues, each tint indicative of the exact stage of decrepitude arrived at, into a neat, clean quadrangle with three-storied, concrete structures for the accommodation of Indians.

Here will be seen astute Marwaris, whose chief business and source of income is money-lending ; mild-spoken Kashmiris and Panjabi dealers in silks, skins and furs ; petty grocers from the plains ; sellers of old and rare coins ; Bhutia pawn-brokers and Cheap-Jacks from whom many an article of *virtu* may be picked up ; Nepalese who deal in curios consisting of turquoise-wear, coral, amber and jade ornaments, kukris, knives and brass-ware (of which the reader has already been warned) ; and last but not least, the affable Parsee who deals in Japanese silver-ware and oilman's stores. In the Daroga Bazar, which leads from the east of the Market Square to Mount Pleasant Road just below the Central Hotel, as well as in the latter road, are located the iron-mongers, and Indian tailors so dear to the hearts of our lady visitors.

On Saturday afternoons vendors trudge in from near and far laden with their stock of market produce for sale at the *hat* held on Sundays when the murmur of voices engaged in barter can be heard a great distance away, while the motley crowd is so dense that it takes no little pilotage to wend one's way through it.

The Pleasaunce.

This park which is situated to the south-west of St. Andrew's Church, and on the flat on which once stood Lloyd's Bank and the old Secretariat Buildings, covers 2½ acres of ground. In the centre are two pavilions, which afford shelter in case of sudden showers of rain, and a bandstand in which on Saturday afternoons during the season, and weather permitting, His Excellency's band by kind permission plays from 4-30 p.m.

The Lloyd Botanic Garden.

The first Botanic Garden, during Sir Ashley Eden's tenure as Lieut.-Governor of Bengal, was laid out in 1876 at Rangiroon (5,700) six miles away and to the east of Darjeeling. It was eventually abandoned in favour of the present one below the Eden Sanitarium owing to the frequent hailstorms which denuded that locality of all foliage. In 1878 the greater part of the present site was presented by Mr. W. Lloyd, the proprietor of the bank, and has no connection with Lt.-General Lloyd, the discoverer of Darjeeling. Such is fame! And, Alas! that it should ever be said of *the* Lloyd in Darjeeling—

"His memory and his name are gone,
Alike unknowing and unknown."

Similarly, of Campbell (of whom it has been recorded "whatever has been done in this district, has been done by Dr. Campbell alone") Oh! that we could say with Burns—

"But I'll remember thee, Glencairn,
And a' that thou hast done for me."

The garden is divided into two main parts, the upper or indigenous section, and the lower or exotic section. Many of the paths intersecting it are lined with the tea plant, the flowers of which are white with a pale yellow centre, reminding one of orange blossoms. The whole plot measuring 14 acres of land is neatly laid out, and contains specimens of nearly all our flora as well as many exotic plants, including the Australian Blue Gum tree (eucalyptus). There is a pavilion for use by picnic parties; while in the hot-house, which stands in the centre of the grounds, is a beautiful wisteria, a Japanese plant, and many varieties of camelia, a native of China, which when in full bloom are a revelation of colour.

The number of exhibits are being added to annually thereby

making it correspondingly interesting to such visitors as are capable of appreciating its contents from either an arboricultural or a botanical point of view. In 1916 over 11,500 plants, over 5,173 dozens of annual seedlings, over 908 bulbs and tubers, and over 417 packets of seeds were either exchanged or distributed to other gardens, while in addition special collections of seeds of Himalayan species from both high and low levels were made. Over 52,000 visitors to the garden were counted during that year, nearly 16,000 of whom were Europeans.

Note.—To get to the garden take the Lochnagar Road just below the Eden Sanitarium and to the north of the Market Square. About 50 yards lower down the path bifurcates, the right leading to the R. C. Chapel, the left after winding round the hill reaches the Botanic Garden.

The Victoria Falls.

It would be well if the trip to the Botanic Garden and this Fall were combined as the west gate of the garden opens out on the Victoria Road. The falls are about ½ a mile to the south, and the ravine through which it rushes headlong down to the reservoir of the electric-power station at Sidrapong is spanned by an ornamental ferro-concrete bridge 110 feet long, which in itself would repay the effort of the visit. During the rains this Fall is a pretty cascade having a sheer drop of 80 feet.

Half a mile to the south of the falls is "Rose Bank," the residence of the Maharajadhiraj of Burdwan, whose ancestors are accredited with having imported the first batch of kites and jackals to aid in the scavenging of the town. The intention was decidedly good ; but if it could have been foreseen that the last would prove more a bane than a boon, for they not only make night hideous with their calls but have also introduced rabies, which has now become endemic, they would have been left to disport themselves in their original haunts. Crows and sparrows were introduced by Dr. Campbell. Lately, many English birds have been imported, and set at liberty, by the Deputy Commissioner, from funds provided for the purpose by the Darjeeling Improvement Fund.

Birch Hill Park.*

The land on which Birch Hill Park stands was acquired by Government in 1877 at a cost of Rs. 30,000/-. Material changes and improvements were effected by the late Sir Ashley Eden in this park, which is 1½ miles from the Chowrasta, and 6,874 feet above sea-level. It has a large pavilion, and a grotto in the grounds. During the spring and summer months the cuckoo is heard all day long calling plaintively to its mate. Where does he winter? Certainly not in Europe, for—

'In May he comes to stay ;†
In June he changes his tune ;
In July he prepares to fly ;
In August go he must'.

Then in October-November when the acorn ripens, the tree-bear, an aggressive little beast, is much in evidence in the early mornings and at dusk. The scenery here is certainly the grandest in the station for the trees are old and stately with knarled barks covered with linchen and moss, which imparts to the landscape a russet-brown hue picked out with silvery specks. But the hand of the despoiler is about to lay his fingers on the flat in this park which is required for another and third recreation ground ; and so the beauties of Birch Hill will shortly be a matter of ancient history.

From the Mall round Birch Hill and back is just 3¼ miles.

---

*See Appendix II.
†In England.

CHAPTER VI.

IMPROVEMENTS TO TOWN.

The Natural History Museum.

This Museum, a three-storied, ferro-concrete structure containing 20 spacious rooms, which stands to the north-west of the Secretariat Buildings and is easily reached through the Mall and the Park, displaced the little cottage which, owing to its location in the Lloyd Botanic Garden, was seldom if ever frequented by the public and so never attained the status of a museum in the true sense of the word. Further, it was not provided with the necessary apparatus for the preservation of the specimens, collected by a very large staff who scoured the entire district and even Sikkim, with the result that the collections deteriorated quickly and ultimately found their way into the dust heap, thereby leaving the impression on the casual visitor that either little or no effort had been made by those in charge to obtain and maintain specimens of fauna and flora in which Darjeeling abounds, or that adequate care had not been bestowed on their preservation : neither of which would be quite accurate.

Darjeeling has to thank His Excellency Lord Carmichael, who is a keen collector himself, for removing this disgrace and allotting sufficient funds for the erection of a suitable building, which was designed by Mr. Crouch, the Architect to the Government of Bengal. The internal arrangements are the care of Dr. Annandale and Mr. F. H. Gravely of the Indian Museum, Calcutta.

The new building, which was completed in 1915, contains a large gallery for exhibition purposes, a basement for storage, and an upper storey designed partly for the exhibition of living insects etc., and partly for original research work. It is understood that the care and management of the fresh specimens will be entrusted to the officers of the Zoological and Anthropological section of the Indian Museum who will appoint an assistant from Calcutta whose knowledge of the care and preservation of specimens will prevent loss and delay and so justify the expenditure of public funds on the new structure which, it is understood, cost half a *lakh* of rupees.

With a view to arouse and sustain public interest and also obtain, if possible, gifts of specimens from residents of the town and outstations an instructive lecture was delivered by Mr. Gravely at the Town Hall which, if numbers are any criterion, for the hall was taxed to its utmost capacity, clearly indicate that the public fully appreciates the interest taken by His Excellency in giving Darjeeling an institution worthy of the name of Museum.

The field being so extensive a one the lecturer had necessarily to confine his remarks to an exceedingly limited group and so chose as his subject the life history of a few bettles, bugs, spiders and scorpions which abound in Darjeeling. As an introduction to the subject Mr. Gravely pointed out that during the glacial period, when icefields doubtless extended as far down as the lower ranges of hills here, certain creatures were driven further south where they have ever since been confined as they could not easily recross the Gangetic plain. He next drew attention to the fact that owing to a break of 80 miles in the Sewalik range (the smaller hills which border the Himalayas) from the Tista Valley to the Raidak* on the east, the clouds swept through this gorge and drenched the higher ranges thereby enriching both its fauna and flora : hence Darjeeling, Sikkim and Tibet, and also Bhutan were so rich in specimens, which were to be had for the asking, and he accordingly hoped the specimens necessary for the new museum would very quickly be contributed by the public.

His Excellency in asking for a vote of thanks to the lecturer indulged his extant humour by quoting an American taradiddle of which he is very fond—

"The May bug has wings of gold
The June bug wings of flame
The bed bug has no wings at all
But he gets there all the same."—

and so shall the specimens for the Natural History Museum.

---

*The chief river of Bhutan.

The Bloomfield Barracks.

The armed police force of this station, which is entirely recruited from the Gurkha tribes of Nepal, is quartered in spacious barracks located at Bloomfield which is just below the Cart Road at West Point, a mile out of the station, and to the south.

The Inspector and European Sergeant have each a bungalow containing four large rooms with lights and water laid on. Below these cottages are situated the arsenal, armoury, guardroom, hospital and office, all located on the border of the flat, fully 2½ acres in size, intended both for drill as well as a recreation ground. Further down are five large barracks each containing 30 rooms 13 feet square, so that the rank and file have healthy surroundings, and at the same time being self-contained will keep them away from the baneful influences at work in the bazar.

Although the station is ordinarily free from brawls and riots (except when the Chinese run amok, when skin and hair literally fly, as on the last occasion which occurred in 1914 when they sent over half a dozen policemen and paharis to hospital dangerously wounded) yet the Inspector's quarters are connected to the town by telephone in case of such emergencies.

The Chinese Club.

The Chinese population of both Kalimpong and Darjeeling appreciably increased in 1912 when the Chinese rabble, called an army, were repatriated from Tibet through British territory. Many were the deserters who hid in the forest along the Tista Valley Road, seeking employment in the Rinchipong block where extensive sawing was being carried on by an European firm until all fear of arrest had passed away, when they flocked into the two towns. In the forest soldiers were to be seen working as carpenters at wages varying from eight annas to a rupee a day, during which all the military formalities were most strictly observed, for privates stood to attention when addressed by officers of superior rank.

The result of the influx into Darjeeling is to be seen in the erection of a three-storied, concrete structure on the Jail Road, and immediately below the Eden Sanitarium, where Chinamen congregate every night indulging in potations of much chow and a little harmless gambling.

This club stands on a spot which hitherto was noted for anything but sanitation and has accordingly improved that quarter of the native town.

The Police Head-Quarters.

The old Volunteer Head-quarters, a most unsightly structure which faced the Goods-shed on the Cart Road, has been demolished and in its place three stone cottages have been erected for occupation by the Inspectors of the City, and District Police and their staff.

The Electro-Hydraulic Scheme.

The Power Station* and Hydraulic Works are situated at the foot of the Sidrapong spur which is roughly 4 miles below the Railway Station and about 3,500 feet above sea-level.

This station, which is the first of its kind erected in India in 1897, by Messrs. Kilburn & Co. of Calcutta, was taken over by the Municipality and added to considerably from time to time. There are at present 4 alternators with a total capacity of 400 kilowats, which generate current at 2,330 volts, single-phase and 83.3 periods. This is transmitted to eight sub-stations in the towns of Darjeeling and Ghum, and then transformed down through static transformers to 230 volts.

The original plant which cost Rs. 1,20,000/- was buried in the great slips which occurred in September, 1899. The town was in consequence plunged in total darkness for a period of two months during which repairs were being effected.

Hydraulic Works.

The water which works the turbines is collected in two reservoirs, of which the first built in 1897 measures 112′ × 47′ × 13′

*I am indebted to Mr. S. N. Mandal, the Assistant Electrician to the Municipality, for details in connection with the Power Station and Reservoirs.

and contains 68,432 cubic feet. The other constructed in 1905 has the following dimensions—209′ × 59′ × 13′ and contains 160,303 cb. ft. The total storage capacity of these two tanks is thus—228,735 cb. ft., which is just sufficient to run a 100 H. P. set for about 15 hours. With all this power generated, the plant at Sidrapong, which brought in a net profit of rupees seventy thousand in 1913-14, was found incapable of meeting the growing demands of the town and the two cantonments. His Excellency Lord Carmichael was accordingly invited on July, 24th, 1914, to visit the Power Station in connection with the new scheme for the supply of current to the Lebong and Jalapahar Cantonments which is estimated to cost Rs. 1,70,000/- when established at Phulbazar in the valley, one of the high-roads to Sikkim.

The above scheme, however, which was formulated by the late Mr. G. P. Robertson, Municipal Engineer, who lost his life while engaged in survey work on the Rangneet river, was held in abeyance pending the full consideration of a much larger scheme by which the needs of the tea gardens throughout the district right down to Dam Dim (Jalpaiguri, Duars) on the east and Nuxalbarie (Siliguri district) on the west, including the town of Siliguri, will be fully met. With this end in view Mr. Stonebridge, whose services were specially engaged, had been touring the Tista Valley the whole of the winter of 1914-15 and has lately submitted proposals and plans for the first of the four proposed stations, *viz.*, the erection of one at the junction of the Little and Great Rangneet rivers just near the Tukvar Tea Estate at an estimated expenditure of Rs. 3,50,000/-. As the whole scheme is so extensive a one it follows that a number of years must elapse before it can be carried out in its entirety. However, when it is completed, tea gardens, which now depend upon the forest for their fuel supplies, will have a clean and economical motive power at command which should materially reduce the working expenses and consequent cost of production, and, it is to be hoped, the market value of the manufactured article—Tea.

The war has, however, compelled a recast of the above scheme, necessitating an addition only to the existing plant, which will generate just half as much again as the present output. This project would have been completed early in 1916 were it not for the sad fate of the first set of machinery ordered which is now somewhere at the bottom of the deep blue sea, thanks to our disciples of frightfulness. The second set was in full working order by the end of October, 1916.

The Town Hall.

The foundation stone of the new Town Hall was laid by His Excellency Lord Ronaldshay, on the 27th October, 1917, on the site once occupied by the Rhododendron Villas on the Mackenzie Road, the main artery of the town. This building which was completed in 1921 is estimated to have cost 2½ *lakhs* of rupees, towards which His Highness the Maharaja of Cooch Behar had contributed just half—on the distinct understanding that the Hall shall form a memorial to his father, Maharaja Sir Nripendra Narain Bhup Bahadur—and had further undertaken collecting donations from his friends, and the admirers of his late father, to the extent of another 40,000 rupees, on the condition that the building should be, in every sense of the term, a public hall, to which the citizens of Darjeeling should have access at all times. From childhood the late Maharaja made this station his summer residence where he was known to, and appreciated by, all classes of the community. Apart from his numerous benefactions, such as the donation of the land on which the Lowis Jubilee Sanitarium stands, and contributions to the Hindu Public Hall &c., his generous and sympathetic temperament and his sportsmanlike qualities endeared him to both Europeans and Indians alike.

The plans of this building were designed by Mr. Morgan, the Municipal Engineer, who had the benefit of the advice of Mr. Crouch, the Government Architect, who designed the Natural History Museum. These plans provide for a spacious building which can accommodate 600 people. The hall, which will contain the bust of the late Sir N. N. Bhup Bahadur, a present from the son to the citizens of Darjeeling, and the reading room measure respectively 88 × 45 and 47 × 15 feet. The surface of the former being of seasoned teak wood, it follows that dancing and other amusements will afford much pleasure to the general public, as the Amusement Club is for the exclusive use of its members.

At the north-west of the building is the square, stone clock tower, which will stand fully 100 feet high including the octagonal gable roof of timber, and a flag-staff which will rise still higher.

To the west and south of the building are the offices of the Municipality.

This hall, which was declared open in the spring of 1921 by Lord Ronaldshay, resounded to the stentorian voice of Mr. "Pussyfoot" Johnson, the American temperance advocate, who tried to induce Darjeeling "to run dry", like his country, thus forgetting that such a condition is an impossibility from a climatic point of view, as also from the personal inclinations of its populace!

Post and Telegraph Offices.

The authorities of the Postal Department had after much casting about for a suitable site decided upon the triangular plot of land in the Beechwood Estate to the north of Madan's 'Palace of Varieties' on which a building (in which the sorting room alone covers 1,400 square feet) in keeping with its requirements was erected in 1920. On the highest floor are the quarters of the staff.

The Heart of the Town.

During the course of his farewell address, Lord Ronaldshay referred to the following projects which the residents are desirous of seeing effected at an early date, namely, the widening of the Railway track so as to do away with the level crossings which are a source of danger to the wheeled traffic and the public generally ; the replacement of the barnlike structure, which for years has served as the passenger station, by a building in keeping with the architectural design of the neighbourhood ; and the removal of the line and goods-shed from the Cart Road.

To effect these improvements it has been agreed to ear-mark a sum of one *lakh* for each of these projects out of the receipts of the Mutual Improvement Fund, which belongs in equal share to the Government and the Railway. The first, which has fallen to the lot of the Government, it is expected will be completed within the next 3 years ; the second, the Railway hopes to complete within 4 years from date (1920) ; while the last will be taken in hand immediately thereafter.

The above sum, it is feared, will be found insufficient for the last two schemes which fall to the lot of the Railway, and so the difference will be made good by the Company from other sources.

New Recreation Ground.

The hand of the despoiler is after all to lay his clutch on Birch Hill Park (which for ages has been considered sacred ground) where a flat is to be denuded of its stately trees in order to form a third recreation ground measuring 480 × 160 yards, overlooking the fact that there are two already in existence, each quite capable of meeting singly the demands made on it, *viz.*, the cricket ground attached to Government House, which ever since the "Shrubbery" was built, has always been placed at the disposal of the public for its sporting fixtures ; and the immense Race Course at Lebong, which is three furlongs in length, where our May and October Meets take place. Wherein the necessity for another recreation ground it is hard, indeed, to see ; and so the expenditure of public funds goes on, on the mere dictum of the powers-that-be, while the rate-payer has to stand by and smile in a non-regulation province wherein election hitherto to its Municipal Board, like kissing, has gone by favour, but which officially is termed 'nomination'. The dictum of the redoubtable editor of 'Capital' (of April, 20th, 1915) on the constitution of the last Viceregal Council applies *mutatis mutandis* to all corporate bodies, and is accordingly quoted here in the hope that a few 'nays,' in place of the usual 'ayes,' will now be heard at the board of our City Fathers when the expenditure of public funds, and the denudation of our cherished hillsides are under consideration.—

"This is what a learned professor of the Fergusson College, where Gokhale was developed, has to say of them :—

'Non-official majorities are no good, although I am not prepared to go so far as to say, as some have said, that a nominated non-official is worse than a nominated official.'

But I have no hesitation in going the whole hog. It is my experience that a nominated non-official sycophant out-herods the most reactionary official and nominated official."

Let these remarks be 'read, marked and inwardly digested' by those in whose hands our interests are vested.

Municipalities.

The Darjeeling Municipality came into being in 1850, while that of Kurseong, which was established as late as 1879, has its affairs administered by a Board consisting of 12 Municipal Commissioners. In the current year (1916) a nomination—*cum*-election system is being tried as an experimental measure in the former: in Kurseong the elective system has been in force for sometime.

Of the 28 commissioners who now form the Municipal Board of Darjeeling 18 are elected, while of the 10 nominated, 5 are reserved for the following officials:—The Deputy Commissioner (the Chairman), the Executive Engineer, the Civil Surgeon, the Superintendent of Police, and the Deputy Conservator of Forests, Darjeeling Division.

The incidence of income of the municipality per head of population is Rs. 17/- in Darjeeling, and only Rs. 7/- in Kurseong. In these circumstances one is in doubt whether to say—poor, or rich Darjeeling.

CHAPTER VII.

SCHOOLS AND COLLEGES.

Darjeeling.

"What, you're a scholar, friend?
I was born so, measter, Feyther kept a grammar-school".—*Sheridan*

No account of the schools in this district would be complete if due mention were not made of the efforts of the Catholic Order and the Christian Missionaries, who as early as 1841 strove to up-lift the population both mentally and spiritually. For the last two decades, however, this duty has primarily devolved on the Church of Scotland Mission into whose hands all contributions to primary education from the two municipalities as well as the Government have been placed.

In 1835, when Darjeeling was acquired, the population numbered about 100 souls only, consequently no one thought of raising the masses by means of education until the advent of the Rev. Mr. Start, a private missionary, and Mother Teresa M. Mons both of whom devoted their lives in this direction with the result that on the one hand a convent was fully established in 1846, to which a vernacular department was attached ; while on the other, the illiterate were made literate, some even holding positions of responsibility, for which they are indebted as well to other workers in this field, the chief being the Rev. Mr. Neible, who composed Lepcha primers, and the Rev. Mr. Macfarlane, who shortly after his arrival discovered that the people could be reached by means of the Hindi tongue which so closely resembles their own. He, therefore, fixed upon Hindi "as the *lingua franca* and in it prepared text-books, some of which to this day are still to be found in use in this district." His next step was quite a statesman-like move, for knowing that the children here are compelled through poverty to earn their living, he prevailed upon the Government to award scholarships, which supplied the deficit in the income of those families whose children were attending the several schools started all over the district. These classes eventually formed the nucleus of the Training School (in existence to this day) at Kalimpong, which, like that at Kurseong, turns out fully qualified teachers. These little beginnings in a short while bore much fruit, for we find that in 1873 "there were no less than 25 Primary schools in the district in which 615 boys and girls received instruction", which by the 31st March, 1917, had assumed colossal proportions, as will be seen from the tabular statement below :—

Schools	Number	Number of Pupils		Total
		Male	Female	
High	2	345	37	382
Middle	6	843	1	844
Primary	215	4,215	749	4,964
Special, including Training, Industrial Schools, etc. ...	22	215	259	474
Total ...	245	5,618	1,046	6,664

Anglo-Vernacular schools were soon established. In 1860 the Government started the Middle English School ; then the Bhutia Boarding School (which is attended by all classes of Indians) followed in 1874, the two eventually being combined in 1891 and raised to the status of a High School.

The education of the Domiciled Community, however, was left entirely to private enterprise, which was not found wanting, for in the course of a few years, that is, as soon as the advantages of a hill climate were understood and appreciated by parents residing in the plains, the schools opened for the reception of the children of Europeans and Anglo-Indians rose to 10 in number, the place of honour being easily secured by the Loreto Convent which came into being in 1846 and St. Paul's, which opened at Jalapahar in 1864 through the efforts of Bishop Cotton. There are now twelve institutions which impart instruction to over 1,600 youths of both sexes. Many of the Old Boys are in this great contest fighting for their Country and their King, while the great majority are holding positions of trust and responsibility both in the service of Government as also in several Mercantile firms in Calcutta.

This defect, however, was remedied by Government by the establishment at Kurseong of the Victoria Boys' (1897), and Dow Hill Girls' Schools (1898) in which the children of its servants receive a good education up to the Eighth Standard.

The credit of being the pioneer in matters relating to industrial and technical education goes to Mrs. F. C. Fooks* of Toong, who in 1880 established the 'St. Agnes Industrial Orphan Home' at Bloomfontein for the reception and education of orphans, and the children of planters. This institution after caring for and launching into useful spheres of life many youths of both sexes, some of whom even to this day are to be seen earning their livelihood in Darjeeling, was forced to close down owing to lack of adequate support. But about three years prior to this event a suggestion was made to this philanthropic lady to transfer her field of labour under the auspices of the Church of Scotland Mission to Nimbong in the Duars, which on a subsequent visit was found to be impracticable owing to want of proper road communications during the rains. This institution doubtless foreshadowed the Colonial Homes (See under Kalimpong) started in 1900, which eventually gave it its death blow. And so in the great glare of this colossal project Mrs. Fooks has been forgotten both by the public as well as by those she fostered, but who now for obvious reasons disclaim any connection with the *home* that gave them that opportunity in life which would otherwise have been denied to them.

Technical education was taken up in right earnest only about 15 years ago, the Victoria School leading with Goethal's a good second. In both these institutions, which are affiliated to the Engineering College, Sibpore, instruction is imparted in

---

*Mrs. Fooks, who was educated in S. Africa, is the daughter of the late Col. John Sutherland, 13th Bombay Cavalry, Governor-General's Agent, Gwalior, and British Resident, Rajputana. See also *'Sal Baree'* under Terai Gardens, to follow.

carpentry, mechanical, electrical and mining engineering, that is, in old and beaten tracts, quite overlooking the fact that there is a dearth of printers in this country. The consequence is that the Government annually import a batch of qualified printers, while private firms have to shift for themselves as best they can. It would, therefore, be to the interest of the domiciled lad if the authorities of these two institutions gave this matter their earliest and best consideration.

The St. Paul's School, which was started in Calcutta in 1845, replaced the High School founded by Archdeacon Corrie in 1830 for the education of European and Anglo-Indian youths of that city. In 1864 it was removed to Jalapahar (where it now stands at an altitude of 7,376 feet) with 130 pupils on its rolls. Students attending this institution are prepared for the examinations for admission to the several public services in India.

The original school was unable to hold its own against its better endowed rivals—The Doveton College* and La Martiniere College—and so the building in which it was located in Chowringhee Road, Calcutta, was sold for Rs. 1,30,000/- with a view to start a school in Darjeeling, as was accomplished in Simla by Bishop Cotton, the Metropolitan of Calcutta, where that institution existed for years and was known as "Bishop Cotton's School." The site on which St. Paul's now stands was acquired, and with a further sum of Rs. 1,12,300/- collected by private subscription to which half was contributed by Government, an endowment was formed and the amount invested in 1864. This school has now four buildings, one of which is exclusively set apart for the classes. A large and well appointed library and reading-room is placed at the disposal of the senior students where their evenings are spent in laying in a stock of knowledge which will stand them in good stead in the near future. In the grounds stands one of the oldest and best known buildings in the Station, *viz.*, 'Bryanstone,' the house in which Dr. (Sir) Joseph D. Hooker lived in 1848, but

*The Parental Academic Institution (which subsequently on receipt of an endowment from Capt. John Doveton became The 'Doveton College') was founded by J. W. Ricketts, who represented the cause of the Domiciled Community before the House of Commons. See "Domiciled Community" under Kalimpong, Part II.

which is now the seat of the Rector of St. Paul's. As an annexe it has a spacious and up-to-date hospital fitted with all the latest medical appliances, and large enough to accommodate 20 patients and a resident nurse, or matron. A special room has been set apart for the use of convalescents, while another is reserved as an Observation ward.

The St. Joseph's College, a large Jesuit institution, was started as the St. Joseph's Seminary, in 'Sunny Bank' (on the site on which the Park Hotel now stands) in 1888 under the direction of the Fathers of the Society of Jesus. It was transferred to its present site at North Point (6,513′) in 1892. From small beginnings it has attained a place among schools of the first rank having 200 pupils on its rolls. Its ordinary curriculum works up to that of a Secondary School, but it has also special branches which prepare youths for the different services, such as the Superior Accounts, Forest &c., as well as for entrance into the Civil Engineering College, Rurki. A museum, which promises to develop in a few specialised lines, and fully established laboratories for training in physical science and chemistry, are the chief features of the instruction imparted at this college.

*The Loreto Convent**. Twelve nuns of the highest attainments and eight lay teachers instruct the 202 pupils of whom 160 are boarders in all that educates girls for their different stations in life. Music, painting and art in all its branches receive due attention as evinced by the entertainments given during the course of the year, as also at the distribution of prizes at the end of the last term.

A well-stocked library, and an up-to-date laboratory in which instruction in elementary physics, chemistry and botany is imparted afford the more advanced pupils an opportunity of obtaining a *finish*. The dormitory is spacious, well ventilated and inviting by its spotless clean accessories. Adjoining it is the dressing-room measuring 75 × 50 feet to which are attached lavatories having both hot and cold water pipes laid on.

This building which is to the north of the Eden Sanitarium

---

*See Plate VIII.

has an ideal situation at an elevation of 6,800 feet, and commands a magnificent view of the Singalia range*. It stands in its own grounds of 15 acres which is intersected by pretty shaded paths over which the children may be seen wandering during play hours thoroughly enjoying themselves.

This convent was founded in 1846 by Mother M. Teresa Mons, one of the three Irish pioneer ladies who laboured in the cause of education in this distant land. The first home of these sisters was in a little cottage named 'Snowy View' to the north of Birch Hill during the period in which the original convent was being built by funds provided by Mr. William Moran (the tea broker), Mr. R. J. Longhnan, I.C.S., the then district judge of Darjeeling, and Capt. Sambler, one of the pioneers of the tea industry. The transfer to the new building took place on October 10th, 1846. For many years following the number on the rolls were few† as the residents were few and far between, and also to the fact that the advantages of a hill climate were not understood by the majority of parents then located in the plains. In the meantime the struggle for existence was severe, indeed: but all this was patiently overcome until it now numbers 202 pupils of whom 160 are boarders. In 1892 the thatched building was replaced by the present imposing stone structure planned and erected by E. J. Morarity, the builder. In 1915 it was found necessary to make further additions to the building to cope with the ever increasing applications for admission; while in the current year a new range has been added, the lower flat being specially set apart as the dining-room.

A special department which admits boys up to 8 years of age was started in Caroline Villa in 1849 and transferred 14 years later to 'Springfield' which adjoins the convent.

---

*The mountain of Alder trees.

†The following appeared in the "Hand Book of Darjeeling":—

Year.	Number of Pupils.	Teachers.	Year.	Number of Pupils.	Teachers.
1846	6	6	1853	29	7
1847	17	5	1854	31	17
1848	24	10	1855	36	17
1849	28	9	1856	42	17
1850	18	9	1857	54	17
1851	18	8	1858	48	17
1852	26	8	1863	45	18

*The Diocesan Girls' High School**. Miss Roby's School after the slip-disaster was taken over by the Clewer Sisters and started in 1904 under the above designation in the spacious building situated just beyond the Old Cemetery on the Lebong (Cart) Road. This institution is under the management of the Sisters of the Community of St. John Baptist, Clewer, England, who are assisted by a competent staff of lay teachers.

The Queen's Hill Girls' School is located about 500 yards to the south of the Railway Station and about 100 feet above the level of the Cart Road. It was opened on March 10th, 1895, and has now 112 pupils on its rolls of whom 86 are boarders. Its curriculum of studies works up to the Higher Secondary Grade. Its success in December, 1915, when 9 out of 10 pupils passed the Cambridge Examination Test, testifies to the ability of its staff.

Annandale to the immediate south of the Station House will very shortly be no more, for on that site a building will be erected at a cost of 4 *lakhs* of rupees to meet the ever expanding requirements of this institution.

The Maharani Girls' School, which was established in 1908 at 'Oak Lodge' as a Primary School, is now an affiliated institution teaching up to the Higher English Standard. Its rolls shew an average attendance of 75 pupils of both sexes. A special department admits boys up to the age of 10 years.

The chief supporters of this school were the Maharani of Cooch Behar, and the Hon'ble Sir Bejay Chand Mahatap, Maharajadhiraj of Burdwan; while among the list of donors were Their Excellencies Lord and Lady Carmichael, the Maharanis of Mourbhanj and Vizanagram, the Rani of Kakina, Sir S. P. Sinha, the Hon'bles Mr. B. C. Mitra and Mr. P. N. Mukerjee. It receives a Government grant-in-aid of Rs. 250/- per mensem.

The Government High School is just below the Station House. The Bhutia Boarding School which was started in 1874 and the Government Middle English School which came into being about the year 1860 were amalgamated in 1891 and raised to the status of a High English School. Since that year, when

---

*This is the only school which failed furnishing necessary details. The above account was, accordingly, gleaned from other sources.

the number on its rolls was only 98, this institution has grown in importance and is now imparting instruction in 8 different languages to 332 pupils (in addition to the ordinary curriculum of the several standards), many of whom doubtless have found the following only too true:—

"Dear Teacher, it is very hard
To write 'mid such a row:
My wits have gone to gather wool,
And addled is my pow.

Pons asinorum I can't cross;
I'm fairly off the line,
Although my eyes look to the skies
In rolling frenzy fine."

The main building and hostels together with the 2½ acres of land on which they stand cost the Government over a *lakh* and a quarter of rupees.

In 1916 the charge for educating each lad at this institution was Rs. 60/- towards which the Government contributed Rs. 42/-. With the exception of High Schools in Calcutta where Rs. 69/- was expended on each pupil, the cost of education in Darjeeling is highest in the province. It would be interesting to know how much is spent by the Government on the education of each child in European schools.

This school has undertaken the education of the indigenous population, which was originally the care of the early Moravian missionaries. It is chiefly attended by Paharis (hill people) with a sprinkling of Bhutia and Hindu youths. Among the first, the Kamis or blacksmith class, stand out pre-eminent as they have forced their way to the front filling the major portion of the clerkships in the station. In the social scale the Kamis hold a very subordinate position, the barriers of which are inexhorable relegating them to contumely for the natural term of life. With a view to obtain better treatment and social recognition the leaders of this community a few years back approached the Maharaja of Sikkim. In reply they were informed that audience would be given them at an open durbar at which their grievances and aspirations could be advanced—an invitation which was declined with thanks, as it was felt that few, if any, for their temerity in wishing to overthrow the caste-system would ever live to return to their native land.

The following pertinent question will therefore force itself forward:—What is the use of higher education if the Orient will not follow the lead of the Occident and permit of its caste-system being broken through by sheer force of ability and polished manners?

Kurseong.

The Victoria Boys' School. The Domiciled Community is indebted to the late Sir Ashley Eden for establishing the Victoria Boys', and Dow Hill Girls' Schools at Kurseong, both of which are maintained by Government for the education of the children of its servants, who otherwise might not be able to afford their offsprings the benefit of a hill climate.

The Boys' School, which is situated at an altitude of 6,000 feet above sea-level on an estate covering fully 100 acres of land, was started in 1879. Addition after addition had to be made to the main building to cope with the ever increasing demands for admission until the current year when the number of pupils on its rolls stands at 190. The curriculum of studies, which at present works up to the Junior Cambridge course only, will shortly be raised to that of the Senior Cambridge; in fact, such a status would have been attained were it not for the war which has set back the hands of the clock in every sphere and calling in life. Pupils after passing the Junior Cambridge Certificate Examination may, if so disposed, put in a further two years for the Technical branches* which include Mechanical,

*The authorities of this institution, like those of the Geothal's Memorial School, very reluctantly were compelled to close down these classes for want of adequate support by the children of the Domiciled Community be they European or Anglo-Indian, who apparently labour under the impression that manual labour and handicrafts are undignified, while quill-driving and servitude behind counters (being softer jobs) carry a better status. And so scheme after scheme based on these lines, including the school started at Calcutta in 1900 by the author and others interested in this community (and subsequently handed over to the two branches of the Christian Associations) have ended in complete failure. It, therefore, appears that the backwardness of this community will last so long as it

Electrical and Mining Courses, the final examinations being held by the Principal at the Sibpur College, Calcutta ; while those desirous of joining the Civil Engineering Course must pass the Sub-Overseer's Examination of the Joint Technical Examination Board.

This school, which is controlled by the Director of Public Instruction, Bengal, and is supervised by the Inspector of European Schools, has the following staff.—A Head Master, seven Assistant Masters, two Lady-teachers for the Lower School Department, two Masters for the Technical Branches, and one Munshi.

The main playground, which is one of the largest in these hills, enables the Cadet Company comprising 112 of all ranks to have its drills within the precincts of the school, and commands some of the grandest views of the snowy range and intervening valleys. Physical culture is developed in an up-to-date gymnasium, while a well-stocked library, which contains over 1,500 standard works and books of reference, affords the pupils, when weather-bound especially, an opportunity of adding to their stock of knowledge.

The Goethals' Memorial. This institution (and also the St. Helen's Convent) which was designed and built by Bro. Molitor fills the void caused by the establishment of the Victoria Boys' School in that it meets the wants of those who are unable to obtain admission in the Government school, and also other schools in these hills owing to the tuition charges being so heavy. It came into being in 1906 mainly through the exertions of Bro. O'Brien, one of the most amiable of Irish Brothers, who stumped Calcutta until the required amount was obtained wherewith to erect a memorial to the memory of the late the Most Reverend Dr. Paul Count Goethals, S. J., Archbishop of Calcutta; in the doing of which he unconsciously also raised unto himself a per-

---

does not come to appreciate the dignity of labour in any form—a condition which the present trend of events, coupled with the scheme at present before the Government for the establishment of a fully equipped Technical College at Jamalpore, E. I. R., must gradually sweep away.

At both these schools the management is still hopeful, and with this end in view are making efforts to get the lads to attend the workshops daily.

manent memorial which testifies to his silent, unostentatious work done during two decades in which his sole thought was the uplifting of the domiciled youth.

This three-storied building, which accommodates 200 boarders, stands on 148 acres of land just two miles to the north of the town of Kurseong, and at an elevation of 5,500 feet above sea-level.

The course of studies pursued is that laid down in the Code of Education for European Schools, Bengal, and includes all the Cambridge Local Examinations.

Its annual sports, which have come to be recognised as permanent fixtures which none should miss, and at which all are more than welcome to its hospital board which literally groans under victuals and viands, are closely contested by the entrants of the school as well as all comers, and enjoyed with an apparent heartiness which affords the onlooker much pleasure. May Bro. O'Brien, and this institution, see many an anniversary is the wish of all residents in stations along the D. H. Railway.

The St. Helen's Convent. This convent, which is a Government-aided institution, imparts instruction up to the Senior Cambridge Course. Though started in February, 1890, only it now has 160 pupils on its roster. To attempt a description of the good work done in this school would be but repeating what has already been recorded under its sister institution, the Loreto Convent, Darjeeling. All that is, therefore, left to be intimated is that the young ladies attending this school are required, in addition to the ordinary curriculum, to pass through a course in Cookery, Sicknursing and Domestic Economy.

The Dow Hill Girls' School is maintained by Government for the education of the daughters of persons of European descent who are employed in any branch of its service. After providing for these, the children of persons not in Government employ are admitted at an uniform rate of Rs. 30/- p.m. for each child. This school, which was started in 1898, has 120 resident pupils on its rolls, to whom instruction is imparted up to the Eighth Standard. Pupils are also prepared for the Junior School Certificate Examination of the University of Cambridge.

The St. Mary's Training College was built in 1889 by the

Belgian Jesuit Fathers of the R. C. Mission of Bengal, for the preparation for Ordination of members of the Society of Jesus of the Bengal and Madura Missions. In this year of grace 1922 there are, besides the 7 Fathers on its Staff, 44 theological students, and 3 Brothers who look after the temporal affairs of the institution. The staff and most of the inmates are Belgians.

Soon after the establishment of this college provision was made for the education of children of the Christian servants attached to it, as also for Indian orphans. This school, now known as the St. Alphonsus School, has developed materially in recent years, and now teaches up to the Lower, and Upper Primary Standards of the Code.

CHAPTER VIII.

Amusements.

> "How small, of all that human hearts endure,
> That part which lords or kings can cause or cure;
> Still to ourselves, in every place consigned,
> Our own felicity we make or find".—*Dr. Johnson.*

The advent of the Administration brings in its train each year the gaieties which tend to make life worth living; during the off season life is dull indeed and *blase*. Our pleasures during the season are many-sided and take the following forms:—weather permitting, cricket, hockey and gymkhanas draw large crowds to each of these functions which are held at the Government House grounds; golf takes its devotees each Sunday right away to the links at Senchal; polo draws fairly large crowds to the Race Course at Lebong; while the Annual Sports of the Colleges, especially St. Joseph's, are attended by fully 500 Europeans and some 3,000 Paharies, dressed in gala attire which adds a picturesqueness to the scenery: our indoor amusements are usually Bioscope Shows at the Palace of Varieties, dancing, rinking, tableaux vivants, theatricals, tennis at the squash courts in the Amusement Club, flower, dog and horse-shows, and carnivals. On golf, a special note has been added, and all that is left to be here intimated is—Golfers are always most welcome on the links after applying to the Hony. Secretary at the Planters' Club. Circuses occasionally spread their canvas in the Market Square where large crowds of Paharies, and not a few Europeans, spend a pleasant time. The last troupe that visited Darjeeling suffered an irreparable loss in that 'jumbo' took a severe cold and died.

The Dog Show.

"Dear Friends, we wish to interest
And let all people know
That in the Poojahs will be held
The first Darjeeling Show.

As we parade the streets and Mall
We note with pitying eyes
A lot of really first class dogs
All yearning for a prize.

You may regard your faithful pet
  As not of the *Haut ton;*
There may be a surprise in store,
  Your duck may prove a swan.

Perhaps you do not own a dog
  Or innocent young pup,
But you can help the show along
  By giving us a cup.

Calcutta, Simla and Bombay
  Hold a good show each year;
Darjeeling it must ne'er be said
  Is lagging in the rear.

Nay, put your shoulder to the wheel,
  And hear our plaintive song :—
Bring forth your dogs, your cups, your cash,
  And help the show along".

The Darjeeling Times—1912.

Tableaux Vivants.

When it was announced that the Loreto Convent under the distinguished patronage of Their Excellencies Lord and Lady Carmichael, intended restaging "Our Empire In Arms," Darjeeling while anticipating a treat was agreeably surprised when the present effort at staging these living pictures surpassed that of the year prior (1915) ; indeed, the posing, and the harmonious blending of the gay costumes of the several units constituting the group of the Allies formed the subject of general comment.

The intention of the Mothers, who staged these tableaux, to depict England's might by gradually weaving round Britannia (the first tableaux) first Ireland, Scotland, Wales and India, who clung closely to her, then the several Colonies and Allies in the order in which they fell into line to crush the militarism of the Huns, was well sustained and carried out without a hitch by the pupils, the very perfection of the mites proving what patience and perseverance can effect with little children. The next series comprised tableaux which similarly grew in size from our soldiers and blue-jackets led by Sir John French and Sir John Jellicoe. The last of the series depicted the restoration of Peace in which poor, crushed and sore-stricken Belgium, over whom was the protecting angel of peace, surrounded by Britannia and the other Powers who were supporting her in the hour of need. As an accompaniment to these tableaux the school orchestra played, and the choir sang the National Anthems of the several Allies, and also "Rule Britannia," "Men of Harlech," "It's a long way to Tipperary," and the "Marseillaise." The national dance of each of the nations on the side of the Allies was gracefully executed by the pupils the one which took most being the Japanese patter by the wee mites. At the conclusion of this function Her Excellency Lady Carmichael kindly presented Miss Sylvia Bourne with a purse of 9 guineas awarded to her by the Trinity College of Music, London, for being the most proficient pupil in all the Colonies, thus testifying to the excellent and sound instruction imparted at this institution.

Dances and Entertainments.

"The dancing pair, that simply sought renown,
By holding out, to tire each other down"—*Goldsmith.*

A 'ghost' dance was given at the Gymkhana Club at which all the guests appeared in white, fantastic costumes, except one *mortal*, who had the temerity to attend in the conventional evening dress. It was not long, however, before he reappeared, arrayed at the hands of unfeeling ghosts, in swaddling clothes of purest white, to the merriment of all.

This novel and uncanny idea was carried out in its entirety, for at the porch each of the sixty guests, including a party from Government House, was met by a ghost and conducted into the ballroom, from the ceiling and walls of which hung snakes, spiders, lizards, owls, bats and all manner of uncanny things.

The Knights-Errant.

The Knights-Errant each year give an entertainment under the direction of their Grand Master, at which over 200 guests, including Their Excellencies attend. In 1914, the programme included a dinner at which over 100 sat, during which the Band of the King's Own played selections, then a variety entertainment, and finally a delightful dance which brought this successful function to a close.

The hall of the Amusement Club was draped in chocolate, relieved by horizontal bands of black, the colours of their escutcheon, while from the ceiling hung streamers of dazzling white, the whole being lit up by Japanese lanterns. *Kala Jagas* there were none, but the sitting-out room with walls of creamy pink was decorated with the delicate shoots of the maling bamboo picked here and there with baskets from which hung deep crimson flowers and trailers of staghorn moss. The theatre was similarly transformed into a drawing-room where lights shone on a mellow green bank of moss and ferns.

These Knights-Errant came into being in 1903 when a small social club was started by the late Maharaja of Cooch Behar and the Officers of the Duke of Wellington's Regiment, and by the bachelors and grass-widowers whose aim was to return hospitality enjoyed. The club since then has grown in numbers until it now counts fully 30 resident knights as well as many dispersed over the country who acknowledge allegiance to the Grand Master.

The Gymkhana Club.

The old Town Hall, an annexe of the Club, was oftener used as a theatre by the Amateur Dramatic Club than by the public for meetings. The members possess histrionic talent of no mean order which probably accounts for the few touring companies which seldom, if ever, find their way up here.

The Gymkhana Rink, and Palace of Varieties.

The rink attached to the Gymkhana Club is for the exclusive use of its members and friends ; the other on Mackenzie Road, which was permanently converted on April 15th, 1916, into a theatre, known as 'The Palace of Varieties' caters for the amusement of the public. The latter building which has the largest and best rinking surface in India has also an unique span of over 80 feet which called forth no end of evil predictions during construction ; but it has stood the test of time and vouches for the mechanical knowledge of Mr. Carl Forstmann, the late proprietor. This building has been thoroughly renovated by the new owners, fitted with comfortable tip-up, plush seats imported from home (a condition which might well and to advantage be emulated by other places of amusement), while separate entrances for the different classes of seat-holders have materially added to the comfort of the European portion of the audiences. Apart from the takings on the opening night, it must have been gratifying to the lessees to know that their efforts at providing for the entertainment of Darjeeling by importing travelling troupes had met with the complete success it deserved. And so the round of pleasure goes on.

The Golf Links.

The idea of forming a Golf Link originated with the Hon'ble Mr. Stevenson-Moore, C.V.O., I.C.S., and a meeting of golfers was called on May 20th, 1905, at which the following were present:—Mr. (now Sir) Robert Carlyle, Messrs W. A. Inglis, H. H. Green, J. H. E. Garrett, R. D. Murray, the Hon'ble Mr. Stevenson-Moore and Col. Sir W. J. Buchanan, K.C.I.E. It was then decided to prepare the ground on which these links stand at Senchal, which prior to the days of golf was visited on the way to Tiger Hill by tourists for a view, if possible, of Mount Everest. So far back as 1844 this spot was chosen unwisely for the erection of a cantonment, but was abandoned shortly after owing, according to tradition, to the number of suicide cases among the troops. This ground being abandoned, the members of this club through Mr. Garrett, the then Deputy Commissioner, obtained a 99 years' lease of the hill-top at a nominal rental. To clear the land of the abandoned ruins of some forty years previous cost a lot of money, but the founders of the club were helped both by the Maharajadhiraj of Burdwan and by the Darjeeling Himalayan Railway.

At first thirteen holes were attempted, but in the course of time these gave place to nine good holes. The members of this club have a right to use the Senchal dak bungalow erected by the Darjeeling Improvement Fund.

The first tee is at the solitary chimney, visible from Darjeeling, and it is a good iron shot to "The Chimney Hole" on the first green; a sliced shot is badly punished by the road below on the right. The bogie for this is an easy four. The second hole is a short iron shot on to a large green. On the ridge near by is the third tee; from here is a splendid drive over a big hill on to a large maidan on the other side. Shorter shots reach the big hill and need another shot, or more, to get on to the maidan below. The fourth tee is on this maidan and a good, long drive is needed to carry a large flat ridge and get on to the further maidan beyond, from which a good lofting shot is needed to get up to the "Pulpit Hole". The bogie is five; it can be done in four, but more often we find six and more recorded.

From the tee beyond the "Pulpit Hole", and at the foot of Tiger Hill the next hole is reached by a good iron shot on to the ridge, bogie four; and from here another good iron or brassy shot will carry the ball on to the green on the flat ridge at the foot of Tiger Hill, called the "Three Chimney Hole". The seventh tee is on this ridge and from it a long drive will be needed to carry the ball on to the first maidan, and from here the seventh green is reached by an approach. The eighth tee is on a high ridge, near the shelter, and from here is a splendid long drive over the left side of the big hill, already mentioned on our way to the third green. It is possible to carry this big hill, but many shots fall short, necessitating another approach shot to the green. The last, or ninth hole, brings us back to a spot below the starting point, and it needs a clear, straight drive to reach the neighbourhood of the green. The bogie score of the nine holes is as follows :—4,3½,4,5,4,4,4,4,4½ = 37.

The Himalayan Challenge Cup (handicap) is played for each October, and for the past two years a "Bogie Cup" has been played for during May and June.

It is needless to say a word about the unique position of the links. The hill well deserves its Tibetan name of "Senchal", or the Hill of Mists, but it takes a good deal of mist to deter keen golfers. The ridge of Senchal is at an altitude of 8,300 ft. To the north can be seen the whole of Kinchenjunga Range, to the north-west over Sandakphu Mount Everest (Plate XVII.) comes into view, and the Makalu Mt. 27,799 ft.; to the south lies Kurseong, while beyond it are the plains of Jalpaiguri.

What is Golf?

Golf, like angling, becomes an obsession with some people, and so the following skit is reproduced :—

Five people were discussing the game of golf.

"Golf might be described as billiards gone to grass", said one.

'Spleen on the green', suggested another.

'The last flicker of the dying fire of athletics,' put in a third, who was himself an ardent footballer.

'The misuse of land and language', was the contribution of a tennis player.

But the fifth man, the only one who ever played golf, declared they were all wrong.

'Golf' he affirmed 'is simply a game wherein the *ball lies badly* and the *player well'*.

Poojah Pastimes.

"There is no time, in all the year,
Like these two pleasant weeks,
As free from care, we breathe the air
That blows from snow-capped peaks.

'Tis good to know that one's alive,
To feel the pulses beat
While from us fall the load that thralls
In Bengal's summer heat.

The sun we cursed, so oft below,
But makes Darjeeling glad;
Dispelled is gloom; with bud and bloom
The mountain sides are clad.

The birds we heard in by-gone years,
Sing for us in the trees,
And violets rise, with purple eyes,
To greet the gentle breeze.

The children play their merry games,
And leap and laugh with glee,
And all the while, the mothers smile
Their bonny bairns to see.

All o'er the hills, the lovers roam,
While cupid shoots his darts;
When gods are blind, they are so kind
To those with loving hearts.

And now and then, the old folks too,
  Would mingle in the fun ;
Oh ! do not tease, but tell them, please,
  Their salad days are done.

Oh ! Mountain Queen ! Within thy realms,
  What potent charms do lie,
Which gives the old a clinging hold
  On things foredoomed to die !

What sights we see upon the Mall,
  When ladies don their best !
How much they show; how can they know
  That fancy sees the rest !

The Flappers flap, to show the boys
  Their ankles trim and neat;
The little fools wear heels like stools
  Which ache their martyred feet.

Ah ! yes, 'tis good to be up here
  In this thrice blessed clime,
Where Jacks and Gills may climb the hills
  And have a jolly time.

'Tis good to watch the babes we love
  Who to our heart chords cling,
To see them grow in beauty's glow,
  Like flowers in the spring.

'Tis good to see the virgin snows,
  No man has ever trod,
The saints alone around His throne,
  May walk the heights of God''.—

The Darjeeling Advertiser, 1917.

CHAPTER IX.

Climate and Health.

"From labour health, from health contentment springs".—*Beattie.*

Darjeeling has been aptly described as 'the children's paradise' for in no hill station in India do they thrive so well. Its climate is most agreeable for the thermometer within doors in summer seldom registers more than 75° in the day, or less than 45° at nights. Snow rarely falls,* and when it does, it never lies. Many of the old residents, however, affirm that 25 years ago when the hillsides were clothed with virgin forest snow covered the landscape with a white mantle for weeks at a time.

Climate.

As falls are now more the exception than the rule this change in climatic conditions has been attributed to the gradual denudation of the hillsides due to the expansion of the town. But this theory appears untenable inasmuch as Jalapahar which is over 1,000 feet higher than Darjeeling has occasional falls of snow. Similarly, snow does not lie on the Singalila range (to the west of the town) below the 10,000 feet level, thereby indicating a gradual but complete change in the climate of the whole district during the last two decades.

On March 18th, 1913, a snow storm which swept the uplands of Tibet caused an unprecedented fall of 8 inches during that night which covered for a whole week the entire district down

Snow Storms.

to the 5,500 feet level, and also caused great damage to the forest from Senchal to the Takdah Cantonments at Hum: indeed, so great was the destruction that the snow-broken trees and branches supplied Darjeeling with its wood fuel for fully 18 months.

The line from Darjeeling to Sonada was covered so deeply by the snow, which in many places was over 3 feet deep, that

Snow Ploughs.

snow-ploughs had to be attached to the engines to clear the line for traffic. The only other occa-

---

*"It is not to be supposed that because the nights are frosty and snow does fall once or twice in the season, that the winter is a severe one." —*The Hand-Book of Darjeeling*—published in 1863.

sion on which these ploughs were requisitioned was in the year 1882-83 when drifts in and around Ghum only caused a temporary block in the traffic.

In this connection early travellers tell us of heavier and more frequent falls. In February, 1828, when Lt.-General Lloyd visited Darjeeling for the first time, snow fell for three successive days covering the station and the adjacent hills with a white mantle for weeks. On revisiting Darjeeling in 1836 a snow-fall covered the ground to the depth of a foot and remained unthawed for over a week.

Observations taken of the snow-line on Kinchenjunga have apparently to the unaided eye conclusively proved that it is gradually receding ; and accordingly at the instance of the Board of Scientific Advice, experiments and observations are being undertaken by the Local Survey Department to determine whether the lowest line of permanent snow on the four chief peaks, and especially on Janu and Kabru (See plate XIX), which are nearer, tends to recede up the mountain-side or not, and with this end in view Mr. J. Burlington-Smith, the photographer, has been deputed to take photographs of high magnitude at stated periods. So far no progress has been made in this direction, while the theodolite work has also not been successful owing to the four selected peaks not being visible at the same time. This work is, however, to be continued for the next ten years, after which the results, if any, will have to be put away for the next decade or so in some pigeon-hole, most probably to be forgotten by the next generation of scientists.

The average maximum and minimum temperatures recorded for some years past prove that the climate of Darjeeling (bar the rains) resembles that of London, the figures being 58° and 48° respectively. On June 12th 1913, however, the heat was intense, the thermometer registering no less than 102° in the open ; and this heat continued for three days. As the actinic power of the rays of the sun cannot be correctly gauged by feeling alone, owing to the cool breezes which always obtain, it behoves new-comers to go about with hats, or *topees*, and not caps of sorts, as some do. The rainfall is 125 inches of which 32 is distributed in July, the rainiest month of the year.

The population of the higher levels, or temperate zone, suffer from chills, fevers, bowel complaints and phthisis, which is a great scourge: those living in the lower ranges and Terai, or tropical zone, are attacked by malaria, the *kala azar* and occasionally black-water fever. During April-May in each year a few sporadic cases of small-pox, measles and chicken-pox occur; but these are invariably imported from the plains where not a few hillmen proceed to during the winter for employment, and bring these diseases back with them. Such cases are promptly segregated and so the infection is stamped out at once.

Public Health.

Beri-Beri has been traced to the eating of rice unfit for consumption; but the black-water fever, from the fact that it chiefly attacks Europeans, planters especially, gives colour to the theory that overdoses of quinine is the primary cause as it produces some disorder of the blood and subsequent complication of the kidneys.

Beri-Beri.

It was left to Major Clayton-Lane, I.M.S., Civil Surgeon of Darjeeling, to determine the cause of emaciation of the ryots in Bengal in general and in the planting areas in particular. Careful study disclosed the fact that fully 90 *per cent* of the population was affected with this parasite, which enters the system through the feet. According to both Ceylon and Indian authorities it is by no means a stubborn disease and is comparatively easy of cure when taken in hand in time. It is at the same time so easily detected by the layman that there would appear to be no excuse for its prolonged continuance amongst a coolie force. Formerly anaemia was generally ascribed to a long-continued period of feverish conditions caused by malaria. It would now appear to be the other way about. The hookworm is now considered to be the first cause; fever and anaemia following as consequences. It is now perfectly well understood that the labour capacity of many gardens could be increased by 25 *per cent* and some by 50, if they were rid of this pernicious parasite. It is, therefore, well worth the strenuous exertions of both the managers of gardens and the medical officers in charge not only to cure the malady but also to remove the cause.

Hookworm Disease.

Health of New-Comers.

The chief and probably the only ailment from which new-comers suffer is the hill-complaint—diarrhœa—,and a few from sunstroke due to neglect of the ordinary precautions mentioned above. The former malady has received due attention at the hands of medical practitioners, while many are the remedies prescribed for its treatment and cure; many also have been the theories advanced as the contributory cause. Among these the mica theory seems to hold its own, for without doubt mica has been found in suspension in our water-supply which is obtained from the springs at Senchal. But whatever the impurity be, there is not the slightest doubt that health will be maintained if the following simple precautions are rigidly observed:—Boil the water and then allow it to stand in an open vessel covered with a thin piece of muslin so as to permit of re-æration which reinstates the water to its tasteless condition, for all know the peculiar flavour it acquires after boiling due to its de-oxidation. After the boiled water has stood for 12 hours only a thin, white opaque layer will be noticed lying at the base of the vessel. It is this deposit, whether of mica or any other subtle substance, which is the chief contributory factor; another being chills contracted either by exposure, or getting caught in one of our sudden showers. As both are avoidable it need hardly be added that to circumvent the second that much-abused but serviceable article, the umbrella, should form an indispensable part of the outfit of new-comers from May to October of each year.

The Water-Supply Scheme.

The authorities have done all that could be desired in this direction, and have given both Darjeeling and Kurseong as pure a water-supply as is possible. The town of Darjeeling, which covers an area of 4.85 square miles, is supplied with water from 26 springs in the Senchal Catchment Area (constructed by Thos. Kenay, the first Engineer to the Municipality) which collects in the large lake, and from thence conveyed through large conduits to the reservoirs established at the St. Paul's School and Rockville, the capacity of the three being

20,000,000; 200,000 and 50,000 gallons respectively. From these reservoirs the water is distributed over the town through pipes of varying calibre, the total length used being nearly 13 miles. From June to December the source of supply is the same; but thereafter the water from these springs, which extend from the lake right up to the foot of Tiger Hill, a distance of 3 miles, is collected at its source in small, pucca cisterns measuring 5′ × 5′ × 5′, strained therein and conducted direct into the reservoirs mentioned, that is, it no longer passes into the lake which by this time has dried up. The lake is 5½ miles away from Darjeeling.

The Town.

Provision has also been made for the supply of pure water at three of the most important stages along the Tista Valley Road which is estimated to cost Rs. 5,000/- for the construction of necessary reservoirs at Tista Bridge, Kalijhora and Sivoke—places the tourist must halt at if he does this trip on foot. In regard to this scheme all that is necessary to add is that it cannot be completed any too soon as it is the highway from Tibet and Sikkim into India, as also owing to the fluctuating population which along the Tista Cart Road during the dry months amounts to nothing short of 5,000 souls who are forced to live under the scantiest of shelters—*lean-tos*—thereby demanding a pure water-supply, the want of which has hitherto been the cause of epidemics along this route during the past eight years to the knowledge of the writer.

Tista Valley.

Mineral Springs.

These springs which are well-known to the indigenous population are situated at a spot called '*Devi Pani,*' or medicinal waters, on the west surface of the hill to the east of the Mall. Sir W. W. Hunter says—"These were formally utilised for medicinal purposes, and a convalescent depot was built near by for the convenience of the troops at Jalapahar. The water, however, is not used at present, and the depot has gone to ruin".

This depot very probably came into existence on receipt by Government of the report on the analysis of the water of Darjeeling by Dr. Hutchinson, who was specially deputed for the purpose in June, 1871. If so, it would be interesting to know why it was abandoned; and also whether the waters from the springs could not be utilised in the manufacture of 'mineral waters' as is done at Jamalpore, E. I. R., from the springs at Sitakund.

Besides this one, which gave its name to the 'Mineral Spring Tea Estate', there are several other such springs in the district, from which the waters ooze out warm, and of a reddish colour with a strong suphurous odour. The hill-people believe in the efficacy of these springs, which each winter draw large crowds to the Rungneet Valley, Sikkim, and also distant Gyantsee for medicinal baths.

CHAPTER X.

HOSPITALS, &c.

The Eden Sanitarium.

Few know of the incident which proved to be the actual foundation stone of this institution, and fewer still remember it. It would, therefore, be well within the scope of such a work as this to revive these reminiscences, and to keep green the memory of the Man to whom both the European and Anglo-Indian communities owe so much; and, indeed, it may be added without any fear of contradiction that during the tenure of no Lieut.-Governor of Bengal were so many institutions of public utility founded the one dove-tailing in purpose with the other.

To begin with, the mortality among maternity cases, which then had only a wing allotted for the purpose in the Medical College, Calcutta, assumed such alarming proportions that the Man of the Hour stepped in and made clear the way for the erection in 1882 of the Eden Hospital, Calcutta. From a consideration of Motherhood to Childhood was but a natural transition; and here again this Man steps in and plans the establishment of schools for the youths of both sexes at Kurseong. The next step, and a very natural one too, was the care of the invalid, both old and young, and lo! on April 22nd, 1883, the Eden Sanitarium*, Darjeeling, which was designed by Mr. Martin, C. E, the Architect to the Government of Bengal, sprang into being. Thus did this much maligned man complete the round of the good Samaritan, and the practical Christian.

The late Sir Ashley Eden while out one morning for his accustomed walk observed an European on the platform of the Darjeeling Station in the grip of death. To see distress was enough for this tenderhearted man, for whereas his predecessors *talked* of things to be, this man of the world said little but *acted*.

---

*Erected by Government at a cost of 2 *lakhs* of rupees = £13,333 and 1/3, at the present rate of exchange.

He spoke to the invalid to learn that he was about returning to the plains as he was unable to get accommodation anywhere within his means. Throughout the remainder of that walk he was *moody* and on getting back to the 'Shrubbery' (as Government House was then called) immediately despatched an A. D. C. to have the invalid admitted anywhere at his expense. But, alas, too late! for the invalid had left for the plains. Subsequent enquiries brought back the sad tidings that the invalid had died at Siliguri, the victim of pneumonia contracted while at Darjeeling. And now be it said to his praise:—Sir Ashley's eyes were suffused with tears when the sad message was conveyed to him. This immediately clinched his decision to have a home for the reception and treatment of such cases. Such were the circumstances which brought into existence the Eden Sanitarium—an everlasting monument to his memory and sympathetic heart.

His broad views of life, and his intimate acquaintance with the needs of the Domiciled Community very soon indicated the lines on which help could be afforded to the middle classes of this body, and the shape this help took was the establishment of schools at Kurseong, where pupils while conning their props would be building up frames to better fit them for the struggle of life, thereby placing both the European and Anglo-Indian under a very deep obligation to the man who after his death was dubbed 'licentious' by those who probably had never heard the addage—"*De mortuis nil nisi bonum*";* and be it known to the shame of both that no protest was lodged to the degradation offered his memory when his statue, which stood at the north-west corner of the Dalhousie Square, Calcutta, (after it was unveiled by Sir Steuart Bailey on April 15th, 1887, when the Hon'ble Mr. Justice H. T. Prinsep delivered the following felicitous speech) was relegated† to a secluded spot within it:—

"To the lasting memory and honour of Sir Ashley Eden be it borne in mind that on more than one occasion, and with some risk to his

---

*"Of the dead be nothing said but what is good."

†To make way and rightly too, for the pure white, octagonal marble column erected during the administration of Lord Curzon to mark the spot in which the bodies of 122 Europeans were cast after the tragedy known as the 'Black Hole', which took place on June 20th, 1757, when 146

personal career, he has courageously stood forth as the redresser of wrongs, the champion of the oppressed, and has been the means of securing liberty and freedom of action to the poorest classes of the community. We are justly proud of such a distinguished public servant, and rejoice to do honour to his memory in India". At the Northbrook Club, London, on July 12th, 1887, Lord Northbrook made the following speech:—"The Indian Civil Service has been rich in able administrators, but I do not think any Indian gentleman will hesitate to agree with me that we have seen of late years no abler administrator than the late Sir Ashley Eden, &c.".

The Eden Sanitarium has 64 beds:—8 first-class, 8 intermediate and 24 each for the second and third classes, the last being accommodated in a dormitory. At a pinch as many as 126 adults and children can be received, as in the year 1912. A tennis court faces the building, while a billiard-table affords recreation to its inmates when the weather does not permit of outdoor exercise being indulged in. The sitting-room has an excellent piano purchased from funds raised by its late steward, Mr. C. H. Richardson. Free quarters are provided for the servants of residents.

This institution, which is maintained at an annual expenditure of about Rs. 50,000/-, is under the control of the Civil Surgeon of the station assisted by an Assistant Surgeon (a member of the Sub. Med. Service) and an European Steward; while the creature comforts are the special care of a number of Sisters. An illustrated pamphlet giving full particulars of charges, etc., can be had from the Secretary.

The Lowis Jubilee Sanitarium.

The honour of being the first to recognise the want of an institution similar to the Eden Sanitarium for the exclusive use of Indians goes to Sir Franklin Prestage (who made the

---

persons were thrust into a room measuring 18 feet square only. The site is marked by brass bands inlaid on the stones forming the pavement adjoining the G. P. Office, Calcutta. But that the statue of the late Sir Ashley Eden should be relegated to a secluded spot within the Dalhousie Square is an unpardonable act toward the memory of the Man who deservedly earned the gratitude of both the European and Anglo-Indian Communities throughout India.

D. H. Railway what it is) whose efforts toward obtaining the necessary funds proved unsuccessful owing to the fact that prior to the opening of the railway to Darjeeling the journey was not only expensive but it also took a big slice out of the amount of leave obtainable by the middle, or working classes. The idea was again taken up by Mr. Edmund Elliott Lowis, the then Commissioner of the Jalpaiguri Division, when in 1886* by the liberality of Maharajah Gobindo Lal Roy a sum of Rs. 90,000/- was placed at his disposal to be expended on any work of public utility. Having obtained the sanction of Sir S. C. Bailey, the Lieut.-Governor of Bengal, to the construction of a sanitarium for the exclusive use of Indians he cast about for a site. The selection rested upon the spot on which this sanitarium now stands comprising 7½ acres which was made over as a deed of gift for the purpose by the late Maharaja of Cooch Behar, father of the present ruler. With these two donations as a nucleus it did not take the management long to raise the necessary amount, for we find that the Lowis Jubilee Sanitarium was completed in 1887. By April 30th, 1912, inclusive of the Government grant-in-aid of Rs. 16,000/- towards the erection of an annexe called the Edward VII House, the total sum of Rs. 3,54,134/- was collected, *viz.*—By donations Rs. 2,60,656/- and by annual subscriptions Rs. 93,478/-.

The foundation stone of the annexe, which is a ferro-concrete structure, was laid on May 27th, 1912, by His Excellency Lord Carmichael, Governor of Bengal. It was estimated that this building would cost Rs. 34,000/- while the new range of kitchens, for the use of the several castes into which this community is divided, would absorb the Rs. 9,000/- subscribed for the purpose. The annexe was completed during the year, and so increased the accommodation of the sanitarium to 118 beds. About Rs. 25,000/- is expended annually on its maintenance.

The Victoria Hospital.

The first Charitable Hospital and Dispensary was started in 1864 in the building lately utilised as the Police Lines. In

*When the D. H. Railway was already an accomplished fact.

1888 it contained 12 beds only which, obviously, was quite inadequate. To meet the ever increasing demands of an expanding population building work to the north of this structure was started, which on completion in 1903 increased the accommodation of the new hospital to 70 beds. In 1905 over 10,000 outdoor patients were attended to, while the operations which were performed numbered 390. It is in charge of a Medical Officer subordinate to the Civil Surgeon of the Station; while the care of the invalids devolves on the Sister in charge. No account of this hospital would be complete without reference being made to the services of the late Rai Nibaran Chandra Sen Bahadur, the Medical Officer, who during his tenure of a number of years raised the efficiency of the staff as well as by his personal influence obtained funds for the erection of the cottage attached to the building.

For sometime past the accommodation has again been found inadequate and unable to cope with the requirements of indoor patients, and so with a view to remove these disabilities the quarters lately occupied by the Sadar Police Lines, which adjoined the building, were handed over to the hospital authorities in order to bring it into line with its sister institution, the Eden Sanitarium. This hospital by the end of 1915 was quite up-to-date, thanks to the keen interest taken in its welfare by Their Excellencies Lord and Lady Carmichael; to the donation of Rs. 3,000/- by the Rajah of Digapatia and to the assignment of funds raised for commemorating the memory of the late Maharajah of Cooch Behar. The following extensions and additions were made:—'The Cooch Behar ward', another for the reception of phthisical patients whose numbers are ever on the increase; while two small cottages, like the one already standing to the north of the hospital, which was erected by Lal Mohun Shaha Shankhanidhi of Dacca at the instance of the late N. C. Sen, has still to be erected with the Digapatia contribution in which paying patients, both European and Indian, will be received at a nominal charge of Rs. 2/12 per day, (or Rs. 70/- per month) which will include medical attention, the use of three rooms and a kitchen, and lighting. Finally, the lines lately occupied by the Police are to be either suitably altered, or rebuilt for the accommodation of the Nursing Staff, which will be augmented and supervised by qualified European Nurses.

Lady Carmichael's Nursing Fund.

Her Excellency's fund, started in 1914, though providing incidentally for trained nurses, aims at a much wider scope. Lady Carmichael had for sometime noticed that mofussil hospitals in Bengal shew, as a whole, a lamentable want of proper nursing owing to the fact that they can barely afford to pay for European nurses, and therefore get no others. She accordingly proposes to provide for the training of Indian nurses, whose service will then be available throughout Bengal at salaries which mofussil hospitals should be able to afford. Their training will be started and mainly carried out in Darjeeling, but will be completed in Calcutta. This will be no mere experiment. There are Indian nurses trained in Darjeeling who are now doing excellent work in mofussil hospitals, and in particular the Mayo Hospital, Calcutta. It is quite certain that there is nursing material available in Darjeeling; but it is equally certain that better use can be made of it than is possible under existing conditions. No one can satisfactorily train a nurse except a thoroughly trained nurse, and it is to provide for the proper and complete training of a number of Indian nurses that Her Excellency is desirous to see the Victoria Hospital provided with English trained nurses of the highest qualifications. Temporary arrangements are being made to house this nursing school in the old thanah building, but this land will shortly be required to provide for extensions to the hospital, and it is essential that more suitable accommodation should be provided for without further delay on a part of the site. The cost of the building is estimated to amount to Rs. 20,000/- and the annual cost of training to about half that sum. Very appreciable and substantial aid has already been received from influential Indian sources, but much more is required to place Her Excellency's scheme on a satisfactory financial footing. All donations for the purpose should be sent to the Secretary, Victoria Hospital Nursing Fund. Separate accounts will be maintained for Her Excellency's Fund, and annual reports will be issued; while donations of Rs. 5,000/- and over will be commemorated by a tablet set in the hospital.

The Small-pox Hospital.

Darjeeling was visited by this scourge in 1904 when fully a fifth of the population was attacked, while a tenth of those stricken, succumbed. This outbreak was exceptional, indeed, for small-pox, like other contagious diseases, does not usually thrive in temperate climates; but once it gets a footing, and owing to the filthy habits of the pahari, it abides and becomes endemic for a time. Happily, neither Darjeeling nor Kurseong have many cases, and the few that come to notice, and are immediately segregated, are invariably imported from the plains. However, as a measure of prevention a special small-pox hospital was built in 1914. Singamarie-way, *i.e.*, beyond the New Cemetery and below the Lebong or Cart Road.

The Glen Eden Laboratory.

Their Excellencies, Lord and Lady Carmichael in June, 1916, visited the recently completed Glen Eden experimental station at Darjeeling.

The phenomenal success achieved by Prof. Sir J. C. Bose in demonstrating by means of screens on which the typical phenomena of irritability in tropical plants were projected in vivid pictures, induced the Secretary of State, at the instance of the Minister of Education and the Governor in Council, to sanction the establishment of a research institute at Darjeeling, wherein these series of experiments and studies may be extended to plants whose habitat range from the temperate to the arctic regions.

In this laboratory several important results have already been obtained on the phenomenon of hibernation, as well as on the effect of low temperatures in retarding morbid reactions. It is understood that experiments are also in progress in the maintenance of tropical and temperate zone plants in a state of continuous irritability throughout the year, irrespective of the usual conditions of light and temperature which are maintained by special automatic electrical appliances.

Sir J. C. Bose's experiments have obtained world-wide recognition, especially in America where the leading Universities are desirous of introducing his methods of investigations in their laboratories.

CHAPTER XI.

CALAMITIES.

Earthquakes.*

All hill stations more or less are subject to slight seismic disturbances: but Dharamsala and Shillong were devastated like San Francisco.† Darjeeling also in June, 1897, suffered from a severe shock of earthquake which caused a good deal of destruction, among which the following properties were badly damaged:—Castleton (in which Wilson started his hotel), River View, Duka's Delight (an annexe of The Dale) and Rockville (then Mrs. Houghton's boarding establishment), which being heavy, stone-built structures, like the buildings in San Francisco, oscillated out of their centres and flattened out like a pack of cards; while the lighter, wooden structures suffered little or no damage. Carlton House was shaken to its very foundations, as evinced by all its arches which were cracked; Craig Mount had its upper storey levelled, while Magnolia, near West Point, in which the boarders of The Darjeeling Boys' School resided, collapsed during the constitutional that its pupils and principal, Major Bomwetsch, were having at Jalaphar at the time, otherwise there would have been a repetition of the slip-disaster, and a greater one too than that which befell the Methodist School during the landslip in 1899. Mr. Holland, the assistant master of this boys' school, had a marvellous escape for he lay ill in the building and just managed to literally crawl out when he saw a part of the premises give way.

These reminiscences involuntarily take us back to personal experiences of the same shock which devasted Shillong, and was felt in Tibet, and throughout the whole of Assam and Bengal right down to Calcutta. The writer was engaged that Sunday

---

*See foot-note under 'Everest,' Tour A—4.

†Nearly as much money was spent in the rehabilitation of San Francisco since the earthquake and fire of 1906 as the Panama Canal will cost when completed. Three hundred and sixty million dollars will be spent upon the canal; and since April 18th, 1906, there has been expended in San Francisco 341,500,000 dollars, practically as much as the canal will cost when completed.

afternoon in angling at the tank in the grounds of the Chitpore Hydraulic Press, Cossipore, Calcutta: at the same hour the Arab portion of the followers of Mahomed turned out for the Mohorum, mourning for the loss of the two sons of the Prophet, while the lower strata of the Christian community residing in Bow Bazar and its purlieus had thronged the main thoroughfares for a sight of this pageant, otherwise the loss to life would have been great indeed.

His attention was first drawn to a deep, dull rumble in the earth which equalled in volume the sound created by 10 train loads of empty wagons being shunted; the next, thousands of bubbles were seen welling up from the bottom of the tank, to be followed by the water being churned as in a maelstrom until whirled over the embankment 3 feet high, while the fishes, from midgets to those weighing fully a maund (82 lbs.), leapt clean out of the water on to the land. The birds swept round in circles giving tongue to plaintive notes, the earth heaved, the chimney attached to this press, which was over 80 feet in height, swayed 4 feet on either side out of plumb, while the wall of the main store-house, which is fully 400 feet long, sinuated like a snake and opened out in large fissures through which the light of day shone. Hastily rushing home, in order to wend his way to town, he found that the partition walls of his home had collapsed: getting into his cart was the work of a few minutes, while the drive in was a record one, as his family was spending the day in town. At the foot of the Chitpore bridge the market had collapsed, the walls of many houses *en route* had cracked and fallen, while not 10 *per cent.* of the parapets were left standing. The spires of the St. Paul's Cathedral and the Sacred Heart of Jesus, Calcutta, had snapped in twain, while many of the dwellings of the poorer order had ceased to exist. Such was the panic in that city that thousands slept in the open parks and public warehouses for the whole of the week following, or until such time as the authorities found suitable accommodation for the homeless.

The severity of the shock was felt throughout the Province of Bengal, from the South Lushai Hills on the east to Shahabad on the west, and from Puri on the south to Sikkim on the north. A. H. Savage Landor, who was at that moment at Garbyang (16,467′) which is on the borders of the Kumaon district and Tibet, also recorded that the oscillations which were severe and passed from S. S. W. to N. N. E. lasted from 5h-20m to 5h-24m-2s, p.m.

Assuming that the focus of disturbance to have been near Cherapunji in Assam, the shock appears to have travelled thence to the western extremity of Bengal and Behar in 6 minutes or less. Its duration varied greatly, according to the reports of local officers, the lowest being 5 seconds, the highest 5 minutes.

In the towns of Rungpore, Bogra, Pubna, Dinajpore, Murshidabad, Berhampore, Dacca, Mymensingh and Cooch Behar nearly all the masonry houses suffered; while in Hughly, Rampur-Boalia and Malda a considerable portion of the larger buildings suffered. In Calcutta over 1300 houses were injured in the town and suburbs ; but only 4 deaths were reported as against 135 throughout the province.

Heavy damage was done to the bridges, buildings and permanent-way on the Assam Bengal and Cooch Behar Railways. The total cost of repairs to, and reconstruction of, Government buildings in the districts and Calcutta was estimated at nearly 13 *lakhs* of rupees, while the losses to private individuals probably amounted to over a *crore*, or 100 *lakhs* of rupees.

The palace of the Raja of Sikkim was also destroyed, while several monasteries in that State had either to be rebuilt, or very materially repaired. In Cooch Behar most serious damage was caused to the Maharaja's palace, the State buildings generally, the State railways, roads and bridges, the total loss being estimated at over 15 *lakhs* of rupees.

Running parallel with, and at a distance of about 100 yards, and throughout the entire length and east of the railway line from Siliguri to Sara Ghat were to be seen geysers (*fumaroles*) from 50 to 100 yards apart throwing up hot water and sand, their points of exit being marked for many a year by small, dome-shaped mounds of earth and sand.

In Shillong, only those who happened to be out of their houses or out for a drive along the margin of the lake, which was 5 miles long, escaped ; all others were either maimed or killed. *The whole lake disappeared,* all the houses were levelled, the jail buried its inmates two of whom alone escaped by crawling under a table. The Catholic Mission established at this station sank vertically over 1,000 ft, and so passed beyond the pale of all help for its edges were precipitous and so could neither be reached from above nor below. Food was, therefore, dropped down in barrels to the imprisoned band numbering over 50 including a priest ; but they gradually succumbed for want of water—an awful fate !

Dharmsala, similarly, a few years after suffered the same fate as Shillong, but in this station the wooden structures took fire and so added materially to the death-roll.

Landslips.

"Who was it scooped these stony waves,
Or scalped the brow of old Cairngorm,
And dug these ever yawning caves ?
'Twas I, the Spirit of the Storm."—*Burns.*

Darjeeling is always subconsciously associated with the loss of the Lee family and other European children, numbering ten in all, who were engulfed in the landslip which submerged the greater part of the building in which the American Methodist School was then located to the east of Observatory Hill on the Rangneet Road. This sad occurrence entirely absorbed public attention and deflected it from a still greater calamity which befell the district and which was caused by an unprecedented rainfall of 27½ inches on Sunday, September 25th, 1899. The following is a summary of the calamity :—In the town of Darjeeling 10 Europeans and 62 Indians perished (of these 45 died on the precipitious eastern side of the hill) ; in Kurseong there were 9 deaths; while in the district no less than 219 souls perished either from exposure that followed the storm, or by being engulfed in falling debris or slips. The railway also suffered considerably, which in some places, notably near 'Mary Ville', had its lines suspended in the air compelling passengers to cross this chasm on a wire-ropeway to which a seat was attached.

During this rain-storm huge boulders said to weigh over

hundreds of tons each went tumbling down the hillside into the Balasan Valley, and caused the bungalows in that locality to rock and sway as if shaken by a mighty earthquake. The rushing waters swept away the heavy machinery and buildings of the old Cedar Tea Estate, not to speak of doors and windows, and landed the debris at the Tirrianna crossing, which is fully 10 miles below in the Terai. The Poole bridge suffered a similar fate, while animals both tame and wild were drowned in the flood. Finally the total loss to property as computed by competent authority has been estimated to amount to one *lakh* of rupees.

To add to the miseries of those who had suffered, as also those engaged in the work of rescue, who necessarily were much handicapped, the town was plunged in total darkness by the electric power station at Sidrapong being engulfed in a large landslip. Every one went about bewildered and dazed, while chaos reigned supreme for days.

The following appeared in The Darjeeling Advertiser* :—

"There is no house, there is no plantation, there is scarcely a road or highway in the district which has not suffered. Owing to the line being washed away at 'Mary Ville' and several other places between Ghum and Darjeeling the up mail was held up at the former station where passengers were forced to shift for themselves and spend the

---

*The late Major Bomwetsch, B.A., V. D., while Principal and proprietor of 'The Darjeeling Boys' School', published *'The Darjeeling Advertiser* royal quarto in size which was printed at a native press in the market, the first issue being in March, 1899. The account of the disaster which was most vividly and pathetically written called for an immediate and special issue numbering 3,500 copies, which did not even then fully meet the demands of those stricken with grief, or of their friends. Encouraged by such beginnings Major Bomwetsch shortly after took over the Scotch Mission Orphan Press, known as "The Albert Press',, and on August 3rd, 1899, brought out an issue printed on royal folio paper, its present size. Since then it has outlived all competitors, and is now filling a decided want in this station where new-comers look out for the weeks' gossip and news while seated on the Chow, ruthlessly criticising both friends and acquaintances alike.

About the same time as *'The Darjeeling Advertiser'* came into being. Mr. John Lord started the original *'Darjeeling Times'* in which many a quaint and original paragraph appeared about persons and their doings much to the chagrin of the authorities, who were then more than autocratic, with the result that Mr. Lord often found himself before the Deputy Commissioner for *Lese-majeste.* Then followed *'The Darjeeling News'*, Edited by Dr. O'Brien, and *'The Chronicle'* which were short-lived, as also the second *'Darjeeling Times'* whose Editor-proprietor relinquished journalism for more remunerative avocations.

night as best they could in all possible discomfort, arriving the following morning in dandies or rickshaws. . . . About 320 privates and Non-Coms of the Munster Fusiliers under Capt. Tizzard and Lt. Henderson worked all Monday and Tuesday in their efforts to unearth the wounded, and dead from the debris of the houses to the east of Observatory Hill which had been engulfed by the landslip."

It is a common occurrence during the monsoons, or rains, for hill-streams, notably the Jhelum at Srinagar, Kashmir, to rise 20 odd feet in one night after a fairly heavy rainfall. But this unprecedented one washed away the village at Tista Bridge (which in those days nestled a little above the water's edge) during the early part of the night and so the loss to life was not great.

The Darjeeling Relief Fund, which was started through the exertions mainly of the Rev. Mr. R. Kilgour and Mr. W. A. M. Lattey, Agent of the Alliance Bank of Simla, disbursed a sum of Rs. 10,692-14-3 among the Europeans, who suffered by this calamity, and Rs. 16,238-14-8 among Indians. Great difficulty was experienced in distributing relief among the latter, as minute enquiries had to be made in many distant places throughout the district.

Again, on August 5th, 1914, both Darjeeling and Kalimpong were struck by a storm which in the former caused a few slips one of which carried away the bridge at Setikhola on the Peshok Road to the Hum Cantonments thereby dislocating the fuel supply of the town, as the charcoal kilns are chiefly located in the forest about this locality; while at the latter place the loss to life and property was great, indeed. This storm caused 8 slips on the adjacent Sikkim hills; in one spot especially the hillside for the width of a ¼ of a mile and from a height of 5,000 feet to the very bed of the Rangneet river was washed away, and with it all the hamlets that studded its sides. It is feared the loss to life was great, indeed, but how many perished will never be known as they were buried 'In God's Acre'.

Just a year after, *i.e.*, on August 8th, 1915, another disaster occurred in Darjeeling. For a week prior to the occurrence the weather had been variable indeed. The last week in July gauged an abnormal rainfall, which gave place to bright, sunny days which contributed not a little on the 4th of August to the attendance at the several Intercessory Services held in the station in connection with the anniversary of the declaration of the war. Since the 6th rain had been general throughout the district, while from 6 p.m. of the 7th till 8 a.m., of the 8th the town was deluged by a continual, steady downpour which aggregated 9½ inches and brought about the following disaster which not only cast a gloom over the station but revived reminiscences of the past when two slips occurred on the same site where Miss Roby's School, (now the Diocesan Girls' High School), was located in the building at present in occupation by the N. B. M. Rifles. In the first, a part of the premises was carried away as well as a small cottage located to the east of that building; in the second, which occurred five years ago only a servant's shanty in which five souls were asleep was buried beneath a large slip: and also of the slip which took place on the east of Observatory Hill, which ended in the great calamity of September 23rd, 1899.

A part of the grounds of the Volunteer Headquarters measuring 80 feet in depth and width, standing over the stables attached to this building and adjoining the tennis court, was carried away at 4 a.m. of August 8th, and crushed, as if made of a pack of cards, this structure which was of ferro-concrete. Of the 11 horses stalled therein 7 were killed, or so badly injured that they had to be shot. Three were buried in the debris, three through the force of impact were shot through the opposite wall and hurled down the khud to the road below, while one, named Brutus, managed to crawl out in a battered condition and was found above Dant Kotee near the Mall and shot. The other 4 animals and two syces who were located at the western end of the stables had a miraculous escape, for they all crawled out of the building, the roof of which was nearly parallel with the ground.

Within a distance of about 15 feet and to the right of the stables, are the quarters of the servants, who fortunately escaped. Had this building been involved in the slip there would have been a loss of human life, as quite a number of families live in it.

It was also reported by natives living Lebong-way that about 9 p.m. on the night of the 9th a great noise as of a heavy slip was heard east of the disaster but right down the valley. The report, however, was never verified.

The permanent-way staff of the railway was commended for the promptitude with which two slips at Sonada and a third at Ghum were cleared, thus avoiding delays in the running of the trains.

The Power of Rushing Water.

From the Jaldakha river, which separates Darjeeling on the east from Bhutan, to Gangtok in Sikkim on the north, a rainfall of over 27 inches was recorded in the first two weeks of August, 1915.

In the Tista Valley Road innumerable small slips occurred along the railway line, which, however, were speedily cleared thereby ensuring no delay whatever in the running of the trains on that road.

In this connection and with a view to exemplify the manner in which our mountain-paths had suffered, the following account will afford some impression of the power of rushing water. The sides of Gel Jhora, where it crosses the Cart Road 2 miles below Tista Bridge, were revetted by the railway authorities with walls 10 feet deep and twenty feet thick to carry the girders of the new line. The boulders which were hurdled down in this torrent actually ground away one of these pier-heads entirely, leaving a clean, smooth surface as if the stones had been designedly polished.

On the Kalimpong side, the roads and mountain-paths along the Leish and Geish rivers were damaged in many places, while slips between Gangtok and Rungpu, in Sikkim, carried away telegraph posts, which caused a temporary but complete block of the traffic, which, however, was promptly re-established. The Jaldakha river, which debouches into the Duars, and flows to the east of Chalsa Station in two small streams running close to and parallel to each other, and which is spanned by two iron bridges, united and assuming one main channel carried away the embankments between the two bridges as also the approach to the east of the further bridge to an extent of over 600 feet, leaving the two structures standing as if they formed the connecting link to a very large structure which had vanished.

To the south of Darjeeling the Mahanady and Balasan rivers had overflowed their embankments, notably the former, which caused temporary inundations at the bridge just outside the town of Siliguri, where the river extended from bank to bank in one swirling, swollen torrent. (See illustration, Plate III, which exhibits the ordinary size of this river).

CHAPTER XII.

Cemeteries.

The following stanzas portray the materialistic, and the spirituelle views held by the two schools in regard to the transition of life to the Unknown:—

"Man doom'd to care, to pain, disease and strife,
Walks his short journey through the vale of life
  Watchful, attends the cradle and the grave,
And passing generations longs to save:
  Last dies himself: yet wherefore should we mourn?
For man must to his kindred dust return;
  Submit to the destroying hand of fate,
As ripen'd ears the harvest-sickle wait".—*Euripides.*

"Life' we have been long together,
  Through pleasant and through cloudy weather;
'Tis hard to part when friends are dear;
  Perhaps 'twill cause a sigh, a tear;
Then steal away, give little warning,
  Choose thine own time,
Say not good-night, but in some brighter clime
  Bid me good-morning".—*Mrs. Barbauld.*

The Old Cemetery which is a mile from the Chowrasta, and through which the Lebong (Cart) Road was cut, was consecrated and opened formally in 1865. It contains the following graves:—

1840—Rachael Preston, aged nine months.

*1842—Alex. Cosma de Koörösi, "a native of Hungary, who, to follow out philological researches, resorted to the east, and for years passed under privation, such as seldom has been endured, and patient labour in the cause of science, compiled a Dictionary and Grammer of the Tibetan

---

*Have mural tablets placed to their memory in the St. Andrew's Church.

language, his lasting and real monument. On his road to H'lassa to resume his labours, he died at Darjeeling on the 11th April, 1842. Aged 44 years."

*1844—Capt. R. Taylor, 65 Regiment, N.I.

*1850—Lieut. J. Gowan, 14th Regiment, N.I.

*1856—Lieut. F. A. Jeune, 25th Regiment, B.N.I.

*1862—Lt.-General Andrew Hearsey, C.B., H.M., Indian Army who died at Darjeeling on the 14th June, 1862, aged 71 years. A prominent figure at Dum Dum, near Calcutta, during the Mutiny.

*1865—Lt.-General George Alymer Lloyd, C.B., in H.M.'s Bengal Army, who died at Darjeeling on the 4th June, 1865, aged 76 years. The discoverer of Darjeeling. And such is fame! and the gratitude of posterity that his name is not preserved in Darjeeling, for the Road and Botanic garden perpetuate the name of Mr. W. Lloyd, the proprietor of a bank of that name.

*: :—Carl Gotlob Niebel, one of the early missionary settlers.

*1873—Capt. Chas. Wood; aged 59 years.

*1876—Mr. Henry Woodrow, M.A., formerly of Caius College, Cambridge, and Director of Public Instruction in Bengal; aged 53 years.

1878—Mr. Mandelli, ornithologist, appointed by the Italian Government to report on birds of the eastern Himalayas.

1881—Mr. William Napier Campbell, son of Dr. D. A. Campbell, Superintendent of Darjeeling; aged 33 years.

Campbell, like Lloyd, is unhonoured by Darjeeling!

1882—Mr. S. Mackintosh
The Wernickes
The Stoelkes } Pioneers in the Tea Industry.

*1889—Gustavus Septimus Judge: aged 73 years, of which more than 50 were passed in India. A pioneer in the Tea Industry, and founder of the Judge Property, of which the upper Beechwood Estate once formed a part.

1893—Col. Crommelin, R.E., one of the early settlers.

1899—The Lee Family, and the children of the late Dr. J. R. Wallace of Calcutta, who were engulfed in the landship.

: :—John White, an old resident, who did much for public institutions.

1913—Sir Chas. Allan, I.C.S., Chairman, Calcutta Corporation.

Among those laid to rest in the New Cemetery (which is 2 miles out of town) are :—

1909—E. J. Morarity, builder and contractor, who designed and built two out of the four buildings constituting St. Paul's School, Jalapahar; as also the main building of the Loreto Convent.

1914—Arthur Gasper, Bar-at-Law.

: :—Capt. John Hay-Burgess, M.D., F.R.C.S., I.M.S., Surgeon to His Excellency the Governor of Bengal.

The Convent Cemetery.

It is difficult to determine the origin of this cemetery in which the remains of the Nuns attached to the convent, who belong to the order of the Institute of the Blessed Virgin Mary, and a few of the pupils attending this school were buried. According to popular belief it came into being owing to the Old Cemetery, which was consecrated in 1865 only, having no plot allotted at the time for the burial of the members of the Catholic faith. The more probable reason being a matter of convenience which governed its origin. Whatever the origin be, this cemetery located at the foot of the grounds attached to the convent was started in the year 1868 to receive the remains of Sister Mary Gouzaga, who was buried on May 24th, in that year. To the extreme west of this graveyard a Mortuary Chapel was erected over a vault built for the reception of 10 defunct nuns. Of these 9 have been utilised leaving one only which has been set apart for an aged and blind Sister who arrived in Darjeeling in 1850, and now desires being laid to rest on the spot on which she has laboured all her life.

The earthquake of 1897 levelled the chapel, leaving only the large marble slab intact on which the following names have been inscribed :—

Sister Mary Gouzaga—24th May, 1868.

,, Mary Teresa Longhlen—14th June, 1876.

,, Mary Alphonso Sheehy—27th August, 1876.

,, Mary Ignatia St. Lawrence—3rd June, 1879.

,, Mary Agnes Daunt—23rd April, 1880.

Sister Mary Regis St. Lawrence—25th July, 1880.

,, Mary Dominica McCarthy—10th July, 1882.

Mother Mary Borgia Culkin—14th April, 1884.

The Ven. Rev. Mother Mary Joseph Hogan, I.B.V.M., Provincial Superior, and the First Superior of the Loreto Convent—27th August, 1884.

In the plot above and to the east of this chapel are laid to rest—

Fr. A. D. R. P. Accurcius, of the Order of St. Francis Capuchin in the year 1885.

Sister S. J. Monica Stone, a widow*, who died on the 27th March, 1892,

and

The Ven. Mother M. Stanislaus Hart on the 24th June, 1894.

The Parsee Cemetery.

The followers of the Zoroastrian creed lay their dead in the Towers of Silence†, which require a number of attendant priests to carry out the last services to loved ones. Accordingly, 'Parsee cemetery' sounds peculiar to ears used to 'Towers of Silence' only. As the community in this station is small, indeed, deaths are few and far between; consequently the upkeep of a sacerdotal establishment is neither necessary nor possible.

There are only three persons buried in this cemetery, which is situated just below the Lebong Road about one and a half miles away from the Market Square, the first being Mrs. Shreen Dewacha, the wife of Lt.-Col. Dewacha, I.M.S., who was buried here in 1907, on a small plot assigned hastily for the purpose by the Forest Department. Through the influence of Mr. G. S. Hart, C.I.E., the then Conservator of Forests, Bengal, (now the I. G. of Forests, India,) the grounds of the cemetery were enlarged to three times its original dimensions.

**This is the first (and probably the last) occasion in which a widow has ever been admitted into the Order.*

†The first Tower of Silence—The Modi Ghandi—was erected on the Poddar Road, Bombay, in 1669. Dr. Fryer, the historian of that presidency, in 1750 also makes mention of only one which was 25 feet in diameter and 12 feet high. This was followed in 1797 by another *Dakhma* erected by Mr. Dadabhai at the foot of Malabar Hill for the use of the Dady family.

Other Cemeteries.

The Chinese cemetery is situated at boundary pillar No. D. M. 14 on the Cart Road about a mile and a half to the south of the railway station.

The Indian Christian Cemetery is alongside the Parsee Cemetery.

The Mahomedan Cemetery is situated a little to the right and above the Hindu Burning Ground.

Burning Grounds.

As soon as life is extinct the Bhutias lash the corpse so as to make it assume a sitting position as their Great Buddha is represented in the contemplative posture. According to the means of the bereaved either 61, 91 or 101 lights burn throughout the night during which conches and whistles are blown continuously to drive away evil spirits.

The first burning ground is situated immediately below St. Paul's School on the Calcutta Road. This ground is used by a sect named Kagaties only who according to custom must raise a *chorten* over the spot on which the remains of their loved one has been cremated. There are two other grounds, the one situated alongside the Monastery at Ghum, the other at Ging Busti. These burning grounds are used promiscuously and so no *chortens* are seen on them.

The Hindu burning ground is located immediately below Butcher Busti, and can be seen from the north of the cottage named North View on the Cart Road near its junction with the Mackenzie Road.

CHAPTER XIII.

The Cantonments.

As early as 1844 detachments of invalid soldiers were quartered in daub and wattle structures in this cantonment.

The cemetery (in which there are graves bearing inscriptions covering a period of 21 years, and 14 nameless ones in which probably rest the bodies of those soldiers who are reported to have committed suicide), and few dilapidated chimneys now mark the spot on which once stood the barracks which were started in 1857, and occupied when partially completed in December, 1860, by H. M's 6th Foot of which Mr. J. White* formed an unit. There were 14 Officers' bungalows and 20 barracks. This cantonment was intended to accommodate a whole regiment of European troops, but further work was stopped in 1863 thereby reducing the accommodation to 500 men only with the usual complement of officers. There were two hospitals, one for 64 men the other for 16 women. Rumour has it that owing to the excessive isolation and bitter cold which obtains at this altitude (8,163′) during the winter there were many cases of suicide among the soldiers and so this cantonment was abandoned in April, 1867, and transferred to Jalapahar.

Senchal.

The Jalapahar† Convalescent Depot (7,701′), which was completed in 1848 and is situated above and a mile and a half to the south of the Station, has accommodation for 550 soldiers each a convalescent from one of the regiments in the plains. In 1863 it contained the following buildings in addition to the usual store-houses and godowns:—The hospital, powder magazine, quarter-guard, the church (R.C.) and quarters for the Commandant, station Staff Officer, the Asst. Surgeon, Sergt.-Major, Quarter-Master Sergeant and about 150 men only.

Jalapahar Cantonment.

---

*See foot note on page 74.

†Jalapahar, which is 3 miles from the Chowrasta, may either be reached by the path off the Calcutta Road to the east of the hill, or by Auckland Road on the west, the return journey being varied by taking the Cart Road from Ghum, which is about 4 miles long.

At the present time it has 37 buildings of which 11 are reserved for married men, the remainder being allotted as follows:—7 form the barracks, 4 are allotted to the institutes and clubs, 2 have been converted into the hospital, 2 serve as the guard-room, while the rest have been reserved for occupation by Officers, Messes, Magazines, and Offices.

Katapahar.

In Katapahar (7,886′) between 150 and 200 men of the Field, and Garrison Artillery are distributed over its 20 buildings, 4 of which are reserved for married men and their families.

The following is a list of the offices in these two cantonments: The G.O.C. 8th (Lucknow) Division, The G.O.C. Presidency Brigade, The Dy. Director Medical Services, The Asst. Director Medical Services, The Station Staff Officer, The Cantonment Magistrate, The Military Works Services, The Supply and Transport, and The Senior Medical Officer.

The following officials are quartered in these cantonments:—The Camp Commandant, The Station Staff Officer, The Officer-in-Charge Station Hospital, The Officer-in-Charge Supply and Transport and the Garrison Engineer.

Lebong.

The cantonment at Lebong* (5,970′), which is 1¾ miles to the north of the town and contains sufficient accommodation for a battalion of British infantry, was constructed after the last Sikkim Expedition (1888). It is easily reached by the Rangneet Road to the east of the Mall, but a trip round Birch Hill, or the Cart Road, which is about 4 miles in length, affords the tourist an opportunity of obtaining splendid views of the valley and scenery of the locality, such as that reproduced on Plate XVI.

Takdah.

The Takdah, or Hum cantonments (5,500′), which is 3 miles from, and to the east of the Peshok Road at 'The 6th-Mile', are occupied by a battalion of Gurkhas. A large recreation ground affords them ample opportunity of indulging in sports of all descriptions. The quarters of the Officers are located along the several paths leading to the cantonments from the main road. Of the two paths, one is

---

*The 'tongue-like' spur.

intended for pedestrians only, as the gradients are heavy ; the other though longer was constructed by the Military authorities in which the gradients are easy permitting of automobiles being run on it.

When it was first proposed to build these cantonments it was pointed out by the planting community of that locality that the site was most unsuitable owing to the mists and clouds which perpetually hang over this spot making it the gloomiest place on these hills, thereby interfering with range practice, which the present war has proved to be of vital necessity. But *cui bono*?

CHAPTER XIV.

The S. P. C. A.

"Remember, He who made thee made the brute
Who gave thee speech and reason, made him mute.
He can't complain, but God's all-seeing eye,
Beholds thy cruelty and hears his cry;
He was designed thy friend and servant, not thy drudge;
And know that his Creator is thy judge".—*Cowper.*

While public health is watched with assiduous care that of the lower animals is not forgotten. In 1906, the S.P.C.A. was formed with branches at the chief sub-divisions of the district in order to obtain and insist upon better treatment being meted out to the beasts of burden, as well as to provide for the treatment of their ailments, such as glanders, rinderpest, and foot-and-mouth disease which annually lay a heavy toll upon horses and kine working in the district, and along the Tista Valley Cart Road,—the numbers in 1903-04 being 43, 800 and 1,400 respectively.

Two of its really good suggestions have for sometime past been under consideration by our City Fathers:—the adoption of a more humane yoke for carts, and the establishment of a weigh-bridge near the Goods-shed here and at Siliguri by which overloading and the resultant cruelty would be abolished for good. As regards the first, it appears that the Act would have to be amended before this desideratum could be enforced on owners of carts. But so far as the second was concerned the Deputy Commissioner who is the head of the administration in the district as also *ex-officio* Chairman of the Municipality, promised at the last annual meeting of this society (1915) to exercise his influence with the commissioners to subscribe substantially towards acquiring such a machine which the society contemplated purchasing, if the difference in funds at its disposal were subscribed by the City Fathers.

It is sometime since both these suggestions were made, and apparently the wheels of the Municipality grind small and slowly like those of the Government.

In regard to the *fixed* drinking troughs, which now number 32 along the main trade routes, the following suggests itself. If these were made after some *lip-up* model contagious diseases, such as glanders, would not have cultural ground to spread as rapidly as it now does. This society may, therefore, give this suggestion its earliest consideration.

CHAPTER XVI.

NATURAL HISTORY.

Flora.

"If thou wouldst learn a lesson that will keep
Thy heart from fainting and thy soul from sleep,
Go to the woods and hills"—*Longfellow.*

A feature of this district is the variety of trees, etc., it contains which is not surprising when the forests, which are reserved and controlled by the Forest Department, cover an area of 445 square miles, or 38 *per cent* of the total area of the district, and are located in two well-marked zones, the tropical up to the 6,000 feet level, and temperate which lies between the 6 and 12,000 feet levels. Besides, owing to a break in the Sewalik range from the Tista Valley to the Raidak, the clouds sweep through this gorge and drench the higher ranges thereby enriching both its fauna and flora.

Forest Conservancy.

Prior to December, 1864, forest conservancy was unknown much to the detriment of the standing crop which was felled without let or hindrance. This defect was remedied in August of the year in question by the appointment of Dr. T. Anderson, M.D., Superintendent of the Royal Botanic Garden, Calcutta, who in 1865 placed the forests in and around Darjeeling, which had been denuded between the 3 and 6,000 feet levels, under the care of Dr. Schlich, Ph.D., the first Conservator of Forests; while the forests of Northern Bengal were for the purposes of control divided into three divisions—British Sikkim, which covered 1,05,000 acres of land, Bhutan Duars, and Assam (prior to the partition of Bengal). In 1880 we find the Conservator busy in making out Working-Plans with a 20-year rotation for the systematic felling of the areas under his control, as well as providing suitably for fire-protection, regeneration, road communications and conservation of the more valuable classes of timber.

Early prospectors, including Lt.-General Lloyd, tell us that the hillsides of this station were clothed from summit to base with virgin forests, which disappeared shortly after the British came into possession of this country. When the hill territory was first acquired, the early settlers, and even the officers of Government, were impressed by the great extent of the forests rather than by the benefits to be obtained from them ; and so for many years their sole aim was to expedite their conversion into timber in order to lay out the clearings as tea estates or cultivated land ; in fact, reckless exploitation ran riot. But with the advent of forest conservancy these defects were remedied by the measures enumerated above. All felling within a radius of 5 miles from the centre of the town was put a stop to, and the crop regenerated by the planting out of the quick-growing cryptomeria, and other valuable species of timber. The altered appearance of the landscape sufficiently attests the valuable work of regeneration and conservation which have been effected by the Forest Department.

Fire-protection was started in 1875-76 by clearing a wide belt along the boundaries, and by fire-tracing the principal roads which divide the blocks into rectangles thereby materially assisting in the plains areas especially in the extraction of all forest produce. This operation included the extermination of all savannah growth, the cause of forest fires in the Terai, Tista Valley and along the Nepal border (See next chapter).

Conservation resulted in the stoppage of valuable timber being felled by ignorant persons for purposes of fuel ; while the Dhobijhora block in the Kurseong division, which was the most backward block in this district, was brought under protection and subsequently worked in accordance with the late Mr. Hatt's working-plan introduced in 1904, which makes due provision for the proper treatment of immature poles and seedlings now growing in it. So far so good !

Similar work was carried out in the three divisions constituting the forest tracts in this district—The Darjeeling, Kalimpong and Kurseong—and also throughout the province by which the number of divisions was increased in 1875 by four—The Jalpaiguri, Palamau and Singhbhum, the Sunderbans, and the Chittagong, thus adding a further area of 2,465 square miles to the reserved forests. Of these, 115 were in Jalpaiguri, 1,118 in Palamau, 885 in the Sunderbans, and 347 in Chittagong.

That our knowledge in Forest Conservancy is limited, and apparently yet in the experimental stage is evinced by the following account which appeared in the 'Statesman' of June, 26th, 1916:—

"To help us solve our timber problem some expert Canadian lumbermen are over here (England) engaged in the scientific method of thinning out certain of our most famous woodlands and hewing and shaping the timber for immediate use.

At present they are marking down and surveying certain tracts of forest land, "blazing" the trees—mainly the soft wood trees of pine and fir—and so arranging their scheme of attack that the beauties of our rural scenes shall not be unnecessarily marred.

In the course of a long walk through the beautiful Forest of Windsor certain parts of which have been ear-marked for slaughter, a *Daily Mail* representative met a little party of pioneers.

They were brown, lithe woodsmen--half-soldier, half-trapper, and wholly romantic. They were diagnosing the cases of certain tall, feathery-topped pines very much as a doctor deals with his patient, and jotting down their calculations in a chartered case-book. Already behind them could be heard the battle-music of saw and axe, broken into now and again by the sudden scream of the steam-driven "circular". Sundry gaps appeared now and again in the dark line of foliage—each gap meant the fall of a giant, and no giant has ever been dismembered so speedily as he. Half-an-hour ago a king of the glade, he was now a neat pile of railway sleepers ready for the track.

"If we had all our tackle here", said one of the pioneers, "I guess we'd be able to turn you out a complete box of matches from the waste product of that tree—and do it while you wait!"

This soft-voiced, keen-eyed young man seemed to know everything there is to know about the trees and the forests of the inhabited globe and how to make the best use of them".

In India, similarly, it would appear to the uninitiated that little or no progress has been made in this direction; and the following questions will, therefore, assert themselves:—

Has any further advance been made in our knowledge of the habits, life-history, as also the respective qualities and bearing strains which are the inherent properties of the several classes of timber trees? In regard to the last, experiments have been conducted in the laboratory at Dehra Doon the head-quarters of the Forest Department, and tabulated; but these data ought to be circulated among the purchasers of forest produce. In regard to the former, it is believed, little or no progress has been made in these most desirable directions.

Although half a century has elapsed since this department came into being the life-history of *Sal,* the chief forest produce of India, like Teak is that of Burma, and the one most in demand, is apparently as little known to-day as when this service was first established as a separate branch of the Administration except the following meagre details, which have been accepted *ex-cathedra* as they found favour in the eyes of the successive heads of the department:—1. that *sal* attains maturity at 120 years, 2. that its seedlings fail to establish themselves in any appreciable numbers under or near the parent tree owing to the deleterious emanations thrown off by its roots, and 3. that there is but one species, the brown in colour, which is ordinarily met with.

In regard to the first, the age limit cannot but be hypothetical inasmuch as the writer has failed to detect the rings by which the age of the plant is determinable in other species although over 9,000 trees have been felled during the course of his business. To account for the second many and varied have been the theories advanced from time to time, the nearest being that formulated by a mere ranger, *viz.*, that the emanations thrown off by the parent tree were nullified *after* the occurrence of superficial or ground fires which consumed the dead leaves and scrub and scorched the earth, and so permitted a few seedlings to establish themselves and thrive. Verily, a half truth, in that such fires provided for a greater amount of light, air and moisture to get at the tender plants. The actual truth, however, was revealed when owing to the stunted and meagre growth of *sal* in a certain tract it was decided to clean-fell the area, and lease it to the husbandman for a period of 5 years; after which it was resumed and planted afresh with *sal* seedlings all of which throve into strong, healthy plants:

i e., an accident revealed the law which applies to ordinary agriculture, *viz.*, that the soil soon exhausts itself of the particular food necessary for the well-being of each class of crop, and so must either have that particular constituent, which has been drawn off the soil, restored, or that a complete rest must follow the harvesting of such a crop in order that the soil may recoup itself—a system to be seen practised on the smallest of holdings where just a third of the land is allowed to lie fallow by the ignorant but practical farmer who has graduated in the school of experience only.

In this, as in various subjects, we might well take a leaf out of the book of the Indian, especially in matters affecting close and accurate observation by which Nature has been forced to divulge many of her secrets,—of which the following are reproduced :—

1. There are two distinct species of *sal*, the white and the brown in colour. The former resembles *Simal* (Bombax malabaricum) so closely that touch has to be resorted to before any definite conclusion can be arrived at; while of the second variety there are 5 distinct classes each determinable by its grain-markings, one of which fetches twice the price of any of the remaining four.

2. That the correct way to season timber is by washing out the contained sap instead of drying it within the interstices of the fibre (as is practised even now at Sukna where a consignment of timber so seasoned awaits despatch to one of the English Universities, as samples of Indian timber), a procedure which has lately been adopted in Europe, chiefly France, and one which might to advantage be adopted by dealers here who ought to be taught the correct method, for example is better than precept.

Power of Observation by Indians.

"It is astonishing how much we go about with our eyes open, and yet see nothing! This is because the organ of vision, like other organs, requires careful training"—*J. S. Blackie.*

The Occident puts all the *action* possible into the day's work, while the Orient allocates a certain part of the day, about noon, for *rest* during which current events are marshalled before the mind's eye, tabulated and pigeon-holed for future use. Both attain the same end—a livelihood, more or less: but the latter scores decidedly in that he at regular intervals recuperates his energies: hence the longevity of the Aryan race.

And so by patient observation has Nature been forced to yield up many of her secrets, even unto the ignorant farmer, as the following will establish:—

1. He will neither cut a bamboo culm during the period that the nights are bright, as otherwise it will be speedily riddled by weevils, nor will he bring it, or any timber, into use until it is seasoned by immersion in the nearest patch of water, be it tank or running stream, in order to *wash out* the sap from the fibre. The converse of this proposition is to be seen daily in process of solution in this district, *viz.*, the sap is by exposure to air *dried within* the interstices of the fibres which at the first contact with moisture expands, to contract again on exposure to the hotter air of summer, thereby absolutely unfitting the wood for delicate work: hence furniture made from timber cut in this district is not worth purchasing.

2. Despite the theory advanced by Col. Sir Ronald Ross, I.M.S., and our leading scientists, he *knows* that it means death to sleep for a period of *three nights* only in a *sal* forest which has burst forth into blossom. Again, Livingstone in his "Travels in South Africa", pp. 375 and 376 writes:—"When the *west* wind blows much fever immediately follows. On the 20th February the westerly wind blew strongly, and on the day following we were brought to a stand, by several of our party being laid up with fever"—that is, *within 24 hours.* Then, wherein the theory of impregnation solely by the anopheles, whose cycle is a *fortnight* ?

3. He well knows also that if a *southerly wind* persists for two days immediately following the transplanting of the paddy (rice) slips, he will harvest but *half* a crop: while

4. The opulent Bengalee when *angling* will, by observing the oscillations of the float, tell with unerring accuracy the particular species of fish nibbling at the bait; and also that no

fish will bite when an *east wind* blows (both of which have been repeatedly proved to the writer, who is himself a devotee of the rod) : facts which do not find a place in amiable Walton's "Complete Angler," nor in any standard work on the subject.

The Occident, therefore, imbued with science to the finger tips asks with supercilious smile—"Wherein the connection between the wind, from any point of the compass, and these alleged physical results? Prove it, man". To which the Orient replies with features as inscrutable as that of the Sphinx—"I know not; I cannot tell; but this I *do* know, the one follows the other as surely as the night the day"—thereby exemplifying the trite saying of Sir Arthur Helps in 'Friends in Council',—"an ounce of practical knowledge is worth a ton of theory".

The only instance that I am aware of in which the Occident knows of the effect of the wind appears in the "Allahabad Farm Manual", and is connected with the curing of meat:—"In clear, bright weather, with a *westerly* wind, the meat can ordinarily be kept at a low temperature—in which condition it absorbs salt freely; but if the weather is cloudy and inclement, and an *easterly* wind prevails, the salt gradually melts away without penetrating the meat, and serious loss results."

While a medical student the writer noticed, especially in the hospitals (now) in the Behar Circle, that wounds took longer to heal than when a westerly wind blew; indeed, gangrene was generally looked for when an *easterly* wind obtained for any lengthy period.

The instances cited above should prove to demonstration that observation and experiment are the only two sources through which man has acquired knowledge, the highest as well as its lowest aim being guidance in *action*, for "the errors in this world come less from illogical reasoning than from inaccurate observation and careless hearing".

Contemplated Appointment of a Commercial Officer.

The contemplated appointment of a Commercial Officer (whether for each division, or one for the whole Circle is one of finance) will entirely, if not in a great measure, remove the following disabilities from which the purchasers of forest produce suffer at present.

It is an open secret that for some years past the chief purchasers of forest produce in this division have laboured under the following grievances which at a certain stage threatened to bring about a deadlock in the negotiations that followed; but which, happily, were temporarily adjusted. But as some of the chief disabilities recur from time to time, the subject will be treated at some length in the hope that, if possible, the grievances from which this class, which contributes no less than a *lakh* of rupees per annum, or one-twelfth of the gross revenue of the department, suffer may be removed finally.

In 1914 a certain timber contractor forwarded samples of Terminalia tomentosa (*pakasaj*) to Calcutta with a view to extend his business. No sooner was a market established than the scheduled price was advanced 100 *per cent.*, which the dealer had to accept in order to complete his contract: to be followed shortly after by the following order—Tomentosa would in future be sold by public auction, like *sal*,—quite overlooking the fact that this tree is not to be found like *sal* in belts but scattered in patches over large areas, and, therefore, not worth purchasing under the same conditions and terms as the latter—result, an absolute deadlock, thereby affecting the revenue of that particular division. But *cui bono*?

Again, the falling off in the demand for soft woods was cursorily disposed of in one of the Administration Reports of this Department with the remark:—'This has not been explained by the divisional officers concerned', although both the public as well as the planting community well knew at the time that the price fixed for these woods would not yield the dealer a fair margin of profit, and so the trade in tea chests has gradually passed into the hands of the United Kingdom and that of Japan which, respectively, supplied the tea industry in 1913-14 with 1,985,238 and 129,259 chests (These figures have been obtained from the Department of Commerce and Industry). Such a condition would ordinarily suggest to a concern run by private enterprise that the price should be sufficiently lowered to ensure speedy sales and so develop the resources of the business on the principle of 'every mickle makes a muckle' rather than allow these trees to over-mature and decay, as well as permit the trade to pass out of India.

Another procedure to which great exception is taken, and one which affects all dealers in timber, is the system of fines inflicted in the guise of compensation realised for damage caused to poles and smaller plants (whose proximity to each other can only be likened to pins in a cushion) which is unavoidable in that in felling trees of the following dimensions it borders on the impossible to drop them in the desired direction—poles from 6 to 12 feet in girth and 50 and more feet in height, with crowns fully 40 to 60 feet in expanse.

Such a system bears all the harder when the tree or pole damaged, and for which compensation has been realised, is not handed over to the dealer but retained as the property of Government. It need hardly be added that if such a transaction occurred between two private individuals or firms it would lead to much litigation. It, therefore, follows that the appointment of a Commercial Officer would be hailed with satisfaction as it would not only place dealers in touch with one imbued with thorough business principles, but also with one who would understand the requirements of each case and so bring about a settlement satisfactory to both parties to the contract—which cannot be said of existing arrangements. Finally, it may safely be predicted that fairer and more considerate treatment would bring about an increase in trade, and also in the revenue of this department.

The following is a list of the Flora of this district:— Accacia, Aconite, Bamboo, Champ, Chestnut, Chilliani, Cinnamomum, Conifers, Criptomeria, Ferns, Grasses, Iron-wood, Katus, Lampati, Laurel, Magnolia, Maple, Michelas, Mosses, Oak, Orchids, Palms (of which there are 7 varieties) Panisaj, Pipli, Rhododendron, Rubber-vine, Sal, Silver-fir, Simul, Sissoo, Teak (in the Bamanpukri block, Kurseong division, in which 477 acres have been planted out with this exotic), Tun and Walnut.

The Criptomeria, which now predominates the district giving the landscape such a stiff appearance, was introduced from China and Japan by Mr. Fortune who brought back with him a quantity of seed which was passed on to Dr. Anderson and planted out in nurseries at Jalapahar. In shape it reminds one of the wooden trees which complete the samples to be found in a child's box of toys. *Sal* has already been referred to in detail. Of the several species of Oak which thrive here, only five yield good timber. The Chestnut produces a small, sweet nut, and good timber, if well seasoned ; otherwise it warps badly. There are two species of Maple and Birch. Sissoo grows in the valley of the Balasan and Rangneet rivers. Tun thrives well but is inferior to the variety which grows in the plains. The Wild Mangoe is found in the tract between Kurseong and Pankabarie. Of Rhododendrons the variety which bears pink flowers flourishes from Darjeeling up to the 12,000 feet level ; the white at lower elevations. Both grow to a gigantic size and flower in April-May. The Walnut is now found chiefly in the Tista Division. Champ, a light yellow, close-grained wood, is well adapted for furniture making. Magnolia trees are large and handsome bearing a profusion of white, sweet-scented flowers in spring. The Lotus tree produces large, white lotus-shaped flowers, and is really the Queen of the Forest, belonging to the Magnolia genus. The Sycamore resembles somewhat the Plane-tree of the N. W. Himalayas and Kashmir. Its leaves are not infrequently used by the natives as a substitute for tea. The Holly is seen in winter in Birch Hill Park to advantage with its load of dark red berries. Then there are the Olive and Simul trees whose timber are utilised in the manufacture of tea chests. Figs, of which there are two species, yield edible fruit in August. The Paper-tree—one variety which bears whitish and pink flowers. yields a good paper pulp and is found up to the 2,000 feet elevation ; the yellow flowering species has its habitat between the two and five thousand feet levels and produces a paper of inferior quality ; while the scarlet flowering variety which grows at elevations from and above Senchal yields the best paper pulp. Firs are to be found only near the Rangneet river ever since the denudation referred to under 'Forest Conservancy' : its place being taken by the stiff and quick growing Criptomeria. Wild Cherries grow abundantly about and below Darjeeling. The Barberry is indigenous to the district, the fruit is fully equal to its English forbear, while the wood is green and is used for dying purposes. The 'stink-wood' is yellow in colour and very durable. Then we come to the tea and coffee plants both of which are exotics. The latter was first planted out in Kurseong where even now a few plants exist. Raspberries cover five varieties, while the Strawberry is full flavoured but slightly tartar than the English variety. Apples, Pears and Plums being exotic will not thrive and ripen. Peaches bear luxuriantly, but the fruit is bitter and fit only for making jam. A wild grape is found on the lower eastern slopes.

Fauna.

The following is a list of the Fauna to be found in this district: Antelope (rare) Bear (black, sloth and sun) Bison, Boar, Cats (civet, jungle and tiger), Deer (barking, hog and spotted), Elephant, Fox, Gaur, Gayal (or Methin, the wild cattle of Bhutan and Burma) Goat (goral and serrow), Hare, Jackal, Leopard (ordinary and black), Lynx (rare), Mongoose, Ounce (Snowleopard), Panther, Porcupine, Rhino (rare), Sambar, Squirrel (flying and ordinary), Tiger, Wild-dog, Wolf; and Snakes, of which there are 47 varieties the chief being the Python,* which often tapes 28 feet, the Adder, Karait, Cobra† [the King Cobra (Hamadryas elaps) which measures 14 feet and more, a pretty green variety with pink hoods, and the black, all of which are exceedingly aggressive attacking at sight] and the Russell's Viper.

---

*These comparatively dwarf into insignificance when compared to the Secury, a water-snake of Brazil, which measures 45 and more in length.

† *Fixed fangs*—Cobras, the Hamadryas elaps, all hooded snakes and all Australian serpents, therefore, strike downwards and forwards, while the poison causes the blood to coagulate. *Folding fangs*—The Daboia and Karait of India, all vipers, rattlesnakes, and the great bulk of African snakes have fangs which curve and lie along the upper jaw when at rest: while they strike horizontally and laterally; the poison causes the blood to become watery.

Feathers.

Of feathered game the following may be shot on the fringe of the forest along the whole of the Terai, and on the scrubby, grass lands bordering the Tista, Mahanady and Balasan rivers which meander through the plains :—duck, florican, geese, green pigeons, the imperial-pigeon, jungle-fowl, partridge, peacock, snipe, teal and woodcock. Green-pigeons and woodcock are also to be had in Darjeeling during the summer and autumn ; the latter, however, is scarce.

CHAPTER XVII.

Fires.

"As from one fatal spark arise
The flames, aspiring to the skies,
And all the crackling wood consumes".—*Pindar.*

Owing to the excessive rainfall in these forest tracts fires are rather the exception than the rule, but when they do occur, and owing to the dense undergrowth and maling bamboo which entirely cover the slopes of the lower hills, large areas are denuded of all vegetation.

In December, 1910, a fire started on the borders between Nepal and Darjeeling (to the west of Ghum) which taxed both the energies of the Forest Department as well as denuded the town very nearly of all its male population who were pressed into service to counter-fire and stamp out the conflagration which raged over an area of 70,000 acres. The town was enshrouded for days with smoke so dense that it reminded one of the mists which hang over the station during the rains, while it rained ashes and even whole, charred bamboo leaves three inches in length which covered Darjeeling in a black mantle. Indeed, so great was this conflagration that the valley at night was lit up with a red glare for a whole week, which caused the more timid to prepare for flight.

Forest Fires

At the end of April, 1914, another fire raged in the Tista Valley which similarly taxed the resources of the Forest officials as also of the Police force in obtaining sufficient labour to stamp out the fire which started in the grass savannahs along the bed of the Rilli river, a tributary of the Tista. The fire gradually crept up the hillside and attacked the *sal* forest growing on either bank of this stream. Here also it rained ashes for days, while the smoke was so dense that the opposite hills could not be seen.

Several fires raged around Kalimpong on March 23rd, 1916. The one at Rangpu was only controlled after a period of 10 days with the help of 1,000 coolies. Another occurred in the Rilli bed, a distance of only 3 miles from Kalimpong, which despite the efforts of the 500 men engaged in counter-firing continued burning for fully a fortnight. In all over 1,000 acres were destroyed. In this instance also the firmament was overcast with smoke while ashes rained over the surrounding country for days.

In 1905 the spacious structure to the west of the Chowrasta which was occupied by Messrs. F. H. Hathaway & Co.; Thos. Paar, the photographer; and Pymm's Stores was burnt down. The present solid stone building was designed and erected on behalf of the first-named firm by E. J. Moriarty, the builder and contractor of Darjeeling, who also designed and built the present Loreto Convent, and two out of the four existing buildings constituting the St. Paul's School, Jalapahar.

Town Fires.

The town of Darjeeling had two narrow escapes from fire in 1914. The first broke out in May in a three-storied structure, used as a stable for hack-ponies, just opposite the Goods-shed. This fire burnt itself out by 2 a.m. after destroying property worth Rs. 30,000/-. It was fortunate, indeed, that the wind which was blowing all the evening from the south veered round to the north just a little before the fire started, otherwise the fate of the cottages in Lloyd's, and Mount Pleasant Road, would have been sealed: indeed, the fir trees adjoining this building and Aloobarie Cottage were charred, and in some cases actually took fire. The glare from this burning wooden structure attracted the notice of the Sergt-Major in charge of the Depot at Jalapahar who with commendable promptitude turned out the whole detachment numbering 200 and marched them down to the scene of the fire where they rendered valuable assistance to the Fire-brigade by dismantling the huts forming a connecting link between the burning building and Aloobarie Cottage.

The powers-that-be are exceedingly fond of indulging in make-shifts, for instead of legislating on the subject and prohibiting the erection of dwellings composed chiefly of wood, we find them busy at putting up alarm bells throughout the town in order to spread quickly the news of the occurrence of a fire, (or landslip). One bell has already been set up at the north-west corner of the Mall immediately above the Dale the peels of which can be distinctly heard at the Saddar Police, the Fire-Brigade Station, and the headquarters of the Conservancy Department in the bazar.

In December of the same year a fire consumed the premises known as Rock House owned by Messrs. Hingun & Sons, tailors. The flames leaped so high that the sentry-box just above this building on the Auckland Road was burnt, also the railings of the short cut from Mackenzie Road to Auckland Road. This fire, the origin of which is still shrouded in mystery, led to no end of litigation.

In 1915 another fire started in one of the cottages in Lloyd's Road due to the careless handling of an oil stove. It was, however, smothered by neighbours attracted by the screams of the person whose carelessness caused it before it could do much damage.

Again, early in 1916, and fortunately during the vacations, the main staircase of the Diocesan Girls' High School was completely destroyed by fire.

PLATE X.

TOWN OF KURSEONG.

PART II.

CHAPTER I.

Kurseong.

Kurseong, the land of the white orchid, is 31 miles from Siliguri and 20 from Darjeeling, and is situated at an altitude of 4,864 feet, and in 26°-53′ north latitude, and 88°-17′ east longitude. The area within municipal limits, which is about two square miles, with a population of fully 5,000 souls, is gradually being extended eastward to Giddapahar. While its climate is more temperate than that of Darjeeling its rainfall is heavier, owing to a break in the Sewalik range to the south of the station through which the clouds sweep in and drench the town; indeed, a fall of 5 inches in as many hours is not an uncommon occurrence. Its average annual fall is 165 inches of which 45 occurs during July against 32 in Darjeeling in the same period.

The European and Anglo-Indian community are deeply indebted to the late Sir Ashley Eden for establishing the Dow Hill Girls' School (5,541′) and the Victoria Boys' School (6,000′); and to the Catholic Order for the Gœthals' Memorial, the St. Helen's Technical School for girls, and the St. Mary's Training College. Just above the Victoria Boys' School is the Forest Officer's bungalow, and the Forest School and hostel attached thereto.

Schools.

An enquiry into the curriculum of studies imparted at the first two schools disclosed the fact that these institutions were working at an anomalous grade which could only be described as Lower Secondary. With a view to raise their status to that of complete secondary schools, as also to bring the practical portion of the curriculum into greater prominence—in the Boys' School, the teaching of manual instruction, and in the Girls', the teaching of domestic economy—His Excellency Lord Carmichael, on June 4th, 1914, accompanied by the Director of Public Instruction and an official of the P. W. Department, inspected the site of both institutions in order that definite plans may be drawn up in this connection.

Hospitals.

The health and care of the pupils attending the schools have also received due attention. Owing to the annual epidemic of mumps, measles, fever and kindred complaints that children have to undergo as a necessary part of existence each of the schools is now provided with a hospital of its own, the last being an up-to-date hospital built at Gœthal's which has accommodation for a nursing staff and 20 beds for patients.

Growth of Town.

Kurseong is growing apace, being now the headquarters of the D. H. Railway. Midway between the town and the St. Helen's Convent, sites were acquired by the railway on which residential quarters for its officers and staff have been constructed. The little station is very quickly putting on an appearance of importance with its spacious Office and Traffic Officers' bungalows.*

Hydro-Electric Scheme.

As the Hydro-Electric Scheme, by which it is hoped the needs of Darjeeling, Kurseong and the tea gardens of the district will be fully met, will doubtless take years before it can be carried out in its entirety, Kurseong has become impatient and has gone in for a scheme of its own. With this end in view it has engaged the services of Mr. C. A. Ansell, than whom few know the district better, for he has been associated with every hydraulic scheme either considered or brought into being during his residence of 45 years in these hills. Mr. Ansell has, therefore, been instructed

---

*Had the project which Major Lindsay, R.E., the Manager of the E. B. Railway, had in mind, when the D. H. Railway was in process of development materialised, the combined E. B. and D. H. Railway Offices would have been located in the buildings at present in occupation by the Dow Hill Girls' School. These quarters were soon found inadequate and then the authorities of the former line hied off to Saidpur from where there was a further exodus to Calcutta.

How business could have been conducted right up in the clouds is beyond ordinary mortals even to conjecture : but this process appears to be a speciality of red-tapism which conducts its affairs from the recesses of the Himalayas. Fortunately some one with a modicum of common sense over-ruled this quizotic scheme at the eleventh hour, and so we have offices within the reach of the public at Sealdah and Kurseong, respectively.

to survey the locality with a view to formulate a practical scheme by which the needs of Kurseong as well as of Mirik (which is 16 miles to the south-west of Kurseong) should it form the summer seat of the Government of Behar and Orissa, will be fully met.

The schools also have not waited but have gone in for installations of their own, Gœthals' leading with a plant which was established at a cost of Rs. 12,000/-, while an installation for the conjoint use of the two Government institutions is at present under consideration by the Director of Public Instruction. It is, therefore, all the more suprising that the railway has not emulated the example set by the schools by having a fully established plant of its own instead of going in for make-shifts, such as disconnecting the generator hitherto attached to the down Mail train and converting it into a power-station, for the exceptional dividends declared each year should enable it to expend the necessary capital on such a plant ; indeed, the travelling public which contributes to these earnings have a right to expect that the several stations on this line should be adequately lit up.

Water-supply.

The water-supply of the town is obtained from a catchment area situated above Dow Hill through 15 springs which yield 60,000 gallons of water daily for the consumption of the population. This supply is distributed over the town through pipes having a length of 4 miles. This area is protected by barbed-wire fencing, and is inspected monthly by a committee appointed by the Chairman of the Municipality.

Buildings.

Its buildings which now number 70 include the Christ (C. E.) and St. Paul's (R. C.) Churches, the Cresswell Institute, the Bloomfield Library, the schools, the Town Hall, the dak bungalow, the railway offices and residential buildings, the kutchery, and Constantia, which was once occupied by the railway (now Government) school, but now the residence of the Sub-divisional Officer.

CHAPTER II.

Kalimpong.

Kalimpong* which is 3,933′ above sea-level has a population of about 1,200 souls. Since April 1st, 1916, it has been raised to the status of a sub-division. Its climate is mild and dry, the annual rainfall being as low as 89½ inches only, so that it should attract a number of fresh settlers under the new development scheme in progress. The main street of the town is laid out in the correct boulevard style with rows of trees. Its buildings include in addition to the Colonial Homes, the MacRobert Clock Tower, which dominates the site of these buildings, and indeed of the surrounding country, a handsome gothic church, in which the gospel is preached in 10 different languages, and the tower erected in 1891 to commemorate the memory of the late Rev. Mr. W. Macfarlane, the pioneer missionary of the Church of Scotland; several Mission houses near the church, a charitable dispensary at which 15,000 patients obtain relief annually, an excellent dak bungalow, and the residence of the Forest Officer; while near the bazar are the Mahomedan mosque, the Hindu temple and Buddhist monastery. This monastery named the Trongsa Gompai is under the jurisdiction of the Kargyupa section of Bhutan, and not like those of Sikkim which are under the guidance of the Pamionchi body. There are differences certainly in the vestments and possibly ceremonies between the different sects, but to the uninitiated the interior of this building is similar to that of the Sikkim institutions. In the centre of the altar are two figures of Buddha—a very large one in the recess, a smaller one in front. On either side are figures of the last Dharmaraja of Bhutan and of the Sangcho Chakor Llama. The interior is decorated with *tanksas* and banners, while the walls are painted in rainbow colours with representations of Buddha and other figures. In the ante-room an aged Tibetan daily earns merit by turning a huge prayer-wheel as an exercise for about eight hours.

---

*Was originally called Dalingkote by the Bhutias.

PLATE XI.

THE MACFARLANE MEMORIAL CHURCH, KALIMPONG.

Beyond the monastery, and about two miles from the town, is the residence of the Bhutan Agent in which the Dalai Llama lived during his exile at Kalimpong. The rooms in which he dwelt are preserved just as he left them with the addition of various gifts he made to the late Minister Raja Ugyen Dorgi as a mark of his appreciation of the hospitality extended to him. In one room there is a library containing a complete copy of the Tibetan scriptures; in another there is the throne on which the Dalai Llama sat, with the vestments he wore and the various ecclesiastical furniture he used; two beautiful prayer-wheels, incense burners, chalices, vessels of holy water, etc. In a corner is the bed on which he slept, while opposite the window is a cabinet containing costly images and emblems; in another corner is an image of the great Llama presented by himself after his return to Lhasa, while the walls are hung with beautiful banners with emblems of the Budda worked upon them in rainbow-coloured silks.

At the north end of the bazar stands the memorial to Queen Victoria, just where the steep path leads down to Melli on the cart road to Sikkim.

A few miles* from the "Homes" is the small chapel of the devoted French catholic Father Desgodines who, after being forced to quit Tibet, where he had worked for a quarter of a century, started afresh a mission in the Daling Sub-division, which has continued for a similar period to minister to the indigenous population.

Daling, of which Kalimpong is the headquarters, covers an area of 524 square miles; of these the Government Estates absorb 401, (213 are under forest and only 10 under tea, which comprises the area of the only four gardens in this Sub-division) the remainder, or 123 have been reserved for cultivation by natives of the sub-division. The population numbers 49,520 souls giving a density of 101 persons to the square mile. The district was taken over after the war with Bhutan in 1866.

---

*At Pedong, which is 12 miles from Kalimpong and 4,760 feet above sea-level. The school started by this mission has over 75 scholars attending the several standards. Traders wend their way through this little station from the Chumbi Valley to the Mart at Kalimpong.

Kalimpong has a fairly large bazar and is the mart of a considerable area, in addition to which it is the centre of the Tibetan trade with Bengal which mainly consists of imports of wool and hides, of which the following is the list for the year 1914 :—

Yak hides	2,000	Sables	3,000	Wolf skins	5,000	Most of these are exported to China
Sheep skins	10,000	Snow leopards	2,000	Fox (brown)	10,000	
Goat skins	3,000			Fox (E)	5,000	
Lamb skins	10,000			Fox (Bc)	5,000	

The chief crop is maize, which covers 38,000 acres or ¾ of the area under cultivation.

Kalimpong is 7 miles from Tista Bridge, 37 from Siliguri, and 29 from Darjeeling. And now that the Tista Valley Railway has been completed as far as Gel jhora (named Kalimpong Road Station) 2 miles from Tista Bridge, it follows that trade will materially develop and in its wake raise the status of Kalimpong from a sub-division to that of a town, apart from the anticipated influx due to its prospective settlers.

Prodigality of Hillmen.

Owing to the prodigality of hillmen in general, and the ryots of the Khas Mahals in Kalimpong in particular, the authorities found it desirable at the settlement of the estates to restrict the ownership of the land to hill tribes as well as make provision by which Lepchas and Bhutias only were allowed to dispose of their land among themselves, in order to prevent the more thrifty and enterprising Nepalese and others from becoming possessors of the land in the district, which to a great extent would have been the case had such provision not been made.

The first and only exception to this rule was made in favour of the Missions, and the Colonial Homes. But as the restriction still applies to Europeans in general, His Excellency Lord Carmichael started the present development scheme by which allotments will shortly be available for Europeans and Anglo-Indians desirous of retiring in Kalimpong, the climate of which owing to its lower elevation is more temperate, while its rainfall is far below that of Darjeeling. With this end in view the Government of India deputed a survey party in 1915, under the direction of Major Hirst, to survey the locations reserved for the purpose, which starts from the 3,000 feet level and will approximately cover an area of 3,000 acres. In connection with this scheme the Sanitary Engineer to the Government of Bengal was also engaged in surveying the trend of the country from Rissisum (6,410′), which is about 15 miles away from the Rinchipong Hill on which these allotments are located with a view to supplying a pure water scheme for intending settlers.

It is understood that new rules are being framed in connection with the Civil Station to be opened shortly on the east side of the hill at 'Durpin Dura'. As both the climate and soil are favourable to the cultivation of all our English fruit, as well as the orange, which is the chief horticultural export, it is expected that these allotments will not go abegging.

Demonstration Farms.

Finally, a word about the efforts of the Home authorities and the Government to improve the status of the ryot.

About the year 1903 two agricultural farms were started, one above the Homes, the other below the bazar, the latter being subsequently converted into a demonstration farm for the benefit of cultivators. As the results obtained were encouraging, the Government stepped in and established an orchard and experimental farm where demonstrations have ever since been given in the use of up-to-date appliances, while samples of seed have been distributed gratis with a view to improving the outturn of the crops. In addition to these benefits a representative of the Agricultural Department has been stumping the country, his last turn to Kurseong being early in 1915, where a stall was established in connection with the Flower Show, which invariably draws crowds of hillmen who love excitement of any description.

Co-operative Credit Society.

With a view to further raise their status a Co-operative Credit Society was established in 1912. The latest figures (1915), giving 2½ *lakhs* balance, shows that the ryot has not been slow to profit from the self-help offered by the scheme. Indeed, the Registrar in his last report says:—"In the matter of co-operative credit societies Kalimpong is now the most advanced Government Estate in the province".

The Colonial Homes.

"The Homes possess 700 acres of land which, like all the land in the surrounding district, is held on lease from Government. The original estate of 100 acres was granted by Government on 24th September, 1900, on a peppercorn rent from a reserved block above Kalimpong bazar. On the 27th June, 1903, Government gave permission to the Board to purchase from the adjoining ryots the tenancy-right of 325 acres additional,—of this land 12 acres were gifted by Rai Ugyen Dorji Bahadur. Subsequently 62 acres of richer agricultural land were similarly acquired below Kalimpong bazar and are used for the Demonstration Farm. In 1911 the Homes were empowered by Government to acquire further land up to a maximum of 200 acres. The rent of the land varies from annas 4 to Re. 1-4-0 per acre. The total cost of the land—Rs. 24,159/- was met by the investment in it of lump-sums paid in advance for the maintenance and education of special pupils. Rs. 20,000/- of the total cost was repaid to the maintenance-in-advance Fund from a legacy left to the Homes by Mr. John White, one of the oldest residents of Darjeeling. The value of land in the district has considerably increased since this estate was acquired."—*The St. Andrew's Colonial Homes Magazine.*

There are now (1919) 35 houses—such as cottages, schools, industrial and farm buildings, the Charteris hospital, the McLeod swimming-bath—and the Ronaldshay Park on this estate, which have sprung into being mainly by the strenuous efforts of Dr. J. A. Graham, D. D., C. I. E., in which instruction is imparted to 600 domiciled European and Anglo-Indian children of both sexes ranging in age from mites of two to youths of eighteen. And what is more, each one feels that these

> "Homes are the resort
> Of love, of joy, of peace and plenty, where,
> Supporting and supported, polish'd friends
> And dear relations mingle into bliss".

Some of the pupils are doing their 'little bit' at the front, others have been drafted into the Navy, while not a few have found an opening in Australia where they are holding their own against all-comers.

These Homes are so well known in India that they need no special description. They are run on the lines associated in England and Scotland with the names of Geo. Müller, of Bernado and of Quarrier. These cottages cost Rs. 25,000 each to build and furnish ; and each is associated with the name of the great man who laid the foundation stone. There is a Woodburn Cottage, an Elliott Cottage, a Hart Cottage, a Laidlaw Cottage, a Canadian Cottage, an Edinburgh Cottage, and many more. There are workshops, a store-room, gymnasium, farm-steading, kitchen, garden, clothing department, etc., and a well-equipped hospital.

The Industrial School is worth more than a visit, for in it lace-making, carpet-weaving, embroidery, carpentry and joinery are taught. Over 50 Nepalese lads are engaged in sawing, planing, carving and cabinet-making. In another shed Nepalese lads and girls are engaged in spinning wool and making beautiful Tibetan carpets, which are dyed by products of the jungle and blended by two women of the latter race who follow indigenous methods. In the Lace school girls and women are to be seen deftly making all kinds of laces—Brussels, Irish, Valencene, and Devonshire, as well as commoner varieties. Inside the rooms the girls are taught embroidery, while the boys go in for general tailoring.

In the Charteris Hospital hill-women are taught nursing in accordance with the scheme started by Lady Carmichæl.

The Training Institution.—Infants are engaged on nature studies ; some may be seen sketching on their slates an orange, or fruit of the season which it is allowed to partake of when the lesson is over ; others are engaged on modelling in clay, while a few are employed in making pictures on the floor with beans. The bigger youths continue these studies by following out from personal observation the cardinal points in the mountains which bound the landscape, and where the sun sets at the different seasons of the year, etc. In connection with this department silk nurseries have been started where experiments in the production and utilisation of cocoons are carried on in the manufacture of silk.

May the Homes, and Dr. Graham see many an anniversary.

Subscriptions for the maintenance of these destitute children would be thankfully received by the Hony. Secretary at Kalimpong.

The Domiciled Community.*

"In this world exists distinctions,.
Of colour and caste;
But death puts us all on a level,
When brief life is past.

We seem to forget a day will come,
When together we'll stand;
The rich, the poor, and the 'country-born',
In Heaven's bright land".—
Alice Foley.

That this community has suffered from (fancied) disabilities ever since the year 1830 when John W. Ricketts on June, 21st and 24th was permitted to advance the cause of his kith and kin in India before a special committee of the House of Commons is admitted by all just thinkers and philanthropists like the late Sir R. Laidlaw, the late Mr. James Luke and Sir William Lee-Warner, G. C. S. I., who at a meeting in London said:—"To-day you are abandoning to ignorance the sons of those who acquired or maintained your Empire in India at the cost of health, nay, of their *blood*—and you leave their descendants to sink to the level The *Kala feringhee*".

The demands of this community for equal rights and privileges with the rulers of the land, which have been based on its birth-right as well as on grounds of equality in thought, aspirations and even education, have from time to time been considered by both the Provincial and Imperial Governments to be as often shelved for consideration at a more convenient season, which I venture to think is the present and accepted time, for it has been brought about by a conjunction of circumstances which primarily inspired the removal of the capital to Delhi, for we have been, and are still passing through a very critical period and are yet far from out of the wood. It were well, therefore, if these legitimate aspirations were acknowledged as an act of grace towards a body ever ready to offer their lives in the defence of the Empire rather than they have these forced or doled out—

*Appeared in 'Capital' of July 9th, 1915.

as others, who have hung back and merely contributed donations, expect at the close of the war when *their* demands for an *equal* share in the administration of the country will by their very moderation 'stagger humanity.'

It will, therefore, be my pleasing duty to prove that these disabilities are more imaginary than real ; that its demands are based on no fanciful data ; and that when a fair field and no favour is the order of the day, the members of the domiciled community, be they blonde or brunette, are fully the equals of their more favoured brothers from across the seas. A cursory review of the several avenues of employment *in the Bengal Presidency alone* will establish the above assertions.

The Mercantile—Be it said to the credit of the late Mr. James Clarke, the jute merchant, that he openly defended his policy of employing none but members of this community solely on the ground that they were a trustworthy, sober and an industrious lot to be fully depended upon although located miles away in the interior of the country purchasing raw material to the tune of *lakhs*. Then, again, a survey of the Calcutta Port Commissioners shews that from the Vice-Chairman (late) downwards many of its departments were officered by the country-born, whose services have even been acknowledged to the extent of Knighthood.

Our next survey covers the following fields:—Accounts, Army, Banking, Civil Service, Engineering, Journalism, Law, Literature, Medicine, Railways, Ship-building, etc.

Accounts.—Fink, Hollingbery, Rivers-Howe, and Cooke will be remembered ; Kiernander and Edwin Kellner rose to be Accountants-General, Bengal ; while Sir George Kellner who received a knighthood was, on retirement, appointed a member of the Cyprus Commission.

The Army has evolved such men as General Jones, who commanded the Bombay Army during the campaigns of 1803-05 ; and Col. Stevenson, who was Quarter-Master-General of the Army for many years. To these should be added the names of Col. Nairn ; Major Deare ; Capts. Routledge, John Doveton (who endowed the Colleges of that name in both Madras and Calcutta), Hyder Young, Hearsey, and Col. James Skinner, who rose from trooper to command the same regiment, subsequently known as 'Skinner's Horse', which did such yeoman service during the mutiny—"All of them distinguished officers, notable for bravery and gallantry in action, capable soldiers and leaders of men in days when war was learned in the field and camp, and not as now-a-days in cramming establishments and in the bureau of a Military Department".*

It is a pleasing reflection that when the Government of India now assemble for Divine worship at Delhi and bend the knee before Almighty God it is in the very church built at his own expense by the once neglected James Skinner in the fulfilment of a vow made as he lay wounded on the field of battle.

In the Great War, Lt. Warner† of the Flying Corps, Elloy of the Medical College, Calcutta, Levery of the St. Joseph's College, Bangalore, and Jolly of the St. Joseph's College, Darjeeling, were among the first to receive that much covetted trophy—The Victoria Cross. This cross was also awarded to Lt. W. L. Robinson of the Worcesters for the destruction of a Zeppelin on the 3rd September, 1916: he was born in Pollibetta, India. Gerald Tartleton of the St. Joseph's College, Darjeeling, received the D. S. O.; while Allan A. Dennis-Jones of 'Sherwood', Naini Tal, (subsequently trained at the Civil Engineering College, Seebpore, Calcutta) received the D. C. M. for gallantry in action.

The Civil Service have given us Platel and Stark, and also

---

*Life of H. L. V. D'Rozio by Thos. Edwards (an European) quondam Sub-Editor, '*The Englishman*'.

"Major Vickers", so says Herbert Compton (See also foot-note on page 5), "was an exceedingly gallant half-caste soldier in Holkar's army. In 1804 he was asked by Holkar to serve in the war against the English, and in consequence of his refusal suffered martyrdom (being beheaded by his treacherous master) rather than take up arms against his father's people". It is one thing to go into battle with a possibility of a return, but quite another to face *certain* death with stoicism, as he did. Truly, a hero worthy of many V. Cs.!

†The Warner Memorial monument was unveiled by Lord Derby, Under-Secretary of State for War, on the 11th July, 1916, at Brompton Cemetery. On the medallion is the following inscription:—"Courage, Initiative, Intrepidity", and below a representation in bas-relief of the gallant act by which he won the Victoria Cross—the destruction of a Zeppelin by means of a bomb dropped from an æroplane of which Warner was the sole occupant. He was 24 years old only; and born in India.

the late A. D. B. Gomes, the first Commissioner of the Sundarbans, whose survey map of that region is the only one still published under authority.

In Engineering, Hefferan has by sheer ability forced his way into a partnership in one of the leading engineering firms in Calcutta. Similarly, Newing from an accountantship rose to be senior partner of a leading Coach-building establishment in India.

Journalism has so many lights that any special mention would be invidious.

The Law is fully represented by such brilliant lights as Ledlie, Bar-at-Law, Robinson, scholar and linguist, who held the appointment of Translator to the High Court, Calcutta ; Fink, the late Registrar, Original side, H. C. ; the late Sir Chas. Paul, Advocate General, Bengal ; and Mr. Robert Belchambers, whose duties when he retired at the ripe age of 60 years were divided between *two* young European lawyers, and who even up to the age of 70 was frequently referred to on matters affecting the Hindu Law of Partition.

Literature has produced Professor Omann, who received an honorary degree from the University of Oxford ; and D'Rozio, who while still a youth had the mantle of Byron thrown over his shoulders ; and be it added that as poet, teacher, philosopher and scientist he shone in a circle of which the Great David Hare was the centre.

In Medicine such brilliant lights as Drs. Solomon and McConnell have not been extinguished in the respective branches in which they specialised.

Railways—Robert Tait rose to be Chief Store-keeper, E. B. Railway, while F. D. Kiernander was Traffic Superintendent on the same line.

Police—The first to reach the highest rungs of the ladder in this department was E. C. Ryland, C.I.E., Deputy Inspector-General of Police, Behar and Orissa.

Ship-building has had one exponent only—Kidd—whose dockyard is still 'The Kidderpore Docks', Calcutta ; while his gift of exotic plants and herbarium as well as an extensive tract of land at Seebpore formed the nucleus of the Royal Botanic Garden, Calcutta.

Survey of India—In a few rapid strides, A. N. James attained the position of Deputy Surveyor General of India, which he successfully held for over a decade.

These were the Men who had their opportunities proving thereby that when there is a fair field and no favour they are fully the equals in thought, aspiration and even education of their more favoured brothers who hail from the homeland.

Finally, all that is left to me is to indicate wherein the interests of the European and the Country-born, be he blonde or brunette, are interminably interwoven. When we review the number of troops in India, we find there is but a paltry 70,000 British regulars to hold and to have the land of our adoption, while against this number there are 250,000 Indian troops, with about double that number in the Feudatory States officered and drilled after the latest European methods. On the other hand, the Militia or Volunteer Force, which has over 90 per cent. of its members recruited from the domiciled community consisting of men and lads, number fully 50,000, and if to this be added those who on principle refuse to enroll themselves, the combined force that Britain could put into the field here would total 125,000, a number which would doubtless emulate the handful of 1857 in deeds of daring. It, therefore, behoves the Government to remember that 'when the face of the waters was troubled' domiciled men straight from their desks sprang into saddles and dashed with Skinner's *regulars* into the thick of battle; that they manned the ramparts and *died* standing shoulder to shoulder with those enured to fight; that their offsprings* defended the citadel of the Martiniere, Lucknow, while, Kavagna, whose intimate knowledge of the slang of the vernacular helped him pierce the cordon, which was being gradually tightened round the neck of the works at Lucknow, guided Outram to the relief of that city, an achievement which

---

**The North Point Annual* (Darjeeling) of 1915:—"In addition to the list given last year of Old Boys at the front or on their way to the front, the following names have reached us"—of which the list of Officers only is appended.

Major—Richard Bradley, I.M.S.
Capts.—Bertram O'Reilly, I.M.S., and Martin Byrne, 10th Middlesex.
Lieuts—*Joyce, V.C.*, 9th Sappers; and Sydney Boyd.

earned him that much covetted trophy—The Victoria Cross—which only another civilian*, the defender of Arrah, has had pinned to his breast.

> "These are the Souls
> To whom high valour gave
> Glory undying."

These and kindred acts prove that the aspirations of this community are based on solid facts, and that in coolness and daring in action the Country-born is not a whit behind his brother from the homeland. Then where are the fancied disabilities, which are but chimerical? I have been at pains to marshall the above facts for the especial benefit of the Military authorities who chiefly stand in the way of this body†. It is to be hoped that the Government will no longer overlook its inalienable rights but extend to it the hand of true fellowship

---

2nd Lieuts.—Gerald Tartleton, D.S.O., Douglas Augier, Alfred McCarthy, Terrence McCarthy, Maurice O'Gorman, John Leys, Richard Clifford, Joseph Stoddard, James J. Salt, Neville B. Tapsell, David. M. Stewart, Leonard Peters, Leo Colley, Maurice H. Colley, Arthur Rice, Harold Lindsay, Edward Villa, and Eric Colin Dozey.

The Victoria Boy's School has also furnished its quota for over 50 are serving with the colours, while the following have obtained commissions :—

Lieuts—D. Frizoni, N. Moorat, B. Petri.

2nd. Lieuts—P. Bapty, A. Viex and V. Watson.

The Colonial Homes, Kalimpong—"No less than 40 per cent. of those who have passed through this Institution are fighting in France; and of these fully 10 per cent. have obtained military medals".

*1. Mr. Vicars Boyle, an engineer connected with the E. I. Railway.

2. Since 1857 the Victoria Cross has been awarded to two Army Chaplains—the Rev. Mr. James Williams Adams for conspicuous bravery in front of Bhagwana in Kabul, and the Rev. Mr. Edward Noel Mellish; and to Messrs. W. R. F. Addison, and T. B. Hardy in the present war.

Military crosses have been awarded to Asst. Surgeons Braganza, Boilard, Messinier and Main—the last named having answered 'The Last Post' when the *Majola* was mined. Elloy has in addition been decorated with the Russian Cross of St. George.

†Early in 1916 sanction was accorded to the formation of Anglo-Indian platoons; but too late, for those with grit, such as Warner, and the above list, had already at their own expense proceeded to the front, and obtained the covetted distinction. "Over 8,000 have already joined the army in the homeland", for the conditions at first imposed, *viz.*, that they could be enlisted in the Indian Army here were repugnant to their feelings. In regard to the offer at the 11th hour, it was felt that the recognition of this community had at last been governed by policy, and a dearth of fighting material. Notwithstanding these slights and hindrances this community has not been found lacking when the Call

and friendship, for a day may dawn, and probably will in the near future when, as sung by a local bard :—

"Ye sons of a handmaid, like Hagar's of old,
 Will yet fill this country in conjunction to hold!
While Britain who sprang you to cast you aside,
 Will one day respect you tho' now she deride"—*E. B. Robertson.*

The Late Rajah Ugyen Dorgi.

Rajah Ugyen Dorgi, a well-known and familiar figure in the social and political circles of Kalimpong, passed away on the morning of June 22nd, 1916, after a brief but serious illness. The Rajah, who felt that the end was drawing near and in order to set his affairs in order, had his only son, a pupil of St. Paul's School, and a contemporary of the present Maharaja of Sikkim, summoned to his bedside to receive his last instructions. The body after being embalmed was conveyed on the 24th idem to Tashisudan, the capital of Bhutan, for the deceased who had held the appointment of British Agent at the Court of Bhutan was also the second cousin and Chief Minister of the present Ruler. His donations to public institutions were many and lavish, while his private benefactions were numberless and done with a stealth which brings back the injunction—let not thy right hand know what thy left hand doeth. That he will be much missed both by the officials as well as the public in general in Kalimpong goes without saying, and especially so by the indigent members of his own community.

A brief review of his career would be interesting. He accompanied his father, the Kazi of Jungtsa, who was deputed by the Bhutan Government to meet the Trades Mission des-

---

to Arms was sounded, for in place of the 240 required from Bengal, Bihar and Orissa, Bengal alone contributed 395 men up to 31st May, of which Jamalpore, E. I. R., gave 48 out of the 78 apprentices in its workshops, while the Civil Engineering College, Seebpore, Calcutta, generously responded with 36 out of the 43 pupils on its rolls. Who, then, dare say that this community either in courage, aspirations or loyalty is one whit behind the home-born? This note is closed in the full assurance that these men and youths will emulate those who have already obtained distinction, and earn, it is to hoped, by their prowess full recognition of the merits and aspirations of those they represent, when Peace is established.

patched in 1864 by the British Government under the direction of Sir Ashley Eden. Of this mission the late Capt. Power, quondam Vice-Chairman of our Municipality and an assistant in the Office of the Private Secretary to the Viceroy, formed an unit. In the fiasco which terminated that memorable meeting in the Durbar Hall of that State, the Kazi prevailed upon the then Rajah to spare the lives of the members of the mission as he had decided having them killed during the retreat to British territory. The members, however, were subjected to the meanest of indignities; Sir Ashley Eden was spat upon by the Chief Minister, and the remaining members of the mission imprisoned in the Daling Fort from which they escaped at dead of night through the instrumentality of Raja Chebu Llama*, —"Faithful only he among the faithless found"—who in 1860 informed the British of the impending advance of the Sikkimese into Darjeeling. War was accordingly declared, and the Bengal and Assam Duars together with the Daling Sub-division, of which Kalimpong is now the head-quarters, annexed.

The lad, Ugyen Dorgi, in the capacity of interpreter rendered valuable assistance to Mr. Paul, I.C.S., Deputy Commissioner, Darjeeling, who had been deputed to organise the newly acquired district. A few years later we find Dorgi again rendering invaluable assistance in transport work during the Tibet Expedition for which the title of 'Rai Bahadur' was conferred upon him. His chief achievement, however, was the consolidation of his own country under the highland chief, Tongso Penlop, which earned him the title of 'Rajah'. Tall in stature and stately in carriage, he was the observed of all observers at public functions. He died in his 61st year, which wore lightly on so amiable a disposition as his, for these years left little or no trace on his frank and open countenance.

---

*For these services the Government made a grant of 74,016 acres, or 49 square miles of land to Chebu Llama, since known as the Rilling Estate which lies to the west of, and between the town of Darjeeling and Phalut in the Singalila range. Chebu Llama, however, did not long enjoy the advantages accruing from this grant for he died in 1866 leaving a brother and an only son whose descendants have since sequestered the estate by litigation.

CHAPTER III.

Siliguri.

The tourist must halt at Siliguri (397′) if he does the Tista Valley trip, and accordingly the following data will be found useful. Siliguri, or the stony plain, according to tradition derived its name from the stones which once lay in myriads on the bed of the Mahanady river which flows to the north of the town, whilst its existence has hitherto been coupled with memories of the last week-end trip to Darjeeling, as well as with the first glimpse of the snowy range from the south end of the platform.

It is roughly in the centre of the Bengal Terai, which was acquired from Sikkim in 1850, and is bounded on the north by the mountain spurs, on the south by Purneah, the east by Jalpaiguri and the west by Nepal. This forest track extends from north to south a distance of 18 miles, and from east to west 16 miles. Of this area 58 square miles are under forest while 230 miles are under tea and ordinary cultivation.

In 1850 the upper tracts were chiefly inhabited by Meches, and the lower or plains portion by Rajbunsis, Santals (who number about 14,000 souls) and Mahomedans, who speak the dialect of the Comilla and Dacca districts.

The town of Siliguri came into being in the year 1878 when the metre-gauge line was completed from Sara Ghat to this station, and became the administrative headquarters of the sub-division when the kutchery was transferred to it from Hansquar near Phansidewan.

As the stones are now embedded in the break-waters of the Hardinge Bridge, Siliguri, which is now the focus of the three narrow-gauge lines—the D. H. Railway, the Kissengunge, and Tista Valley Extensions—will no longer be coupled with the last week-end trip to the hills, but will assume a place worthy of being the centre of the trade with Darjeeling, Nepal and Tibet, if not, also of the Northern Duars; as well as of the timber trade of which she has been the mistress for at least two decades. With this end in view the astute and monied classes have not been slow to grasp the possibilities created by the new feeder lines and have already started building structures on every available piece of land in the station as well as at Matigora, 3 miles away from Siliguri, and the real terminus of the Kissengunge line, where stores have sprung up like mushrooms against the material increase in the imports of jute, which according to rough computation is expected at least to treble the past output.

If the following figures are any criterion of the possible expansion of Siliguri then it may be safely predicted that within the next decade she will have attained the position anticipated by her capitalists. Shortly after the D. H. Railway was opened (1881) the traffic consisted of :—

Year.	Passengers.	Goods.
1882	8,000	380 tons.
1905	29,000	31,570 do.
1916-17	2,39,696*	59,740 do.

In 1915 the earnings for the week ending the 21st August were Rs. 26,722/- (or about 12,82,656/- *per annum*) as against Rs. 17,291/- for the corresponding period of the year prior ; while the gross earnings for the financial year ending the 31st March, 1917, amounted to Rs. 13,01,592/-, thereby indicating the manner in which railways develop the resources of the country.

The traffic over the two Extensions were :—

	Year.	Passengers.	Goods.
Kissengunge	1916	76,478†	27,920 tons.
Tista Valley	1916	48,071	15,589 do.

---

*Of these were		
1st Class		7,226
2nd do.		29,103
3rd do.		203,367

*Principal commodities :—

Edible grains, flour, rice, &c.	17,804 tons.
Tea	5,354 do.
Potatoes	3,824 do.
Salt	1,634 do.
Sugar	894 do.
Metals (owing to war, as low as)	915 do.

†Nearly all were 3rd class passengers.

The gross earnings of the former line were Rs. 2,11,449/-, while that of the latter Rs. 1,21,480/- only.

Trade accordingly must in its wake increase both the population as well as develop the town, which hitherto has been left to itself and the devices of the members of its rural municipality. Its future care, however, appears to devolve on the Darjeeling Improvement Fund which, it is understood, has earmarked a sum of Rs. 40,000/- for the construction of an up-to-date hospital ; and has also taken in hand the sanitation of the town, which sadly needs drainage, etc.

The town contains a sub-jail, the kutchery, post office, the Sub-divisional Officer's bungalow, a dispensary, at which over 4,000 patients are treated annually, and an excellent dak bungalow containing four large rooms.

CHAPTER IV.

Industries.

TEA.

"Here, thou great Anna!
  Whom three realms obey,
Dost sometimes council take,
  And sometimes tea"—*Rape of the Lock.*

Early History.

The earliest mention that we have of this beverage (*Thea*) is in a letter from Tom Coryat (see Pic-nics and Tours to follow) to a friend dated, Surat, 1617, which formed part of the dowry of Catherine of Braganza on her marriage in 1662 to Charles II, King of England, and thus proved to be the beginning of our power in India.

The earliest evidence of tea having reached England is a notice which appeared in 1658 in the *Mercurius Politicus;* while Tom Pepys in his journal, dated September 25th, 1661, makes mention that he sent for a cup of tea—"a Chinese drink of which I have never drunk before". And, mark you, the tea in those days was sold at the 'coffee-houses' fully boiled (as is done even now by the indigenous population of Darjeeling), and not in the dry state. Teapots, however, had found their way into England a few years previous to this. In the Hardwicke accounts there is an item, dated 1583, by the well-known Bess of Hardwicke, Countess of Shrewsbury, which runs:—"A note of my plate", under which is included the surprising article—'a tee pott'.

Although the East India Company was founded in 1590, it was 1615, according to Birdwood's "Report on the Old Records of the India Office," before any term representing tea appeared on the books of the company. On June 27, 1615, R. Wickham, who was the company's agent at Tirando, Japan, wrote a letter to Mr. Eaton at Macao, China, in which he asked for "a pot of the best sort of chow."

The taste for tea (of Chinese manufacture) increased throughout England until the year 1720 when the East India Company imported one million pounds, which was retailed at 30*s*. the lb. Five years later the imports rose to five million pounds. In 1773, the company having over seventeen million pounds in its warehouses, obtained permission to export the surplus to America, which brought about the famous 'Boston Tea Party', when 342 chests were thrown into the harbour by the irritated Americans, and thus proved one of the chief causes of the 'American Rebellion' !

Knotty Problems.

The problems which for the past five years (1917) have been engaging public attention and that of the planting community in particular are the fillip expected in the tea industry owing to the drink problem having been finally solved, the concessions recently obtained by a syndicate for the cultivation of tea in Bhutan, and the extension of the broad-gauge from Santahar to Siliguri.

The last has been commented upon in Part IV, and it has been proved to demonstration that the expectations of the several Tea Associations so far as this extension goes must be confined within the bounds of possibility, much as it may be desired, for it would not be equitable to demand more from a State Railway than one run by private enterprise which would necessarily extend its connections, irrespective of public opinion, in conformity with its reserve funds. It, therefore, devolves on us to calmly and critically analyse the factors which play so important a part both in the output of the manufactured article (tea) as also its market value.

Tea Culture.

Such a consideration necessarily leads to an enquiry into the origin of the culture of the tea plant in India, as also a retrospect of the industry from the time it was established on a commercial basis to the present day ; and with this end in view the history of the cultivation will be lightly touched upon to show the extraordinary expansion and consequent setback it received.

The Chinese originally held the monopoly of the trade in tea with Europe, while its retail in the United Kingdom formed a part, indeed, the most valuable part of the transactions of the East India Company until the renewal of the Charter in the early part of the 19th century (1813) when the monopoly in this commodity passed over to the Crown. The astute directors of this Company, therefore, cast about for a rival source of supply which would be entirely under its control, especially as there were indications that China would follow the lead of Japan and break off all trading connections with the West.

It was already a well known fact that the tea plant throve under very widely varying conditions of climate and soil, for it had been naturalised in Brazil, in St. Helena, in Java, in Sumatra, in Penang, and other places. Accordingly, the Government of Lord William Bentinck was prevailed upon to appoint in January, 1834, a committee, "to consider the question of importing seeds and plants from China ; to decide upon the most favourable localities for growing them ; and to make immediate arrangements for giving effect thereto". In March following the committee issued a circular inviting opinions which were likely to be of value, as well as arranged that one of their number—Mr. G. J. Gordon—should proceed at once to China to obtain the necessary plants and operatives to start the venture. The replies received, which in the main were based on the analogy of climate and soil, convinced the members of the committee that the most suitable localities were :—1. On the lower hills and valleys of the Himalayan range, 2. On our eastern frontier, and 3. On the Nilgiris, etc. By the Himalayan range it is quite evident that only Mussoorie and Dehra Dün were implied, for Darjeeling did not come into our possession before 1835, while the eastern Frontier could not have included Assam, for even the Government were ignorant of the fact (or rather ignored it) that the tea plant was indigenous to that province. The first and third predictions at least have been verified for we find that the tea plant now carpets the hillsides of the Himalayas, its valleys, and outlying plains from sea-level to the 6,000 feet elevation.

And now, mark you! all these solemn conclaves, deliberations and voluminous minutes by the Tea Committee in 1834 when since 1815, the latest, it was well known to Capt. Jenkins, the then Commissioner of Lower Assam, and other residents in that province, that not only was the tea plant found indigenous in the following localities throughout Assam, but its leaves were used in brewing tea manufactured after the Burmese method:—In the Singpoh hill tracts in Upper Assam, and other places like Gabro Parbut at the foot of the Naga Hills, where they formed a part of the ordinary flora of the country; scattered throughout the land to the south of the Brahmaputra river, and from Sadiya and Beesa on the one hand to the Chinese province of Younan (a whole month's march) on the other; indigenous in the Muttock country between the Debru and Dehing rivers of Assam, and often met with in such regular patches as to indicate that they had been planted out.

The Government deliberately ignored the above data as long as it was possible to simulate a belief in the non-indigenous tea plant although reference was made to these conditions as early as 1815 by Col. Latter; three years later by a Mr. Gardner, and again in 1824 by Major Bruce (who commanded a division of gunboats in U. Assam during the first Burmese war) who two years later and on his own initiative started a nursery of tea in the grounds attached to his bungalow at Sadiya. Again, repeatedly did Mr. David Scott, the Commissioner of Assam, and Major Bruce send plants down to Calcutta for identification; but it was not till November 8th, 1834, when Lt. Charlton, who assisted Bruce, forwarded samples of locally manufactured tea, and also fruits, flowers and seeds of the plant that it was at last identified as belonging to the same genus but of a different species to that cultivated in China, which grows to a height of 15 feet, while the indigenous variety often attained the height of 30, and more, feet.

Thus convinced the Mission to China was recalled, and a Scientific Mission (consisting of Dr. Wallich, Supdt. Royal

Botanic Gardens, Calcutta ; Mr. William Griffiths, one of the most distinguished botanists that ever worked in India ; and Mr. McCleland, a geologist) despatched on August 29th, 1835, to Sadiya to investigate and report upon whether the tea plant was actually indigenous to Assam or not ; were existing conditions such as to make it probable that a tea industry would succeed; and if it was considered necessary at all to import Chinese tea seeds.

The result of this deputation committed the Government to a definite policy of furthering the tea culture in Assam, and Major Bruce was accordingly appointed Superintendent of this industry.

The first tolerable samples of tea which were manufactured by primitive methods (*i.e.*, dried over charcoal fires and according to the process used for black tea) and forwarded to Calcutta early in 1836, and amongst others were pronounced by Lord Auckland, who had also tasted the brew, to be of good quality. In the following year both the quality and quantity increased to such an extent that it was pronounced to be a mercantile commodity ; while great were the rejoicings of those who originally induced the Government to take this subject up seriously when on May 6th, 1838, Capt. Jenkins announced that *8 chests* containing 350 lbs. of tea had been despatched to England for sale !

By 1839 this industry was well established in that province, the Assam Tea Co. being the first (1837), and is still the largest concern in India. In 1840 it produced 10,000 lbs. of tea which by 1858 rose to 7,70,000 lbs.

First Auction Sale.

On January 10th, 1839, the above chests were sold by the East India Company at the Commercial sale rooms, Mincing Lane, in the following lots which realised phenomenal prices :—

Lot.	Quality		Price per lb.	Purchaser.
1.	Souchong	...	21s.	Capt. Pidding.
2.	,,	...	20s.	,,
3.	,,	...	16s.	,,

1.	Pekoe	...	24*s*.	Capt. Pidding.
2.	,,	...	25*s*.	,,
3.	,,	...	27*s*. 6*d*.	,,
4.	,,	...	28*s*. 6*d*.	,,
5.	,,	...	34*s*.	,,

Note.—These teas were pronounced by the Tea brokers to be "not of good quality, but a curiosity".

The year following, that is, on March 17th, 1840, 85 chests out of 95 despatched to England were sold at the same Mart and realised on the average 9*s*. 6*d*. per lb., except a very coarse lot termed *toychong*, which fetched 4*s*. 6*d*. the lb.

Apparently the report of the brokers, quoted above, was instrumental in Dr. Chapman obtaining sanction to give the Chinese variety* a chance, and accordingly the first lot of seeds and plants were imported into Darjeeling in 1841, along with a number of Chinamen to teach the pioneers in this industry how to lay out gardens and manufacture tea. But if the records left by Fooks (mentioned later on) are to be credited, and if the condition of the gardens in Hope Town, as he found them, are any criterion of the method adopted by these instructors, it is quite evident that jealousy lest the monopoly pass out of the hands of China formed no small part of the directions given them before they left their native land. Patience and perseverance, however, soon overcame all difficulties for we find that by 1856 the industry was well established in Darjeeling, while within the next six years it was gradually extended into the Terai.

Hill Gardens.

The Makaibarie and Aloobarie gardens were planted out in 1857 to be followed two years later by the Takvar Tea Company, Mundakoti, and the Darjeeling Tea Company. In 1860 the Neej Kaman (since re-named the Cedars), and the Rangmuk Tea Estate in Sonada were laid out by Mrs. H. C. Taylor and Dr.

---

*The curse of the Indian Tea Industry, according to Dr. Harold H. Mann, late Scientific Officer to the Indian Tea Association (1900-1907) to whom I am indebted for details in connection with the culture of this plant in Assam.

Roberts of Raneejunge, respectively. In 1862 the Dooteria, Nahore, and Margaret's Hope gardens were planted, while the year following the Lebong Tea Company, and the Himalayan Tea Company came into being. In the slump that followed the collapse of the Hope Town scheme the Dooteria garden, which is alleged to have cost over 8 lakhs in its outlay, was purchased at an auction held at Calcutta by Dr. Brougham of the General Hospital for a sum of Rs. 20,000 only, and Asst. Surgeon Malins (his descendants are still connected with tea) appointed to manage it.

In 1866, *i.e.*, only ten years after the establishment of the industry on a commercial basis, there were 39 gardens each having an average acreage of 256½ acres and an aggregate yield of 133,000 lbs. of tea. In 1870 the number of gardens rose to 56 covering an area of 11,000 acres on which 8,000 operatives were employed in the yield of 1,700,000 lbs. of tea. Between the years 1866 and 1874 the number of gardens was trebled, the area increased by 80 per cent. while the outturn was multiplied ten times.

In Kurseong in 1871 Springfield, and Castleton were laid out, the latter being supervised by Dr. Chas. Graham who threw up his practice in Calcutta for tea culture. Eden Vale in Toong was established by Mr. Grazebrooke, while the Maharanee Tea Estate was laid out in 1874 by Major Keane, as well as Avondale in Sonada (which has since been acquired by the Kingsleys). These were left to his sons J. P., and R. Keane. The widow of the former subsequently married J. Kenay and now directs the affairs of that garden as well as Gyrebong (which was started by Mr. MacArthur) and Eden Vale.

Terai Gardens.

The first two gardens started by H. Hancock, at Upper Puntunghar, date back to 1861 ; then the Champta was planted shortly after (1862) the Singel Tea Estate had been laid out by Mr. James White in Kurseong ; in 1866 Messrs. Patterson, Mandelli and Martin owned a garden at Manja near Panighatta ; then Fallowdhi came into being—a combination of the first letters of the names of the owners, *viz.*, Flemsted, Lloyd and Hill; Atulpore in 1871 was owned by Lloyd, the banker of Darjeeling; by 1872 there were 14 gardens in all, one of which Chota Cheng was flourishing under Smallwood (subsequently Smallwood and Lloyd the Tea Brokers of Calcutta); while Sal Kotee (now a part of Wingfield Tea Estate) was laid out in 1873 by Mrs. F. C. Fooks (a grand old lady of over 82 years who is now living at Bloomfontein in Toong), to be followed the year after by 26 gardens.

Owing to increased facilities in transit, the years 1878-88 were the palmiest days for the Terai. The E. B. Railway had been extended to Siliguri in the cold weather of 1878, the D. H. Railway had reached its terminus in 1881, and the Garidura and Nuxalbarie P. W. D. roads were opened for traffic in 1883.

The management of the present day would scarcely credit that the staff in those easy, harum-scarum times consisted of at least 3 Europeans on each garden, which in a few instances rose to 11 ! ; while the bungalows were built within hail of each other at Awwal, where no trace of a building is now left.

Rapid Expansions.

Owing to these rapid expansions the industry experienced a severe setback in 1897, the chief contributory cause being over-production brought about by expansions in India, Ceylon, Japan, Java and Sumatra; while a rise in the tea duty imposed by Great Britain added not a little to the depression, as the cost of production, owing to all operations, which were then conducted by manual labour, was as high as 11*d*. the lb. Managers of tea estates, therefore, turned their attention to the patent devices of the late Mr. William Jackson which reduced the cost to 3*d*. the lb. The impetus thus given the industry enabled it in a short time to practically spread over the whole district between the 3 and 6 thousand feet levels (the remainder or about ⅓rd being still either forest or waste lands attached to tea estates). By 1905 we find that it covered no less than 50,000 acres or 79 square miles, with an output of 12,477,471 lbs. of tea, which employed 64,000 resident operatives, or one-third of the entire population. This figure at times of pressure, i.e., when the flush had to be harvested within a given period, rose to over 90,000 the surplus being children, who are even now to be seen bending over the bushes deftly plucking the tender shoots. In 1915 there were 159 gardens covering 53,178 acres of land with an output of 17,990,786 lbs. of tea which gave employment to 42,308 operatives—the fall in numbers being due to Mr. W. Jackson's patent devices.

Having practically exhausted the available labour supply so far as this district is concerned and with a view to induce an influx of labour from the plains, plots of waste land attached to these gardens were allotted to fresh immigrants, who soon were taught that they had acquired tenancy rights with the result that many will not work on the gardens but eke out an existence from the land too easily handed over to them. It will, therefore, be seen that this experiment had ended in failure, and that any further expansions here must necessarily lead to a deterioration of the standing crop for want of proper and prompt attention, and is therefore to be deprecated until such time as recruitment for the Gurkha Regiments and the Armed Police Force from among the tribes of Nepal is stopped by the Government in compliance with the memorials submitted by the Indian Tea Association—which, however, does not appear to be within the bounds of possibility as the requirements of the Government are the first consideration. In the meanwhile the planting community, while bemoaning its fate, has not sat idle but with the same acreage at command has gone in for intensive cultivation which yields a larger crop, which can well be attended to by the present labour staff and at the same time satisfy the shareholders by giving them larger outturns, and therefore dividends, the measure of the capacity of their respective managers.

In addition to these difficulties and disabilities this industry is further confronted with the concession lately granted an English Syndicate by the Bhutan State which spells overproduction. Then, again, the enticement question is calling for legislation, for obviously more labour cannot well be drawn off other industries, such as the manufacture of quinine and other alkaloids, which absorb some thousands of operatives. These conflicting interests promise to cause the Local Government and the several Tea Associations no end of trouble, truly a case of the Gordian knot. And so amid these conflicting influences it might well be said that the managers of tea estates are between the devil and the deep sea.

The tables overleaf will shew at a glance the marvellous expansion of this industry in Assam, Bengal and all India during the past two decades, which in a great measure was brought about by the incalculable benefits conferred upon it chiefly by the patent devices of the late Mr. William Jackson, and also by Mr. G. W. Christison, who in his 79 year (1916) had just retired after playing an unique part for over fifty-two years in the building up of this industry in Darjeeling.

Year	Acres under Cultivation			Outturn in Lbs.			India	Exported to United Kingdom from		
	Assam	Bengal	India	Assam	Bengal	India		Java	Japan	Formosa
1867-68	*	*	*	*	*	*	7,811,429	*	*	*
1892-93	247,192	92,864	347,869	84,221,132	30,302,869	121,994,274	114,722,447	*	*	*
1914-15	376,048	159,054	622,628	208,227,104	88,346,832	321,976,208	302,557,900†	61,939,000†	38,184,000†	22,936,000†

*Figures not obtainable.

†The major portion of these exports were distributed in the following manner. But with a view to establish the depressing effects of the war figures for the year 1913 and 1914, are given in juxtaposition.

Countries	1913	1914	Net Result	Remarks
United Kingdom	209,073,152	237,303,792	28,230,640	The only increases have occurred in the United Kingdom and United States, while Russia's imports have roughly decreased by 14 millions : similarly, other countries including Canada and China, both of which have not the submarine peril.
Russia	33,398,209	19,636,087	—13,762,122	
Egypt	1,593,680	686,062	—907,618	
Canada	11,564,565	10,950,615	—613,950	
United States	1,942,237	2,737,534	795,297	
China	10,950,205	8,288,630	—2,661,575	
Turkey	2,829,625	1,229,826	—1,599,799	
Afganistan	1,325,296	682,864	—642,432	
Total ..	2,72,676,969	2,81,515,410	8,838,441	

Year	Province	Number of Plantations	Acreage		Outturn	Operatives			Highest average outturn per acre
			Area cultivated	Waste land attached		Permanent	Temporary	Total	
1914	Assam ...	762‡	376,048	914,755	208,227,104	429,317	40,108	469,425	Darrang (Assam) 691 lbs,
	Bengal 1. Darjeeling ...	156	53,778	79,082	17,990,786	30,167	12,141	42,308	Duars 613 ,,
	Bengal 2. Duars ...	118	101,284	154,848	68,704,442	67,012	17,259	84,271	Darjeeling 353 ,,
	Bengal 3. Remainder ...	25	4,592	16,124	1,651,604	3,419	440	3,859	
	Total 1, 2, 3 ...	299	159,954	250,054	88,346,832	100,598	29,840	130,438	
	All India ...	4405	622,628	1,268,356	312,976,208	5,87,898	88,602	676.500	

‡From the figures given by the Department of Statistics for 1915, there were 300 tea gardens in Bengal, 779 in Assam and 268 in Southern India, and the total area under tea was 636,200 acres of which Assam had 383,800 and Bengal 161,300. The total production of black and green teas was about 371½ million pounds, that of Assam being about 245 and of Bengal 85½ millions, respectively.

Tea Planting.

In Darjeeling, the tea seed is sown about the beginning of the year, each seed being placed about two inches apart. The nursery is well shaded, while the ground undergoes frequent weeding. The tender shoots are not interfered with for about eighteen months. They are then transplanted at the commencement of the rainy season into holes three feet apart and two feet deep in parallel rows facing east and west, thus growing 2,982 plants to the acre. These holes are at first only half filled in, and gradually added to as the plant gets deeply rooted.

While moisture is indispensable for the well-being of the plant, the drainage must be complete so that water should not be in contact with the roots for any length of time. Hoeing and weeding are constantly carried on. It follows that in order to obtain luxuriant crops manuring must be heavy as well as applied direct to the tender roots. Consequently nitrogenous green crops are trenched in between the rows immediately after, and preceding the rains to follow.

When the tea plant grows naturally, the China variety grows to a height of about 15 feet, while the Assam, which is more a tree in form, grows to a height of 25 to 30 feet. For the purpose of tea cultivation, it must be kept in the form of low bushes, not higher than 3 feet, although 2 feet is the most useful height; a result obtained by pruning and cutting back.

The picking of leaves commences in the third year, and is carried on from April to October, when from six to sixteen pounds of green leaves are collected daily per acre, according to the productiveness of the ground. Four pounds of green leaves usually yield one pound of the manufactured article. The annual outturn per acre varies according to the age of the plantation, but it may safely be taken to average from one to four maunds. It follows that the tender leaves make delicate brews, while the coarser shoots produce teas with *body*. The 'orange pekoe' and 'broken orange pekoe' are obtained from the bud, the next tender leaves make 'pekoe', while the coarser leaves produce 'pekoe souchong'.

Manufacture.

Black Tea.

The green leaf undergoes the following process before it is placed on the market as 'tea' :—withering, rolling, fermentation, drying, sifting and packing.

Withering is the first process in which the leaves are spread out in thin layers for about 20 hours in order to develop and increase the *enzyme*, its most active constituent.

Rolling, which was formerly done by hand, is now accomplished by machinery which bruises the leaf and so brings the sap to the surface.

Fermentation starts as soon as the sap comes to the surface and in contact with the air, causing the leaf to assume the coppery tint, which infused leaves exhibit to a marked degree. It requires about 5 hours to complete this process during which the temperature is maintained at 80°F.

*Drying** is effected by machinery through which hot air passes at a temperature of 240°F. The fuel consumed in such an operation in a garden of 1,000 acres is 500 tons.

Sifting brings about the different grades and qualities ; while

Packing is done in large, lead-lined chests carefully soldered, as the leaf is very susceptible to moisture, in order to retain its flavour and aroma. "Caddies" should, therefore, be used, in which tea should be transferred the moment a packet is opened.

Note.—The managers of many of the tea gardens about Darjeeling would be glad to shew tourists round, by appointment.

---

*The method by which the Chinese dry their tea so perfectly can be found in some of the earliest "tea books"—Col. Money's and others.

Chinese tea leaves partly cured are bought from peasants, and refined in a dealer's stores. The tea is put into bamboo drums, say 1½ feet in diameter by 2 feet in length. These drums are stacked on racks, 3 to 4-foot passages are left between these racks. On the floor at intervals of 10 to 20 feet there are open charcoal fires. The house is closed so that the whole of the inside is kept at a moderately high temperature and perfectly dry. The tea is left for several days, and is thus dried perfectly without excessive heat.

But as the trade is satisfied, and pays for the usual 3% of free water it would be unwise to change, unless of course, as in the present crisis, (war) the tea must be kept longer than usual and long enough to restart fermentation or moulds.

Green Tea.

This tea produces a dark, strong brew much appreciated by the Chinese, and hill tribes. It is manufactured chiefly in China from where it is exported in the shape of bricks (each 4 lbs. in weight) : hence, is often referred to as brick-tea. This variety of tea is obtained by throwing the leaves direct into the pan without undergoing the withering process.

Blights.

Numerous are the pests and blights which attack the tea plant, the chief being the red spider, the mosquito blight* and the green fly, while red rust, root-rot and fungi are not uncommon. The red spider first appeared in 1876 in the valley of the Little Rangneet river (thereby attracting the attention of Mr. Christison) but is now general throughout the Terai and the hills. The mosquito blight, for which apparently there is no remedy, has caused serious damage throughout the district, notably in the lower elevations. The green fly on the other hand is looked upon with some favour (its habitat being in and around Kurseong chiefly), because although it affects the outturn to a certain extent, its action is such as to produce conditions favourable to the production of an exceptional quality of tea which commands extraordinary prices in the home market.

In the course of Mr. Christison's investigations on the blight caused by red spiders he remembered that sulphur was largely used as a specific for this pest in the vineyards in Scotland and elsewhere, and forthwith tried its effects on tea. This was in 1878. But like all innovations it was many years before his example was followed to any appreciable extent. It is now universally applied in all Indian Tea districts, producing results of incalculable value.

In this connection, however, it ought to be added that in the Terai the remedial properties of sulphur are either nullified by climatic conditions, or else the red spiders found there are of a hardier variety, for once they establish themselves in a

---

*It has been established beyond all doubt that where the percentage of phosphoric acid in the soil is high that the garden is less likely to suffer from the effects of the mosquito blight than others where the percentage is lower.

garden the proprietors have no other course open to them but to close down for a number of years. Indeed, in one instance a plantation, which cost over Rs. 80,000/- in laying out, owing to the continued attacks of these pests, was sold for Rs. 12,000/- only to an enterprising Indian. The year following the purchase the pests died off without any remedial measures being applied, and the owner has ever since reaped a golden harvest!

Patent Devices.

The late Mr. William Jackson, as the inventor of many patent devices, conferred an incalculable benefit upon the tea industry, which but for the application of his inventions could not possibly have attained its present immense proportions. When Mr. Jackson first came to India the industry was at that primitive stage when the leaf was rolled by hand, dried over charcoal fires and trampled into chests by the naked feet. Being of an inventive turn of mind, Mr. Jackson in 1872 improvised a tea rolling machine which was installed on the Hurlekat garden in Assam. During the year it rolled 64,000 lbs. of tea, a wonderful achievement in those days. The rapid development of this process which followed, reduced the cost of manufacture in India to a very great extent and had the effect of gradually relegating the once formidable Chinese rival to an inferior position, for we find that China in 1913 actually imported 10,950,615 lbs. of Indian tea. Prior to 1872, the cost of production was 11*d*. the lb. Overproduction and expansions in India and elsewhere caused expenses to be cut down to the minimum which by the aid of these devices was eventually reduced to 3*d*. the lb. These inventions now form part of the equipment of almost every garden in the country; and by their aid in 1912 no less than 500 million lbs. of tea, or 214,000 tons, were manufactured. In 1913 there were fully 8,000 of Mr. Jackson's machines at work accomplishing what otherwise would have employed 1,600,000 operatives!

Planting Reforms.

The measures adopted by Mr. Christison for preventing the erosion of soil on steep hill surfaces, and for resisting the effects of drought, have contributed in no small degree to the continued prosperity of the gardens in the Darjeeling district. Pruning even was treated as a fine art, for his policy was to prolong the life of the tea bush to 20 years and more by treating the plant on scientific lines.

The preservation of standing timber as well as afforestation on his tea garden was his constant care, while the evil effects of deforestation in this district, and in Sikkim, was a subject which evoked from this otherwise mild and retiring man vehement speech and writing. Indeed, for the past decade it has been the acerbity of his pen that has so far preserved Birch Hill* from the hands of the despoiler : and now that he has retired the probabilities are that this lovely spot will be levelled to form a third and unnecessary recreation ground. (See page 93).

Freight Crusade.

The exhorbitant rates charged by the D. H. Railway next occupied his attention. With his usual thoroughness he patiently collected data on these heads from the managers of mountain railways in Europe, Asia and the United States before entering the ring single-handed. After a prolonged battle, in which the authorities of the D. H. Railway were worsted, he caused reductions to be made in the rates for both the passenger and goods traffic. In the latter a reduction of no less than 33 *per cent* was made on coal, 25 on rice, and 10 on tea. Not satisfied with this achievement he next addressed the authorities of the *lines* in the plains and similarly obtained concessions on tea and tea stores.

Profits.

The report issued by Messrs. Barry & Co. of Calcutta in June, 1915, establishes the fact that investments in tea have produced an average profit of 20.7 *per cent.* on the capital involved (in one instance to the writer's knowledge the percentage was as high as 50) while the report of the Department of Statistics, India, comments on the future of this industry in the following terms :—"The prospects of the tea industry continues

---

*See Appendix II.

bright. The demand for the supplies to troops of the Allies coupled with the prohibition of the manufacture of *absinthe* in France, the sale of *vodka* in Russia, and the restriction placed upon the sale of spirituous liquors in the United Kingdom will no doubt result in a larger demand and (according to some) a demand which may temporarily outstrip production''.

The above optimistic view is certainly not borne out by the figures given under the distribution statement (p. 201), for the only two instances in which an increase in consumption had occurred are the U. Kingdom and the U. States, shewing a net increase of 8,838,441 lbs. of tea in 1914; while the countries which the war had not directly affected have shewn a marked decline due doubtless to the fact that necessaries only can be obtained now, and for a good many years to follow the Declaration of Peace during which taxation will be at high-water level thus placing a ban on luxuries in general and tea in particular. Further, history has repeated itself. When the duty during the Boer war was raised from 5 to 8*d*. the lb. the consumption of tea in the U. Kingdom fell from 6.17 lbs. per head of population to 5.99 lbs.: it began to recover only in 1906 when the duty was again reduced to 5*d*. In November, 1914, the duty was raised to 8*d*., while in the second War Budget introduced on November 21st, 1915, the duty was enhanced to 1*s*. It, therefore, follows that if the duty of 8*d*. caused so appreciable a fall in the consumption, a shilling, together with the duty imposed on the import of machinery rererred to below, will, when the exceptional fillip given the industry wears off, bring about a very severe setback, which will last so long as heavy taxations are the order of the day wherewith the Debt* of Nations is to be liquidated, if possible.

---

*On the fourth anniversary of the war the total expenditure of all the belligerents had risen to £32,000,000,000, which conveys little or no meaning to the average citizen, who thinks in hundreds if he is a professional man or in thousands if a munitioner. It has been left to an American paper to express this gigantic figure in comprehensible terms. Each period of five weeks would pay for the entire cost of the Franco-Prussian war. The thirty-two thousand millions would pay for 400 Panama Canals, or 92 world-encircling railways could be constructed with it. Translated into one-dollar notes, placed end to end, the money would stretch 75 times round the world. Last, but not least, it would purchase 160,000,000 Ford cars.

According to Mr. George Sherwood Eddy, 2/3rds of the population of the world were at war at a cost of £22,000,000 every day, or £20,000

The tax on modern tea-making machinery is a direct one on progress and so obvious that the argument would scarcely need elaboration had not the Government already announced it.

Those companies and private individuals who have already established their factories and are at present owing to high prices well able to pay taxes, will pay nothing of this tax at any rate for a number of years to come till their machinery needs repairs or replacing. Private companies and individuals who have invested capital under the impression that they would receive encouragement from Government, especially at the present time of financial stress and that immediately following the war and have not yet erected their factories or bought machinery, will stand aghast at the reckless legislation which will force them to re-estimate and increase their capital expenditure at a period when money is scarce. And it is at such a time when Britain is organising a trade campaign against the Huns and struggling to retain her hold of the markets of the world that the Government with singular want of forethought has thrown an extra burden, not on properties but on those investors who, relying on due notice of such financial legislation, have invested their money in land and its developments and cannot now draw back.

It, therefore, behoves those interested in tea to proceed most cautiously so far as further expansions go lest bankruptcy follow such undertakings in the great game of grab.

Pioneers in Tea.

"With them the seeds of Wisdom did I sow,
And with my own hand wrought to make it grow;
And this was all the harvest that I reap'd—
'I came like water, and like wind I go' "—*Omar Khayyam.*

Dr. A. D. Campbell, Capt. J. Masson, Messrs. Samler, Brine,

every minute. Forty milions were with the colours, and about 3,000 were killed or wounded daily. Of one regiment of 1,100 men, only 136 came through the first engagement. The British Empire sent 9,496,370 men—6,211,427 from Britain, 1,605,527 from the Dominions and Colonies, and 1,679,416 from India—and the total casualties including 964,023 deaths, totalled 3,266,362. In one week 400,000 school boys of Germany were sent to the front. There were in the Autumn of 1918—17,000,000 more women than men in Europe.

Fooks and Martin will be remembered among those who lead the forlorn hope, who planted the banners of civilisation and industry on these mountains; and in sowing the seeds of the tea plant have laid the foundations of India's increased prosperity.

Francis. Colbrook. Fooks.

From records placed at the disposal of the writer it appears that the industry in this district at least is not a little indebted to Mr. Fooks. Accordingly, a short account of his career, and connection with tea are here given.

Fooks, who hailed from the Isle of Wight, landed in India in 1857 and was immediately drafted into the Yeoman Cavalry which subsequently proved not only useful in rounding up the rebels but also in pressing hard on the heels of the infamous Nana Sahib (the author of the massacres at Cawnpore), who eventualy found an asylum as well as his last resting place in the dense forests of the Nepal Terai into which he had been driven.

After the mutiny, Fooks' services were transferred to the New Police Force at Mymensingh where he subsequently met Mr. Wm. Taylor (son of Mrs. H. C. Taylor, one of the pioneers of the H. T. Scheme), the Dy. Magistrate, and was influenced by him in 1866 to buy the 'Neej Kaman' garden at Sonada on the hire-purchase system. On arriving at Sonada, and to his great surprise, he found the following conditions obtaining:—1. The Hope Town Scheme had ended in complete failure, 2. all the gardens had been deserted by their managers, and allowed to revert to scrub jungle, and 3. the tea bushes had been laid out in *irregular* patches and about 10 feet apart in order to enable the projectors to advertise their gardens as covering so many acres of land with a view to impose on the credulity of purchasers—as in those days it took the best part of a week and much trouble to get to Sonada.

Fooks, whose father was head gardener at the Royal Gardens at Osborne, very early imbibed a certain amount of agricultural knowledge which stood him in good stead at this critical juncture; and so with a view to better supervise a smaller area he had the tea bushes uprooted and laid out in parallel rows 3 feet apart and facing due east and west near his *shanty*, as bungalows did not exist in those days. But before replanting them he had the tap-roots cut off, thus treating the plants as one does fruit trees and rose bushes. The result, as anticipated by him, proved exceptional for the outturn increased 100-fold, although nothing but failure was predicted by LeMesurier in the Terai and others in Darjeeling. He may, therefore, be considered the pioneer (whatever the Chinese, who were imported, may have taught the projectors of the H. T. Scheme in the way of planting out tea) in this district who was the first to recognise the utility of planting out in parallel rows facing due east and west in order that the plants should obtain the greatest amount of heat and light so necessary for their well-being, conditions so essential for growth and reproduction. The cutting off of the tap-roots is so opposed to practice and current literature on the subject that it appears to be worth consideration at the hands of the Scientific Officer of the Indian Tea Association, especially in view of the fact that if found to yield the advantages claimed by Fooks it would obviate the necessity of deep trenching, as practised at present, and thereby materially reduce the cost of production.

While running his own garden, Fooks found the time to supervise the Willows at Hope Town, and Atulpore, Chota Cheng, and Sal Kotee in the Terai. Overwork coupled with a climate more notorious in those days than now soon sowed the seeds of a breakdown, and he was in consequence compelled to retire at Toong in 1879, where he built 'Bloomfontein'.

Life in Early Seventies.

"Ah, make the most of what we yet may spend,
Before we too into the Dust descend;
Dust unto Dust, and under Dust to lie
Sans Wine, sans Song, sans Singer, and—sans End"—*Omar Khayyam.*

In those days sport was the order of the day. Those of the old school could play cricket, polo, shoot, gamble and ride. If one was known to have a new case of wine or whiskey, his neighbours would assemble and empty it. Physically strong were these men, as none but the fittest survived malaria, drink and the damp climate. Late night after night these planters would ride back to their bungalows helter-skelter ; there were no roads and no bridges, and this in the rains meant crossing a dangerous rockstrewn torrent like the Balasan (See Bridges, page 35).

There must have been awful orgies in those riotous, harum-skarum old days to judge from the following stories given verbatim by a contemporary. Practical joking was inevitable when a few of these kindred spirits met, or on the arrival of a griffin, or visitor from the metropolis, for they kicked up such a bobbery that they came to be known far and near, even to the very confines of the Maharatta Ditch (round Calcutta), under the soubriquet of—'The Blue Devils'.

Herein an instance of a harmless prank. One day Messrs Hurt, Feltwell (not assumed names) and others went down the line from Siliguri. At several stations they got out of the train and went round to the different carriages collecting tickets, advising passengers how to arrive at their various destinations, including changes of trains, especially the one from Paddington and the north, and otherwise amusing themselves.

The driver determined to give them a 'Roland for their Oliver', and so suddenly steamed out of a station while they were thus tomfooling. Hurt and Feltwell made a rush for their carriage; but the former fell, and were it not for being rescued by his pal would certainly have been badly hurt, if not killed. The railway staff, noticing the accident, stopped the train for enquiries, names and addresses. On asking Hurt his name, he truly replied—'I am Hurt'. 'Yes, yes', the staff said, 'but what is your name?' To all these he replied, 'I am Hurt' ; and so the valiant Indian Station Master turned his attention to Feltwell. When the latter assured him that he was 'Feltwell', the fat was in the fire, as the staff thought its legs were being pulled ; and so these two youths were more or less placed under arrest until the mystery was solved. Ultimately they were both fined Rs. 25 each for boarding a train in motion.

Few tales could cap the following, which used to be related with much gusto by J. C., a wild old blood, who on one occasion put to sleep an artless griffin by liberal potations of 'Tiger's milk', which was recommended as a preventative of the deadly malaria ; and then had him put to bed between the corpse of two coolies who had that day died in the lines. The morning following a climax was put to the horror of the youngster when told between the paroxysms of a headache that as he had killed these two men a matter of a couple of rupees to each of the widows would hush up the matter. The face of that youngster was a picture to see! 'What', gasped he, 'Did we, did *I*, kill them?' 'Oh! That's nothing', said the old reprobate, 'we often kill them for fun!'

In less than no time that youngster bundled up his belongings, then having literally shaken the dust from off his feet mounted his nag and emulated John Gilpin by not drawing rein until he had reached the nearest railway station, and so placed a safe and respectable distance between himself and that haunted garden.

Tales of a similar nature still recounted by some of the old school put the achievements of those whom we know, and who are far from tame even now, completely in the shade ; and so each succeeding generation in turn regrets its palmy days in the oft-repeated saying—'Oh! for the dear, good old days'—in which the planter was looked upon as 'The Protector of the Poor' and a benefactor, although justice was meted out in a rough and ready fashion ; and so a community of interest bound the peasant and the planter in a friendly intercourse.

It, accordingly, followed that if a planter was popular he could wield enormous power for in his own person he combined the offices of judge, jury, law-giver and the dispenser of justice.

So in drawing up an indictment against the old school if we are guided by—

"To their virtues be very kind,

To their faults a little blind'—we cannot but arrive at the following verdict—Each generation has its own work cut out for it and to be accomplished in its own way, for are not customs and fashions irresistably bound to change with the circumstances and the times?

These old bloods have given place to a more sober and sedate generation for the qualities that ensured success in the pioneers are little needed by their successors, who now live under a reign of law and order—conditions which 50 years ago would have been scouted both as impossible and improbable—for roads now intersect the country in all directions, schools have been established in every large village, while the education of the ryot has been rounded off by those harpies of society (the Vakil), and so the garden coolie and factory (Indigo) hand now fully know their legal rights and accordingly are far from disposed to yield these up readily as in the days of old ; indeed, they are not slow to assert them under the guidance of their pseudo friends (the Vakil). Thus has the planter fallen from his high estate ! indeed, all that he now accomplishes for the betterment of the labourers on his garden is no longer considered by them as benefits actuated by goodwill, but as those which form a part of their birthright. So much for making the illiterate, literate, and thus from a contented albeit poor ryot he has been converted into a most litigious individual ever ready to contest his rights, real or imaginary, against all and sundry in the courts of law !

Medical Officers.

In June, 1871, Dr. Hutchinson was deputed by the Government to analyse and report upon the water-supply of Darjeeling. He was met at Kurseong, on his way up from Pankabarie, and without dismounting proceeded on to Toong to attend Fooks who was lying dangerously ill suffering from a severe attack of malaria, due to neglect as in these days the nearest medical officer was located at Jalpaiguri, which was over 40 miles away. On his return to headquarters the fiat went forth that all tea gardens in future must have a qualified medical attendant attached to each estate.

In compliance with this order we find that Dr. James O'Donoghue (whose heirs now own Pattabong, North Point and Thealand gardens in Darjeeling) was appointed Medical

Officer to the Terai gardens owned by Lloyd, the banker. It was he who built the original Alice Villa, and also a two-storied structure on the hill on which the Eden Sanitarium was subsequently erected during Sir Ashley Eden's tenure as Lieutenant-Governor of Bengal.

Substitutes for Tea and Coffee.*

The leaves of the Sycamore are not infrequently used by the indigenous population of the Darjeeling district as a stimulating beverage, while the Matte (*Ilex Paraguayiensis*) is to the southern Republics, Chili, Paraguay, Brazil and Argentine, what tea is to the European. It is even drunk more in many places than its rival coffee. The infusions are green in colour.

This bush, or rather tree, varies from 12 to 25 feet in height, and is found between the 1,500 and 3,000 feet altitudes. Each bush produces some 200 lbs. of leaves and fine stalks, which is reduced in the factory to about 90 lbs. of herbs. The annual consumption per head of population is 10 lbs.

The following being taken into consideration the wonder is that it has not driven tea at least off the market. It is being sold in some parts of Europe, and even in some parts of England at 9*d*. the lb. Each quart of the prepared beverage costs $\frac{1}{10}$th of a penny! It is claimed for Matte that while tea affects the nervous system as well as the digestion, the former possesses the following beneficent properties—It is a tonic, nutrient, stimulant, and diuretic, and according to medical opinion, a febrifuge, capable of preventing intermittent fever. It is also a great aid against alcoholism, and excites the appetite and assists the digestion. It stimulates the nervous system so gently that no ill effects follow. It is eminently the beverage for all; the brain-worker, the field labourer, the soldier or the miner. Analysis shews that while out of 1,000 parts it contains only 12.28 *per cent*. of tannin (the harmful ingredient of tea), green tea heads the list with 178.00, next comes black tea with 128.80; while coffee has 16.39 *per cent*. Obviously, tea according to the above ought to be discarded, as

*Brazil in 1911—J. C. Oakenfull.

it is deleterious to the constitution. And yet the British are so conservative as not to give Matte 'a fair field and no favour' ; at the same time they seem content to swallow the proverbial camel and strain at a gnat in that they drink 'coffee' by the ton, which is far from the natural product.

Coffee.

In 1905, there were in Italy 23 manufactories of coffee substitutes, and in Austria and Hungary at present exist no fewer than 412 making fig-coffee, 142 using chicory, and 14 barley. In Germany there are 723 factories, and in France 166, while in Belgium 60,000 tons of imitation coffee are produced annually. In England, Russia, Spain, etc., chicory is the usual substitute, but the quantity used is not very great.

CINCHONA PLANTATIONS.

Cinchona is known commercially as 'Jesuit's Bark' and 'Peruvian Bark', the former indicating the source by which Europe came to learn of its properties, the latter the locality in which it is indigenous. It is now universally spoken of as cinchona, after the Countess Chinchon, the then Spanish Vicerine of Peru, who was cured by it of the fever in 1638. Our Vicerine, Lady Canning, however, was not so fortunate for she succumbed to the deadly malaria contracted during a few hours' halt in the Terai for the purpose of sketching, and was buried in the grounds of the Barrackpore Park (formerly the week-end resort of the Viceroy of India) on November 18th, 1861. Her epitaph which was written on the 22nd idem by Lord Canning runs as follows :— "At a lovely bend of the river—Lady Canning's favourite haunt —her body rests. Honours and praises, written on a tomb are, at best, a vainglory".

About the same time, that is, 1664, Surgeon C. Dellon of the French Navy sailed in the course of duty to Madagascar and eventually found himself in Western India where he made a study of tropical diseases, including small-pox, which he found very prevalent, and the malaria. His description of malaria is full and accurate, but in discussing the treatment he makes no mention of 'Jesuit's Bark'. The fact is also recalled that as early as 1754 an eminent Frenchman of science, M. Job, described the anopheles larva which he had discovered in a reservoir in Paris. And yet, although the proper treatment of malaria has been known for more than two centuries, it awaited the advent of Col. Sir Ronald Ross, I.M.S., to discover the cause of malaria, which was traced to the mosquito (anopheles) which impregnates its victims with deadly germs causing the spleen to enlarge, and subsequently general complications which end in pneumonia and death.

The fen districts in Cambridgeshire and Lincolnshire, Romney Marsh in Kent, and the marshy districts of Somerset have now lost their evil reputation for ague. In England it was once very prevalent. James I died of 'a tertian ague' at Theobalds, near London, and Cromwell succumbed at Whitehall to a 'bastard tertian ague' in 1658, a year in which the malaria was very widely spread and very malignant.

The Quest for Quinine.

The historian Prescott tells us that the Incas of Peru knew of the medicinal value of the cinchona bark long before their land was subjugated by the able Spaniard Pizarro in the year 1525. The prophylactic properties of this bark on being divulged to the Jesuit order was speedily in turn disseminated throughout Europe ; but all quest for the bark, and the localities in which the plants were indigenous were frustrated by the Indians.

In 1738, however, La Condamine and Jessieu of the French Scientific Expedition, which was sent to Loxa in Eucador, succeeded in discovering these localities ; but their effort to send over some of these plants ended disastrously for the whole consignment was washed off the deck of the vessel during a severe storm. Their researches in this direction established the following.—There are 14 or 15 different varieties. Eucador was the home of the 'red bark' (*Cinchona Succirubra*) ; Loxa produced its *C. Officinalis;* further south the 'grey yielding bark' was found (but of little or no value); while in Peru the 'yellow bark' (*C. Calisaya*) came into prominence on the drug being extracted from it in 1820.

A period of quiescence then followed until the eminent French chemist, Waddell, between the years 1843-45 found the yellow bark tree indigenous in Bolivia and Brazil at an elevation of 6,000 and 5,000 feet, respectively.

Its Active Principles.

The Russian chemist, Reuss, made in 1815 a tolerable analysis ; but it was left to Gomess, a Portuguese naval surgeon, to isolate cinchonine. These achievements were followed in 1820 by the French chemists, Pelletier and Caventon, isolating *quinine*, and in 1852 by Pasteur discovering quinidine, and cinchonidine.

Its Subsequent Culture.

As early as 1819 we find Dr. Ainsle insisting upon the introduction of the plant into India—but as usual the Government of India took 99 years to wake up to its responsibilities in this direction. Again, and although Dr. Royle (the only exponent on the fibres of India) in 1839 pressed its introduction into Bengal, no action appears to have been taken until the year 1857 when the Secretary of State for India appointed Mr. (Sir) Clements Robert Markham*—(who was only 29 years of age at the time, but who had 'already grown old' in traversing the whole of S. America) to obtain and furnish India with supplies of this tree. While thus engaged the Government of Bengal, to the surprise of not a few, deputed Dr. T. Anderson, Superintendent of the Royal Botanic Garden, Calcutta, to proceed to Java† (where the cultivation of the cinchona plant had already been established on a sound commercial basis by 1854) and inspect the plantations and process of manufacture. By the combined

---

*Was Knighted on becoming President of the Royal Geographical Society in 1893.

†Justus Karl Hasskari, the Dutch botanist, in 1848 brought 49 cinchona plants from Callao to Java and had them planted out at an elevation of 5,000 feet in Tjibodas. The *Calysaya*, followed by *Ledgeriana* specie, was subsequently found to be richest in quinine and have, accordingly, been solely utilised in the manufacture of sulphates and salts, such as, chlorohydrates and bromohydrates; while the *Officinalis* and *Succirubra* are reserved for cinchona febrifuges and wines. The yield of bark in 1907 amounted to 8,985 tons.

efforts of Markham and Anderson we find the tree established in 1861 in the Nilgiris ; and nurseries started at Dimsong in Sikkim and Senchal in Darjeeling in the year following. By 1878 the plot at Dimsong covered 2,200 acres and yielded a considerable outturn of bark, the crop amounting to no less than 340,000 lbs. ; at the latter the elevation proving unfavourable a permanent habitation in 1863 was allotted the cinchona at Mongpu (5,200′) in the Riang Valley, 18 miles south-east of Darjeeling, and 5 miles east of Serail. Its cultivation was intensified in 1864 on Dr. Anderson assuming charge of the Forest Department, and in 1881 new plots were laid out at Labdah and Sitong on the southern slopes of the same valley. The cultivation was further increased owing to the great demand for quinine in Bengal until in 1890 there were no fewer that 4½ million plants (some eventually attaining a height of 30 feet) yielding quinine and febrifuge. Yet with all these colossal numbers the demands made on this bark were found to be insufficient for the needs of India, and so much bark was imported from Java up to the close of 1914.

The following plantations existed in 1915 :—The Rangpu Valley block, consisting of the Rungbi and Mongpu divisions, which together cover an area of 900 acres, on which nearly 2 million trees have been established ; 2. the Reang Valley block, consisting of the Labdah and Sitong divisions, which together comprise an area of 600 acres ; and 3. the Rangpu Valley block comprising the Mungsong division.

Col. Sir Ronald Ross, who was engaged at the War Office on special malarial work, celebrated on August 20th, the twentyfifth anniversary of his discovery of the malarial parasite. It was on August 20th, 1897, at Secundrabad, India, that his long researches were rewarded by the finding of the parasite of the anopheles mosquito. He is reported to have been so moved by the discovery that he gave vent to his feelings in the following lines :—

'Seeking His great secret deeds
  With tears and toiling breath,
I find thy cunning seeds,
  O million-murdering death..

I know this little thing
A myriad men will save,
Oh Death, where is thy sting?
Thy victory, Oh Grave?"

The preventive measures adopted against malaria, through the knowledge of the source of disease, have saved untold lives in the tropics, and have proved of inestimable value during the war safeguarding the health of the British troops in India, Mesopotamia, East Africa and Salonika.

There are 190 species of the mosquito in the museum in Rio Janeiro. The female of the variety termed *Stegomyia fasciata* produces 'yellow-fever' which wellnigh depopulated Central America; while the *Culex Fatigans* is the cause of that terrible disease—Filiarisis (known to science by name only, as no remedy has yet been discovered) which induces either chyluria, which saps the body of its vitality, or causes elephantiasis or white-leg.

The process of manufacture is too technical and therefore finds no place here; but the following details may prove of interest:—Quinine is supplied to the Civil, and Military Medical Stores, the Postal Department, which through its innumerable post and sub-post offices sells it in packets containing five tablets of 3 and ⅛th grains each for an anna (penny), and the Juvenile Jail at Calcutta which in a single year distributed in Behar and Assam no less than 14,544 lbs. which was made into 125,825 boxes containing 200 tablets each of 3 and ⅛th grains. In 1912-13 six million tablets were sold, while in 1913-14 the demand was so great that 24 million tablets passed through the hands of this Jail alone.

Some impression from these figures may be drawn of the ravages of the malaria fever in Bengal, Behar and Assam.

In Bengal twenty 4-grain tablets in glass tubes are sold for four annas (four pence). The number of 4-grain tablets which passed through the hands of the Juvenile Jail, Alipore, Calcutta, for sale in Bengal during the years 1914, 1915, and 1916, was 21,302,800; 12,301,600; and 19,317,400, respectively.

In Madras the plantations in 1914-15 yielded 683,054 lbs

which were worked up into 29,422 lbs. of quinine sulphate, and produced a net profit of Rs. 371,488/-. These figures speak for themselves!

BREWERY.

The Victoria Brewery at Sonada, which was started in 1888, forms one of many established by the same company at Simla, Kasauli, Murree and other hill stations. Its output per annum varies from 75,000 to 100,000 gallons which is chiefly consumed by the troops located at the three cantonments of Jalapahar, Katapahar and Lebong.

GEOLOGY*.

"Confusedly hurl'd,
The ruins of an earlier world."

The rocks of the Darjeeling district according to Mr. F. R. Mallet are divisible into five groups:—gneiss, the Daling and Buxa series, Gondwanas, and the Tertiary system.

"Gneiss varies from a foliated granitoid rock composed of quartz, felspar and biotite to a more or less pure mica-schist. The Daling series covers a large area in the northern and eastern parts of the district. It consists of phyllite, slate, and quartzite with some hernblend-schists and very subordinate bands of dolomite and crystalline limestone. Copper ore is frequently found disseminating through the slates and schists. The Buxa series, which is largely developed in the Western Duars, occurs only at the extreme eastern end of the Darjeeling district. It consists of slates, quartzites, and dolomites, the preponderance of the latter rock serving as a means of distinction from the Daling series. The Gondwana beds crop out near the base of the hills and constitute a narrow band between the Daling and the Tertiaries, running from Pankabarie to Dalingkote. They consist chiefly of sandstone, shale and coal, all of which have been intensely crushed and faulted. Owing to this crushing, the coal-seams vary much in thickness, and occasionally cut out altogether by faults. The Tertiary beds fringe the older rocks continuously from close to the Mechi river

---

***The Darjeeling Gazetteer* by L. S. S. O' Malley, I.C.S.

eastward nearly as far as Dalingkote†. They are chiefly composed of soft, massive, 'pepper-salt' sandstones, containing mica and felspar, &c."

MINERALOGY.

Mica, though crushed and faulted, is found in large pockets throughout the Daling series, and in Nepal just over the western border ; and, accordingly, should command a ready market since, being a non-conductor of heat, it has for sometime past been used as a coating for boilers, thus helping, in however small a measure, in the conservation of our stocks of wood and coal.

Copper occurs in the same series as mica, and has for ages yielded ore in paying quantities along the left bank of the Rangneet river to the enterprising Nepalese who work at it according to primitive methods. He has proved to be an able craftsman fashioning his vessels and bric-a-brac, and giving them the appearance of great age in order to delude tourists especially into the belief that they have formed a part of the chattels in connection with the ancient ritual of Buddism. Lately, however, a concession has been granted to a well-known European firm in Calcutta which has been working the mines situated at Rangpu (Sikkim), on the borders of British territory, under the latest scientific methods ; but whether this venture will turn out a financial success is still a matter of conjecture.

Coal was first discovered near Pankabarie in 1849 by Dr. Hooker, and the analysis obtained on the sample sent to Calcutta was pronounced upon favourably. It occurs in beds in the Gondwanas ; at Kalijhora, Tista Valley ; and at Dalingkote overlooking the Duars ; but is of such poor quality that it is fit only for bricket-making—an industry which has still to be established in this country.

Lime is found in many parts of the district, especially in the Duars ; in the Buxa and Tertiary series ; and calcareous tufa. The limestone, however, is hardly used probably owing to the purity of the tufa, which contains 98 per cent of carbonate of lime, which is deposited by springs issuing chiefly along the line of junction of the Gondwanas with the Tertiary rocks.

---

†The name of the Kalimpong sub-division when it formed part of Bhutan prior to the war of 1864-65.

CHAPTER V.

Agriculture.

As the area of the district is divisible into three distinct tracts, *viz,* the level stretches at the foot of the hills where the soil is alluvial, and the submontane and mountainous portions, it follows that the conditions of agriculture in these regions are varied in the extreme.

As the hills rise higher and higher the slopes become so stony that little or nothing will grow on them ; while on the gentler slopes, which are more fertile, tea has entirely covered the hillsides, indeed, so much so that with the exception of Chebu Llama's Grant ("The Rhilling Estate"), which comprises 74,016 acres of land, the cultivation of this beverage absorbs more than two-thirds of the rural population. The soil necessarily varies in these tracts and, according to Dr. Hope, the Scientific Officer of the Indian Tea Association, should be both chemically and mechanically analysed in order to determine the particular crop which would thrive on any particular spot :—"In the Darjeeling district the original composition of the rock has been a very important factor in determining the types of soil to be derived from it, because throughout the district there is generally a fairly similar climate, and the nature of the chemical changes which take place during these weatherings are fairly uniform, but on the other hand the varieties of rock is very great containing as these mountains do such different materials as sandstone, limestone, gneiss, &c., and many varieties of soil are found in consequence. A chemical analysis of the various soils to be met with shews a remarkable uniformity, while the few mechanical analysis which have been made prove that as regards mechanical composition soils of every variety exist".

At the settlement concluded in 1898 it was found that the area under cultivation in the Terai had shrunk considerably owing to its malarious climate, while in the Kurseong sub-division it had increased so rapidly owing to the influx of Nepalese labourers and settlers that further extensions were restricted by legislation so as to create reserved lands for grazing, fodder, fuel, &c.

In the Terai, eliminating the area under forest, tea covers 8,000 acres, rice is planted on 45,000, while other crops are grown on 16,000 acres; the total being just half of the area comprising healthy tracts.

Rice Crops.

These crops are known by the season in which planted and harvested—thus, that sown in May and harvested in December is the *Aman* rice, while the crop sown in the winter and harvested in August-September is the *Aus* variety.

The procedure of cultivation is as follows—The land, which is enclosed by ridges in order to retain the rainfall at a height of at least 8 inches, is ploughed after the first showers in April, and thereafter kept constantly mulched during the excessive falls of rain during June-July until the soil becomes a puddle, when the young seedlings, which are raised in nurseries round the homestead of the ryot, are transplanted into the manured and prepared soil. From daylight to dark is he to be seen standing knee-deep in water, and bending until his face is on a level with it, dibbling in the shoots about 6 inches apart: in sunshine or rain this labour goes on for weeks during which he is exposed to the inclemencies of the weather to eke out after the harvest is gathered in normal years, but an existence; in abnormal years he starves and then goes in quest of roots and bulbs to be found in the surrounding jungles. Such is his life!

The monsoon supplies the necessary irrigation, for the roots of this crop must stand in not less than 4 inches of water otherwise the ears will not mature. When the rainfall is deficient, or fails entirely, he has to starve, or, if there be a patch of water close by, to conduct it by means of channels, or by bamboo piping (the culms of which are hollow) to his fields. This is not his only trial, for experience has proved that if a *southerly* wind persists for two consecutive days following the transplanting of these shoots he will harvest but *half* a crop.

While elevation determines the class of cereal grown it also seems to govern the races which work at them, for we find the Lepcha engaged on the lower levels, while the Bhutia and Gurung being pastoral in habit prefer the higher ranges. Racial distinctions are also observable in their methods of working for the enterprising Nepalese cultivates every square inch of soil, obtaining the necessary manure and fuel somehow; the Bhutia and the Lepcha invariably reserve a part of their holding as scrub-jungle for their fuel supply.

Maize and Cardamomum.

The former has existed from a time veiled in the Ages of the Past for it was found growing in Brazil by the first navigators, and was known by the name of Abati by the Indians of that continent. Those savages, like our own population, soon discovered its utility in the manufacture of fermented beverages as well as flour. It is planted generally on any soil which is unfitted for other cereals. The kind most generally known and planted is the common yellow maize, popular not only by reason of its abundant production, but also for its resistance to the disease called *calandragranaria*. There are no less than 19 varieties of this cereal found growing in the different zones of the world; and no proper classification has been made beyond the commonly known fact that white maize resists drought better than all the other varieties.

While maize thrives between the 1 and 7 thousand feet levels, the cardamomum, which is raised in rich, black loam at the bottom of the valleys, or on the sides of hill streams, luxuriates with its roots under a constant flow of water, as well as heavy shade above. It flourishes between the 1 and 5 thousand feet levels, and demands much labour and care which, however, is repaid by the steady and high market it commands. The yield starts in the fourth year, progressing until the eighth year after which it begins to decline until the fifteenth year, when the whole field is replanted. The cardamomum is a root-bulb which blossoms in May and is harvested in August, and then dried in kilns before being placed on the market.

The other important crops are:—Jute and mustard, which respectively cover about 3,000 acres each; oilseeds, pulse and sugarcane absorb about 2,000 acres, while thatching-grass covers fully 4,000 acres, or 5.5 per cent of the area cultivated.

CHAPTER VI.

Himalayan Resources.

The exploitation of the rich and partially tapped resources of the mountain and sub-montane portions of the district has been retarded by at least two decades owing to the want of proper road communications, and the paucity of draft-cattle. These defects, however, it is expected will in the near future be remedied, for India has awoke to the possibility of a complete expansion of her resources, and the place that she aspires to in the conclave of nations, and especially so in regard to her position as a colony of the Crown. Such being the case these notes, it is hoped, will be found of some interest to the general reader, if they do not prove of use to those on the look-out for fresh avenues of enterprise.

Timber.

Sal furnishes sleepers for the several railways in Northern Bengal, while the soft-woods (too numerous to mention) are exploited by petty dealers in timber. *Bombax malibaricum* (cotton-wood) deserves more attention than that given it in the past, for it is admirably suited for planking in the manufacture of *shukes* (tea chests) of which India has been in such need during the war, and so brought in the use of cartoons, and the packing of tea in lead sheets only. It follows that even in pre-war days, if the following figures are any criterion of India's needs in this direction, a fortune awaits the capitalist who will invest in machinery for the manufacture of these shukes:—The imports of tea chests into India from the United Kingdom and Japan, respectively, in the year 1913-14, amounted to no less than 1,985,238 and 129,259—which should, and could have been supplied locally had we but the appliances.

Bamboo.

The next in importance is *Bambusa vulgaris* (bamboo) which enabled man in the East to rise to the first stage of civilisation ;

and which now supplies the entire wants of the rural population of the tropical zone. With it, his homestead and all the contained furniture are constructed even unto the tiny cradle in which his progeny is put away at nights, or placed in the strong sunlight to bask.

In 1914, its exploitation at Phalut (to the north-west of Darjeeling, and on the borders of Nepal) ended in complete failure due to gross mismanagement on the part of those entrusted with the scheme, which included its extraction and subsequent floating down of its culms on the Rangneet and Tista rivers until they reached Sivoke, where the latter river debouches into the plains of Jalpaiguri, and where a factory was to have been established for the manufacture of wood-pulp.

Fibre.

Ramie, the fibre of the ordinary nettle, is the most valuable product that we have. It springs up in large patches at every nook and corner of the district (and is eaten as spinach by the people) and though a weed possesses a fibre thin, silky in lustre and of a delicate texture thus lending itself readily to the adulteration of silks now on the market, especially those imported from China where the cultivation of this crop is carried on extensively. A fortune, therefore, awaits the experimentalist who succeeds in decorticating this fibre by means other than retting, which necessarily lowers its market value. Yet, withal, samples prepared by the latter process in 1908 had a quotation of Rs. 30 the maund from one of the mills at Cawnpore. That the fibre can be extracted by the aid of chemicals, or other means, is proved by the silken band of ramie exhibited in the Economic Section of the Indian Museum, which was sent in by a lady residing in the Tirhut district who, sad to relate, went mad (probably through joy at her success) shortly after she achieved this wonderful success. And so the secret died with her!

CHAPTER VII.

Tropical Fruits.

Although the district covers a climate suitable for the cultivation of almost every kind of fruit yet the indigenous population will neither plant these nor will it hire any waste-lands for the purpose. Consequently all that is done in this direction is the planting out of orange groves (for the word culture is unknown to him), and in a few instances the cultivation of the pineapple (*annanaz*).

The Orange.

Over six millions of these fruits are exported annually to Calcutta from the orchards of Sikkim, Kalimpong and Darjeeling. The price ranges from Rs. 1-8-0 to as much as Rs. 7-0-0 per hundred during Xmas, which leaves an exceedingly large margin of profit per acre.

That the quality and size of the fruit can be improved by culture is indisputable ; but the Indian being conservative, and cursed with a phlegmatic temperament, knows not what innovation means, and so follows in blind faith the lines adopted by his forebears, with the result that his crops suffer from all manner of blights and pests which not infrequently sweep away the entire fields.

Plants are propagated from cuttings, known locally as 'ghuttys'. These should be set out at the commencement of the rains at least 12 feet apart, and in rows facing due east and west. In the third year the trees bear about 20 fruit each, but which in the fourth year of bearing increases to 500 and more fruit until the fertility of the plant may top anything between 2,000 to 4,000 fruits. The tree is exceedingly hardy, and needs only two manurings each year, the first before the rains set in, the next shortly after the harvest has been gathered in order to recoup the energy of the plant. On the other hand scrupulous attention must be devoted to the warding off of attacks by insects—each plant being scrutinised twice each year.

Among the pests which attack the citrus family are—

1. Black rust, which is held in check by liberal applications of kerosine spray, and heavy pruning.

2. Black insect, or *mawa*, which exudes a sweetish fluid, succumbs to infusions of tobacco.

3. Scale insect, which first appears in whitish-yellow bands and subsequently become black on bark and leaves, yields to the following mixture—8 lbs of resin to 4 of washing-soda well-boiled and sprayed over affected parts.

4. Borer-worm is responsible for the loss of 20 per cent of the crops. A small quantity of asafoetida and Boris root (Buckh) boiled in oil, and then poured into the orifices drive the insects out.

5. Foot-rot being due to over-manuring, the remedy is obvious.

6. Gum disease, *i.e.*, exudation of sap from the base of the trunk, is stopped by liberal applications of a mixture composed of 4 parts of resin, or shellac, to 1 of wax, followed by judicious pruning.

7. As a preventative against attacks by insects, whose name is legion, and which ascend the trees from the base, grease-bands renewed twice each year and wound round the stem near the root keep them off.

The Pineapple

which is propagated from suckers, should be planted out 3 × 4 feet apart in parallel rows just before the rains set in. Each plant bears fruit in the second year after the rains that follow, and at the same time throws out from 2 to 4 suckers, which should be removed as early as possible and planted out, thus ever increasing the extent and outturn of the orchard.

Fruit of Plains.

Almost all the fruit of the plains, such as the guava, plantain, mangoe, loquat, lichee, papaya, peeches, and even pears, apples, plums, grapes, etc., have been successfully raised at Gyabarie, which is just below Kurseong and only 2,700 feet above sea-level.

Other Produce.

Aconite (the deadly night-shade) which is largly exported for medicinal purposes, grows at an elevation of 10,000 feet, while the maginta (which is a creeper) yields the colour of commerce; the cherita (a tonic plant) grows wild round every homestead; and the myrobolam (soap-nut) is shipped by the ton.

CHAPTER VIII.

Pastoral Industry.

With regard to pastoral conditions, Darjeeling must be divided into three zones, *i.e.*, tropical, semi-tropical, and temperate, where grasses of a hundred species could, and should be raised by the Forest Department. But of this there is little or nothing to be had, and so the meat and milk supply is meagre and very nearly unfit for human consumption.

Cattle, &c.

In the plains portion the cattle do not differ from those raised in Bengal, *viz.*, oxen which are exclusively used for agricultural purposes; while the buffalo, goat and pig are raised for food. In the hills we have two distinct breeds of cattle, the Siri and Nepali, and a cross-breed between the Siri bull and Nepali cow, termed *Kutcha-Siri*. The Bhutia being pastoral in habit goes in for grazing chiefly, even when they take to agriculture. Pigs are reared in localities where Lepcha and Limboo predominate as they are inordinately fond of the flesh of this animal. Droves of sheep are tended to by the Gurung, who, to avoid the ravages of the leech during the rains, take them up to, and beyond the 12,000 feet level.

Ponies, &c.

The indigenous breed is the well-known Bhutia, a short, sturdy, thick-set animal which never seems to tire. They are bred in Tibet and Bhutan and are annually imported along with mules. Asses and donkeys are also bred in the Kalimpong sub-division.

CHAPTER IX.

Trade—Local.

Necessarily the chief trade is carried on with Calcutta, the export being cardamomum, gunny-bags, jute, maize and tea, and the imports cotton yarn, kerosine-oil, piece-goods, rice and salt. Coal and coke are imported from the fields at Raneegunge. With Nepal food-grains, cotton piece-goods, manufactured wool, raw hides, potatoes, sheep, goats, cattle and poultry are imported in exchange for European piece-goods, cotton-twist, salt, kerosine-oil, tobacoo and food-grains.

Trade—Transfrontier.

The transfrontier trade of Bengal with Sikkim, Nepal, Tibet, and Bhutan is at present registered at 14 stations of which 8 are located on the frontier of the Darjeeling District—Sukiapukri (near Ghum) registers the trade with Nepal; Phulbazar, Singla and Rangneet (below the St. Joseph's College) that with both Nepal and Sikkim; 15th-mile Rangneet and Mellighat with Sikkim only; and Pedong and Laba (Kalimpong way) with Sikkim and Bhutan: while of the remaining 6 stations 4 are located in the Jalpaiguri district and register the traffic with Bhutan alone, and 2, *viz.*, Gangtok in Sikkim, and Chema in Chumbi Valley, account for the trade with Tibet solely.

The magnitude of the transactions with these States may be gauged by the figures in the following statement :—

Imports (1916-17).

	Tibet.	Nepal.	Sikkim.	Bhutan.
Horses	167,770	1,250	23,582	54,663
Cattle	...	311,508	98,002	21,502
Sheep	74,630	143,757	190,507	24,183
Animals	...	1,122,683	179,413	69,123
Fruit	10,416	1,048,316	802,735	39,745
Hides	...	32,175	28,970	4,317
Skins	162,071	...	2,079	298
Musk	4,420	...	...	12,649
Butter	...	113,229	155,625	13,748
Grease	10,375	89,443	169,059	1,662
Spices	...	9,445	408,165	5,191
Wool	2,102,803	...	2,304	...
Silver Coins ...	315,083	156,519	62,534	2,000

Exports (1916-17).

	Tibet.	Nepal.	Sikkim.	Bhutan.
Apparel	104,354	230	2,777	630
Yarn	13,952	41,837	79,919	164
Piece-goods (F) ...	170,240	27,859	29,284	39,028
Fruit	41,465	...	33,353	416
Piece-goods (I) ...	132,220	126,499	164,962	895
Oil	2,545	9,006	41,189	1,587
Lubricants ...	557	21,857	144,591	2,087
Salt	...	29,365	76,605	2,801
Silks	101,872	...	7,484	2,569
Silver Coins ...	60,100	87,932	21,302	4,448
Sugar	38,068	12,383	101,419	7,512
Tobacco	61,048	4,719	70,239	12,038
Wax	...	...	40,054	...
Woollen Fabrics ...	81,370	...	...	...

The transfrontier trade of Bengal with Sikkim, Nepal and Tibet was affected by the war during the year 1914-15 to the extent of only 12 per cent. According to the returns just issued by the Department of Statistics, the total value of exports and imports together amounted to 108 *lakhs* of rupees as compared with 123 *lakhs* in the preceding year. The trade of 1914-15 is still considerably ahead of that in 1912-13, when its total value stood at 93 lakhs. The falling off in the traffic including that in hides and skins, cotton manufactures and sugar, is scarcely more than might have been expected in the first year of the conditions imposed by the war on foreign trade through Calcutta. There was a small increase in the imports of wool from Tibet. The quantity received during the year was 47,224 maunds, valued at a trifle over 14 *lakhs* of rupees. The increase in quantity was only 4 per cent., but the rise in value was 10 per cent. Raw wool constitutes the main staple export from Tibet. As the trade in other commodities has declined owing to the war, the Tibetans are more than likely to take advantage of the high prices obtaining at present and develop the export of wool in the future. (See Tista Valley Extension, Part IV).

PART III.

CHAPTER I.

Pic-nics and Tours.

"Come hither, you that walk along the way,
See how the pilgrims fare that go astray;
They catched are in an entangled net,
'Cause they good counsel lightly did forget :"—*Bunyan.*

The best of hill stations begins to pall after a visit or two, but not so Darjeeling which has this advantage over other sanitaria in that it is the starting-point for sceneries of unsurpassed beauty, as far as your stamina or your purse can carry you, even unto the very confines of Sikkim on the one hand and, if one of the fortunate ones, to Gyantse (145 miles from Lhasa), the outpost station where the British Trade Agent resides and where the absolute power of Tibet starts, on the other. For those unable to get the necessary permit and whose time is more limited a lesser circle with Gangtok in its periphery is recommended; or a trip along the Nepal frontier.

The following itinerary is accordingly inserted for those who have the time at their disposal to undertake excursions in and about the district, and in Sikkim which now, owing to the present Maharaja being under the tutelage of a Political Officer, can be accomplished in comfort and security. But such was not the experience of the earlier tourists, for hindrances in every conceivable form were offered to exploring parties, which worked wonders! This procedure, however, had apparently no effect upon two adventurous spirits who determined upon reaching Kinchenjunga, if not, to cross the mighty Himalayas by the Chumbi Valley. The above policy forced them to retire for a while; but nothing daunted they returned to the charge and essayed the journey for the second time armed on this occasion with a sufficiency of provisions. The authorities of that State finding themselves outwitted very kindly informed these travellers that to save them the trouble and unnecessary fatigue of the return journey they would have them bound hand and foot and dropped into the river—a famous mode of punishment which to this day obtains in Tibet. And so all attempts at crossing the borders were discouraged by the Government lest political complications arise. Happily, these days have passed never to return, and the tourist may now traverse the following routes in the full knowledge that in place of the usual hindrances every facility will be afforded him.

The Prince of Pedestrians.

Ye, tourists, who now travel with every convenience and facility at hand, Ye know not of the hardships and privations which dogged the steps of Mungo Park, Bruce, Marco Polo and Tom Coryat ('not only the first globe-trotter but the Prince of Pedestrians, and the only European who *walked* out to India') who at the close of day rested not in well-appointed hotels, or dak bungalows but in *serais*, or walled enclosures, with ordinary mendicants, cut-throats, and way-farers. The pace was necessarily slow, the impressions deep, while the impulse to record and make permanent some semblance of what engaged their attention or wakened their imagination so strong that they could not be stifled; and so in the case of the last we have *"The Crudities,"* being an account of his journeys through Germany, Italy, the Alps, Syria, Turkey and Egypt which subsequent travellers have verified to the very letter—

> "Time but the impressions deeper make,
> As streams their channels deeper wear".

In 1612 he set out to *do* Europe, Asia, China and the far East, but got as far as Surat only where he, sad to say, died from a deep indulgence of *arrack* in 1617, having completed only five out of the ten years he had set apart for travelling, like Ulysses of old. In his journeys in Asia he covered the distance from Skanderun to Surat—3,000 miles—on foot, a greater feat than Captain Grant's big walk across the African continent. He can, therefore, throw down the gauntlet to all travellers on foot, and no man shall take it up. And now be it remembered that these hardships were not endured by a coarse-bred man, but by a refined gentleman, a companion to the then Prince of Wales, by a scholar who, we are told, discussed Greek and Latin with Causabon in Paris, with Gruter at Heildelburg, with Grynaeus at Basle; as well as acquired nine different languages during the course of his travels of which he could read and write six, excluding his mother-tongue which 'he wrote with a genuine ring of the Elizabethan period'. Unfortunately his notes of the journey in Asia were destroyed, or burnt with his effects by the factory hands at Surat. Although no mound or sepulchre marks the spot where his bones were laid to rest, yet his fame will last so long as the following lines find a place in our literature:—

"Here lies the wanderer of his age,
Who living did rejoice,
Not out of need but choice,
To make his life a pilgrimage".

The Dak Bungalow.

To fully understand the comforts attending a stay at one of these rest-houses, a visit to the *serai* facing Ghum Station, is recommended. Yet while enjoying these advantages of modern travel, how few ever enquire into their origin.

About the year 250 B. C. Asoka was the first to construct countless traveller's rest houses throughout his kingdom. The pattern was improved upon by Arungzeb during his reign of turmoil and endless wars first with his brothers and then with the Rajputs, Maharattas and even the Shiahs of his own religion. His realm in 1659 embraced the provinces of Hindustan, and included Kandahar and Kabul on the west, Bengal on the east, Kashmir beside the Himalayas, and Khandesh in the Deccan; and so from Kandahar to Travancore he built dak bungalows wherein to rest his weary body until he died at Ahmednagar in the Deccan in 1707 fighting to the last!

Dak Bungalow Rules.*

1. Tourists unless provided with a pass by the Deputy Commissioner, Darjeeling, will not be allowed beyond the frontier.

2. Passes for all bungalows† except the following are issued from the office of the Deputy Commissioner:—Pedong, Peshok, Kalijhora, Birrik, Riang, and Tista Bridge which are under the charge of the Executive Engineer, Darjeeling Division, to whom application should be made for their occupation.

3. For those situated in Sikkim, application should be made to the Political Officer of that State (residing at Gangtok), or through the Deputy Commissioner, Darjeeling, which means a loss of time. Such application should be made at least a month in advance, and especially during the *poojahs*, and October-November, when many decide upon touring.

Passes.

4. Application for passes should be addressed to these officials by designation, and not by name, and should be forwarded to their offices and not private residences.

5. Each tourist must be provided with a separate pass for each bungalow, whether going or returning. Persons occupying bungalows without passes will be required to pay double fees, provided there is accommodation.

6. Passes may be cancelled by the local authorities without payment of compensation.

7. Passes must be made over to the chowkidar‡ of the bungalow occupied.

8. A list of *dak* bungalows, furniture, accommodation, &c., are given under each tour.

---

*The rules, and the mileage, altitude and accommodation at the stages of the tour routes in Sikkim have been reproduced from the printed slip issued by the office of the Dy. Commissioner, Darjeeling. With the exception of the first, these have been recast under the several routes in which they lie, and so form a handy reference.

†Many of these roadside stations are built on commanding and picturesque spots. It is unfortunate that the rules prohibit a longer stay than 24 hours.

‡The chowkidars are either Bhutias or Lepchas; but there are a few Indians who invariably worry for 'bakshis' (tips).

1. A fee of eight annas will be charged for occupation by day, up to a maximum charge of Rs. 8/- for a party. The fee for occupation of 24 hours, or one night, is Re. 1/- per head, up to a maximum of Rs. 4/- per party.

2. At Senchal, Rangiroon and Badamtam the charge is annas four only for each person, up to a maximum of Rs. 4/- per party.

Fees.

3. Refund of bungalow fees is not allowed after issue of a pass, unless it is cancelled.

4. Fees for such occupation must be paid in advance to the Deputy Commissioner, or the Executive Engineer, as the case may be.

5. Out-station cheques in payment of fees should include annas four for every Rs. 25/- or part thereof, as discount.

Furniture.

Beds, tables, chairs, lamps and wicks, candlesticks, glasses and kitchen utensils are provided at each bungalow. Cutlery is provided in all Sikkim bungalows, but no *mattresses*. Tourists should therefore take their own bedding, linen, candles, oil for lamps, provisions, and, in the Darjeeling district, *cutlery*.

Provisions.

Ordinary bazar supplies are obtainable at Jorepukri, Dentam, Kalimpong, Tista Bridge, Pedong, Namchi, Pakyong, and Rhenock, 3 miles from Ari (see Kalimpong tours). The quicker one gets reconciled to tinned provisions the better.

Firewood.

Firewood is supplied free of charge in the Nepal frontier road bungalows. At Kalimpong and Gangtok the charge is annas four a maund, and in bungalows in Sikkim, except Gangtok, annas two a maund, which is payable in advance.

Servants.

1. A sweeper can be hired at Kalimpong, Jorepukri, Tista Bridge, Rungpu, Sankokhola, Gangtok, Pakyong, Namchi, and Rhenock.

2. Elsewhere tourists must take a sweeper with them, as no pass will be issued except on this condition.

3. There is no resident khansama (cook) at any bungalow.

A table of rates is obtainable from the Vice-Chairman of the Municipality.

Porters.

Eight annas a day (but they will not stir under 10 to 12 annas) is the average charge for each porter hired in Darjeeling; annas six if hired at Kalimpong or in Sikkim.

Frontier Passes.

Two passes are needed, one for entering and another for leaving Sikkim, at a cost of annas eight each for each person, in addition to the usual bungalow passes.

Shooting Permits in Sikkim.

For large game Rs. 30/- has to be paid to the Superintendent of this State, Gangtok; and Rs. 10/- for small or feathered game. Carnivora and pig may be shot without such permits.

CHAPTER II.

Pic-nics.

"We that live to please, must please to live".—*Dr. Johnson.*

1. Lloyd Botanic Garden—see page 91.
2. The Victoria Falls —,, ,, 92.
3. Birch Hill Park —,, ,, 93.
4. Observatory Hill (7,163′). Darjeeling, derives its name from 'Dorge,' the Llama in charge in 1835 of the Tibetan monastery, which was built on this hill just 156 years ago. In 1860-61 this monastery was transferred to the flat to the north-east corner of St. Andrew's Church, and in 1878-79 was finally removed to Bhutia Busty where it still exists. The numerous flags on the summit of this hill shew that it is still revered by the Buddist who weekly proceed to it in gay parties composed chiefly of women. There are two caves on the western side of the hill, the lower and larger one according to tradition leads to Tibet. But there is a phenomenon well-worth visiting; and that is the natural stone bridge over the Ramman river at its junction with the combined streamlets—the Ratho and Sri. In the present Gompa, or monastery at Bhutia Busty, which is two-storied, the priests live in the upper flat, while the lower contains numerous praying wheels one of which is over 6 feet in height to which is attached two bells. When revolved it does produce most weird and uncanny sounds! The following account by Sir J. D. Hooker of the devotions performed at these monasteries answers in general for all the monasteries to be met with in the country :—

"We were awakened at daylight by discordant orisons of the Llama; these commenced by the boys beating drums and the great tambourine, then the blowing of conch-shells, and finally the trumpets and thigh-bones. Shortly after the Llama entered, clad in scarlet, shorn and barefooted, wearing a red mitre, a loose gown girt round the middle, and an undergarment of questionable colours, possibly once purple. He walked along slowly muttering his prayers, to the end of the compartment, whence he took a brass bell and a dorge, and sitting down cross-legged, commenced matins, counting his beads, ringing a bell and uttering most dismal prayers. After various disposal of cups, a large bell was violently rung for some minutes, himself snapping his fingers and uttering most unearthly sounds. Finally, incense was brought of charcoal with juniper twigs—it was swung about, and concluded the morning service—to our great relief, for the noises were quite intolerable".

This hill is probably for the great majority of visitors the easiest and best place from which to see the snowy range, for from its ridge more than 32 peaks 24,000 feet in height are visible. The ascent if made a little before break of day repays the trouble involved for the sight that greets the vision baffles description, and we stand in silent wonder at the work of the Great I Am. The snowy range appears at first as a pale, cold gray mass until kissed by the first rays of the rising sun which causes it to blush in shades of light purple and pink to be followed by a rich golden sheen which in turn fades away into the dazzling white mantle it wears throughout the day; to be renewed at the shade of eventide by the same tints of the morning, but oh ! so subdued.

This range seems to be so near. A reference to the Sketch Map of Tours (Plate XIII) however will shew that the peaks, Janu, Kabru, Kinchenjunga and Pandim which appear to be in a straight line are not so due to the dazzling whiteness which causes all sense of perspective and proportion to be lost. As a matter of fact the dual-pointed Kinchenjunga,* the highest of these four peaks, is 8 miles behind Kabru, and fully 12 behind Pandim. The mountain range in Sikkim, *i.e.*, the peaks we see, is widest between Kinchenjunga and Kabru and tapers away in either direction, which in the east terminates at Narsing (19,250′). During summer the permanent snow line stands at

---

*All attempts to scale the heights of Kinchenjunga, including the last by a party of Americans led by a Swiss guide in October, 1898, have ended in failure. See also Appendix V.

16,000 feet, which during the winter advances to the 13,000 feet level.

Immediately below the spectator, and to the left of Lebong, the Rammian and Little Rangneet rivers combine and flow into the Great Rangneet which about 1½ miles above the Tista Bridge merges with the Tista, which rises on the further side of the Himalayas in lake Chalamu (17,500′) 74 miles to the north-east of Darjeeling. To the west is the Singalila range, which, with the Mechi river, forms the boundary between Darjeeling and Nepal; while on the east is the Takdah Spur (on which the Gurkha cantonments have been erected) over which we can see the plains of Jalpaiguri in the dim distance; and beyond and to the north-east on a clear day may be seen the cottages of the Colonial Homes in Kalimpong. These homes may also be seen from the Mall just above the Volunteer Headquarters.

Our reveries will probably by the time these observations have been made and noted be disturbed by the rays of the rising sun warming up unpleasantly; or by the advent of some devotees at the Llamaserai; but we shall retrace our steps feeling all the better for this one silent hour during which we have been face to face with the Great Unknown—

"What art thou, Mighty One! and where thy seat?
  Thou broodest in the calm that cheers the lands,
And thou dost bear within thine awful hands
  The rolling thunders and the lightning fleet.
In the drear silence of the polar span
  Dost thou repose? or in the solitude?
Vain thought! the confines of his throne to trace
  Who glows through all the fields of boundless space".—

H. K. White.

5. Senchal [A. 8,163′]* is 5 miles while Tiger Hill (Plate XII) is 7 miles to the south-east of the town. To see

---

*Capital letters, or numerals within brackets immediately following the names of the several tour-stages indicate their position on The Sketch Map of Tours. These should enable the tourist to work out the routes decided upon without any difficulty whatever; indeed, it is to be hoped that the map will be found useful.

the sun rise, and also Everest (the lot of the happy few) one must either awake at 3 a.m., and proceed there on ponies or dandies, or sleep over-night at the Senchal bungalow. The ascent starts a little beyond Jorebungalow, and although the path is steep and over 3 miles long, it is broad enough to admit two horsemen to ride abreast of each other. At the summit and to the north is the bungalow ; the solitary, dilapidated chimney which marks the site of the first military barracks and the Golf links lie to the south. From this spot, or Tiger Hill (8,515′, where there is only a pavilion and tower) we may see Everest, which is fully 107 miles away, over the Singalila range and a little to the left of Phalut, apparently standing between but really miles behind the two other peaks, which though actually smaller look the larger of the two. Facing Kinchenjunga, the highest glaciers* in the world (13,000′) can be seen by the unaided eye. Indeed, in 1913, from the town itself a large black mass (probably a huge boulder) could be seen daily slipping lower and lower for a period of three months until it fell over the glacier into the depths below. Silvery, snow-fed streams may also be seen meandering down the sides of these mountains until they flow into the Ramman, Little and Great Rangneet rivers. To the south stands Kurseong perched on either slope of '*Eagles Crag*' ; further on the plains are seen as through a glass darkly, while some even maintain that river steamers may be watched plying on the Ganges ; but the Mechi, Balasan, Mahanadi and Tista rivers shine out quite distinct like silver bands. Immediately below the observer range after range, placed like terraces, one above the other, and peak after peak with beautiful valleys between arrest the attention ; beyond are seen upland and dell, thorpe and towering crag, smooth slope and jagged ravine, all massed with romantic imagery, all budding with eager life ; while the panorama of blue-grey appears in the dim distance to melt into one great chain on which the play of sunshine and shadow, broken here and there

---

*Four glaciers radiate from this peak :—The Zemu, 18 miles long, and the Tangla, both of which drain into the river Tista ; the Kinchen, 15 miles long, and the Yalung which drain into the Arun and Kosi rivers in Nepal, respectively.

PLATE XII.

SUNRISE FROM TIGER HILL.

"I stood upon the hills when the heaven's wide arch
Was glorious with the sun's returning march
And woods were brightened, and soft gales
Went forth to kiss the sun-clad vales,
The clouds were far beneath me".—*Longfellow.*

by bright, flashing cascades which rush headlong through wooded ridges scoured by landslip and torrent, are sights never to be forgotten. Turning in the opposite direction, we see the cantonments of Katapahar and Jalapahar with the cottages of Darjeeling standing out most prominently in the lurid glare of day. On the return journey a visit to the Catchment Area and settling tanks, which collect the water for consumption of the inhabitants of the town from 26 springs, would well repay the time spent in walking over their boundaries.

6. Rangiroon [B. (5,700′)] is 6¼ miles from Darjeeling on the Peshok Road, but as it is much below the main road is seldom, if ever, visited. The original Botanic Garden was laid out here in 1876, but owing to the locality being subject to frequent hailstorms the site was abandoned in favour of the one now located in the town.

7. Badamtam [C. (2,500′)] is on the road which skirts the Great Rangneet river, and on the route to the Tista Bridge. It is 7½ miles from the Mall. The old cane (Calamus) structure which acted as a bridge has given place to one of iron with a span of 300 feet. The river at this point is fully 250 feet wide, and although these cane structures were erected 40 feet above normal level yet they were often washed away by a sudden rise of the river, thereby giving one an idea of the heavy rainfall our hills are subject to. The way is steep, the valley narrow, making the heat during summer unbearable, for it is fully 4,000 feet below Darjeeling. And now for a tip worth remembering. On no account be persuaded to have a dip in the river for it is not only treacherous* but the water also is so cold that many a chill has been contracted to be followed by inflammation of the liver.

---

*The late Mr. G. P. Robertson, Engineer to the Municipality, was drowned early in 1915 while engaged in surveying this river in a jolly boat, which was never seen again notwithstanding its air-tight compartments.

WEEK-END TRIPS.

About Darjeeling.

Admission to the following bungalows is granted by the Forest Officer, Darjeeling Division, to whom application should be made at the Kutchery :—

Bungalows.		*Altitude.*	*Miles.*	*From.*
Battassi	...	6,958′	5	N.-W. of Jorapukri.
Debripani	...	6,000′	2½	S. of Do.
Lepchajagat	...	7,000′	5	W. of Ghum.
Palmajua	...	5,900′	4	N. of Tonglu.
Rambi	...	6,250′	5	S.-E. of Ghum.
Ramman	...	7,500′	7	S.-E. of Phalut.
Rimbick	...	7,980′	6¼	N. of Palmajua.

Off the Peshok Road.

Bungalows.		*Altitude.*	*Miles.*	*From.*
Jaisi	...	4,200′	2	N. of Lopchu.

Toong.

Babukhola	...	5,978′	4	E. of Toong.

About Kalimpong.

The following Khas Mehal bungalows* and that at Tarkhola (at the 9th-mile on the cart road to Sikkim) are in charge of the Divisional Forest Officer, Kalimpong Division :—

Dalopchan.	Paten Godok.
Gorubathan.	Samthar.
Kumai.	Sinjee.
Mongpong (near Sivoke).	Siokbir.
Nimbong.	Targta.
Pagriabong.	Tarkhola.
Pankasari.	Tolo.

***Note.**—Each of these is about 5 miles apart.

Tips to Tourists.

"Cheerful at morn he wakes from short repose,
Breathes the keen air, and carols as he goes".—*Goldsmith.*

Touring is best undertaken from the latter half of October till the end of January. Altitudes higher than 12,000 feet should be avoided lest one gets snowed up in the passes. February is always misty, while March brings in the usual east wind, so dreaded at home. April ushers in the spring with its occasional showers against which a good thick mackintosh should be provided; to be followed by May which is ideal in regard to both climate and scenery, for the hillsides and fields have burst forth into blossom, the rhododendron and sweet scented magnolia predominating. Therefore, choose November for the majestic grandure of its scenery, and May for botanical revelations in colour.

Seasons for Touring.

The active and hardy walk the entire distance, and so renew their vitality; the more opulent usually ride, while ladies can be carried all the way in dandies, which require 6 bearers, 3 in each relay. Ladies may with full confidence undertake these journeys alone as the coolie-sirdars, who accompany such parties, consider their safety a personal matter.

Locomotion.

As variations in temperature are extreme touring should be done in shirt-sleeves and 'shorts', with a heavy overcoat ready to hand on the saddle, or carried by a follower, for use when heights are climbed. The 'shorts' should be just long enough to tuck into the putties or gaiters when the path lies through undergrowth in forest tracts to prevent leeches getting at one. An extra pair of boots with hobnails, such as 'ruggers' use, preferably an old one for comfort, should be worn, with a spare one at hand, for the mountain paths are sharp and wear through these in no time. To those not used to much walking the following tip is worth bearing in mind:—Dust French chalk into the footwear each morning before starting, and rub the heels and toes of the socks with the end of a tallow candle, both of which will help materially in avoiding

Clothing, &c.

Care of Feet.

blistered feet. This is what the 'regulars' do when on the march: a tip I have followed to advantage. Also remember that in going downhill especially the strain is over the toes and instep just where the lacing catches the instep. So avoid sore feet, or else the pleasures of the trip will be marred, if it does not bring it to an early close.

Outfit.

The outfit should consist of the following (to which each one can add as best suits him or her):—a large luncheon basket, a thermos, large bottle of water, cutlery for day's use, enamel plates and glasses, a few glass bottles (such as those in which Pascal's jams are sold) into which the contents of sealed tins may be tipped as soon as opened as otherwise they are likely to cause an awful mess in the tiffin basket, a holdall, mosquito-net (when travelling in the valleys), a mackintosh and a heavy overcoat. Ladies should make provision for their apparel as only rough washing will be done by camp followers.

Camp Followers.

Any old experienced servant in the station can produce a reliable coolie-sirdar who will furnish the required number of porters, who should not number more than 6 a head of the party; while J. F. Madan (in Post Office Road), the well-known provision merchant, will in a trice work out for the tourist his exact requirements for each trip, or round.

When touring, the charge should not exceed Rs. 10/- per head per day; and, obviously, the larger the party the cost should proportionately be less. Thus:—*Kit* Re. 1/- to 1/8 per day, *Khansama* the same, Sweeper annas twelve to Re. 1/-; the remainder on coolies, who demand annas twelve each day, although the tariff fixed by the municipality is annas eight. The above, of course, does not include the hire of ponies or horses which varies from Rs. 3/- to Rs. 5/- per day according to the season in which engaged, that is, the latter amount is demanded during the poojahs.

Pests.

Coming in contact with porters by means of the *impedimenta,* one is liable to get infested with vermin; therefore, the underlinen especially should be examined every morning before setting out. No known specific helps keep them off. Leeches get into the shoes, &c. through the eyelet holes. Never pluck them off, but just drop a pinch of salt over their mouths and they will fall off immediately; then press the bleeding wound (which continues bleeding owing to the exudation caused by suction) until it stops. Tree-tricks, which are small, brown creatures, get on to the lower limbs chiefly by the score when going through heavy undergrowth. Similarly, never pluck them off as they leave their heads behind in the cuticle and so cause nasty little ulcers; just cut their bodies off with a pair of scissors when the head and thorax will wriggle and fall off. Mosquitoes and sand-flies, also a little insect, known locally as 'pipsies', can be easily warded of by anointing the exposed parts with Citronella oil. Lastly, towards dusk always keep your eye well on the path lest you stumble on a reptile, which, if left alone will clear out of the way.

Medicine Chest.

The medicine chest should contain the following (to which each one can add as he thinks best) :—Rubini's tincture of camphor, vegetable tabloids, asperine or chlorate of potash for mountain sickness, (or homœopathic remedies mentioned at the beginning of the work), quinine in solution with sulphuric acid (as its action is thereby increased), boracic acid powder, cotton wool, bandages, chlorodyne, a small flask of brandy, carbolised wool, vaseline, an ounce of permanganate of potash, a sharp scalpel, and a pair of scissors.

Reading Matter.

The unwritten law demands that each tourist shall leave behind magazines, books, &c., which he has read, at the several dak bungalows, thereby forming a fresh library for those to follow. The following books of reference may be consulted with advantage before undertaking the trip, or round :—

Hooker's—'Himalayan Art Journals' published in 1854.

Gazetteer of Sikkim (1894) which has an interesting introduction by H. H. Risley.

J. C. White's (the 1st Political Officer at Sikkim)—'Sikkim and Bhutan'.

Waddell's—'Among the Himalayas'.

Bridle-paths, which intersect the whole country, lead to every place of interest; while the dak bungalows, which are separated by easy stages, are adequately furnished to meet all requirements. It should, however, be noted that the beds in all Sikkim bungalows are covered with cotton webbing, which requires a *razai*, or cotton quilt, thrown over them to make them comfortable and warm. To this may be added the holdall, which helps keep off the damp feeling one experiences in the higher altitudes.

Rest-Houses.

PLATE XIII.

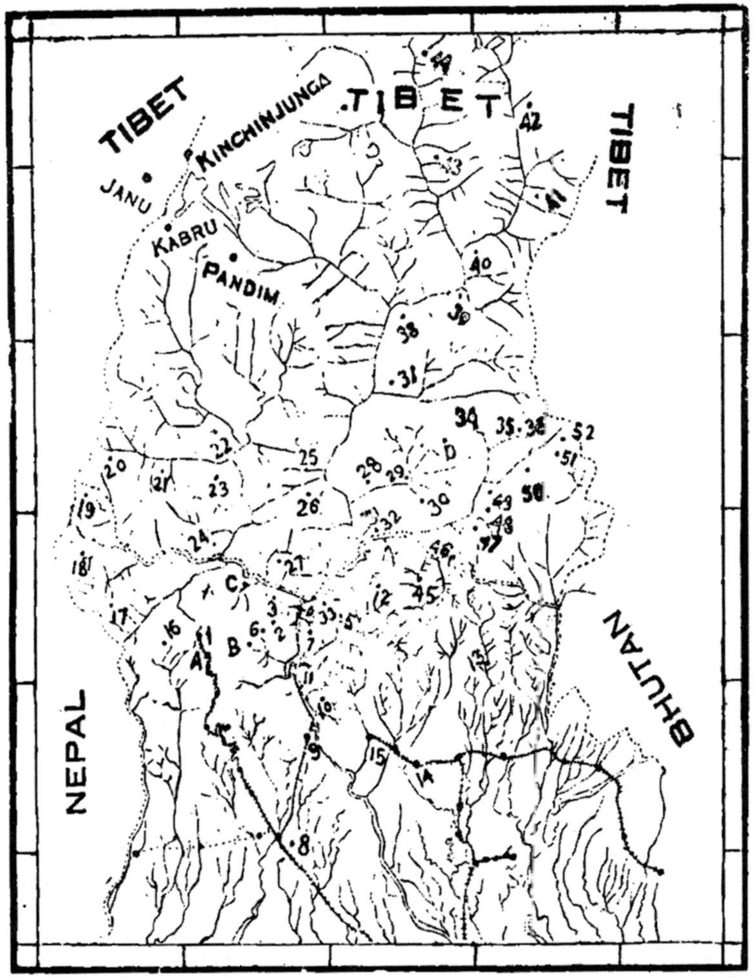

Key to Map.

Pic-nics.

A = Senchal
B = Rangiroon
C = Badamtam

Tours.

Darjeeling (x) to Kalimpong (5)
via Peshok Road
1 = Ghum   3 = Peshok
B = Rangiroon   4 = Tista Bridge
2 = Lopchu   5 = Kalimpong
via Rangneet River
C = Badamtam
Along river
4 = Tista Bridge
5 = Kalimpong

Darjeeling (x) to Riang (7)
via 6th. Mile   6 = Rangli Rangliot
B = Rangiroon   7 = Reang

Siliguri to Tista Bridge
8 = Siliguri   11 = Birrik
9 = Sivoke   7 = Riang
10 = Kalijhora   4 = Tista Bridge

Kalimpong to Plains
5 = Kalimpong   or
12 = Rissisum   15 = Bagrakote
13 = Daling Fort   9 = Sivoke
14 = Dam Dim,   8 = Siliguri
Jalpaiguri,

Nepal Frontier, and Back
1 = Ghum
16 = Jorepukri
17 = Tonglu
18 = Sandakphu
19 = Phalut
20 = Chiabhunjan
21 = Dentam
22 = Pamionchi— 23 = Rinchipong
24 = Chakung
x = Darjeeling.
25 = Pamionchi— 25 = Kewsing
26 = Temi
27 = Namchi
C = Badamtam
x = Darjeeling.

Tours. (*Contd.*)

Darjeeling (x) to Gangtok (D)
C = Badamtam   D = Gangtok
27 = Namchi   30 = Pakyong
26 = Nemi   31 = Sankokhola, or
28 = Sond   32 = Rangpu
29 = Shamdong   33 = Melli, and back to Darjeeling by Tista Bridge and Rangneet River, or the Peshok Road.

Gangtok (D) to Natu Pass (35)
D = Gangtok
34 = Karponang
35 = Changu
36 = Natu Pass

Gangtok (D) to Lachen Pass (43)
D = Gangtok
37 = Dichu
38 = Singhi
39 = Toong
40 = Chungtang— 41 = Lachung
42 = Yeumthang
43 = Chungtang— Lachen
44 = Thangu

Kalimpong (5) to Gangtok (D)
5 = Kalimpong
4 = Tista Bridge   30 = Pakyong
32 = Rungpu   D = Gangtok

Kalimpong (5) to Jelap Pass (52)
45 = Pedong   50 = Gnatong
46 = Ari   51 = Kuphu
47 = Rongli   52 = Jelap Pass
48 = Sendochen
49 = Lingtu

Darjeeling (x) to Jelap Pass (52)
by Rangneet, or Peshok Road
4 = Tista Bridge
32 = Rungpu
47 = Rongli
48 = Sendochen
49 = Lingtu
50 = Gnatong
51 = Kuphu
52 = Jelap Pass

CHAPTER III.

List of Tours.

A—In the Darjeeling District.
- 1. Darjeeling to Kalimpong—
  - (*a*) *via* Peshok Road,
  - (*b*) *do*. Rangneet Road.
- 2. Darjeeling to Riang.
- 3. Siliguri to Tista Bridge.
- 4. Kalimpong to Plains—in the Duars.

B—Nepal Frontier and Back.

C—In Sikkim.
- 1. Darjeeling to Gangtok—
  - (*a*) *via* Singla Bazar,
  - (*b*) *do*. Badamtam.
- 2. Gangtok to Natu Pass.
- 3. Gangtok to Lachen Pass.
- 4. Kalimpong to Gangtok—
  - (*b*) *do*. Pedong.
- 5. Kalimpong to Jelap Pass.
- 6. Tista Bridge to Jelap Pass.

D—To Gyantse,—and the Beyond.

Tours.

Plate XIII.

Stages.	Distance between Stages. Miles.	Altitude in Feet.	Accommodation. Rooms.	Beds.	Mat-tresses.
A—Darjeeling District.					
1. Darjeeling to Kalimpong					
(*a*) *via* Ghum (1) to Rangiroon (B)	6½	5700	2	5	0
Lopchu (2)	7¾	5300	2	5	4
Peshok (3)	4¼	2600	4	6	0
Tista Bridge (4)	3¾	710	3	3	0
Kalimpong (5)	7	3933	6	8	8
(*b*) *via* Badamtam (C)	7	2500	2	5	0
Along Rangneet River*					
Tista Bridge (4)	18	710	3	3	0
Kalimpong (5	7	3933	6	8	8
2. Darjeeling to Riang (7) *via* Rangiroon (B) and 6th-Mile on Peshok Road					
Rangli Rungliot to Riang	23½	625	4	4	0

*At the 12th-mile is Margitar (1,906′).

TOUR A—I (a).

Darjeeling to Kalimpong.

"If thou wouldst learn a lesson, that will keep
Thy heart from fainting and thy soul from sleep,
Go to the woods and hills".—*Longfellow.*

The first stage is Lopchu, which is 14½ miles away.

At the first mile on the road, which runs due east from Ghum, is an unique trough on the retaining wall of which are two grotesque figures, the one representing Hanuman, the monkey-god, with a ponderous club with which he defeated the giants of Ceylon and so rethroned its king ; the other, a *Saisnag,* or serpent-god*. A mile and a half further, and on the left of the road, will be seen the bridle-path leading to the P. W. D. and Forest bungalows at Rangiroon, which are fully a mile below; hence they are seldom, if ever, visited. It was here that the original Botanic Garden was laid out. At the third-mile, and in the seat of the saddle of the hill, are tea-shops where your porters will doubtless stop to refresh themselves; and you may likewise give yourself a rest also. From here the road turns to the right of the ridge and continues on until the sixth-mile is reached, where there is a diversion due east to the Hum cantonments. Proceeding due north the Peshok road, which leads to Tista Bridge, is struck. At the tenth-mile is Lopchu,

---

*The oldest religious beliefs, that is, those that obtained among aboriginal tribes and Aryans, are connected with the worship of the spirits, the seasons and of Nagas or serpent deities, supposed to preside over springs, lakes, rivers, etc.; hence they correspond closely with the classical Naiads or Potameids.

We find that as in Burma, so here. If, unlike most of his countrymen, the paharie has succeeded in accumulating some wealth, his aim is to distribute it in good works. And if any worldly desire survives in his heart, it is to win the title of a builder of a monastery, or in a lesser degree the builder of a serai, or fount; titles to be bestowed on him (or his shades) by his fellow countrymen as an expression of respect, and dearer to him as implying a spiritual attainment than such earthly titles as Khan Bahadur, or even a C.I.E.-ship—

Oh, gentle shades; oh, gentle cool retreat
From all the immoderate Heat,
In which the frantick World does burn and sweat—

as the rippling waters overflowing from one terrace to another seem to personally invite the tired wayfarer to stay awhile and rest.

where there is a two-roomed, well-furnished house, with stables both above and below the road—which should be visited after off-saddling to see that your mount has had its full quantum of fodder. And now a word regarding the extreme hospitality of the people. I was once stranded for accommodation on my way up (the first in the many years which I have used this route) as I found the bungalow in occupation by a party of ladies; and as the night was fast closing in and bitterly cold I had to approach an old Bhutia lady, who lived in a small two-storied stone hamlet, and ask her for shelter ; or sleep in the native grog-shop. The hearty response was a surprise, while we parted the following morning both pleased with each other: I with the exceedingly comfortable night's rest, and she with what I handed her for the accommodation, though much against her will. On another occasion while travelling along the Riang route, *viz.*, Hum cantonments, an old man offered me a long drink of pure milk and a few oranges, both of which were most acceptable as the day was inordinately warm.

These kindnesses recalled—

> "But deep this truth impressed my mind,
>   Through all his works abroad,
> The heart benevolent and kind
>   The most resembles God".—*Burns.*

To resume.

From the verandah of the Lopchu bungalow one of the grandest and prettiest of views of the snowy range is obtainable. On the last occasion (1918) that I halted at this place a greater medley of colours, which perfectly harmonised, have I never seen although an old resident of these parts. Furthermore, as I had the time to *moon,* I intently watched the sun rise ; and that which struck me as novel at first was easily solved on reflection. This range appeared to be ever so much higher and grander than that ordinarily seen from Darjeeling, due to the fact that Lopchu is higher than the intervening hills, consequently more of the base of the snowy range comes into view thereby causing it to look larger and more majestic than when seen from other places in the district. At break of day the hills wore a coat of purple-gray; below the Rangneet and Tista rivers (which are about 850 feet above the level of the sea) were hidden from view by a soft, sinuous bank of fleecy mist (which rises during the winter from the hot streams) which floated hither and thither by the ever shifting wind. Then the rays lit up the peaks in touches of orange and gold, a marked contrast to the lower spurs which were still steeped in russet-browns; and finally, the peaks gradually and almost imperceptibly changed from gold to tints of the palest sea-green which were reflected on the delicate clouds which hovered over them. Such delicate greens above, such browns below are seldom seen.

From this bungalow the path while working its way through the several tea estates is so steep that further progress is usually accomplished on foot. Peshok, which is 4½ miles away, and at which there is a large roomy bungalow, is in a clearing of the forest. If you get so far, and are pressed for accommodation, push on sharp to the one at Tista Bridge where you are sure to get a room, as owing to its low altitude and its proximity to the native town is seldom, if ever, occupied. But hurry on as the darkness of this path is *feelable,* while it is at the same time the steepest on this route. 'View Point' which is ¾ of a mile from the last stage (Peshok) commands a view of the junction of the Tista and Rangeet rivers: hence its name. Lunch is often partaken of by tourists under this canopy while on their way back from Kalimpong.

From Peshok to the Bridge is 3½ miles, and thence to Kalimpong 9 by the cart road, and 7 by the bridle-path. It is best to dismount and cross the bridge on foot as animals are liable to get restive owing to the oscillation as its span is over 300 feet. Across the river, and at the ¼ mile post, is the turning of the path to Kalimpong, which breaks off abruptly and runs south just at the bend. This path is availed of by riders when entering Kalimpong, while the cart road is used on the return journey, as owing to the steep and stony nature of the track riding becomes impossible.

At the first mile is the *argard,* where the carters who ply for traffic along the valley live; at the second is a tea-shop at which you will more than probably find your porters refreshing themselves with this beverage. For the next 2½ miles the path intersects cultivated terraces of maize chiefly, and continues on until it meets the cart road at the 6½-mile. From here Peshok, Badamtam, the Railway Station, and the Tista gorge are seen distinctly. The last 2½ miles are done along the cart road, over which the going is easy. A quarter of a mile out of the town a path leads to the Circuit House (dak bungalow) which, as it is frequently occupied by the Governor of Bengal when he visits that station, is necessarily neat and scrupulously maintained. It takes just 2 hours to cover these 7 miles up-hill.

Time.—To Peshok and Back *via* Ghum or Badamtam—3 days.
To Kalimpong and Back *via* Ghum or Badamtam—4 days.

Tour A—I (b).

In addition to the reasons already given against "Badamtam," page 243, the journey along the bed of the Rangneet river to the Bridge is not recommended as this road invariably suffers from slips during the rains and cannot, therefore, be depended upon.

Plate XIII.

Stages.	Distances between Stages. Miles.	Altitute in Feet.	ACCOMMODATION Rooms.	Beds.	Mattresses
3. Siliguri (S) to Tista Bridge*					
Sivoke (9)	12½	500	No Bungalow		
Kalijhora (10)	5	550	3	4	0
Birrik (11)	4½	570	3	4	0
Riang (7)	3	625	4	4	0
Tista Bridge (4)	7	710	3	3	0
4. Kalimpong (5) to Plains					
via Rissum (12)	12	6410	4	4	0
Daling (13)	12	3350	No Bungalow.		
Dam Dim (14) in Duars	12	510		do.	
Thence Jalpaiguri, or Sivoke *via* Bagrakote.					

*Capital letters, or numerals within brackets immediately following the names of the several tour-stages indicate their position on The Sketch Map of Tours. These should enable the tourist to work out the routes decided upon without any difficulty whatever; indeed, it is to be hoped that the map will be found useful.

Tour A—3.

Plate XIII.

Siliguri to Tista Bridge.

If this journey is undertaken from the Bridge, the stages will of course be reversed, when the following account will be found of some use.

At present the Tista Valley train steams out of the platform just half an hour after the departure of the Darjeeling Mail, so that the tourist has ample time at his disposal. From Siliguri Road Station, which is reached within a couple of minutes from the time of starting, the line deflects from the main line to the north-east for the first five miles during which it passes through fields under cultivation, and along the cart road where from each bend are to be seen in the distance "towering high above the dark ramparts of the outer Himalayas, and glittering in the sunshine, the white fangs of India's icy sentinels, over 20,000 feet above sea-level".

At the fifth mile the train runs through the tall and stately belt of *Sal* forest which affords a cool and shady avenue several miles in length, being interspersed with other soft-woods, the chief being the *Khair,* or Catechu. At the ninth mile a forest track branches off the main road and runs due east to the village of Chamukdangi, the *El Dorado* of the huntsman. The track at the eleventh mile works its way through a deep cutting where the humus, the collection of ages, is seen lying 18 inches thick and black as coal, as also cane-brakes, the haunt of the tiger and the savage black panther. Emerging from this belt the Gorge of Sivoke (in what was once known as British Sikkim) is reached, while across the river is seen the outer ridges of the Kalimpong Sub-division which once formed a part of Bhutan proper, but which was annexed by us after the war of 1864-65. Below these spurs is the undulating country extending to Jalpaiguri on the one hand and the Duars on the other, which has been converted from dense jungle by British enterprise into flourishing tea estates.

This narrow, deep gorge through which the Tista flows

has by the Lepcha been well named Sivoke (The Gate of the Winds) for from 5 p.m. each day until 9 a.m., each morning the piercing, cold winds sweep dense masses of mist into the plains; the one taking its rise in the snow-capped mountains, the other born of the warmth of the flowing stream; both conducing to make the tract of country through which they sweep notorious as fever-laden and unhealthy in the extreme. Here, to the right of the little station will be seen a small village consisting of about 15 huts, which during the winter is populated by a motley crowd made up of hillmen from Darjeeling, who work as navvies on the line; Bhutias who find their way to the plains to beg in the most abject of postures as well as to lay their hands on everything within reach; Tibetans from the Land of Mystery engaged in bartering either ponies, mules, or shaggy dogs, called 'Chows,' which are exceedingly ferocicus and treacherous—marvellously like the Scotch Collie in appearance, for—

> "His breast was white, his touzy back
> Weel clad in coat of glossy black.
> His goucie tail, wi' upward curl,
> Hung ower his hurdies wi' a swirl".—

Gurungs with droves of sheep being rushed to the Mart at Matigora 3 miles out of the town of Siliguri; and pedlars from Sikkim offering bric-a-brac, and furs for sale.

The rushing waters of the river no longer confined by its walls of granite, nor obstructed by sunken rocks, spread out in a wide expanse over the plains which it fertilises by the alluvial deposit brought down from the mountains above. It eventually divides into three parts (Trisrota-Tista)—the Atrai, Purnabhadra and Karotoya which flow into the Ganges and the Brahmaputra, respectively.

On leaving Sivoke the train worms its way along the old cart road (which was aligned shortly after the district was annexed in 1850) which after the unprecedented flood of 1899 was abandoned for the new one* which is located a good deal

---

*This road which is fully 300 feet above the level of the river was completed in 1908-09 at a cost of 5 *lakhs* of rupees.

higher, and over which the pedestrian trudges his way from Siliguri to Gangtok, the capital of Sikkim, and even 49 miles beyond to the passes on the north-east which open out into Tibet.

Throughout the remainder of its length the line is laid on the right bank of the river, and about 100 feet above its level; and through dense jungle which laps the very edge of the stream, thus carrying one through the most magnificent river-scenery that it is possible to behold, with ever changing views and an endless succession of perfect pictures. In the clearings, especially at Kalijhora (Plate XV) and Riang, and even in some remote corners, collections of huts standing in twos and threes, and even solitary, surrounded by patches of cultivation consisting chiefly of maize, the staple product of the Lepcha, will frequently catch the eye.

This cart track was widened out of a much narrower one by the Madras Sappers in 1888 for the expedition commanded by General Graham, to drive back the Tibetans who had invaded Sikkim. It is reported that at that time many of its precipices were spanned by logs supported on frail posts driven into the ever shifting shaly soil; but these conditions no longer exist, for the road ever since the writer remembers it these 20 years and more, is well spanned by substantial bridges whose girders measure over 100 feet.

At the fifth mile from Sivoke is Kalijhora (the black stream) which takes its name from the coal seam at Daling, which lies midway between the Government Cinchona Gardens at Mongpu and Riang. At the latter station may often be seen tons of bark wrapped up in loose gunnybags, and innumerable drums of crude petroleum ether by means of which the quinine is extracted; while below the station are the two old pierheads over which a bridge once spanned the Riang streamlet. This structure, and a great part of the old road about this locality, were washed away by a rainfall of 27½ inches which fell in a single night throughout the district in 1899 and caused the disasters in Darjeeling, as also swept away the whole village at Tista Bridge.

The next run of 5 miles lands the tourist at Kalimpong

Road Station, the present terminus of this line. From here the Bridge is only a couple of miles further north, where a tolerable dak bungalow stands at 701′ feet above sea-level. Across the bridge, and 7 miles up-hill are the Colonial Homes referred to under "Kalimpong, Chapter II, Part II."

Fishing Grounds.

In the backwash at this spot the writer has seen a 60 pound masheer neatly gaffed after a couple hours' play. To leeward of this spot you will see a school of masheer feeding on the minnows that hang on the edges of the sunken rocks. Now for a good, long cast which will drop the fly over them. Let the baited hook sink a foot or so before drawing it up with a fluttering motion. They will see it and turn to grab at it; and soon a swift silvergrey gleam in the depths will be seen accompanied by a sudden swirl on the surface: you strike sharply and then the fish is matching its strength against the spring of the rod.

Its size can be gauged as it breaks water by the breadth of the tail—1 lb. of weight to every inch of tail, that is the accepted standard of measure. But wait till you have it fairly on the scales, for our trophies are usually magnified in conformity with 'the wish being father to the thought'.

A good bait for masheer fishing is made up as follows:—Fry rice until it assumes a light golden tint, then have it pounded fine and kneaded into boiled rice until the mass attains a putty-like consistence, by which the bait is enabled to hold on to the hook for hours. The ground should also be well strewn with particles of this bait, as the aroma draws fishes, as no other bait does. This simple bait has secured in this locality more fish than all the patent devices known to anglers.

(a) The other fishing grounds are:—

A. Following the course of the Tista northward from Riang:—

1. At the junction of the Rangneet, about 1½ miles above the Bridge.
2. At Melli, which is at the 3rd-mile post on T. V. Cart road.

3. At the junction of the Rongli, which is 14½ miles from the Bridge.
4. At Sakankhola, which is 23½ miles from the Bridge.

B. Following the course of the Rangneet westward from the Bridge:—

1. Badamtam, about 7 miles from the Bridge, and same distance from Darjeeling.
2. At the junction of the Little and Great Rangneet rivers, about same distance to the north-west of Darjeeling.
3. At Singla Bazar.
4. At the junction of the Ramman and Rangneet rivers to the N.N-W. of Darjeeling.

The following are well worth remembering:—

1. "Just there, where the water, dark and cool,
Lingers a moment in yonder pool,
The dainty trout are at play;
And now and then one leaps in sight,
With sides aglow in the golden light
Of the long, *sweet summer day.*"

2. "When the stream be low and bright,
Be zure you put on the Blue Upright.
When rain has fallen and water's high,
The March Brown then be zure to try.
Don't be killing little uns when nobody's by
Or big uns 'll be scarce before you die."

3. This do indite—
When an *east* wind blows
No fish will bite;
So, cease from trying
Or you 'll soon be swearing
At the picture true
That Dr. Johnson drew,*
Of the disappointed angler.

The following is worth bearing in mind:—Never lift any article in the closet attached to this bungalow† (or, for that

*"Angling", he said, was "a fool at one end of the rod, and a float at the other".

†This bungalow has lately been demolished.

matter, any bungalow along this route) as you are likely to disturb a reptile. The writer once had a narrow escape from a cobra which lay coiled up behind the wash-bowl which he thoughtlessly lifted up. Therefore disturb such pieces of furniture with a stick before handling them.

The bungalow at Birrik is all that can be desired, indeed, it is one of the best, if not the best in Bengal; and no wonder, for it was fitted up to receive the bride of a P. W. D. *burrah sahib* (person of consequence) thereby earning it the soubriquet of 'Honeymoon House'.

The next bungalow is at Kalijhora, which like that at Riang, is situated at the junction of the black streamlet—Kalijhora—and the Tista. The final stage must be Siliguri, as there is no dak bungalow at Sivoke where the Tista debouches into the plains. If disposed to walk 12½ miles the tourist should entrain as far as Sivoke in order to march into Siliguri. On a full moon night no grander sight is possible, for the scenery of the forests in the Terai must be seen to be fully appreciated. When camping on the Sivoke ground the writer has essayed many such tramps leaving camp at 2 a.m. in order to catch the Darjeeling Mail at 7 o'clock, followed only by his gun-bearer and horse. On one occasion at the 7th-mile he had to wend his way with his heart in his mouth, as the saying goes, through a herd of wild elephants, numbering fully 60, which was feeding on either side of the road. As a rule these animals are harmless, but when they go must, or turn rogues they kill at sight and destroy whole villages.

Tour A—4.

Kalimpong to Plains.

PLATE XIII.

This route is only attempted by those provided with tents as there is no dak bungalow at Daling Fort, or intermediate stages.

The dak bungalow at Dam Dim is about a mile and a half to the south of the railway station of the same name. From here the traveller may entrain for Barnes Junction (see Part IV), cross the Tista in a ferry-boat at Karla Ghat and enter Jalpaiguri to catch the Down Darjeeling Mail; or he may proceed from Dam Dim to Bagrakote, walk 6 miles to the banks of the Tista and by 3 p.m. be crossed over in a dug-out, which is quite safe, to Sivoke station to await the down train to Siliguri, which connects with the E. B. Railway.

Tour B.

Nepal Frontier and Back.

PLATE XIII.

Stages.	Distance between Stages. Miles.	Altitute in Feet.	Accommodation Rooms.	Beds.	Mattresses
B—Nepal Frontier & Back.					
Ghum (1) to Jorepukhri (16)	12½	7400	3	7	6
Tonglu (17)	10	10074	3	7	6
Sandakphu (18)	14	11929	3	6	6
Phalut (19)	12	11811	3	7	5
via Chiabhunjan (20)		9000			
Dentam (21)	17	4500	3	4	0
Pamionchi (22) to	10	6920	3	4	0
(*a*) Rinchipong (23)	10	6000	3	4	0
Chakung (24)	11	5100	3	4	0
Darjeeling, or	20	6812	..	..	..
(*b*) Kewsing (25)	10	6000	3	4	0
Temi (26)	10	5000	2	4	0
Namchi (27)	10	5200	2	4	0
Badamtam (6)	10	2500	2	0	0
Darjeeling	7	6812	..	..	..

Note.—1. Animals should be tethered while grazing as they are likely to nibble the aconite, or deadly nightshade, which grows at these altitudes, and die.

2. Jorepukri or the two Pools, Tonglu or the Hill of Fire, Sandakphu or the Home of the Aconite, and Phalut or the Denuded Peak.

PLATE XIV.

Sectional View of Tour B—Nepal Frontier and Back.

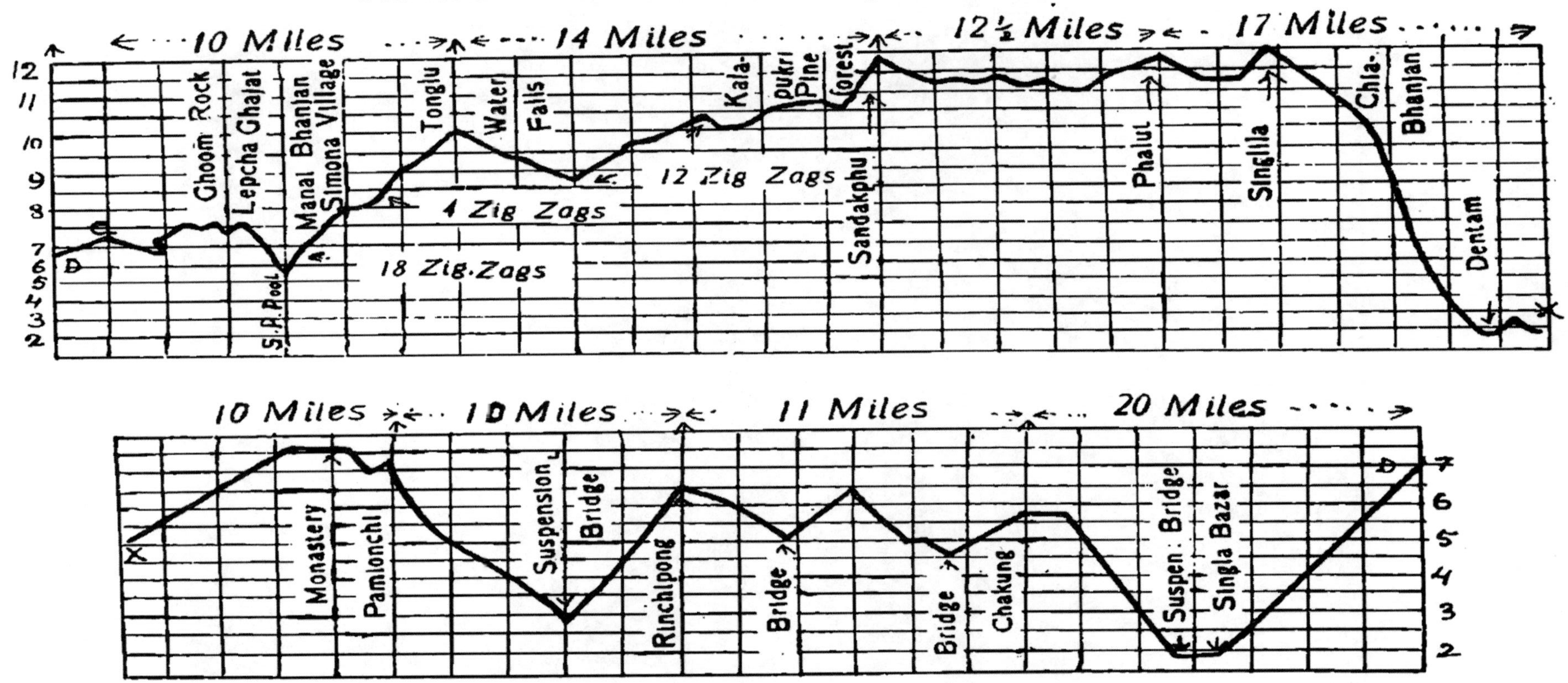

1. Numerals on side of blocks denote the altitude in thousands of feet.
2. Spaces between vertical lines denote an hour's march.
3. Distances between the respective halting stages are given at the head of each division marked by arrows.
4. For details see—"Extract from Diary of a Tourist."
5. Similar drawings to scale may be made by the Tourist from altitudes furnished under each tour.

Note.—This is the only complete Sectional Map ever offered the public: others have only the first part ending with Phalut.

PLATE XV.

KALIJHORA—TISTA VALLEY.

Extract from the Diary of a Tourist.

The traveller who can bring himself to endure the slight inconveniences which a separation from the flesh-pots of civilisation entails for a period of ten days only during which the round of the trip along the Nepal frontier is usually accomplished will become an enthusiast in mountaineering, and more than probably induce him on some future occasion to essay tours in Sikkim, 'the land of rice and fruit', whose llamas still desire it to be as esoteric as its religion—Buddism—but which progress has ordained otherwise. It should be borne in mind that only those enured to hard walking should attempt this tour on foot.

"Left Darjeeling (walking) at 8 a.m., passed through Ghum *via* Jalapahar at 9 o'clock, reached Sukiapukri in the valley at 11, from where the frontier Fort of Elam can be seen distinctly, and arrived at Siman at 12-30 p.m. From this spot there is a drop of two miles to the valley, below and thereafter a steady pull up to the *Tonglu* bungalow, which was reached at 5 p.m. The whole of the Kinchenjunga group is seen in a setting hardly to be matched elsewhere in the Himalayas. Leaving the following morning at 8 o'clock, and passing many a pretty landscape arrived at a small cluster of huts situated at the edge of a pool at 10 where a hasty repast was partaken of before attempting the climb to *Sandakphu,* which was eventually reached after essaying 25 steep zig-zags at the 32nd-mile at 2-30 p.m.: the heavy laden coolies arriving just an hour after. The panorama seen from the rising ground behind this bungalow as the sun rises over the 'Dome of the World', the grandest that human eyes can rest on inspired the following pulsating lines of Capt. F. A. M. Webster:—

Hast thou lain lonely on the hills at Dawn,
  To watch the splendour of the sun arise
Up from the stillness of his couch of morn—
  A heavenly wonder bared before thine eyes?

Or hast thou watched with trembling fear, to see
  Slim, groping, death-pale, primrose fingers clutch

The low-hung pall of Night's dim tapestry,
  Beheld the darkness quiver at their touch?

Saw'st thou one purest hyacinthine ray
  Projected far across an amber sky,
To light the glorious Angels of the Day
  Along the path where deep, black shadows lie?

Hast thou, unfriended, faced the cold, stark light;
  Laid bare thine inmost soul before thy God;
With upflung head, at passing of the night,
  Prepared to take the path the dead have trod?

I, too, have stood upon the beetling height—
  The restless, rolling waves surged to and fro—
And thrilled with awesome wonder at the sight
  Of Dawn upon the waters far below.

From here Phalut, and Everest, Mahakalu and Kinchenjunga—the first, third and fourth highest peaks respectively, and more than twelve other peaks higher than any in the word—can be seen. Starting from Sandakphu at 7 the following morning reached *Phalut* at 1 p.m. Weather permitting a bird's-eye-view of Darjeeling may be had, and by climbing another 600 feet on the ridge behind this bungalow one may, if lucky, obtain an excellent view of Everest. Passed a lake on the way which during the winter admits of skating on its frozen surface.

Braced by the exhilarating air of the past three days, the tourist turns gladly to the descent to Dentam. Sallying forth at 7 a.m. passed through Singalila at 8-30. On the ridge here stands a cairn built of stones which have been carried to the summit from the valley below by Buddist piety. Here the cold was intense, the air tingled the skin while the wind howled through the scrub and undergrowth, and even penetrated the hairy coats of the animals and made them shiver. From Singalila the road rises about 100 feet in the first half mile and then gradually drops to Chiabhunjan which is four miles away, and which is reached at about 10-30. From this point on to

PLATE XVI.

THE SNOWY RANGE.

Dentam, which was entered at 2-25 p.m. the way is so steep and rocky that if riding it were best to dismount for the gradient drops 5,500 feet in 4 miles, to rise again and drop once more another 500 feet respectively in the next 2 miles. Dentam is the main pass from the eastern valleys of Nepal into Sikkim. The bungalow here is perched on a hillock surrounded by rice-fields through which a hill-stream, which rises below Chiabhunjan, meanders and flows on until it merges in the Ramman river. Milk and eggs are obtainable here, while herds of cattle and sheep browse over its fertile fields. In the march from Singalila to Dentam a descent of over 6,500 feet must be made in one stretch before a first acquaintance with the beauties of Sikkim can be formed:—valleys, roads, waterfalls, flowers and all the varied changes in the fauna and flora which intervene between the Sub-Alpine and the Tropical; the first doubtless during summer and the rains being quite as trying to the temper as the muggy heat of the plains of Bengal. Leaving Dentam at 7 a.m. covered the 12 miles, which separates it from *Pamionchi,* by 1 p.m. First there is a rise of 300 feet over the crest of the hill to drop another 400 feet in the space of a mile then a fresh start for a steady climb of 3,000 feet in the next 6 miles, when from the ridge you see just two miles away the first monastery at an elevation of 6,920 feet. Of these Singachela is the larger of the two, while Pamionchi is the oldest in Sikkim. On entering either you will see drums placed on both sides of the entrance, and vessels containing holy water. The altar is at the extreme end of the hall, which is divided by two rows of wooden columns, into the nave and aisles, which are richly carved and painted in gorgeous colours, while the ceiling and walls are frescoed. On the altar are placed the images, usually the Trinity of the llamas, and before these are arranged the articles of their ritual, the seven bowls, the holy-water sprayer, named the Everlasting Tree, lighted lamps, incense-burners, &c. Behind the images are nitches in the wall in which are placed the sacred books and scrolls. The best time to visit these monasteries is between 2 and 3 p.m. (for an account of their mode of worship see Sir J. D. Hooker's description). From here as well as Kewsing, the peak of Janu is hidden behind Kabru (Plate XIII), and so Little Kabru is often mistaken for the greater. About 2 miles below, or some 1,700 feet vertically lies the bazar. The next stage, at the end of which lies *Rinchipong* (from which the British force was driven back to Darjeeling by the Sikkimese in November, 1860) just takes five hours to accomplish. In the first four miles the road drops 300 feet and lands one at the suspension bridge where the path is so narrow and curved that a dandy in use cannot pass. From this point onward, and for the next two miles, the climb is stiff over short zig-zags, while in the two following miles the gradient is easy over the 1,000 feet to be scaled before the bungalow is reached. Starting the following morning at sunrise, and passing over a series of low hillocks, reached *Chakung* at 2 p.m. Riding may be indulged in for the first three miles during which a drop of 1,500 feet takes place before the bridge is crossed: while in the next five miles the road rises another 1,500 feet to drop again some 2,000 feet when the second bridge is crossed; and finally another rise of 2,000 feet before the Chakung bungalow is entered. The next, and final stage can be done in 6½ hours. Leaving the bungalow at 5-30 a.m. reached Singla Bazar at 7 o'clock. Of the 7¼ miles which separates these two places, the road is level for about two miles, after which the descent to the suspension bridge over the Balasan river is gradual but steep, for in the remaining 5¼ miles the drop is 3,500 feet. On the other side of the bridge relief ponies may be had at Barnes Beg for the ascent to *Darjeeling*, which in the 8½ miles rises from 1,400 to 6,812 feet. Reached home tired and worn out at noon".

It will thus be seen that in endless succession high ridges are traversed and descents made into apparently bottomless valleys. On many of the ridges the icy blasts have denuded the landscape of all foliage: in the valleys the birds, blossoms, butterflies, the luxuriance of the foliage, and the gurgling of the streams—all, all suggest peace. While at the end of each day there is a sufficiency of food, a blazing fire to warm and to cheer, a clean bed, and that oblivion in sleep such as can only be induced by fatigue following these exhilarating marches.

Such are the allurements of mountain travelling; and if the tourist finds that he is able to contend against both privations and

PLATE XVII.

MOUNT EVEREST FROM SANDAKPHU.

strains which form voluntarily a part of his lot during such journeys it is more than probable that he will essay longer trips into Sikkim. There is Gangtok, the capital; and thence to the passes of over 14,000 feet elevation, which lead into Tibet; or he may strike off northward in the direction of Jangri, where the dak bungalow is unknown thereby necessitating the use of tents, which makes the pace much slower.

Time usually taken: Phalut and back 8 days: ditto *via* Pamionchi 9 days.

If Everest, which is 90 miles away, was unseeable at Senchal the tourist is sure to get a view of this, the highest known peak in the world from Sandakphu as shewn in Plate XVII. Being further away than Mahakalu (to the right of the picture) it appears the smaller of the two. This peak was named after Col. Sir George Everest, the founder of the Trigonometrical Survey of India. As it lies on the borders of the two closed lands—Nepal and Tibet—very little is known about it, or its surroundings. At Phalut, where the three States meet—Nepal, Sikkim and Darjeeling—the entire snowy range is visible, which from Kinchenjunga stretches away to Donkia (23,176′) and Sipmoochi (14,509′) on the borders of Bhutan on the east, and to Everest and the beyond on the west.

Everest (29,141′) was first noticed as late as 1849, and its height determined in 1852 only. Of the 75 peaks over 24,000 feet in height in the Himalayan range, 32 are located in the Nepal portion, and are easily seen by the unaided eye. It would be interesting here to record the height of the other known peaks of the world:—S. America can boast of its Aconcagua 22,800′, (Chili), Chimbarazo 20,500′ (Peru), and Klimani 22,000′ (Bolivia); while N. America comes next with its Mt. McKinley which is 20,464′ high; Brazil has its Popocatepetl 17,782′; and Japan's only snow-clad peak—Mt. Fuji-san—rises to a height of 12,395′. In Europe we have Mt. Blanc 15,760′ and Mt. Rosa 17,127′; New Zealand's Mt. Cook stands at 12,349′; while in the British Isles we have Ben Nevis 4,406′ and Snowdon 3,560′.

The thoughtful reader will have observed that the highest

peaks lie within the equatorial belt, while the others gradually decrease in height, (and especially toward the north pole), as they recede toward the nodal points—a fact which determined both the theory of their origin, as also that of earthquakes*.

As the tourist usually arrives at each stage at the close of day, when this range is covered by mists, all that is left to enjoy are the sunsets and sunrises, such as are only seen on these mountains. Nature at close of day is still, as if breathing its evening prayer, while mists nestle in the valleys below as if in sweet repose. Here we see a fleecy mass imperceptibly rising to soothe the wind-tossed summit; there a dark mass of cloud joining earth and heaven. On yon mountain summit each facet is scintilating with the hues of the rainbow, there a silver lining, beyond a touch of flaring red which gradually dies away into a golden sheen, while the emerald blue above is flecked with fleecy masses being whirled away nowhere. Where shall we turn and gaze in this ever changing kaleidoscope for the imagination runs riot, and we sit back to reflect on the wondrous works of Him who created all.

Then in the dusk of eventide the range stands out dark, clear and magnified: silence reigns for a brief period between the transition of day to night which is soon broken by the *whirr* of insects thereby intensifying the stillness of the night

---

*The luscious apple has thrice played an important part in the history of the world in that it was the cause of the downfall of Adam (*cum grano salis*), while its own fall enabled Newton to determine the Law of Gravity, and incidentally that of the rise and fall of tides; and also a later English scientist (whose name I can't recall) to set at rest for ever the preposterous theory of the origin of mountains, which, prior to his time, was ascribed to upheavals by a force which, if it did exist, would have shattered our planet into fragments.

On closely observing an apple drying his attention was drawn (1) to ridges which deepened as the fruit became drier, (2) that they lay within a central band, and (3) became less pronounced, especially on the upper half, as they advanced toward the nodal points or poles.

With these facts staring him in the face (and its repetition on our own globe) he proved to the satisfaction of the Learned Society of Europe that our mountains came into being by shrinkage alone: thus also proving incidentally that as the central portion of the earth cooled and shrank so also large crusts of its surface no longer having sufficient support fractured and fell, until brought up with a jerk, on to the molten mass thus causing 'quakes', as well as, by the extreme and sudden pressure exerted on the interior of the earth, volcanic eruptions. See also note on following page.

vaulted in by an emerald arch through which the twinkling stars shine out resplendent.

"A hush in the scented valley
  Packed full of purple shades;
A streak in the far horizon
  Where the last red glimmer fades.

A glimpse of the night's fair lady
  Descending her golden stairs,
To stretch her wide arms seaward
  In hallowing tender prayer".—*Gerve Baronti.*

Nature is now reposing against the breaking of the coming dawn, when the shadows fade away and life once more is on its daily round. What a spectacle is again presented to our gaze! In icy paleness the whole of the range shines out bright and clear to assume delicate mauve and rosy tints as soon as the facets of each peak are kissed by the rays of the rising sun.

Tour B—(b).

(*Page 260.*)

In lieu of this tour we shall here give that from Darjeeling to Kewsing (which virtually takes these stages in reverse order) then Temi, Singtam, Rangpu, Tista Bridge and Darjeeling.

You proceed along the Rangneet road, to the east of the Mall, and after passing through the Cantonment of Lebong get a splendid view of the Rangmo streamlet (through the ever shifting mists which rise from its waters) which flows from Senchal to the east of Darjeeling. A little beyond the towers

---

On August 26th, 1883, the volcano at Krakatoa in the Sunda Straits burst forth with such a terrific explosion that the sound was heard as far as the island of Rodriguez, 3,080 miles away! This island is between Sumatra and Java. Stones and ashes, according to competent authority, were hurled 17 miles high, while the finer palpable dust was borne nearly all round the world. Every village and town upon its coasts were smashed to atoms, and about 40,000 people were killed. Within a radius of 100 miles the sea itself was covered with lava, which scraped clean the sides of the vessels which were making for that once port. This catastrophy, which was one of the greatest in the history of the world, was described by a wag on his way to Australia, thus:—'Krakatoa cracked into two, and the Straits of Sunda burst asunder'.

of the old fort of Darwa Garat, through which our small force beat a hasty retreat in 1861, is seen standing boldly out against the sky-line; while below and in the valley is the suspension bridge at Badamtam, on crossing which you are challenged by the police located at Margitar on the further side for the frontier pass. From this village the road rises through dense forest composed of the stately *Sal* (*Shorea robusta*) which clothes the Terai, and the hill surfaces, up to the 2,500 feet level until you reach the bungalow built by the hospitable landlord, where lunch is usually partaken of prior to attempting the climb to the village of Kittam. From points of vantage along the road good views of the Rangneet and its valley are obtained; the right bank with its dark green tea bushes, with here and there the white cottages of the respective planters, stands out in bold relief—Badamtam, then Lopchu and Peshok—on the left bank are the holdings of the Nepalese and the hamlets of the aboriginal Lepchas surrounded by patches of verdant green cultivation which consists mainly of maize, millet and rice crops. Kittam is composed of about 20 hamlets very Swisslike in appearance with each supporting a balcony, or verandah of its own.

As you ascend the hill, and when nearing Namchi, the landscape unfolds itself; and on the Rinchipong range to the east stand out the Scots' Kirk with the Colonial Homes a little above and to its north-east on the Deola Hill, all shining in the rays of the setting sun. At last the dak bungalow, which is a clean, comfortable place having two bedrooms and a sitting-room.

Early the following morning by ascending a slight eminence above the bungalow you get a view of the undulating downs of the Sikkim valley whose base are covered with cultivation while the crowns are clothed in trees, and each in turn rising higher and higher in terraces. On the right is the Tedong spur fully 8,000 feet above the Rangneet, which in turn is 1,000 feet above sea level. Climbing another 1,000 feet, and about a mile away is a monastery in the upper storey of which are treasured the 100 and odd volumes of the Kanjur. Getting over Tedong a climb through dense forest stares one in the face before you get to Damthong—then another stiff ascent fully 5 miles in length before an elevation from which looking back on Darjeeling you see Senchal with Tiger Hill in the background, and possibly, if the day be fair, a view of the houses in Darjeeling: turning to the north you see the Tista with its mountain range behind which nestles Gangtok, the capital of Sikkim. From this last point of vantage a descent of 3 miles must be made before the Kewsing-bungalow is reached, and from which you can see to the west Pamionchi with Sanga Choling above it, and on the Phalut spur; on the east is the Darting monastery, and beyond the valley is Ralong with Sonook facing it; while below rests the great monastery of Tahsiding.

Starting very early the next morning so as to get through as much of the distance as possible during the cool hours of the day, you descend to cross the Ralong streamlet by means of a bamboo bridge before reaching Pamionchi. To get to this stream the path descends nearly 4,000 feet, which consumes fully an hour and a half. It is only about 35 yards wide. The ascent from its bank is very steep and over stone steps which zig-zag up the surface of the hillside. Tahsiding although the second oldest monastery in this State has acquired a sanctity peculiar to itself and has in consequence drawn devotees from Mongolia, China, Tibet, Nepal and Bhutan thereby adding to the magnitude of its cemetery, which is covered with *chortens*. In the centre of this monastery are enshrined a very large image of the Budda with two of his most devoted disciples, one on either side. But the image which attracts attention is that of Chenrezie with its thousand hands and eyes, the former being arranged in a circle round its torso, and in the multiplicity of its arms recalls the Hindu god Kali which has four only ; thus proving how the two religions in contiguous proximity gradually absorbed the ritual of its neighbour.

Descending from this sacred hill the Ratong is reached, to essay another climb of 500 feet over steep surfaces, which will land you at the day's goal, a distance of 20 miles in all, but which has consumed 9 solid hours. The morning following comes the reward for hard climbing—as grand a sight as one could wish for. Straight before you, and facing the verandah of the bungalow, rise Kabru, Pandim, and Kinchenjunga with Narsing on its left, with the intervening valley of the Ratong unfolding itself in all its pristine grandeur. Here is a little monastery called Dubdi, or 'the hermit's cell', perched on the mountain side ; while 3 miles higher up is the Changachelling monastery built over 300 years ago. From its platform Senchal with Tiger Hill behind is easily seen by the unaided eye, while if the morning be clear Darjeeling also comes into the landscape. Finally, Pamionchi, the oldest monastery of Sikkim, as it was erected in 1450 A. D., with its 20 odd attendant llamas and monks whose head-gear is peculiar. Those worn by the former are red and mitre-shaped, while that of the latter is curved and dropping in front with lapels on either side.

The next stage is 21 miles away. You must first descend to the banks of the Rangneet, which is 4,500 feet below, by a path which covers 6 miles. On the way down a *mandong,* or a sermon in stone, which was built by the fourth Maharaja of Sikkim, is passed. The river is crossed by a frail bamboo bridge before starting the ascent to Kewsing on the opposite spur where lunch is gladly partaken of, before attempting the final climb, which lands one at an elevation of fully 6,000 feet above sea level, and from where the following places are seen:— Tahsiding immediately below with Senin behind it; then Pamionchi in the distance with Changachelling above and beyond in the dim distance; while Ralong is in the near foreground, and Dorling only 3 miles further off.

From Kewsing you rise slowly through 3 miles of forest to get to Danthong and the summit to Temi beyond. Close to the last is the first European habitation—that of Mr. and Mrs. Mackean of the Scots' Mission—the sharp defining line between the land under the sway of Buddism and Christianity.

From the Temi bungalow the stately firs are seen which demarcate the road to Song and Gangtok. Five miles beyond is the Keri stream; 2 miles further is the Kotol suspension bridge which spans the Tista at the Singtam bazar. Proceeding another 7 miles to the south Sankonkhola is reached, which is the next stage to Rangpu (on the Rongli rivulet which separates

British territory from the Sikkim State) a mart of some size resting on a flat to the north-east of which lies the bungalow on a knoll, while to the south-west stands the cottages built for the staff of the Telegraph Department when the Sikkim Expedition of 1888 took place, and which once more came into use when our Armed Mission crossed over the Jelap Pass in 1903 on its way to Lhasa. Thereafter, the site proving extremely malarious, the staff was transferred to Gangtok. Here are the copper mines worked now under the latest European methods by an enterprising firm in Calcutta which has obtained concessions on this, and other monopolies from the Sikkim Durbar.

The next stage is Melli 10½ miles further south (or a push on the Peshok 17 miles away so as to be above the malarial zone), then Lopchu or Darjeeling, according to the stamina of the traveller.

IN SIKKIM.

Tour C.

PLATE XIII.

Stages.	Distance between Stages. Miles.	Altitude in Feet.	Accommodation Rooms.	Beds.	Mattresses
C—In Sikkim.					
(1) Darjeeling to Gangtok					
Badamtam (C)	7	2500	2	5	0
Namchi (27)	10	5200	3	4	0
Temi (Turko) (26)	10	5000	3	4	0
Song (28)	11	4500	3	4	0
Shamdong (29)	4	2300	2	4	0
Gangtok (& Back)	12	5800	5	4	0
Pakyong (30) to	10	4700	2	4	0
Sankokhola (31), or	10	1400	3	4	0
Rungpu (32)	10	1200	4	4	0
Melli (33), and back to	10	800	2	4	0
Darjeeling		6812	—	—	—
(1) (*a*)—Darjeeling *via* Tista Bridge.	Inverse order of above.				
(2) Gangtok to Natu Pass (36)					

Stages.	Distance between Stages. Miles.	Altitude in Feet	Accommodation Rooms.	Beds.	Mattresses.
Karponang (34)	10	9500	2	4	0
Changu (35)	10	12600	2	4	0
Natu Pass (36)	8	14300	details	not	obtainable.
(3) Gangtok to Lachen Pass (43)					
Dickchu (37)	13	2150	2	4	0
Singhi (38)	11	4600	2	4	0
Toong (39)	9	4800	2	4	0
Chungtang (40)	5	5350	2	4	0
(*a*) Lachung (41)	10	8800	2	4	0
Yeumthang (42)	9	13000	details	not	obtainable.
(*b*) Lachen (43)	12	8800	2	4	0
Thangu (44)	13	12800	2	4	0
(4) Kalimpong (5) to Gangtok					
Tista Bridge (4)	7	710	3	3	0
Rungpu (32)	14½	1200	4	4	0
Shamdong (29)	12	2300	2	4	0
Gangtok	12	5800	3	4	0
(5) Kalimpong (5) to Jelap Pass (52)					
Pedong (45)	12	4766	6	4	0
Ari (46)	8	4700	3	4	0
Rongli (47)	4	2700	3	4	0
Sendochen (48)	8	6500	3	4	0
Lingtu (49)	8	12617	—	—	—
Gnatong (50)	7	12210	3	4	0
Kuphu (51)	5	13200	2	2	0
Jelap Pass (52)	4	14390	—	—	—

(6) Tista Bridge (4) to Jelap Pass (52)

Stages.	Altitude. in Feet.	Distances Intermediate Miles.	Total Miles.
Tista Bridge (4)	710	:	:
Tarkola	910	9	9
Rangpu (32)	1200	6	14½
Rongli (47)	2700	10	24½
Sendochen (48)	6500	8	32

Stages.	Altitude. in Feet.	DISTANCES Intermediate Miles.	Total Miles.
Lingtu (49)	12617	8	40
Gnatong (50)	12210	7	47½
Kuphu (51)	13200	5	52
Jelap Pass (52)	14390	4	56½
D—To Gyantse—and the Beyond.			
Jelap Pass	14390	—	56½
Chumbi	9780	14½	71
Phari Jong	14570	29½	100
Tangla Pass	15200	9½	110
Tuna	14700	9½	119½
Dochen	14900	12	131½
Kala Lake	14700	12	143½
Gyantse	13200	52	195½
Nagartse	15000	61	256½
Kambo Pass	16500	33	289½
Lhasa	11830	43	332½

The State of Sikkim.

"To breath the air of Sikkim free
To wander by her purling rills,
And seek the beauty of her hills,
The blueness of her skies—."
Lay of Lachen—Colman Macaulay.

The hill State of Sikkim lies due north of Darjeeling (see dotted line running due east and west in Plate XIII), in the heart of the Himalayas, and is approximately 60 and 40 miles from north to south, and from east to west, respectively.

Although its present area covered 2,400 sq. miles, formerly the boundaries extended much further and included the Limbu country on the west and the Chumbi Valley on the east. Though small in size it contains the Kinchenjunga range, and scenery which is unsurpassed in the world for grandeur. Its population is 87,920, of which about 8,000 are Lepchas.

The aboriginal inhabitants are Lepchas,* or as they call themselves, the Rongpa or Ravine-folk; a most charming people whose origin is obscure, though it is thought they migrated to their present abode along the foothills of the Himalayas from the east, and not from Tibet across this range. They are a distinct race, with a language, both spoken and written, of their own, and with very marked characteristics. Their features are distinctly aquiline, a marked contrast to the usual Mongolian type seen about these parts where flat noses and high cheek bones predominate. They are great naturalists having names for every species of tree, plant, butterfly and insect: in religion they were in the 17th century converted from Animism to Buddism, which is very nominal for they still worship all manner of spirits, generally those connected with Nature, such as the Spirit of the Snows, of the Mountain Peaks, of Rivers, of Forests, &c.; beliefs induced by the grandeur and majesty of the scenes which surround them in their mountain fastnesses. As might be expected of such people, they have a large stock of folk-lore. On the other hand their prodigality is so great that, rather than provide for a bad year, they prefer, should the crops fail, to migrate further into the jungles to pick up a precarious livelihood on roots and berries, or what they can snare in the shape of birds and beasts.

They inhabit the middle and lower heights of the mountain regions, while their houses are seldom found above the 5,000 feet level and deep in the recesses of these inaccessible valleys. No place worthy of the name of town exists in Sikkim, not even its capital, Gangtok; but by the time the next census is taken the latter will probably rise to that status. There are 315 villages in all containing about 17,000 dwellings, which would be termed 'huts', with an average of 4 to 5 souls in each, thus exemplifying the saying:—God made the country and man made the town.

The next race to enter Sikkim was the Tibetan, who came over in two waves. The first hailed from the Tibetan monasteries of Sakhya and Ralung. These soon settled in the new country, dominated the effeminate Lepcha, became the ruling

*According to Mr. J. C. White, the first Political Officer attached to this State.

race, and founded the present line of rulers and aristocracy. They rarely intermarried with the aborigines, and occasionally sought wives from the homeland. The next wave came over from the Chumbi Valley sometime after. Their descendants profess the religion of Budda, and look to Lhasa for spiritual guidance.

These Tibetans prefer trade to agriculture, or keep herds of cattle and yak, and cultivate patches adjoining their little holdings, in which chiefly wheat, barley and a few vegetables are grown.

Subsequent to these two migration waves hillmen from the over-congested areas of Nepal everran the country, and now form three-fourths of the entire population. These have proved to be an exceedingly industrious people and excellent agriculturists, and have settled down quietly amongst their Buddist neighbours, although at first there was considerable friction owing to divergence of customs between the two races. One of the main causes of the prolific trouble being that while the Lepcha (and Bhutia) fenced in his fields, the Nepalese did not do, so that the cattle of the former did immense damage to the crops of the latter. These Nepalese, a much more prolific and thrifty people, must eventually everrun the country, for they are migrating east along the foothills into Bhutan, where they already form a considerable colony.

The physical features of the country are quite exceptional. Sikkim, which lies in the line of the south-west monsoons, receives a very heavy rainfall varying from 300 inches on the outlying hills above the plains, to 6 inches and less in the higher valleys beyond the snows. The result of this rainfall, combined with the difference in the altitude of the mountains, is the varied and beautiful scenery to be found in Sikkim, which is unrivalled in the whole world. The lower hills and valleys are densely and richly clothed with vegetation; lower down the vegetation assumes a sub-tropical nature, amongst which palms, tree-ferns, canes and gigantic creepers abound, gradually changing in the more temperate regions to oaks and chestnuts, and finally as the mountains are scaled to pines, larches and junipers, ending in dwarf rhododendrons at an altitude of 13 to 14 thousand feet.

The lower valleys, many of which are not higher than 500 feet above sea level, are hot and steamy during the rains, which lasts from April to October, while the middle heights are cool, although the atmosphere during these months is almost always at saturation point, while a dry climate is only obtained in the high valleys amongst or beyond the snow-line.

With heights varying as they do from 500 to 28,000 feet with immense deep and narrow valleys, it follows that the scenery baffles description. Owing to the moisture in the atmosphere the middle and far distance is always seen through the softest and most ethereal of blues, deepening in the shadows to indigo; and this combined with the richness of the forest colourings, the wonderful brilliance of the snows, the ever varying clouds and mists, shadow and sunshine, must be seen to be appreciated for they are beyond the power of description.

Flora of Sikkim.

The flora in this State lies in three belts, the tropical, temperate and the Alpine. Sir J. D. Hooker collected no less than 2,920 out of the 4,000 species of plants enumerated by botanists subsequently. Orchids cover more than 320 varieties, 20 species of bamboo are found, while the rhododendron, which numbers 30 varieties, varies in size from mere dwarfs some 2 feet in height to massive trees over 40 feet long. Fir, pine, maple, chestnut, oak and magnolia make up the remainder.

Fauna of Sikkim.

Butterflies and Moths. Of the former over 500 varieties have been enumerated, the papilie, or swallow-tails, accounting for over 40 kinds, and are met with up to the 12,000 feet level. Indeed, it is difficult to determine how high these gossamer creatures can be found, for in 1910 for a whole day countless myriads of white butterflies flew over Darjeeling on their way to the east, and so dense were these clouds that distinct shadows were cast on the town. Similarly, along the Tista Valley Line as the train goes by in June-July millions of dark-brown flies are disturbed and take to wing. The oak-leaf, the croaker, the leaf and cane-insect, which looks exactly like a bit of cane, and bettles which likewise run into hundreds of varieties make up the remainder. The moths number fully 2,000 varieties of which the Atlas, which spans 10 inches across its wings, with its veinings of black and pale pink, and the Death's-Head are the chief and prettiest. Spiders, again, and scorpions add to the wonders of nature. The former is seen almost at every yard casting its net for the unsuspicious fly, but it is the female, for the male measures only ¼ of an inch and is a bright red in colour. Of the scorpions, the whiptail variety with the round head fetches as much as £2 to £3 each, while the square-headed one is fairly common.

Birds. There are between 5 to 6 hundred species including the giant eagle with its span of 10 feet from tip to tip of wing, while the wee honey-sucker less than 2 inches in length closes the scale. These tiny wonders in blue, green and gold are to be seen between 9 and 10, just when the sun has driven off the heavy dew, darting over the honey-suckle to and fro so rapidly that it is hard to follow their movements with the eye. Having selected a tempting looking flower they hover over it and sip the nectar while on the wing which vibrates so fast that it cannot be seen and so leaves an impression on the mind of a poised palpitating body, as large as a big bumble-bee only, with a dizzy halo on either side of it. It is not until satiated that these iridescent creatures come to rest with closed wings on a tender spray that they once again turn into wee feathered birds. And thus bathed in sunlight each seems to live—"A loving little life of sweet small works".

Beasts include the Himalayan black bear, the panther, pig, goral (Indian chamois), wild sheep (*ovis ammon*), snow leopard (ounce), fox, lynx and serrow, and others too numerous to mention.

Our Relations with Sikkim*

By a provision of the treaty signed by the aged Sikimputti on March 28th, 1861, it was agreed that a road should be constructed through Sikkim for the development of commercial transactions with Tibet from our territories. Accordingly, the construction of a bridge over the Tista, and a survey of the following routes from Darjeeling in connection with the Northern Bengal Railway (which was started in 1873, and since renamed the Eastern Bengal Railway), which was in the course of extension to Siliguri, was ordered *via* Pedong, which is 41 miles from Darjeeling, the Jelap Pass (93 miles) and thence on to the Chumbi Valley.

This project was, however, held in abeyance for want of funds until the year 1886 when under the orders of the British Foreign Office, Mr. Coleman Macaulay was directed to organise and assemble a mixed political and scientific mission at Darjeeling with the object of proceeding through Sikkim to Lhasa to confer with the Chinese Resident there and the Lhasa Government on the free admission of Indian traders to Tibet, and the removal of obstruction to the trade route through Sikkim to Darjeeling, it being understood that no proposal for the general admission of Europeans would be brought forward.

In the meanwhile negotiations had started with China concerning the north-eastern frontier of Upper Burma, then recently annexed, and in deference to Chinese susceptibilities the Government of India consented to forgo their intention of despatching this mission. This forbearance on our part was interpreted in true Asiatic fashion as one of fear by the monastic party in Tibet, whose desire to promote a policy of exclusion, and to maintain their own monopoly of trade with India, was connived at by the Chinese Resident. Thus emboldened the Tibetans threw a small body of militia armed with bows and arrows and obsolete guns into Lingtu, on the top of a peak which crossed our road to the Jelap Pass in the Chola range. Here the invaders constructed, at an elevation of 12,617 feet

---

* Abridged from the interesting introduction to the Gazetteer of Sikkim by H. H. Risley.

above sea-level, a stone fort, blocking and commanding the road with a view to stopping trade by that route.

These Tibetans not only held their ground obstinately, but also refused to enter into negotiations with us, a circumstance which then produced an alarming effect in Sikkim. The Raja of this State was in consequence called upon in June, 1887, to confer with Sir Steuart Bayley, the Lieutenant-Governor of Bengal, with a view to modify his relations with Tibet, and to return to his previous friendly relations and policy. After exhausting all Oriental excuses possible, the Raja at last replied that "he and his people had in 1886 signed a treaty declaring that Sikkim was subject only to China and Tibet," and was, therefore, unable to come to Darjeeling without the express permission of the Tibetan Government.

Political matters had assumed such proportions and had clearly gone so far that, unless we bestirred ourselves in a speedy manner, Sikkim would either be once for all a province of Tibet, or, if we were not prepared to acquiesce in that solution of the difficulty, it would have to be conquered by us. The Tibetans were, therefore, warned that unless they vacated the post at Lingtu by March 14th, they would be driven out by force of arms; and the 32nd Pioneers were accordingly sent forward to bridge the Rongli river. His Excellency the Viceroy in the meanwhile addressed a letter to the Dalai Llama, explaining the reasons which actuated our policy.

In pursuance of this policy General Graham, who was directed on no account to pursue the enemy beyond the frontier of Sikkim, commenced operations in March, 1888, which ended in the engagement of September 24th of that year. The stockade of Jelap was carried on March 20th, and Lingtu taken the next day. On May 22nd the Tibetans attacked Gnatong and although vast in numbers, were, as expected, beaten with heavy loss and driven over the Jelap Pass. Our forces were then halted, in accordance with orders. As our forbearance was still being mistaken for timidity, the Tibetans soon were busy collecting their forces from the entire province for a final throw of the dice, to meet which General Graham by the middle of August had at his command at Gnatong a wing of the Derbyshires, the 32nd Pioneers (Sikhs), one newly-raised Gurkha regiment, and 6 mountain guns—in all nearly 2,000 rank and file. On the morning of September 24th the enemy, which numbered over 11,000, had advanced 4 miles from their camp and occupied the Turkhola ridge, 13,350 feet above sea-level, and 1,500 feet higher than Gnatong, and had entrenched themselves behind a stonewall 2 miles in length along the crest of the hill which they had raised during the night prior. Approaching this peak by a route which covered them from the fire of the defenders, the Gurkhas carried the position with a rush, and their attack, combined with a parallel advance by the Pioneers, swept the Tibetans from the ridge.

This expedition brought about the Anglo-Chinese Agreement of 1890 by which the boundaries between Sikkim and Tibet were settled according to our contentions; a protectorate over Sikkim was recognised, with *exclusive* control over its internal administration and its foreign relations.

So far as Sikkim is concerned, the effect has been admirable; the country has ever since been progressing peacefully and rapidly, untroubled by Tibetan aggressiveness.

The reforms included in the above Agreement were:—The appointment of a Political Agent (Mr. J. C. White being the first Political Officer) at Gangtok to assist the Raja in Council with his advice in the administration of affairs, the establishment of a Council for the conduct of ordinary, civil, criminal and revenue work, &c., and the preservation of *sal* forests by bringing them under the direct control of the *durbar*.

All went well until 1891 when the Raja refused to return to Gangtok, the capital fixed by the British Government, and also declined to remove his eldest son, Tchoda Namgyel, from Tibet for the purpose of having him educated, as became his station, in Darjeeling, along with his younger brother, Chotal (who was considered an *avatar*, or incarnation of the founder of the Phodang monastery) and the sons of Raja Tenduk. In March, 1892, the Raja left Pamionchi ostensibly for his return to Gangtok but in reality his intention was to find his way into

Tibet *via* Nepal. As soon as he crossed the borders, he was arrested by the authorities of that State and escorted into Kurseong, where he was detained under surveillance throughout 1892-93. In the interim the affairs of the State were conducted by the members of its Council and the Assistant Political Officer.

No change took place in the attitude of the Raja until the year 1895 when he was removed to Darjeeling, where on expressing regret for his past conduct and subscribing to a document in which he complied unreservedly with the conditions of restoration imposed by the British Government he was subsequently allowed to return to Sikkim. The Raja immediately (and his descendants subsequently) associated himself with the Council in the administration of the State, which has been conducted ever since under the advice and general supervision of a Political Officer.

Shortly after Sir Andrew Fraser assumed charge as Lieutenant-Governor of Bengal, it was decided as a matter of political expediency, that the Political Officer of Sikkim should be subject to the control of the Government of India, owing to that State being bounded by Nepal, Tibet and Bhutan (See Plate XIII) by which our frontier policy was raised to more than provincial importance. And so the control of Sikkim passed over on April 1st, 1906, from the Government of Bengal to that of the Government of India.

This change has brought about material advantages, chief of which is an appreciable increase in the population. According to the last census it stands at 87,920 souls, which is about 50 *per cent.* of an increase over that taken a decade ago. Even making allowances for incompleteness of prior records, the increase is due to the large influx of Nepalese settlers, who have been attracted to Sikkim as fear no longer exists of Tibetan raids, or misgovernment.

TO GANGTOK.

Tour C—1.

PLATE XIII.

Time:—1. Gangtok *via* Badamtam—10 days.
2. Ditto and Back *via* Kalimpong 12 days.
3. Ditto and ditto *via* Phalut 15 days.

Gangtok is well worth a visit. The stages from Darjeeling and Kalimpong are given in the tables above, as also those to the Nathu, Lachen and Jelap Passes. It takes just 15 days to get to the first named pass *via* Badamtam.

To Gangtok via Tista Bridge.

The following are the bungalows, with distances, along this route:—Lopchu (2) 14½ miles from Darjeeling, Peshok (3) 4¼ ditto from last stage, Tista Bridge (4) 3¾ ditto, Melli 3 miles from (4), Tarkhola which is 6 miles further is in charge of the Forest Officer, Kalimpong division, Rangpu (32) at the junction of the Rongli and Tista rivers and about 1200 feet above sea level, is 5½ miles further north, then comes Shamdong, or Middle Camp (29) 12 miles away, while Gangtok (D) is just the same distance to the north of the last stage.

Those whose time is limited usually push on to Peshok, and even Tista Bridge, the first day, reach Rongpu the second, Shamdong on the third, and arrive at Gangtok the next day.

As ponies can be hired at Re. 1/- per day and carry 2 maunds of luggage, besides keep up with the tourist, it were best to hire beasts than be troubled with porters, who, unless under the guidance of a reliable sirdar, give no end of trouble.

While proceeding along the cart road the following are passed:—A quarter of a mile beyond the bridge a narrow path suddenly doubles back to the pony track which leads to Kalimpong; at the 1½ mile post the junction of the Rangneet and Tista rivers is passed to lead on to Melli and its suspension bridge which is at the 3rd mile, and Tarkhola, or 'clearing in the forest'; and finally the village of Rangpu. By this you have noticed—

The Orange Traffic.

Along the route from Rangpu to Tista Bridge during the winter months, and from daylight to dark, an endless chain of human beings will be seen crawling along. They are all hill people of the poorer sort who carry planks, or baskets of oranges up to 164 lbs. in weight, and are in consequence by mid-day crushed down by their grievous burdens, when their gait resembles more than of stumbling beasts than the walk of a human being. The pace is necessarily slow with enforced halts at short distances, while the lungs are choked by the dust of the road which also turns the hair on the face and head white, and lies as a plaster wetted by the sweat in the furrows of the skin. The path being narrow they walk in single file as do ants, and when it narrows into a mere ledge they needs must laboriously proceed by a side-step. In a single day no less than 1,000 men, women and children so engaged have passed my camp, each creeping along at a snail's pace, with their dull, strained eyes fixed upon either the rough stony path or upon the stooping back of the creature that crawls in front. In addition to this load (which earns them a bare pittance) you will see either on their heads, or hanging over their backs their few and sorry possessions—cooking-pots, sticks gathered for the fire by the wayside, a water-gourd and a blanket or sheep's skin to cover them from the bleak winds and feverladen mists which blow down the gorges, or from the sharp frost while lying under a sheltering tree during the last few hours of the night, for each in his effort to reach the goal first robs night of its fair share of rest. And to sustain this awful strain on their strength the diet is frugal in the extreme being wholly composed of maize flour worked into a dough with water and then baked over the embers of a fire of brushwood, which at the same time helps to keep them warm to some extent under such trying conditions.

Although their daily round for months on end is the same yet never a murmur escapes their lips though their souls doubtless cry out in the depths of anguish—

"God! we living ones—what of our tears
When a single day seems a thousand years"?—

as in the dust of that weary track have they seen hundreds of their number droop, drop and die, for they "live forgotten and die forlorn."

Watching them thus from day to day it has often occurred to me that if the carriers of the planks especially, which are straddled horizontally over the backs, were but to place one vertical to the load that each of them would be carrying his own cross to some far off place of crucifixion—and thus end his misery!

Some idea may be formed of the numbers engaged in this traffic, and the number of trips accomplished by each when it is borne in mind that 6 million oranges and more are despatched from Tista Bridge to Calcutta, while a load for an adult varies from 300 to 400 fruit and that of children from 100 to 150 only.

To resume.

It is best to do the day's journey (or ride) of from 8 to 12 miles in the early forenoon. The roads are in fairly good repair yet withal the highland coolie prefers *pakdandies*, or goat tracks, often as not arriving at the next stage before you. He scales perpendicular passes and slides down dales with his load securely fastened to his forehead by a strap or *lamlo* of plaited fibre. 'Middle camp' is a walled place with immense ramparts. Though dawn breaks in these high elevations about 4 a.m. in the summer yet the sun is seldom seen before 10 o'clock, and then as a red, lurid glow striving to break through the mists and clouds. From this camp to Gangtok* is a pleasant ride, during which the preponderating feature of the landscape is the innumerable *gompas* or monasteries scattered over the whole country, like the *pagodas* in Burma. They, however, represent a religion which leads to the superficial impression that it is different from those obtaining either in Ceylon or Burma. It certainly is more engaging and attracts more converts by its images, impressive services, gorgeous pageant and ritual than the austere simplicity of the silent cloisters of Ceylon, or Burma. A short journey lands you at the celebrated De-dong monastery or Llamasarai. The Llamas

*Mutton, fowls, eggs, rice and oilman's stores may be had at Gangtok.

wend their way through the tortuous streets and passages which intersect these villages explaining the mystery of the life after death in deep, rumbling, cavernous tones, which requires prolonged practice to attain perfect intonation:—"Om! ma-ni pad-me Hung!"—Hail! Jewel (Lord of Mercy) in the Lotus-Flower!"

From every cairn, from every coign of vantage these six sacred mystic syllables of Buddism, which claims 415,000,000 followers, or more than a quarter of the population of the world, are chanted from the shores of Japan in the extreme east, through Mongolia, across the inhospitable *Changtang,* China, Tibet, Burma, Siam and India until the echo is heard in distant Ceylon and the Straits Settlement. Printed in black on coloured streamers to flap and crack by the rushing winds, one can fancy these words uttered by many millions of voices being borne across the desolate plains of Tibet to bring happiness and blessings to the devotees of Budda, and especially to the pilgrims who crowd over the passes, some of them situated as high as 17,802 feet above sea-level, on their way to some sacred shrine. Similarly, *manis or mandongs,* (sermons in stones) strew the path of the pilgrim throughout Tibet; while huge cairns perched on mountain tops guide these devotees, as surely as does our compass, over seas of sand and ice which abound in the great *Chang-tang.*

Owing to the rigour of the climate the people of these regions clothe themselves heavily, their *bokhu* being a replica of the *phirun* worn by the Ladakies and Kashmiris: their ablutions are also few and far between as recorded by all explorers and travellers. Their chief luxury is a light beer, a delightful beverage, drawn off the kodu or millet, which is sucked through a reed, like lemon squash, from bamboo bottles.

The King Edward Memorial.

On the Ridge at Gangtok will be seen the memorial to the late King Edward VII which was unveiled by His Highness the Maharaja of Sikkim in June, 1917. The bronze bust of His late Majesty stands on a masonry pillar which has four brass plates let into it bearing the following inscription in English, Tibetan, Nepalese and Bhutia:

"To the memory of His late Majesty Edward VII, King-Emperor. Erected by His loyal subjects in Sikkim".

These plates are embellished by emblematic designs of the sun, moon, the national flower of Sikkim, and a rhododendron. Below the inscription is the eight-spoked wheel of Tibet with a scroll and motto. The floor of the Kiosk is of polished coloured tiles, while the octagonal roof of wood and its railings are beautifully carved and painted by Tibetan artists who have blended, with pleasing effect both as regards colour and proportion, their different mystical signs.

When the Ridge is fully embellished, as it will soon be, with carved Chinese arches at either end, avenues of trees, graceful feathery bamboos, and flowering shrubs, the silent memorial will stand to the memory of a great King perfect in its picturesque surroundings and beauty.

The Memorial Hospital.

This fine, up-to-date hospital built at Gangtok as a memorial to His late Highness Sir Thethub Namgyel, was opened by His Higness the Maharaja Tashi Ñamgyel on September 24th, 1917. This hospital is the first of its kind in Sikkim and is fitted with every modern convenience, with surgical and medical wards, operating theatre, and detached wards for infectious diseases ; the plan and designs being thoroughly practical and well-thought-out by Mr. H. C. Dracott, the State Engineer, and Dr. Turner, Civil Surgeon of the State.

The correspondence of the Durbar at Gangtok is maintained with the Llamasaries in Tibetan, while that with the British Government is conducted in English. Here, as well as at Kalimpong, a fair idea may be drawn of the volume of trade which finds its way to and from India through passes loaded with caravanserais owned and lead by Chinese.

TO JELAP PASS.

Tour C—6.

Via Tista Bridge—Plate XIII.

Time—14 days.

To proceed to the Jelap Pass the tourist must return to Rangpu and then follow these stages :—Rongli (47), Sendochen

(48), Gnatong (50), Kuphu (51) which lies just below the Pass, to reach which a stiff climb up the bridle-path taxes the energies of most pedestrians.

From Rangpu the road skirts the stream for 16 miles to *Rongli,* along a valley some 2,700 feet above sea-level, which within the next 15 miles increases to 10,000 feet, and so transports one from the stifling heat of the plains to the cold blasts of the mountains. At the 10th mile above Rangpu the river is crossed by the substantial bridge thrown across it in 1888 by the Madras Pioneers; below are the copper mines, the green ore of which is worked by Nepalese lessees. Throughout this dale the path winds its way between rice fields and orange groves, but when it strikes the mountains it becomes a sheer ladder of stone steps over which propulsion is limited to about 1½ miles per hour. In this small stretch of country the vegetation is exceedingly varied ranging from tropical to temperate and finally alpine.

The next stiff climb is to Lingtu (12,617′), the margin of the highland plateau on which Tibet is situated. The path which by now has contracted considerably runs through a thickly wooded cliff above a torrent with a rocky wall on one side and a deep precipice on the other until *Sendochen* is reached. From this stage the road passes through magnificent forests of oak and chestnut, which for the next 5 miles is but an ascent over stone steps. Then comes the rhododendron zone which works up to the confines of Lingtu from where you can see *Kin* and *Koben.* At *Gnatong* (where 15 soldiers who fell in the first Sikkim Expedition lie buried in graves bearing dates from 1888 to 1890) the houses resemble Swiss chalets of the ruder sort with miniature fir trees planted on the roofs from which as usual flutter the flap-prayers.

Just a mile and a half further on is the Tuko Pass from which you descend during the next two miles to *Kuphu.* On the north-west of the path lies lake Bidentzo with a moraine to its northwest. The silence of this region, which would otherwise have been palpable, is only broken by the cry of the red-billed cloughs, the commonest of the *Corvidae.*

The approach to the *Jelap* is over broken rock and shale, and on its summit stands a row of cairns covered with its flags and bits of votive raiment. Far away to the north-east lies *Chumulari* (23,930′) with its white dome resembling an immense snow-capped cathedral; in the valley lies *Chumbi* and the road to Lhasa.

TO JELAP PASS.

Tour C—5.

Via Kalimpong.

Time—14 days.

As this journey taxes the strength of the most robust it should be accomplished on horse or mule-back, the latter being the more sure-footed. The *impedimenta* should not exceed a coolie-load, or 60 pounds, nor the followers more than a groom, a bearer and a cook, who should by preference be a Tibetan, or Nepalese. Hindustani will carry the traveller far into the Himalayas, where the Trident of Hinduism and the Cross of the Christian are slowly gaining the ascendency. From Darjeeling to Tista Bridge and thence to Kalimpong is 29 miles. Shortly after leaving this spot a steep climb has to be negotiated over steps, which here pass for a road, before Pedong is reached. Let us halt here awhile and go over the ground on which the chapel built by Fr. T. Desgodines, the French R. C. Vicar Apostolic of the R. C. Mission to Western Tibet stands. His residence, the presbytery and chapel are planted in the midst of waving maize-fields whose verdure is of the deepest spring-green, and amidst which thatched llama's houses and low-roofed *gompas* are studded. Behind the presbytery rise terraces of rice-fields irrigated by the freshets of the prior rains, and bordered by artemesia scrub which in the warmth of the sunshine throws out an aromatic odour. Arriving in India in 1857 his journey to Tibet was cut short at Agra where he formed an unit in the defence of that city during the mutiny. After tranquillity was restored he soon found his way to Khanam in Western Tibet, but was shortly after arrival deputed to go further ahead into Chinese territory where he laboured for 22 years in establishing the mission at Batang and Bonga. In the confusion that followed in the attempt on the part of Tibet to throw off the suzerainty of China he was burnt out and forced to wend his way back to India *via* Chumbi Valley, and on reaching Pedong decided to restart his mission at that spot—as Pro-Vicar of the Western Tibet Mission.

Although only 12 miles away from Kalimpong it takes 6 hours to cover the distance. From here the path descends to the Rongli river, which separates Sikkim proper from British territory ; and from which another stiff climb lands one at Ari, where the frontier pass must be produced. Leaving Ari at 9 a.m. the Rongli river and market-place are passed at about noon. With the exception of bread in any form almost every commestible save tinned provisions can be had ; therefore, lay these in for the next week's consumption, that is, until Gangtok is reached. The road to Sendochen is tolerable and wends through scenery unsurpassed by any between Darjeeling and Kalimpong, while bird-life is represented by fully 50 different species of varied and brilliant colouring. The ascent from the bridge to the 6,500 feet level takes fully 6½ hours to accomplish. Although the climb to Lingtu is trying in the extreme, for in 8 miles the elevation rises another 6,000 feet, one is rewarded by probably the most majestic view of the snowy range to be ever had. As there is no accommodation here the tourist must push on to Gnatong, where there is a fairly large Bhutia busti (village) and the means for being once more in touch with civilisation, for in this outlandish place is a sub-post office ; so arrange for your home papers and letters to await you here. Time may be devoted to going over the ruins of the foundations of the fort demolished after our engagement with the Sikkimese on the 24th September, 1888. The road between the last two stages passes over long undulating swells in the shady recesses of which snow fully three feet deep lies throughout the winter. Three miles to the north-west of Gnatong, but six by road, lies lake Bidentzo (12,700′) which is 1 by ½ a mile in dimensions. Kuphu is 5 miles further, 990 feet higher; and 4 miles below the Jelap Pass, where the highest civilised cantonment in the world was built in 1888 for the accommodation of the Derbyshire regiment. This cantonment was renovated in

1903 when our Armed Mission crossed the borders on its way to Lhasa.

To get to the pass and back takes 4 hours; and from which if armed with a very special permit the Chumbi Valley is entered. However, we can from its summit have a grand panoramic view of this valley and its scattered Chinese villages, the hamlets of which appear no larger than tiny white dots ; to the north Phari Jong or fort, built in 1792 at the base of the Mo river, and the large Buddist monasteries, or *gompas,* are distinctly seen by the unaided eye; while Chumulari, the sacred peak of both the Tibetans and Bhutias, stands out in bold relief behind Phari Jong.

The return journey may be varied by going to Changu (35) which is reached from Kuphu in 6 hours during which the road passes through forests of dwarfed pines standing no higher than 4 feet, which scent the atmosphere with a fragrance. Locally, it is termed *Dhupi,* and as it takes the place of frankinsence in all religious rituals fetches as much as a rupee (16 *d.*) per seer (2 lbs.). A little below the dak bungalow is lake Changu (12,600′) of about the same dimensions as the last, which freezes to a thickness of fully 6 inches during the winter. A short climb above the bungalow to the Changu peak affords a grand view both of the snowy range and of the Nathu La Pass. Leaving here at 9 a.m., Karponang is passed at 2 p.m, after traversing paths lined by ordinary pines ; while Gangtok is entered the same evening at 5-30 p.m.

A policeman invariably follows one at a distance from here to the pass, and back, lest by crossing the frontier international complications arise.

To Gyantse—and the Beyond.

Beyond the Jelap Pass lies Tibet. As entry into this 'forbidden land' by travellers of any nationality, including Indians, is prohibited by treaty with the Grand Llama, no permits are issued by the Government for tours in this region. To proceed even to Gyantse, the last British Outpost Station, which is 137 miles from the pass, requires no little influence to move the Government for the necessary permit. Few tourists even if provided with such a permit could undertake the journey owing to the barren nature of the country to be traversed, as also the silent opposition offered, which thereby necessitates the employment of an army of porters to keep up the supply of provisions, which must be carried from either Sikkim or Siliguri along with the requisite baggage and tents. To tour beyond this outpost, or to proceed to Lhasa, the City of Mysteries, borders on the impossible, for even the application of the famous Swedish explorer, Dr. Sven Hedin, when backed by his Ambassador at London elicited the following reply from Sir John Morley, the Prime Minister, through Lord Minto, the Viceroy of India:—The Prime Minister, desires that the following message be communicated to Sven Hedin: "I sincerely regret that I cannot, for reasons which have doubtless been explained to you by the Indian Government, grant you the desired assistance for your journey to and in Tibet. This assistance has also been refused to the Royal Geographical Society in London, and likewise to British officers in the service of the Government of India".—*Trans-Himalaya by Sven Hedin.*

As the majority of tourists invariably desire knowing something about the 'forbidden land,' the itinerary of the journeys performed by the Superintendent of the Base (Field) Post Office, and Waddell, who accompanied the Military Mission into that land, has been abridged and reproduced in the next chapter.

CHAPTER IV.

To Lhasa, the Rome of the East.

Objection to incursions by 'Foreign Devils' in Tibet is comparatively modern. Two hundred years ago, that is, before China assumed suzerainty over Tibet in 1720, the same freedom was accorded to Europeans as to those of other nationalities to enter the (now forbidden) capital of Tibet. And so contrary to the general, popular belief, a few Europeans have succeeded in reaching Lhasa, who though never welcomed were not only permitted to reside in this city of mysteries but were also suffered to establish missions and even build chapels.

The following is a list of those daring explorers, with dates, who from time to time have endeavoured to draw the veil aside from the doors of the Vatican of the East:—

In 1330 Friar Orderic a Franciscan of Perdone entered Lhasa from China, while in

1660 Father Antonio de Andrada trod the same path.

1662 Johannes Grueber, an Austrian, accompanied by the Belgian Count Albert de Dorville, who died at Agra on his way back the same year, entered this city by the same route as their predecessors. The mission started by the former existed for a period of 38 years.

1706 The Capuchin Fathers J. de Asculi and F. de Tour worked their way to Lhasa through Kashmir and Leh Ladak, to be followed in

1716 in the same route by the Jesuits Desideri and Freyre. The former is alleged to have lived in Lhasa from 1716-29.

1719 The Capuchin monk Horace Della Penna entered this city from Nepal, founded a mission which existed for 50 years, and built a chapel in it.

1736 Of all the missionaries who entered Lhasa, Samuel Van der Putte apparently ingratiated himself with the authorities for we find that he not only lived at Lhasa but also formed a part of the deputation of Tibetans sent to the Court of Pekin.

1774 George Bogle of the Civil Service, and Dr. Hamilton, a member of the Indian Medical Service, were deputed by Warren Hastings to visit the capitals of Bhutan and Tibet *via* Buxa Duars and Punaka the capital of the former country. They returned in June of the following year having failed to get far into Tibet.

1783 Capt. Turner, a relative of Warren Hastings, it is alleged entered Lhasa and saw the new incarnation of the Grand Llama—an infant 18 months old.

1811 Thos. Manning, a friend of Chas. Lamb of the Chinese branch of the East India Company, London, was the only Englishman ever known to enter Tibet and Lhasa prior to our Mission of 1903.

1846 MM. Huc and Gabot, who lost his nose and ears from frost bite while crossing these bleak regions, also sojourned in that city foı a while.

1856-59 The extreme west of Tibet was explored by the two brothers Schlagintweit, who in 1865 were followed by Johnson.

1866 Nain Sing, C.I.E., a surveyor, with crude instruments improvised for the occasion to defeat the scrutiny of the ever vigilant officials who guard the passes, succeeded in accurately maping out a very large tract of the country, which subsequent surveys made during the last Mission merely verified. He entered Tibet from the north-east corner of Nepal. He accomplished much under most trying circumstances and succeeded in determining 276 degrees of latitude, the mapping of 1,200 miles of an unknown and bleak region and in recording 497 observations for altitude with the boiling-point thermometer, as well as taking a series of meteorological observations.

1872 Col. Prjivalski, a Russian, failed in his attempt from over the Pamirs. His next sojourn in this land extended from August, 1876 to July, 1877, and from March, 1879 to November, 1880. During these three attempts he covered 7,350, 2,650, and 4,750 miles. His final effort was made from October to December, 1883, when he traversed another 4,850 miles.

1873-74 Forsyth's venture is merely recorded.

1874 Nain Sing for the second time entered Lhasa through Ladak and mapped the central, or lake region.

1878 Kishen Singh (A.K.), Rai Bahadur, triangulated the upper portion of Tibet and has given us the best and most accurate map of that land. He did herculean work for the geography of North Tibet; ground over which Huc, Gabot, Beonlevat and Prince Henry of Orleans have also wandered.

1880 Kintup, a native of Sikkim, and a member of the Survey of India, entered Tibet with a Chinese Llama who treacherously sold him to the head of a monastery for a sum of Rs. 50/- only and then hied off to his own country. After suffering untold hardships he succeeded in evading his captors and carrying out the special duty with which he was entrusted, namely, to drop marked logs into the river, which was conjectured to be the source of the Brahmaputra, and which proved these conjectures to be correct. He returned to India after an absence of four years.

,, Llama Ugyen Gyatsho succeeded in smuggling

Sarat Chandra Das, a Bengalee, into Lhasa. The bare account of that city by the latter obtained for him a C. I. E.-ship.

1885-87 Carey and Dalgleish were turned back without being able to add much to our meagre knowledge of the country.

1889 Mr. Rockhill failed getting to Lhasa, although a distinguished Tibetan scholar.

1890 M. Beonlevat and Prince Henry of Orleans got as far as 95 miles to the north of Lhasa, when they were compelled to turn back.

1891 Capt. Bower succeeded in getting only as far as the 200th mile north-west of that city.

1892 Mr. Rockhill reached the 110th mile north of Lhasa, while Miss Anne Taylor in the same year reached the 168th mile to the south of that city.

1893 The ill-fated M. Jules Leon Dutreuil de Rhins was treacherously murdered and his body thrown into the river.

1895 Mr. and Mrs. Littledale got as far as 70 miles to the south-east of Lhasa.

1896 Capt. H. H. P. Deasy surveyed fully 24,000 miles of Tibetan territory having got in from Leh Ladak. He and Dr. Stein have done much to clear away the mists and clouds which hung over this Land of Mystery.

1897 A. H. Savage-Landor after undergoing innumerable hardships, and cruel tortures at Taddju or Toxem was ejected from Tibet. Leaving Almorah in May, and passing through Garbyang (16,467′) on the borders of British territory, he succeeded in penetrating the passes and highland of Tibet to within five days' march of Lhasa, the Vatican of the East ; (*a*) compiling a complete map of South-Western Tibet, which covers an area of 12,500 square miles between 29°-0′ and 31°-54′ north latitude, and between 80°-25′ and 85°-30′ east longitude; and (*b*) fixing definitely two of the principal sources of the Brahmaputra river. During the course of these journeys, which extended from May to October, he scaled passes 22,000 feet high, which certainly stands high among records.

1901 Dr. Sven Hedin got to within a few days' march of Lhasa, *i.e.*, about 150 miles N.N-W.

1902 M. Tysbikoff, a Russian, succeeded in bringing back photographs of that city, while the Japanese priest Kawaguchi who was discovered in Lhasa had to flee for his life.

1915, that is, *after* the Expeditionary Mission, Mr. and Mrs. Percy Brown of the Government School of Art, Calcutta, were permitted to tour in Tibet as far as Gyantse in search of Art productions of which they have now a fairly large collection. Mrs. Brown may, therefore, claim to be the first English lady who has travelled much and far in Tibet.

1920, November 1st—Mr. C. A. Bell, I.C.S., Political Officer, Sikkim, left Yatung for Lhasa. This is the first occasion a recognised British Official has on invitation visited the capital of Tibet.

1921 The Tibetan Government permitted the expedition led by Col. Howard Bury to enter the 'forbidden land' in order to assail the heights of Everest (29,141′), which proved unconquerable for Mallory, one of the party, succeeded in climbing to a height of 23,000′ only. It returned to Darjeeling on October 25th after having surveyed 12,000 miles of land, and revised 4,000 square miles of survey work in Sikkim.

Although Tibet, and its capital Lhasa, have been visited by quite a number of Europeans yet no definite data were recorded of the mystic and mysterious Vatican of the East until the Armed Mission despatched by the Government of India during the administration of Lord Curzon, which produced a complete and fascinating history of that unknown land by Waddell.

Between the two highest chains of mountain—the Kwen-lun and the Himalayas—is the Tibetan highlands just south of the great *Chang-Tang,* a vast, lofty desert ice-bound plateau standing at an average elevation of 13,000 feet, and bounded on the north and south respectively by the Pamirs and the Himalayas. This plateau is about 1,500 miles long with an approximate width of 600 miles tapering to 100 at its western boundary and 350 on its eastern side; its total area is about 7,70,000 square miles which in its inhospitable regions supports a population of 4,000,000 souls only.

As the Tibetan authorities deliberately failed meeting our first peaceful Mission under the guidance of Sir (Col.) Francis Younghusband, it was decided, owing to Russian intrigues of which definite proof had been obtained, to push an Armed Mission under the command of Brigadier-General J. A. L. Macdonald (of which the famous explorer Kintup was a member) over the border in December 1903.

Before proceeding with Waddell into this unknown land it were well to have a bird's-eye-view of the trend of the country.

Crossing over from Sikkim into Tibet, immediately the high snow regions are passed, the scene changes wonderfully, the hills become rounded and less precipitous and the spaces between the ranges are wider and more open; the rainfall almost ceases, and there is practically no vegetation, only some very scanty grass.

The geological strata have also changed and, leaving behind gneiss and granite of which the lighter snow peaks are formed, we now see limestones and shale, in both of which fossils are found, shewing that these elevated plateaus and mountains were once formed under the sea.

Among these limestone hills there are some magnificent types of castles, the one at Kamba Jong dominating the country for miles. The cloister will, however, call for its devotees, for we find nuns at Tatshang, which is situated some twenty miles to the east of Kamba Jong, in a desolate spot, from which not a single human habitation is visible; but they are extremely dirty, and must lead, to our ideas, a most dismal existence.

The whole of this country immediately to the north of the snows is of the same character but with more rounded hills, wide valleys, broad plains and numerous lakes, no trees and very little rainfall. Formerly the rainfall must have been heavier, and this is shewn by the old lake shores high above the level of the present water-line, the diminishing glaciers, and the very large number of deserted villages. As the country is penetrated further and the central range of the Himalayas is entered the very dry zone is passed and the moisture in the air which has escaped precipitation by the snows again forms and the rainfall is heavier. The valleys will now be seen to contract again and the cultivation more prevalent, and on reaching the Gyantse Valley, at an elevation of about 13,000 feet, the crops raised are excellent, barley, wheat, peas and broad-beans grow luxuriantly in the fields which are irrigated by a well-planned system of canals and small channels, and trees, such as the poplar and willows, abound around every homestead.

The country on to Lhasa has the same characteristics—all the low valleys being extensively cultivated; but the country is generally a poor one, as the crops grow only in the valleys, the mountains being bare and bleak.

The strata vary from time to time—slate and limestone outcrops, as well as shale and granite intrusions are met with.

The following were the stages in this bleak and doubly inhospitable land.

A little below *Jelap Pass* is a small lake and streamlet, while at Langram (12,100′), there is a Chinese colony. Further down is Yatung (13,200′); still further on is Richengang (9,530′) where there is a collection of about 40 well-built houses. *Chumbi* lies in this valley, at the end of which is Byema another Chinese colony. *Phari Jong** or fort, built in 1792 is 29½ miles higher up at the base of the Mo river. It dominates the great trade routes to Ladak, Nepal and China on the one hand, and to Assam and Bengal on the other. The town below the fort consists of 200 mean houses, low-roofed and windowless whose entrances look like subterranean passages owing to the accumulation of the sweepings of ages which have been deposited on the main thoroughfares in front of each dwelling. Phari Jong is 123 miles from Darjeeling and 104 from Kalimpong: it is on the southern or Indian side of the Himalayas. About midway to the next stage a steep ascent 5 miles in length takes you over the *Tangla Pass* (15,200′) from which you gradually descend to *Tuna* on the great plateau which is 19 miles away in Tibet proper, and 15,000 feet above sea level but which owing to its bleak climate contains a population of 30 inhabitants only, and a fort encircled by hills. *Garu*, where the first brush with our Armed Mission took place at an altitude of 15,000 feet, is on Lake Rham which is about 15 miles long and from 4 to 5 miles in width. *Do-chen* is 4 miles beyond Garu, while as many miles below is the *Kala* Lake 8 miles in length and about 2½ miles in breadth. Then comes *Gyantse*† which although defended by 7,000 Tibetans was stormed on the 6th July, 1904, by a comparative handful of British and Indian troops. It is the junction of the trade routes from India and Bhutan, and also of Ladak and Asia; is celebrated for its woollen cloths and carpet manufactories, and is besides the official residence of one of the two Governors of Western Tibet. Its garrison consists of 500 rank and file. The gompas about the surrounding hills are most numerous. The largest accommodates 600 llamas, followers of both the red and yellow sects into which Buddism

---

*The Tibetan equivalent is Phag-Rhi or pig hill. It stands at an elevation of 15,100 feet above sea-level, and is thus the highest dwelling place in the world if we except the hamlet of Pascoe in Mexico which doubtless claims township rights.

†At this outpost is the gilt-roofed fortified monastery of Gândho-la supposed to be a replica of the one at Bodh-Gayâ. It is about 100 feet high with a base of 600 feet, and is built in five terraced steps on the plan of the vimânas of Indian temples.

is divided. This pagoda which is 100 feet high has a circular base measuring fully 200 yards. It is eight stories high. Here are also several nunneries. Owing to the scarcity of fuel only the llamas, and cases of death through infectious diseases, are burnt; others are left out to be devoured by the innumerable packs of semi-wild dogs which infest this land. The Tse-chen gompa has quarters for 2,000 monks of the yellow-sect. Eighteen miles beyond Gyantse lies *Ralung* (14,500′); thirty-seven miles further is *Kharo*, or the wide-mouthed pass in which the Nojin glacier is situated at an altitude of 16,600 feet. Further on, again, is *Nagartse* in the basin of the Yamdok or turquoise lake, an inland sea at an elevation of 14,850 feet with a circuit of about 150 miles which would take over a fortnight to traverse. To get to *Tsangpo* (12,100′), the next stage, the *Kamba Pass*, 16,500 feet high, has to be crossed. From the summit of this pass, which is in central Tibet, there is a steep descent of 4,000 feet in the first 4 miles where lies *Chaksam*, which is only 43 miles from Lhasa. *Tsangpo* is situated on the great central river of Tibet of the same name, which near the town is spanned by an iron chain suspension bridge, like those met with in western China. It was completed in the 15th century, is 150 yards long, 15 feet wide and about the same height above high water-level. Its pierheads are chorten-shaped. This structure as a whole reminds one of the suspension bridge at Rumbi, Tista Valley. After crossing the river Tsangpo the great monastery of Dapung looms in the distance; it is the largest in the world and has several gilded roofs. The Tsangpo is believed to be the upper source of the Brahmaputra river. A little beyond one debouches through a gorge which at the 6th mile opens out into the Kyi Valley and takes its name from the river which flows past the walls of *Lhasa* which was entered on the 3rd August, 1904, by only 650 British and 4,000 Indian troops and followers over the Tiling bridge and then through a mighty chorten whose solid, square base is pierced by a large and strong gateway.

Thus was the veil of mysticism and mystery, which had hung for centuries over Lhasa, rent asunder and the naked city has been revealed in all its weird barbarity.

Lhasa.

"At last, Lhasa, the Hermit City, the Rome of Central Asia ! From first to last, from far and near this imposing pile on the Potala* hill dominates the landscape and holds the eye. This palace of the Buddist Pope which faces east is a mass of lofty buildings covering the hillsides about 300 feet high with terraces from top to bottom of many-storied, many-windowed houses, and buttressed masonry battlements and retaining walls, and forming a gigantic structure of stately architectural proportions on the most picturesque of craggy sites. The central cluster of buildings, crowning the summit and resplendent with its five golden pavilions on its roofs, was of dull crimson, that gives it the name of the 'Red Palace', while those on the other flank were of dazzling whiteness ; and the great stairway on each side, leading down to the chief entrance and gardens below, zig-zagging outwards to enclose a diamond-shaped design, recalled a similar one at the summer palace of Pekin. A mysterious effect was given to the central portion of the building by long curtains of dark purple yak-hair cloth which draped the verandahs to protect the frescoes from the rain and sun, but which seemed to muffle the rooms in secrecy..................The population which is 30,000, or a fifth of the entire population, includes no less than 20,000 monks, the remainder being chiefly women who are polyandrous. This city is 354½ miles from Darjeeling, which in turn is 386 miles from Calcutta"—*Waddell.*

Lhasa†, the capital of Tibet, covers roughly an area of two square miles, and stands at an elevation of about 12,600 feet. Its main thoroughfares are fairly wide, while its lanes which are narrow in the extreme and unpaved do not improve the sanitation of the city. The houses are for the most part three-storied with flat roofs, and erected in stone and brick. The first floor

---

*'Potala', after the name of a rocky hill overlooking the harbour at Cape Komorin in the extreme tip of the Indian continent, which the Indians fancied was the extreme end of the world. The Potala is a monastery as well as a palace, and can accommodate 500 monks of which the Dalai Llama is the abbot.

†The writer is indebted to the Chief Ministers of the Dalai Llama for these details. See next chapter.

of these quaint buildings are reserved for shops whose stalls abut the streets. The walls are whitewashed while the wood-work including doors and windows are usually picked out in bright, variegated colours which impart a picturesqueness quite peculiar to this land. The rooms of the upper classes are richly painted and have frescoes profusely inlaid in the plastering of the walls, the ceilings are usually daubed with green paint, and supported by highly polished pillars of cinnabar, while the floors are constructed either of wood, or glazed mortar. The seats are three feet square covered with mattresses varying from 6 to 10 inches in thickness over which rich and beautiful Tibetan and Chinese carpets are spread. Silk and fur cushions are not infrequently seen supporting the backs of the loungers who sit cross-legged.

Owing to the extreme rigour of its climate agriculture and stock-farming are in a rudimentary state, though grain and vegetables are raised in sufficient quantities to satisfy the demands of its population, which however subsists chiefly on the yield of the large herds of sheep and yak, which take the place of kine in India. Its imports, therefore, exceed its exports. Of the former pulse, rice and grain are received from India through Sikkim, also cotton, woollen cloth of European manufacture, fancy-goods, toilet requisites, patent medicines, gramophones and other musical instruments, *bric-a-brac* and Brummagem-ware ; silks, brick-tea and jewels from China ; and salt and gold dust from the Chang-tang plateau. The exports are necessarily confined to the limited products of the country, which includes wool and its manufactured articles, namely, woollen cloths, rugs and carpets, and also hides, yaks' tails and musk.

Lhasa was founded early in the 7th century by King Srong Tsan Gampo who married a Chinese Princess, and also a daughter of the King of Nepal. The present city is built on the ancient site which according to tradition was erected on a lake, which was filled in with earth fetched from a great distance by goats: hence it was known as 'Ra-sa' or goat-land. After the holy image of Budda (Sakyamuni) was brought to this city by the Chinese consort of the king it was renamed 'Lhasa' or

PLATE XVIII.

HIS HOLINESS THE DALAI LLAMA.

'place of heaven'. Buddism has not only gradually driven fetishism or 'Bon' worship into the remote provinces, where its followers still indulge in demon-worship, but has also taken so great a hold of the land ever since the 11th century that it has covered its surface with innumerable monasteries some of which, like those named Sera, Drepung, Ganden and Tahsilhumpo, house thousands of monks, of whom the Dalai Llama is the head as well as the Pope of Tibet, Mongolia and other Llamaist States in Asia.

Since 1910 the Tibetans have striven to throw off the suzerainty of China ; and the opposing forces of both nations are to *this day* confronting each other in Eastern Tibet. These wars, including that with the British in 1904, have if anything accentuated the hostile feeling, which has existed ever since the 17th century, against the 'foreign devil', including all Asiatics: on the other hand, the wily Tibetan fully appreciates the advantages accruing from an alliance with the British Government, and more so since his rude awakening as to the real intentions of his pseudo benefactor, the Russian.

His Holiness The Dalai Llama.

In 1910 the Dalai Llama* owing to an invasion of Tibet by the Chinese had to flee for his life to Darjeeling and seek the protection of the British Government. While he resided at 'Hillside', his chief ministers lived at Sadie Villa† for 18 months during which negotiations were in progress between the three governments.

Shortly after his arrival on March 3rd (and it is an open secret) a gang of about 20 Chinamen also arrived with the avowed object of bringing about a fresh reincarnation‡ of the 'man-

---

*According to Waddell, the Mongolian prince, Gouri Khan, conquered Tibet, and made it a present to Ge-lugpa the Grand Llama, who in 1650 was confirmed in his sovereignty by the Chinese Emperor and given the title of 'Dalai, or (vast as) the ocean'—a title little known to the Tibetans who call these Grand Llamas—"The Great Gem of Majesty". 'Dalai' is Mongolian; Gyatsho is the Tibetan equivalent.

†See Plate III.

‡The present Dalai Llama is the thirteenth in the line of succession ; his predecessors being spirited away by means known to orientalists alone.

"It is the worship of a living, rather than a dead deity, that marks deity'. These diabolical intentions were, however, frustrated by the vigilance of the police who guarded his abode carefully. Finding that the plot did not work, a distinguished Chinese linguist named Yang Feng found his way from Calcutta into Darjeeling accompanied by a few retainers purporting to be monks desiring entry into one of the monasteries in Tibet. With this end in view an application, obviously under an assumed name, was submitted to the Deputy Commissioner, Darjeeling ; the intention being to waylay the Dalai Llama on his way back to Tibet in one of the many passes and there carry out the work with which they were entrusted, for his deposition was placarded so far back as August 3rd, 1904, by the Chinese Amban at Lhasa when the British force entered that city.

How the representatives of the Associated Press at Calcutta, the headquarters, got scent of the arrival of Yang Feng history deponeth not, but this much is certain—its Darjeeling representative (the writer) was duly informed by wire and asked, if possible, to trace and unmask this individual. As neither the police nor members of the political department would vouchsafe a reply to the queries of the pressman, a member of each of these departments was shadowed by a shrewd urchin, with the result that Yang Feng through them was traced to the premises behind the Government Printing Press on the Cart Road in occupation by a Mongolian compositor who had harboured, in ignorance, this alleged gang of monks. The press representative next cast about for an interpreter, and on succeeding immediately called on these filthy-looking llamas. After the ceremonies usually indulged in, in the East had been gone through, the ball was started rolling by the intimation that the interviewer owned the house in which the chief ministers of the Dalai Llama lived. The bait took, for the eyes of the pseudo servant (to the other monks) was

---

the difference of the forms of Buddism in India and Tibet. Out of Tibet no incarnation of Budda is believed to have taken place since the death of Sakyamuni; in India, therefore, they have been content to worship images of the departed, or relics which recall his presence. In Tibet, where their divinity is still present among them, continually transmigrating, but never dying, of course such a form of worship is absurd; no relic of a living god can logically exist, and the chaityas of the Great Llamas are honoured and worshipped in the monasteries occupied by their successors."

observed to twitch and twinkle, while those of the supposed head monk were listless. At this stage an officer of the political service arrived and joined in the general conversation, thus giving the pressman further opportunities to study the features of the pseudo servant. Satisfied that whoever he may have been, he was certainly no servant, the pressman told the political man :—"You also have been in search of Yang Feng. There he is" ; at the same time addressing the supposed servant with "Own up, Yang Feng" ; which to the surprise of all, he did, finding the game up, in faultless English. And now for a greater surprise in store for all. The room in which these men put up contained no boxes or furniture save a few squalid bundles and bedding. Yet an hour later Yang Feng, like Brett Harte's heathen Chinee, who had all the trumps tucked up his sleeves, turned out dressed after the latest European fashion in a silk suit, patent leather boots and a panama straw hat in response to the mandate of the Deputy Commissioner. Needless to add that Yang Feng was bundled out of Darjeeling by the next outgoing train and deported from Calcutta to China under police escort.

The spiritual affairs of Tibet are guided by the Dalai and Tashi Llamas, who are spoken of with bated breath by the Northern Buddists under the following grandiloquent titles :— "The Great Gem of Majesty" and "The God of the Boundless Life", respectively.

The suite of the former is comprised of a Prime Minister, two chief Ministers and three Sappos or Councillors who daily bring enough in their portfolios to cause the Dalai to lead a most strenuous life in order to keep abreast of the affairs of the State ; as well as to give audience to numberless devotees, each of whom is required to present a scarf of silk and 'Peter's Pence' (which is never less than eight pence) so that the coffers of the Exchequer are never low. In return they are given a silk thread, which is worn round the neck, and a longevity-pill which while extending the lives of the recipients somehow failed to affect that of the priest-donors, whose predecessors were most miraculously spirited away. The present Dalai Llama, however, is a remarkbly suspicious person for his daily menu is tasted by a number of officials in his presence before he will partake of a meal, and so defers a fresh incarnation. The only exercise in which he indulges is walking, doing from 3 to 6 miles each afternoon at a brisk pace but with a slightly bent gait, which is probably the result of the posture assumed for hours at a time in imitation of the contemplative Budda.

Shortly after his arrival in Darjeeling he gave audience to over 10,000 devotees, including many Ruling Chiefs who had come from far lands to be blest.

In December, 1905, the Tashi Llama returned to India to have audience with the Prince of Wales (since King George) and the Viceroy. Prior to his return to Tibet he was toured all over India, and at Rawalpindi was present at a review of 55,000 British troops, which doubtless, and in a great measure, governed the subsequent policy of this State, and taught it to respect the British Arms! At the invitation of the Dalai Llama, Mr. C. A. Bell, I.C.S., Political Officer, Sikkim, proceeded on November 1st, 1920, to Lhasa *via* Yatung. Such overtures coming from this hitherto 'closed land' is suggestive of British influence in Central Asia at a time when all is flux and every Asiatic government stands in terror of Bolshevism, regarded rather as a robber force than a political organisation. This invitation may not have been unconnected with the modernist influences which have lately affected Tibet; but that it clearly indicates a desire to throw off the seclusion of ages brought about by the return of its English-trained mechanics goes without saying. It, accordingly, is within the bounds of probability that the scheme for connection with India by railway will materialise in the near future especially as this State desires utilising its present chief exports and establishing State woollen factories at Lhasa.

Travellers have commented upon the habits of these Tibetans, the chief being their innate apathy to ablutions, to which the writer adds his quota. Although Sadie Villa, a newly built house which had never been occupied before, had its doors repainted and its walls, which were encrusted to a height of 5 feet with greasy stains, washed down *six times* with fuller's earth, yet the malodour imparted to the building by a residence of 18 months only by these ministers would not depart despite the strong smell of fresh paint, which pervades the atmosphere for weeks. What then must be the sanitary condition of the Potala, or at least that portion of this edifice occupied by these officers, can better be imagined than described!

Waddell remarks—"And who will say that the Tibetans neglect their toilet when it is seen that 720 lbs of soap and 6,694 towels crossed the borders in three months" of 1899, that is, during the chief period that the passes into Tibet are open. Thus proving the charge. Fancy, 729 lbs. of soap consumed in one, whole year by a population of 150,000 souls!

PART IV.

Railway Extensions in Northern Bengal.

Much ink has been shed over the present and prospective disabilities which the extension of the broad-gauge to Santahar only has caused, and is likely to cause, but little or nothing has been advanced about the efforts of those interested in the floating of feeder-lines, as well as by the Government, to tap the resources of Northern Bengal with a view to improve incidentally the condition of the tiller of the soil, the first obligation of any Administration worthy of the name.

In regard to the disabilities referred to, it is understood that the protest lodged with the Railway Board and the Government of India by the several Tea Associations, coupled with the complaints of the public, has borne fruit in that the Secretary to the Railway Board will shortly inspect Santahar and its connections with the Hardinge Bridge. Attention has accordingly to be invited to the following:—Apparently little or no fore-thought—a rare commodity now-a-days—was exercised by the Management of the E. B. Railway which had no less than 5 years wherein to link the line for a distance of 60 miles only from the Bridge to Santahar, as well as erect suitable accommodation for the passenger traffic at that station.

That it has failed egregiously in the latter is too apparent to need further comment; but that the new line is a model of construction is more than questionable, for we have it on good authority that the broad-gauge, which approximately runs parallel between these stations with the metre-gauge, is not only 9 inches below the level of the latter but also forms a *cul de sac* for the retention of water which at present percolates through the new unsettled line, but which in the near future will cause breaches*

Broad-Gauge to Santahar.

*It should in all fairness be added that if breaches have occurred these have been repaired without any delay or inconvenience being caused to the passenger traffic.

in the broad-gauge thereby necessitating transhipment at Isshurdy, a condition of affairs which was predicted at the time of linking. It were well if the Secretary had these facts before him when inspecting the line.

In regard to the remaining disabilities, such as the late transhipment that takes place during the journey to and fro, and the speedy extension of the broad-gauge to Siliguri, it appears to the writer that the first could be easily overcome by recasting the time tables of the connected services, while the second much as it may be desired, is governed by three factors—time and funds, as well as one in which the supply of sleepers plays an important part, for either our forests are unable to cope with the demand, or else the price offered is not sufficient to attract fresh contractors into the field. However this may be, it is incumbent on the public to shape its demands within the bounds of possibility and not expect more from a State Railway than from one run by private enterprise which would necessarily extend its connections in conformity with its reserve funds.

The above forecast has proved correct in that it has taken 7 years for the extension project to materialise. At the meeting of the Legislative Council held in January, 1922, the Hon'ble Nawab Saiyid Nawab Ali Choudhry Khan Bahadur, in reply to Mr. W. L. Travers (O.B.E., M.L.C., and Vice-President, Duars Planters' Association) intimated that in accordance with sanction received for the extension of the broad-gauge from Santahar to Parbatipur (64 miles) earth-work had been completed, rails and sleepers collected, and orders placed for bridge girders ; while estimates for the conversion of the remainder of the line to Siliguri (85 miles) had been submitted to the Railway Board for sanction. It follows that if the progress of railway construction in the past is any criterion on which the public may build its hopes (see footnote on page 9) it will take fully 5 years from date before the traveller will entrain at Sealdah and complete the journey to the foot of the hills without transhipment.

During the years 1917—19 the following projects, for tapping the resources of the country in general, and the trade of Nepal, Sikkim and incidentally Tibet, had been sanctioned:—The Kissengunge-Matigora line, The Tista Valley line, The line to Gangtok (Sikkim). The Jalpaiguri-Dinajpur line, The Nuxalbari-Mirik line, and The Nuxalbari-Santahar line; while the following is still under consideration by both the Bengal Duars and the Darjeeling Himalayan Railway authorities, *viz., the extension of* the B. D. Line from Bagrakote to the river Tista at Sivoke where the D. H. Railway has spanned the river with a wire-rope, the nucleus of the wire suspension-bridge, which will ultimately span the Tista at this spot.

Other Lines.

Of those mentioned, the Kissengunge-Matigora line, which connects Siliguri *via* Nuxalbarie and Kissengunge, and which is on the narrow-gauge, has been completed and is now (1915) open to traffic throughout its entire length of 66 miles. The tract of country through which it passes is a rich one. The stretch of country to Islampore, a distance of 22 miles from Siliguri, previously opened for traffic, gave exceptional returns, and now that the entire line is open to traffic a material increase in jute alone for Calcutta may be expected. The rolling stock includes bogie-wagons and a type of engine built specially by Messrs. Sharp, Stewart & Co., of Glasgow for these feeder-lines (like those of the metre-gauge lines) which is capable of drawing an 800 ton load.

Kissengunge Line.

In 1916-17, 3,76,478 third-class passengers were carried over this line, which crosses the Balasan and Mahanady rivers, the former being spanned by a bridge having 14 spans each 40 feet long, while the latter is bridged by one having 7 spans each 80 feet in length.

Two factors played an important part in delaying the completion of the Tista Valley Line:—the heavy blasting operations which were found necessary during its construction, and which have ever since caused innumerable slips, as also the war which had materially interfered with the delivery of bridge material. The line was opened for traffic as far as Riang on the 15th May, 1915, which is 22 miles from Siliguri, and when these setbacks are borne in mind Mr. G. B. Cresswell,

PLATE XIX.

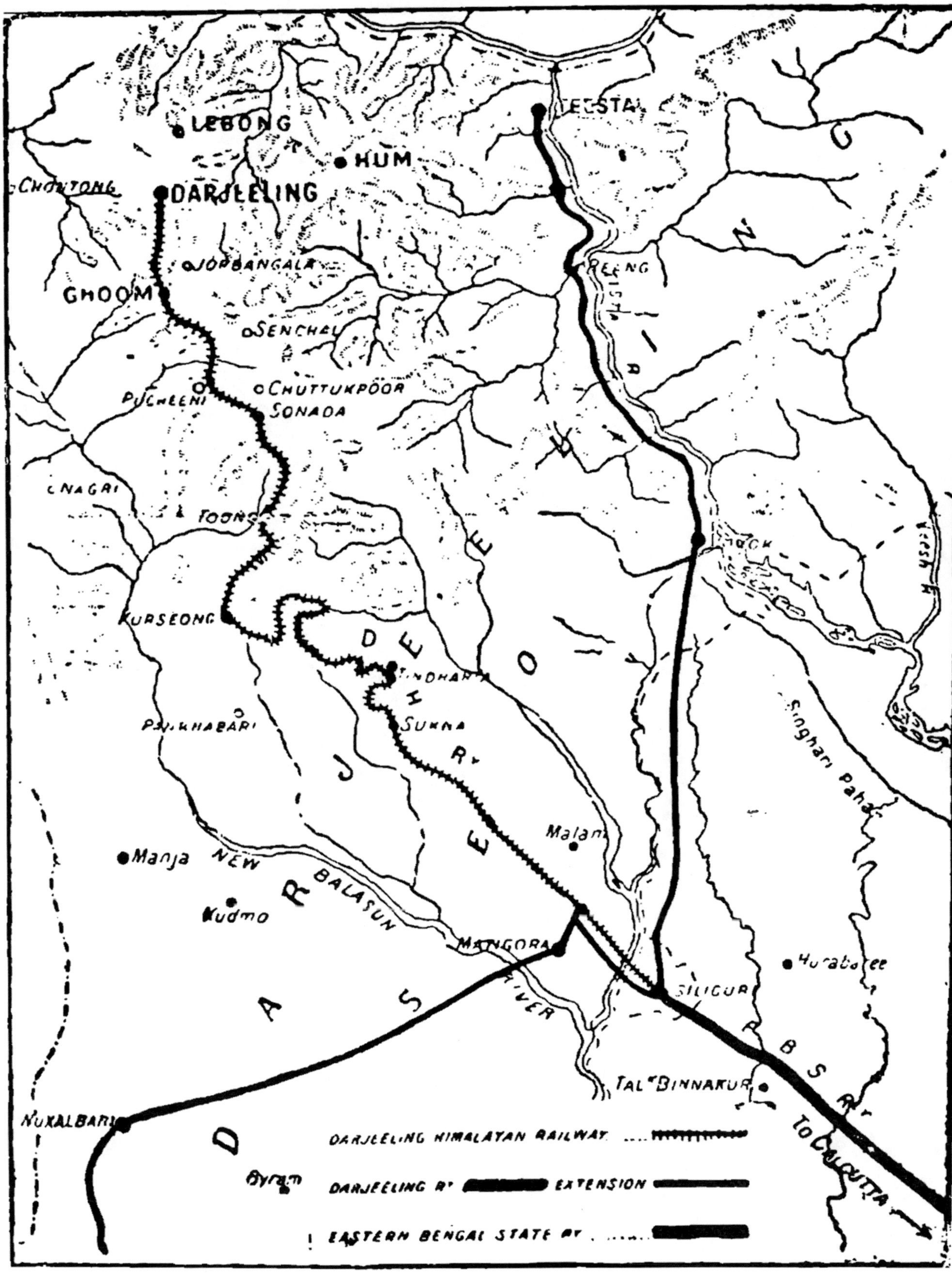

D. H. RAILWAY AND EXTENSIONS.

the late General Manager of the D. H. Railway, might well be proud of the achievement. For 16 miles the line worms its way along the hillside when it reaches its present terminus, Kalimpong Road Station 2 miles from the Tista Bridge. This line will tap the resources of Sikkim and incidentally that of Tibet, through the mart at Kalimpong which annually receives no less than 4¼ *lakhs* of maunds of merchandise. But with the fresh facilities afforded by railway traction it is estimated that in the very near future fully 8 to 10 *lakhs* of maunds of freight will pass over this line in either direction.

Tista Valley Line.

The Tista Valley line passes through an ever-varying succession of beautiful scenery reminding one of the Jhelum Valley Road connecting Rawalpindi and Srinagar in Kashmir, which likewise winds its way a little above and on the right bank of the Jhelum river. Although the Tista Valley line is primarily intended for goods traffic, the journey from Siliguri to Tista Bridge and thence Kalimpong, or Darjeeling *via* Peshok and Ghum, as the case may be, is so picturesque that there is not the slight doubt it will be patronised by tourists on an ever-increasing scale. From Sivoke, where the line emerges from the Terai, to the Tista Bridge the toy-train winds its way in and out of the spurs only 100 feet above the level of the river, which during the rains is a mighty, swirling, muddy torrent, while in the winter its waters are deep, clear and of a pale sea-green colour. At Sivoke the Tista is about 750 feet wide, and it is at this point that a wire-rope has already been stretched across it, the nucleus of the suspension bridge to follow wherewith to tap the resources of the tea gardens between Bagrakote station on the B. D. Railway and the Tista.

On either side of the line rise high mountains clothed in dense forest which, with the placid, green waters below, presents a picture not unlike that met with in Norway. On a clear day when nearing Riang station a glimpse of the snowy range may be obtained. The line works on alternate gradients reminding one of a huge switchback, while the approach to Riang is achieved by a series of bends and curves which can best be likened to the spiral twists of a corkscrew. Several fine bridges (see Plates

XV and XX) each having a span of 100 feet, have been thrown across the rivulets and gorges, the chief ones being located at Sivoke (with approach embankments of ⅛th. of a mile each) Kalijhora, Riang and Gel Jhora. It is expected that this line will be opened for traffic throughout its entire length by the end of 1925 thus landing tourists at Tista Bridge within a few hours after leaving Siliguri, and within easy reach of Kalimpong, which is but 7 miles up the hill, and to the east of the Bridge.

Other Extensions.

The Sikkim Line.

The project of opening out trade-routes with Bhutan and Tibet *via* Sikkim was first formulated by Warren Hastings when Mr. George Boyle of the Civil Service and Dr. Hamilton, a member of the Indian Medical Service, were deputed in 1774 to visit Bhutan and Tibet *via* the Bhutan Duars and Punaka the capital of the former State. It was taken up again in 1864 when the Mission to Bhutan under the guidance of Sir Ashley Eden as envoy ended in such contumely that it forced on the war with that country which terminated in the annexation of 524 square miles of territory which included the Bengal Duars and the Daling Sub-division of which Kalimpong is now the headquarters. This raised the area of the Darjeeling district from 640 to 1,164 square miles. The project has been steadily borne in mind by successive administrations, the last being the deputation sent by the Government of India under Mr. Coleman Macaulay to China which ultimately ended in the Anglo-Chinese Convention of 1890 by which our protectorate over Sikkim was acknowledged and which also gave us exclusive control over its internal affairs and its foreign relations.

These projects paved the way to the sanction now to the D. H. Railway to extend the Tista Valley Line by 34½ miles beyond its present terminus to Gangtok, the capital of Sikkim, *via* the cart-road and Rangpu which lies on the borders of British territory. Operations in connection with the preliminary survey, which has been in hand since the winter months of 1917-18 will include the construction of a girder-bridge over the

PLATE XX.

SIVOKE—TISTA VALLEY.

river Tista near its junction with the Great Rangneet river, in place of the suspension bridge, over 300 feet in length, which has met existing conditions ever since its erection in 1880, and also considerable revetments along the entire projected route, especially at the 1st, 3rd. and 5th. miles respectively, spots which for the past few years owing to the huge slips which take place throughout the rains have caused frequent dislocations in the traffic.

It is expected that within six years of the cessation of hostilities, when bridge and other material will be available, this line will be completed and opened to traffic having stations at the following spots by which the resources of Sikkim at least will be tapped :—Melli at the 3rd-mile, Tarkhola at the 9th-mile, Rangpu at the 14½-mile (where there will be a large siding for railway stock), Sankokhola at the 24½-mile, and finally Gangtok, the capital.

The Mirik Line.

With regard to the Mirik project the statistics collected during the two years 1916-17 concerning the three locations which appeared to the authorities of the Behar and Orissa Government most suitable for a summer resort have not proved conclusive. Mirik has, therefore, again a staff of subordinates busy collecting fresh data. This may be coupled with the fact that sanction has been accorded to the D. H. Railway to survey a line from Nuxalbarie *via* Panighatta and Namsu to Mirik, and leads to the belief that the ultimate choice will end in favour of Mirik, and incidentally the completion of this line within a measurable distance of time.

Junction of B. D. and T. V. Lines.

Regarding the Bagrakote project the following may be predicted :—The Tista Valley Line emerges through the forest at Sivoke, a distance of 12½ miles from Siliguri. The B. D. Line from Mal stops at Bagrakote, a distance of 6 miles from Sivoke, the Tista intervening. The D. H. Railway has however taken the initiative by throwing a wire-rope across the river, the nucleus of a suspension bridge to follow, by which communication with Mal will be established, thereby providing an outlet for the traffic which at present reaches Jalpaiguri *via* Barnes Junction, or the E. B. Railway at Lalmanirhat. Although the mileage will not be appreciably effected yet an important factor, *viz.*, the crossing of the Tista, will play an important part in deflecting the traffic to the T. V. Line over the suspension bridge at Sivoke. That the passenger traffic will be materially affected goes without saying, for the journey to Darjeeling will be completed in a much shorter time and in consequence availed of by the planting community, if not, by the public in general.

The Bengal Duars Railway.

To visit the tea area in the Duars, or the doors to the hills, the tourist must stop the night at Jalpaiguri where the dak bungalow is certainly neither the best nor the most comfortable to be met with on this side of India. But these inconveniences and discomforts are forgotten the moment foot is set on the violas, or ferry boats, which convey passengers over the Tista to Barnes Junction. From the Tista on a clear day the grandest view of the snowy range is available, for fully 150 miles of this panorama forces itself and its majesty upon the vision of the traveller. The early rising sun lights up its surface in pinkish-mauve tints which gradually fade away into a pale gold to eventually settle down into the usual dull dead white so familiar to those who have gazed at Kinchenjunga from Darjeeling. Then the wide, swirling river with its eddies caused by hidden sandbanks absorb the attention until the opposite bank is reached. From here the train proceeds to Domohani, the headquarters of the line, which apparently was chosen as being the most forsaken spot on earth by the projectors of the line. The monotony and feeling of dullness imparted by this station soon give place to interest, for the track from here runs through virgin forests where not infrequently elephants and bears in ignoring the whistle of the advancing train have met with a sad fate: the former have been known to charge the train much to their detriment, while the latter are frequently run over and killed. Once the forest belt is passed the train traverses miles of country under tea cultivation of which many an estate covers no less than 1,500 acres, which require a resident establishment of 700 to 800 operatives to cope with the outturn. Mal, the northernmost point of this line, is reached at 12-30 p.m. where refreshments may be had. Here the line curves away both to the west and east, the former terminating at Bagrakote, while the latter proceeds along the base of the hills at a gradient of 1 in 40 feet until Chalsa, the prettiest spot in the Duars, is reached. Here the line sends out a feeder branch running due north and 5.30 miles in length to Matelli by which the resources of the plantations at the foot of these hills as also that of the southern portion of the Daling Sub-division, of which Kalimpong is the head-quarters, will be tapped. From Chalsa the line debouches into the plains and after passing through miles of the Tendu forest pulls up at its eastern terminus—Madarihat—which is 136 miles from Lalmanirhat, the southern terminus of the line.

No account of this line, which is worked entirely by a native staff officered by Europeans, and under the able management of Mr. J. A. Polwhele, would be either complete or accurate without reference being made to the extreme regularity of its running, for intending travellers, bar accidents, may safely depend upon reaching their destination on scheduled time—which cannot be said of all railways in Bengal. Finally, its waiting-rooms are replete with excellent furniture, except beds.

The stations of this railway, starting from its junction with the Eastern Bengal, are:—

Stations—Mileage.

	Lalmanirhat	38	Baura	83	Neora Naddi	118	Banarhat
6	Aditmari	45	Patgram	87	Baradighi	122	Binnaguri
13	Kakina	53	Changrabandha	92	Mal Junction	127	Dalgaon
16	Tushbhander	59	Bhotepatti	97	Chalsa	131	Mujnai
21	Bhotemari	66	Barnes Junc.	106	Nagrakata	136	Madarihat
28	Hatibandha	71	Domohani	110	Carron		
34	Barakhata	80	Lataguri Junc.	112	Chengmari		

The Cooch Behar Railway.

This railway runs almost due north into the Alipore Duars toward the Military outpost at the foot of the Bhutan Hills, but there is no junction with the B. D. Railway. If the small stretch of country between the two lines were linked up, there would be a complete circle of railways in the Duars giving two outlets for its traffic ; and in the event of a washout, as occurred in 1915 only when the approaches of the Jaldakha bridge on the B. D. Railway for about 600 yards were washed away by an unprecedented flood following an abnormal rainfall of 20 inches in one night, the traffic from the affected area could be deflected to the undamaged line and so reach its mart in time, instead of being held up for months until the breach was spanned.

APPENDIX I.

Hooker's Visit to Darjeeling.

Hooker's visit to Darjeeling produced his 'Journey Through The Terai', and 'The Himalayan Art Journals', both of which are engrossing reading and full of scientific information.

Hooker, who was a close friend of the erudite J. W. Grant, (See page 2) came out from England as his guest. It was not long before this scientist was launched on his famous trip to the hills, and incidentally Sikkim where he spent the years 1848-50 in search of specimens; and also in materially assisting Brian Houghton Hodgson in his translation of the Buddist documents, which were collected at a great expenditure of money and energy.

Hooker left Grant's hospitable bungalow on the 8th April, 1848, and embarked in a frail boat from Bhagulpur to drift down the Ganges to Colgong where the dangerous crossing at the junction of the Kosi river (of Nepal) had to be accomplished before Karagola Ghat could be reached, and thereafter a tiresome journey by palki dak *via* Purnea, Kissengunge, Titalya and Siliguri to Pankabarie before he could get to Kurseong. We shall now let Hooker speak of his experiences in order that the traveller, who now does the journey in comfort, may have some idea of the discomforts experienced by the pioneers in this direction. Having arrived at Kissengunge, where there was no dak bungalow in those days, he was shewn hospitality by Mr. Percy, the Assistant Magistrate.

"I had just got into bed at night when the bearers arrived, so bidding a hurried adieu to my host I proceeded on my journey. April 12th, 1848, I awoke at 4 a.m. and found my *palkee* on the ground, and the bearers cooly smoking their *hokahs* under a tree. It was raining hard: they had carried me the length of their stage, twelve miles, and there were no others to take me on. I had paid £24 for my *dak* from Cargola to the hills, to which I had been obliged to add a handsome douceur, so I lost all patience. After waiting and entreating during several hours I found the headman of a neighbouring village, and by a further disbursement induced six out of the twelve bearers to carry the *palkee,* whilst I should walk to the next stage; or till we should meet some others. They agreed, and cutting the thick and spongy sheaths of the banana, used them for shoulder pads: they also wrapped them round the palkee-poles to ease their aching clavicles. Walking along I picked up a few plants, and 14 miles further on, came again to the banks of the Mahanuddy, whose bed was strewn with pebbles and small boulders brought thus far from the mountains (about 30 miles distant). Here again I had to apply to the headman of a village, and pay for bearers to take me to Titalya, the next stage (14 miles). Some curious long low sheds puzzled me very much, and on examining them they proved to be for the growth of awn (modern *pan-leaf*) or betel pepper, another proof of the moisture of the climate..............I found no difficulty in procuring bearers to proceed to Siligoree, where I arrived at 6 a.m. on the 13th. Hitherto I had not seen the mountains, so uniformly had they been shrouded by dense wreaths of vapour: here, however, when within 8 miles of the base, I caught the first glimpse of the outer range—sombre masses of far from picturesque outline, dotted everywhere with dusky forest".

After Siliguri the road, says Hooker, "winds through a thick brushwood, choked with long grasses." (This is now a wide P. W. D. high road passing through rice fields or grass pasture land, and the railway to Kissengunge runs beside it as far as Mattigora). "I crossed the beds of many small streams: some were dry and all were very tortuous. Fatal as this district is, and especially to Europeans, a race inhabits it with impunity, who, if not numerous, do not owe their paucity to any climatic causes. These are the Mechis, often described as squalid, unhealthy people, who are typical of the region they frequent, but who are, in reality, more robust than Europeans in India; and whose disagreeably sallow complexion is deceptive as indicating a sickly constitution. They are a mild inoffensive people, industrious for Orientals, living by annually burning the Terai jungle and cultivating the cleared spots, and though so sequestered and isolated, they rather court than avoid intercourse with those whites whom they know to be kindly disposed".

"After proceeding some six miles along the gradually ascending path I came to a considerable stream with cliffs on each side, 15 to 20 feet high. The road here suddenly ascends a steep gravelly hill, and opens out on a short flat, or spur, from which to east and west as far as the eye could reach were range base. The little bungalow of Punkabari, my immediate destination, nestled in the woods crowning a lateral knoll, above which the Himalaya rise abruptly clothed with forest from the after range of wooded mountains 6,000 to 8,000 feet high."

These slopes are now covered by the tea-estates of Longview, Kalabari, Punkabari, Fallodhi, Garidhura and Rhoni. The *dak* bungalow at Punkabari is still in use as an inspection bungalow. It was so named because of the large *pankas* or leaf fans used there.

APPENDIX I A.

Characteristics Of The Paharie.

In these tribes, and, indeed, in the whole Mongolian race, the liveliness and happiness of the race is crossed by no flaw. The sheer joy of life abides in them, and they seem to be perpetually at play: hence the impression that they are lazy. And never was there so great a mistake made, for there is such a thing as laziness *and laziness*. There is the laziness of the man who shirks work and goes about with an attenuated frame and a blank mind; one who is driven to put in his tale of labour, the slave of circumstances. There is also the laziness, the *Laissez faire* of the manly fellow endowed with a gay nature and a lively fancy, and one whose being is saturated with a philosophic contempt for the accumulation of material wealth, with a deep-rooted desire to bestow all that is over and above his present needs (thus carrying out one of *our* own injunctions) in charity and in good works. At a fair, or feast he will be seen basking in the sunlight on the hillside enjoying the Nirvana of complete idleness—not because he is lazy, but for the simple reason that he is an artist and a philosopher; because before his eyes there is the blue of the sky and the dazzling whiteness of the snows at which he can gaze and gain inspiration; because the mere earning of wages with him is a triviality when compared with the joy of living.

As with the Spaniard, so with the Paharie. He holds the most optimistic views of the future. To-morrow (Mañana!) for him is the day of days. On that day the rough places will be made smooth, and the crooked ways will be made straight. Everything, therefore, is laid aside for to-morrow. This to-morrow means more than the day-to-come; it means the future that is dim and far away—the future that is not yet to be defined—a time of haze and golden opportunities.

Utopia is his, for he possesses nearly all it can offer—leisure, independence, the nearest approach to a perfect distribution of wealth, and last, and chiefest, a fount of happiness from which he draws even in adversity. The Occident on the other hand is still vainly casting about to solve the problems of life including pauperism and over-crowding, and looking about for what the Orient, exemplified in the hillman at least, has attained as a whole !

What he does lack is 'grit', *i.e.*, the lack of persistent effort. The explanation is not far to seek, for he is still an Unspoilt Child of Nature, with much aptitude and a singular sweetness of disposition; but withal this to his credit, he possesses a passionate temper, and the wanton cruelty inherent in all children.

And what of his religion ? It is true that it is circumscribed in a great measure, for he is more concerned with the devil (against whom is notched all the ills that flesh is heir to) than with the Great Cause whose power unhappily, according to his views, is usurped by this power of darkness. And so he comes to connect each illness with a particular *deota*. If asked where these spirits reside, he will cheerfully, and with a broad wave of his hand, say : "Everywhere ; in the air, in the jhoras, in the woods, in the caves ; sometimes behind that hill at others behind another, and in the mountains".

While the Breath of Life is passing away they blow whistles and conches in order to drive away the evil spirit and so give the shade of the departing one a fair chance to pass on unmolested; and when the obsequies have been duly performed they hastily desert that abode, and immediately try to propitiate that particular *deota* with sacrificial offerings (each according to his means) which vary from a buffalo to that emblem of love which on its return buoyed up the hearts of those imprisoned in the Ark. And last of all, after he has laid his offerings of flowers and vegetables on the altar of the monastery, he takes away a stereotyped prayer stamped on paper banner or flag to hang it on a pole above his new abode in order that the flutter of each waft of wind will cause it to vibrate in the void of space until it is heard by the Great I Am, and answered. Such is his primitive yet withal ardent and living religion : to him a great reality.

APPENDIX II.

On Religions.

According to the latest Religious Census of the World

Christians number	...	468,650,000	(Obviously, incorrect as the populations of the Central and S. American States are shewn as Christians whereas the great majority, including the Haitians and Liberians, are 'heathens'.)
Buddists ...	...	415,000,000	
Muhamadans	...	255,000,000	
Hindus ...	...	220,000,000	
Israelites ...	...	13,000,000	
Confucians and Taoists ...	...	40,000,000	(the former is the State religion and that of the educated classes only: the latter is mixed with Buddism.)
Other Sects	...	200,000,000	
Total	...	1,611,650,000	

So, Christianity and Buddism are the two beliefs which are about equally followed by half the population of the world.

From prehistoric times man has gradually and intuitively evolved for himself some conception of the many attributes of the Deity (the aborigines to this day worship Him under the manifestation of the power exhibited by the sun) each stage adding to the knowledge revealed of the Trinity who was worshipped 'in the spirit and the truth' until schisms have given us the following religions, each claiming for itself divine revelation.

"In every clime from pole to pole,
A creed is found that holds control.

Up every stairway rough or smooth,
The priest ascends with creed to soothe!

Most them good men; but who is right?
For each religion differs quite!

And each avows *his* creed is true—
Implicitly believes it too!

And claims to sway confiding youth
He stands upon the Rock of Truth'—*J. A. Keble.*

The conception of the Trinity of the Godhead has been put so tersely by Keble that I quote him at length.

THE TRINITY.	CREEDS.
"The Christians' ONE GOD TRINITY!	Christianity.
The THREE IN ONE, Great mystery!	
The Hindus too have Trinity,	Hinduism
Great Brahma, Vishnu, Siva,—Three;	
How very like this Trinity	Greek Mythology
To ancient Greek mythology!—	
First Clothe spun the thread of life,	
Then Lachesis joined man and wife;	
But Atropos cut through life's thread,	
And both were numbered with the dead.	
A Trinity unique is found,	Buddism
Among Tibetans, fast creed bound:	
Lord Buddha, Dhurma Queen, and Sunga;	
For whose joy-gifts all Buddists hunger.	
Then Old Osiris, and Isis, Horus—	Egyptian.
God, Virgin, Child, a Triune for us;	
Long awed the world in ages past	
With sacred rites, mid temples vast.	
Another Triad, that of Ista,	Love, Light & Death
The Queen of Love, and Death's dread vista;	
With Shama's god of yearly suns,	
And Sin the moon-god, both her sons.	
Assyrian Trinities as well,	Assyrian.
The highest, Anu, Hoa, Bel;	
First god of heaven who glorifies,	
Then Bel of earth, that 'neath them lies,	
Last, Hoa god of all the seas—	
The hoariest of all the trinities".	

Religions of the World.

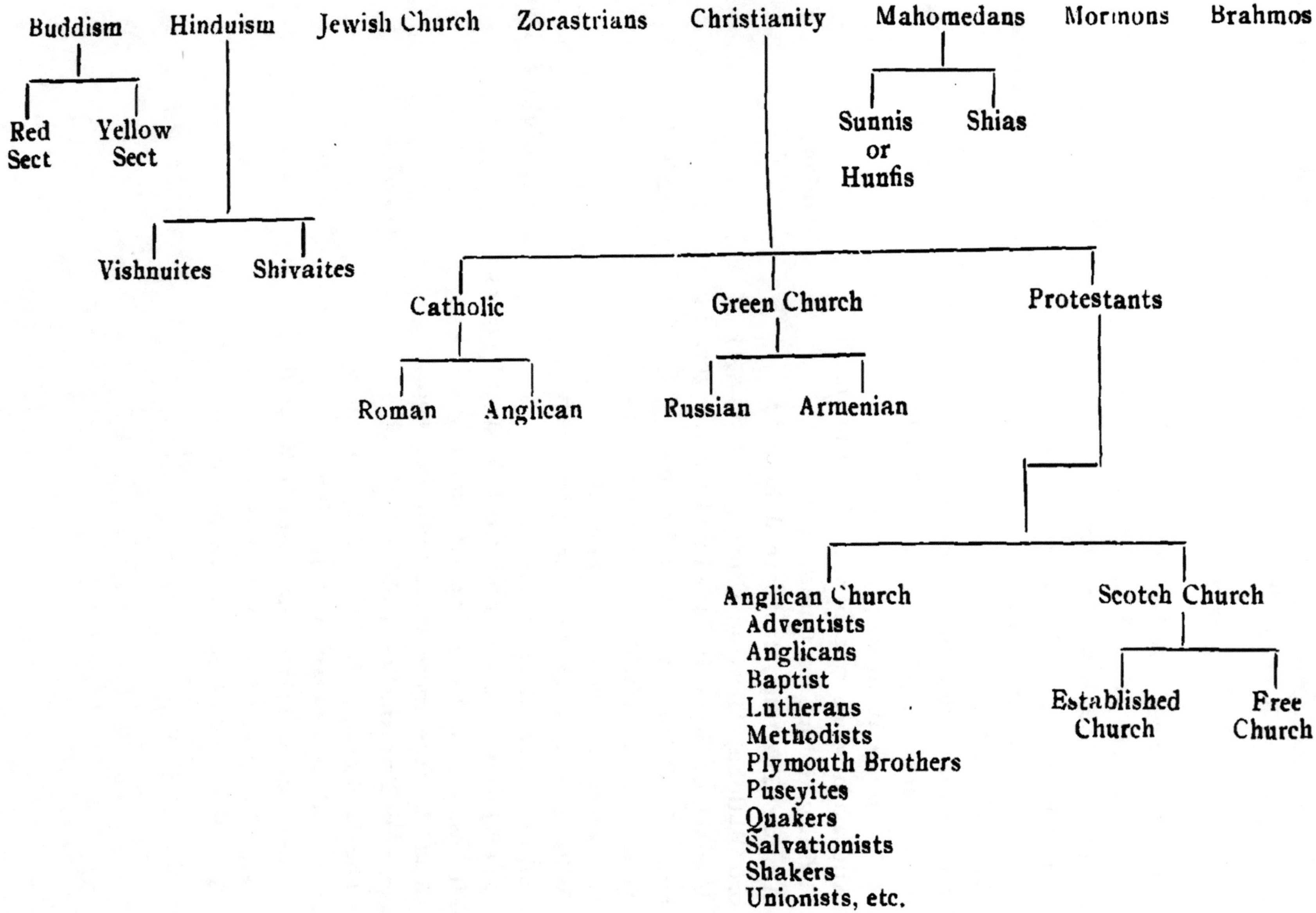

THE WORLD'S GREAT NEED.

"So many gods, so many creeds,
So many paths that wind and wind,
While just the art of being kind,
Is all the sad world needs."

"Above the chants of priests, above
The blatant voice of braying doubt,
He hears the still, small voice of Love,
Which sends its simple message out.

And clearer, sweeter, day by day,
Its mandate echoes from the skies,
"Go roll the stone of self away,
And let the *Christ* within thee rise."

APPENDIX II. A.

On Buddism.*

Its Systems & Philosophy.

(Being the latest views on the Subject).

Our knowledge of Buddism was until very recently mostly derived from what is known as the Pali Canons (the language of the Hina-yana or southern system of Buddism), and from the writings of Buddist philosophers and scholars in Pali.

This school of Buddism seems to deny immortality to the soul, the existence of an Absolute Cause (God) ; and also the existence of a reincarnating Ego. It teaches that the ultimate goal of man's higher aspirations is extinction or Nirvana. What Nirvana is according to this system is hard, indeed, to understand ; but in the teachings we must distinguish between an ethical Nirvana and a metaphysical one, for it has been noticed that the Budda when interrogated about it either waved the question or gave an ethical reply to a metaphysical query—as when he affirmed that Nirvana meant extinction of 'lust', 'anger', 'clinging to existence', dependance upon 'name and form,' etc. And so metaphysically we should say the Hina-yana teaching absolute extinction in Nirvana, denying the Absolute Cause (God), even considered in an impersonal aspect and admitting Nirvana to be inexpressibly (no other conclusion seems possible) and void of all attributes of form and conceptual qualities no other conclusion is possible.

It emphasises that an ethical life is all that matters, and, in fact, considers metaphysics in so far as it is not nihilistic a hindrance and an evil.

It is one of the great illusions this notion of the soul as immortal, and one of the fetters that must be broken before freedom can be attained.

---

*I am indebted to Dr. H. Holst, M.D., quondam representative of the Buddist Society at Chicago, for this valuable note on the systems and philosophy of Buddism.

The Northern or Maha-yana school of Buddism, which claims to be as original as the Hina-yana, is yet too little known for a correct deduction to be drawn of its tenets. The little, however, that is known goes to shew that its system is far more in harmony with the metaphysics of the Vedanta School of thought in India than is the case of the Hina-yana.

The immortality of the soul (as an offset of the Absolute), the final unity with the Absolute, and the existence for aeons to come of a re-incarnating Ego, is taken for granted. The Goal to be striven after is not extinction but perfection of Budda qualities (Buddisattvahood) and a struggle through aeons of incarnate existence to help others to enlightenment and Buddisattvahood. In this system the Budda instead of being merely a perfect teacher becomes a *norm* of existence, the Absolute, the Tathagatabuta corresponding closely to the neuter Brahman of the Vedanta System, the 'Ding au sich' of Kant.

It has long been held that the Maha-yana System originated at the time of Kanishka, the Indo-Scythian king, who came from the north and ruled in the first and second century of our age. It was he who convoked the great Ecclesiastical Council to determine and settle the doctrines and teachings of that floating and more or less amorphic mass of tradition prevalent in northern India and purporting to be the teachings of Budda. Thus, the fact of the presence of 500 prominent monks at this conference, and the union and agreement among them proves that the teachings and traditions of the Maha-yana System were even then both wide-spread and extensively believed, and, therefore, must have had a long history and accordingly can lay claim to be as early and, as far as tradition goes, as original as the Hina-yana.

That the Maha-yana is old, and possibly as old as the Hina-yana, will appear from the reading of the Asoka Edicts on the Bairât pillar. This king holds the same place in Buddistic 'church'-history as Constantine does in Christian church-history, though it must be admitted that the former towers shoulders above the latter so far as morals and character are concerned.

Asoka favoured the Buddistic teachings and, though in no wise intolerant or iconoclastic, strove to make it the religion of his subjects by moral suasion and arguments of reason alone. To this end he raised pillars and other monuments throughout his kingdom and on these had his edicts engraved in regard to what his people should believe and do, or leave undone.

On the pillar referred to, this king and (wonder of wonders) Hina-yana convert, *orders* 7 canonical works to be memorised and preached by every monk of Buddistic faith. And mark you, five out of these seven were recognised as belonging to the Maha-yana School! This, therefore, clearly indicates that even at this early date the Maha-yana teachings and traditions were accepted as 'true Buddistic'.

Besides spreading the teachings of Budda in India, he sent missionaries into distant lands including among others Egypt, Syria, Epirus and Macedonia. What possible influence their teachings could have had upon the Christian traditions and religion is for future investigators to determine: readers, however, who are interested in this subject are referred to Lillie's—"Buddism in Christendom". See List of Works attached.

Its Rise And Fall.

Buddism appealed to the aborigines* or Turanian Dasyus, and to the mixed races, both of whom fell under the category of *Sudras* (servants) in the iron-bound caste system of Hinduism, as it not only acknowledged the *equality* of all men in the social scale but also afforded immediate deliverance from wearisome bondage of caste observances and the depressing prospects of interminable transmigrations. It thus attracted untold numbers to its fold, and in time and through the efforts of Asoka was established on a basis by which it lasted supreme for nearly a thousand years.

After the defeat of the Rajputs by the Moguls on the banks of the Ghahar in 1193 A.D., these classes went bodily over to Muhamadanism as each of the Hindu kings were subjugated or forced to acknowledge suzerainty of the new ruling race: hence the sudden and yet permanent hold the new religion had over the lower orders as a whole for it offered the same equality to all

*Bhils, Gonds, Khands, Oraons, Hos, Kols, Sonthals, Nagas and other mountain and forest tribes.

and thus freed them from the exactions of the dominant priesthood, as well as a physical heaven, in place of Nirvana (or extinction of the *ego* by its absorption into the Great First Cause), in which *houris* tended to the wants of the thrice-born.

Buddist Fanes.

India owes the introduction of the use of stone for architectural purposes, as she does Buddism as a religion, to the Great Asoka who reigned about B. C. 265 to 228. At this period India of course, had magnificent structures, but these were of wood, like the historic buildings and pagodas of Burma which exist to this day.

For a correct understanding of the architecture of this period it has been found expedient to follow the classification adopted by the majority of writers on the subject.

1st. Stambhas or Lâts.—These pillars were employed by the Buddists to bear inscriptions on their shafts, with emblems of animals on the capitals. The same use, however, was put upon these shafts by the Jains, Vaishnavas, Saivas, etc.

2nd. Stûpas or Tôpes—may be divided thus

(*a*) Stûpas proper, or monuments containing relics of the Budda, or of Buddists saints; and

(*b*) Stûpas or towers erected to commemorate some event, or mark some sacred spot.

In Nepal, unfortunately, these stûpas, though somewhat different in form, are called chaityas, and thus differs from the nomenclature adopted in India. In Ceylon, these are known as Dâgobas and reach immense proportions, such as those in the Ruanweli, Jetawarama and Abhayagiri.

Type examples of these are to be found at Sanchi, Saranath and Bharaut.

3rd. Rails, which are to be found surrounding topes, sacred trees, temples, etc.

4th. Chaityas or Assembly Halls.—This term is usually applied to monuments of a religious nature, but would more correctly be applied if held to designate Stûpas of the second order. In the early periods these were mostly excavated out of rocks as for instance those at Karlê, Ajântâ, etc., in the Bombay Presidency, wherein the monks used to congregate for discussion on ecclesiastical matters and for worship. Probably the most typical example is at Karlê near Lanowly on the Bombay-Poona railway section of the G. I. P. Railway. This chaitya, of the same form as the early Christian Basilika (query : Is the Basilika derived from these?) has a central nave and two aisles ending in an ambulatory behind a small Stûpa or Dâgoba in the apse of the nave, just as in Christian churches and the ambulatory is found behind the altar. The earliest chaityas had no image of the Budda sculptured on them but were surmounted by a *Tee* bearing the holy Triratna. From being used originally as dormitories, in which each monk had a cubicle set apart for his exclusive use, they eventually came to be used as places of worship.

5th. Viharas or Monasteries.—With the Buddist, so with the Jain, the monks met at these halls and walked therein : sometimes they became the centres of monastic establishments, and eventually also came to be used as temples. Like the chaityas, they resemble very closely the corresponding institutions among Christians.

Architecture.

The architecture of these fanes fall under three main divisions —The Chaitya, the Viharas and the Pagoda. Obviously, for the following cogent reasons, we find the first two are purer in style than the last which is *the* pattern in Burma and Mongolian countries, and now closely copied in Nepal.

Up to the year 1204 A.D., that is, before the gates of Behar and Bengal were closed by the Muhamadan conquest of these provinces, the architects of Nepal gave their places of worship the same form as that which obtained in India : thereafter, they were compelled to turn to China, the suzerain power, for inspiration, and so we find the buildings erecter from this period downward take the pagoda-shape.

These Buddist temples are usually found erected on high ground or cliff to the portals of which access is gained after a stiff climb up (the plinth) of as much as 1840 granite steps, as to the Etwehera Dâgoba in Ceylon dedicated to the memory of Melinda the royal apostle of Budda ; and so equal in height and size (but having a much higher order of architecture) the well-known Pyramids of Egypt. Indeed, Fa Hein, the Buddist Beadeker, tells us of stûpas erected by Kanishka at Peshawar more than 470 in height.

The most prominent and distinctive features of these structures lie in a tesselated spire surmounted by a gilt umbrella-shaped cone which springs from a square base (the sides of which are ornated with a pair of large eyes which for a thousand years and more have gazed on the void) which in turn rests on a semicircular dome projecting high above a square structure in which are located the nave, aisles, etc.; and all stand on a massive plinth.

Worship.

If we enter the fane at Ghum with the surging crowd, we shall at least return impressed with the deep abiding faith so strongly portrayed on the faces of the devotees—a no mean lesson when it comes to the performance of our own devotions.

At the entrance to this fane will be seen a familiar figure—a blind beggar—fiddling his lays supported by his wife on a base-fiddle. The great crowd ever surges on ; a crowd of monks, little children, while-haired old men, wrinkled old women like skeletons at a feast whose physiognomy is accentuated by pretty young women dressed in gala garb : the aged with slow of step, the young impetuous : all their faces stamped with either sadness and the weariness of life, or faces of laughter and love-lit eyes, each according to his disposition : voices mumbling the never-ending litany of sorrow—Aneitsa, Dhooka, Ananta—Change, Sorrow, Unreality. All pass under the shade of the painted arch to do obeisance to the raised image of the Budda within.

Here come all to pause and kneel on the spread carpets in rear of the earlier worshipers ; the men in front the women behind. Beyond the heads bowed in prayer a long trough of flowers is seen, then paper pennons above, then rows of flickering lights, and last of all, and seated high up but shrouded in tremulous gloom, is the figure of the Budda.

They come and go, passing right across the scene: some rise to leave while others bend to pray: each unconscious of the rest plays his part in the moving drama. Near at hand, see that woman with a tray of flowers, which she holds up toward the sacred image as she kneels; while her child, a mere infant hardly able to stand, clutches at her arm and throws its quota of white petals as her share of the fervid offering; the two making a picture of artless devotion as no country in the world can rival.

Flowers form one of the chief features in the Buddistic ritual, as also of most religions, while the faint tinkle of bells is heard in the deep recess of the cloisters, which instinctively carries the mind like a flash over the 6,000 miles that separate these monasteries in Himalayan heights and those summons to service floating over the meadows in England—a touch of nature which makes the whole world kin.

"Ave Maria, Blessed be the hour,
The time, the clime, the spot where I so oft
Have felt that moment in its fullest power
Sink o'er the earth so beautiful and soft,
While swung the deep bell in the distant tower,
Of the faint dying day hymn stole aloft,
And not a breath crept through the rosy air,
And yet the forest leaves seem'd stirr'd with prayer."

Hina-yana Texts In English.

Dhammapada in Sacred Books of the East Series. Oxford University Press.

Jataka Stories. Cowell. Cambridge University Press. 6 Vol.

Buddist Suttas do. do. do. do.

Questions of King Melinda do. do. do.

Warren: Buddism in Translation. Harvard Oriental Series.

Rhys Davids: Dialogues of the Budda. Oxford University Press.

Rhys Davids, Caroline: Dhamma-Sangani (B. Psychology) R. A. Society Publication.

Silacara. The first 50 Discourses from the Majjhima Nikaya. Luzac, London.

Rhys Davids, edited by: Sacred Books Of The Buddists. Ditto in German.

Neumann. Munchen 1907. Full Translation of the Majjhima Nikaya.

Bhikkhu Nanatiloka. Breslau 1911. The Augutara Nikaya.
Mahayana Texts In English.

Sadharma Pundarika (Lotus of the Law) Sacred Books of the East. Oxford University Press.

Mahayana Text (Budda Karita, etc.) Oxford University Press.

Lalitavistara by Mitra, Calcutta 1881.

Acvagasha. Faith in the Mahayana. Eng. Tr. Suzuki. Court Pbl. Co., Chicago.

Arya Sura. Gataka Mala. Oxf. Univ. Press.

Richard, T; D. D. The New Testament of Higher Buddism. T. & T. Clark, London.

General Works on Buddism.

Oldenberg. Budda His Life & Order. London.

Rhys Davids. Buddism. Society for Promoting Christian Knowledge London.

Hopkins. Religions of India. Boston 1908.

Kern. A Manual Of Indian Buddism. London.

Beal, S. Buddism In China. Society for P. C. Knowledge, London.

Starr. Korean Buddism. Boston 1918.

Reischauer. Studies In Japanese Buddism. New York, 1817.

Waddell, Buddism In Tibet. London 1895.

Suzuki. Outlines Of Maha-yana. Luzac. Lond.

Lillie, A. The Popular Life Of Budda. Trübner. London.

Lillie, A. Buddism In Christianity. Trübner. London.

Narasu. The Essence Of Buddism. Madras 1907.

Wilson, H. Vishnu Purana. Trübner. London.

Sastri. Bhagavad Gita with Sankara's Comment. Mysore 1901.

Ballantyne. Samkhya-Aphorisms. Trübner. London.

Avalon. Mahanirvana Tantra (Shakta Work) Luzac, London.

Sacred Books of the Hindus. Panini Office, Allahabad.

General Works.

Barth. Religions of India. Trübner, London.

Max Muller. Six Systems of Indian Philosophy. Longmans & Green London.

Deussen. System of the Vedanta. Luzac, London.

Deussen. Philosophy of the Upanishads. T. & T. Clark, London.

Vivekananda, Works of, 5 Vol. Adwaita-Ashrama. Mayavati. Almora. India.

Oman. Brahmins, Theists, and Muslims of India. Fisher-Unwin, London.

Oman. Mystics, Ascetics and Saints of India. Fisher-Unwin, London.

Oman. Cults, Customs and Superstitions of India. Fisher-Unwin, London.

Bhattacharrya. Hindu Castes and Sects. Thacker Spink & Co., Calcutta.

Warren. Jainism. Thompson Co., 33 Popham's Broadway, Madras.

Wilson, H. H. Essays on the Religion of the Hindus. Trübner, Lon.

Fergusson. Eastern Architecture. Murray, London.

Note : For a short synopsis of the best in these different religious, the "Wisdom of the East" series may be consulted. Murray, London; for the literature of India—Fraser's History of Literature in India (Unwin, London).

APPENDIX III.

On Hinduism.

This appendix is inserted for the benefit of tourists in general, and for those Americans in particular who have "embraced' the tenets of Hinduism, a religion which claims among its adherents just a fourth of the population of the world; and also for those who, though they have hitherto not taken the trouble to investigate the doctrines of this religion, are now disposed to do so.

On Effigies.

Reader, let us ask ourselves honestly—Can we even *subjectively* have any conception of what a Spirit is, much less what The Great I Am is? If not, and it cannot be otherwise, we are compelled to fall back upon one or other forms of worship:—To accept and believe that He is Omniscient and Omnipresent and approach Him 'in the spirit and the truth'; or to make unto ourselves an *objective* expression of His attributes, which has to be resorted to by about one-eighth of the population of the world, who in this manner alone can be helped to form some idea of the Godhead. Hence, the many grotesque images which we see daily around us. But all the same, ignorant as these worshippers may be, each and all will say that they do not bow down to these effigies made of hands, but to the manifestation that these images represent.

And now ask yourself with all candour:—What about the crucifix placed on the altars of the High (Anglican) Churches, and in all Roman Catholic Churches, to which the knee is bent during the repeating of the Creed? Is it not an image; and is it in keeping with the injunctions—"Thou shall not make unto thyself any graven image &c. Thou shalt not bow down to them &c?"

The East has conceived for itself the idea of God pervading

everything, and so we find HIM manifested in the Three Kingdoms of Nature, as given below.

HINDUISM.

		Symbolised by,	Manifestation.
1.	Brahma (Saraswati*) The Creator.	*The Earth.	Universal manifested existence of 'The Simple Infinite Being'.
2.	Vishnu, or Narayana (Lukshmi* or Radha* one who gives riches, and Tulsi) The Preserver.	*Water (one who lives in).	Ditto, when manifested on earth.
3.	Siva† (Parbati*), Mahadeo (Durga*) The Destroyer.	*Fire (one who causes desolation and lamentation).	When it again dissolves itself into 'The Simple Infinite Being'.

ROMAN.

Jupiter (Juno‡ the goddess of wealth)
The Creator.

Neptune (who lives in the sea and carries a trident)
The Preserver.

Pluto (Proserpine) whose abode is Hades.
The Destroyer.

The Hindus worship the above three attributes of the Godhead separately, and also in one as a trinity, which has one body, that of a man, with three heads, which their pundits, or priests, explain as follows—These three are one, Siva is the heart of Vishnu, and Vishnu the heart of Brahma: it is one lamp with three wicks.

In some of the churches in London, the chancel and the altar are railed in from floor to ceiling, thus forming a 'holy of holies' to which access is obtained through iron doors, and then only after felt slippers are donned ; and notably at Willesden Green where life-size figures of The Christ and his two loved apostles hang from this iron barricade. Therefore, be thou, reader, candid ; slow to draw the mote out of thy brother's eye ;

*The names within brackets are the wives of the Trinity.

†Siva's emblem of fructifying virility is the *Linga* : while *sakti* is the emblem of Siva's female complement.

‡The goddess, to manifest the reproductive power in nature, thereby bringing about and completing the Trinity.

and refrain from applying epithets to him which apply all the more to you in that while he is but *conforming* to the tenets of *his* religion *you are deliberately breaking those enjoined by yours.*

Brahma is the creator of all things, the dispenser of all favours, the disposer of the destiny of man (*Cf.* "Those whom I have predestinated"). Vishnu is the redeemer and preserver of all things, Siva, the destroyer, dissolves all things back into the 'Simple Infinite Being'. The Earth is the common mother of all things, which by the aid of water brings forth plenteously, that is, the preserver and continuer of life ; but which without warmth would never cause generation. The last when in action alone, destroys. These are the underlying beliefs of India, which has its harvest and water festivals also.

Siva is worshipped under several forms :—Rudra (Roarer) of the Vedas ; Bhima or the Dread One ; he is the Maha-deva or the Great God : his symbol of worship is the Lingan, or male emblem of the organ of reproduction ; his sacred beast, the bull, conveys the same idea : he is represented also as a fair-skinned man, with a symbol of the fertilising Ganges above his head ; in other representations he is depicted seated with a necklace of human skulls, a scarf of two serpents entwined, seated on a tiger-skin with a club in his hand at the extremity of which is a human head : he has five faces and four arms. His wife is Devi = the Goddess ; appears in her Brahmanical aspect as Uma = Light, a gentle goddess ; as Durga, a light creamy coloured woman, she is depicted as beautiful but austere riding on a tiger, and in her non-Aryan character as Kali, a black fury, of hideous countenance, dripping with blood, crowned with snakes and hung about with skulls.

How to Distinguish Hindu Gods.

Brahma, who was born of a water-lily, rides on a swan ; Vishnu, which has four arms, rides on an eagle (like Jupiter) called the *guruda* ; Siva rides on a bull, and carries a trident or trisula in his hand. Rama and Krishna are other incarnations of Vishnu, while Siva is represented also by the Lingan = the

Baelpoer or Belphogor of the Moabites = Priapus of the Romans = the Phallus of the Egyptian = the Reproductive forces of nature, the generative source of all living things.

The devotees of Vishnu dress in a shrimp-pink *choga,* on their foreheads they wear the three lines which converge to the base of the nose, the central line being red while the lateral ones are white: when travelling they carry a brass gong and a conch shell.

There are 13 Sivaite sects, each representing some special characteristic of this deity. Of these the three chief sects are given, as the remainder follow rather reprehensible practices:—The *Smarta* Brahmans, who are the disciples of Sankara, still lead a plain monastic life of great piety in Southern India; the *Dandis,* or ascetics, who bury their dead or consign the body to the first sacred stream; the *Aghoris,* who while subjecting the body to much mortification indulge in such ghoulish rites as the eating of carrion, etc.

The lesser gods are—Ganesh, the son of Siva, who is represented with a man's body and an elephant's head. As he is the god of all obstacles, he is accordingly propitiated first at all ceremonies. The next is Indra who carries the lightning and a knife in his hands. Then comes Jagannath or Krishna, a god with a most indistinct human torso, armless and without legs, who is the lord of the universe. Annually he is taken out on a car from temples, especially at Puri* where he is specially venerated: indeed, so much so, that almost any European, if he be prepared to remove his shoes may enter an ordinary temple to view the contained deities, yet Lord Curzon it is alleged was flately refused even a sight of this god when visiting Puri.

---

*This temple was erected by the followers of Budda: See under "Buddist Monasteries", para 2 page 79.

Gods of Second Rank.

Gods	Seated on	Weapon Carried	Colour of Garment Worn	REMARKS
Agni	Ram	Sakt†	Voilet	†Like the Greek gods each has a weapon, also a particular animal sacred to it. The names of these weapons cannot be translated into English as each has a particular shape of its own, and in no way resembles any European weapon.
Indra	Elephant	Vajra	Red	
Yama	Buffalo	Danda	Orange	
Neiruta	Man	Kunta	Dark Yellow	
Varuna	Crocodile	Pasa	White	
Vayu	Antelope	Dwaja	Blue	
Kubera	Horse	Khadja	Pink	
Isana	Bull	Trisula	Gray	

Manifestation in Nature.

Hindus.

Animate World

Hunuman (Monkey-God)

Bull (worshipped by Shaivites)

Reptiles

Cobra

Birds

Guruda

Trees

Fig (the female) } Manifestations
Pipul (the male) } of Vishnu.

Inanimate World

The Salagrama Stone, a metamorphosis of Vishnu. It is ornamented with tree-like markings.

Egyptians.

Animate World

The Sphinx.

Bull (worshipped in Rome also)

Reptiles

Crocodile

Birds

Ibis

Trees

Nil.

Inanimate World

Nil.

Hinduism.

English translations of the Sacred Texts are to be found in the Sacred Books of the East, including the Rig Veda, Atharva Veda, Upanishads, Vedanta-Sutras with commentaries of Sankara and Ramanuja, The Bhagavad Gita, and the law books.

Religions of India.

1. **Jains** ...
   - Swetambara
   - Digambara
2. **Buddism** ...
   - Hina-yana
   - Maha-yana
     - Tibetan
       - Red Sect.
       - Yellow Sect.
       - Black Sect.
     - Japanese
       - Tendai.
       - Shingon.
       - Jodo.
       - Nichiren.
       - Zen.
     - Chinese—Fo, intermixed with Taoism.
3. **Hinduism** ...
   - Vaishnavas
     - Ramanujas.
     - Ramanands.
     - Kabir-Panthis.
     - Rai Dasis.
     - Vallabhacharis.
     - Madhwacharis.
     - Chaitanyas.
     - Rhada Valabhis.
     - Nimavats.
     - Mike Bais.
     - Ascetics.
   - Saivas
     - Northern
       - Lay.
       - Ascetics.
     - Southern
       - Smartas.
       - Lingayats.
       - Ascetics.
   - Saktas
     - Saiva
       - Dakshina.
       - Vamacharis.
     - Vaishnava
       - Dakshina.
       - Vamacharis.
4. **Brahmoism** ...
   - Sauras
   - Adi-Samaj
   - Brahmo-Samaj
   - Sadaharan-Samaj
   - Arya-Samaj.
5. **Zoroastrians**
6. **Muhamadans**

I am indebted to Dr. H. Holst, M.D., for above details.

APPENDIX IV.

Birch Hill Park.

Copy of a letter No. 2704 dated the 21st. October, 1876* from the Assistant Secretary in the Government of Bengal, Revenue Department, (Land Revenue) to the Secretary to the Board of Revenue, Miscellaneous Revenue Department.

As the Lieutenant Governor desires to acquire the 8 lots of Darjeeling, detailed in the margin, for public purposes, *viz*: partly as sites for *public buildings*, and partly for *purposes of forest conservancy*, I am directed to request that, with the permission of the Member in charge, the local officers may be instructed to submit a draft Declaration for publication in the Calcutta Gazette†.

Name of site.	Area.	Probable price.	Owner.
Birch Hill No. 3	7-3-19		
Birch Hill No. 2	13-2-32		
Birch Hill No. 1	10-0-12		Mr. Lloyd Trustee for
Fern Hill	9-0-24	Rs. 25,000	Dr. Withecombe
Prospect	6-2-27		and
Primrose Hill	5-0-28		Mr. Smith's estate.
Darjeeling Hotel	14-2-37		
Lockinvar	5-3-27		

COURT OF DEPUTY COMMISSIONER OF DARJEELING.
August 1877.

Proceedings under Act X of 1870.

Two declarations were published in the Gazette of the 20th December, 1876 under date of 19th December, to the effect

---

*I am indebted for copies of above documents to W. R. Gourlay, Esq; I.C.S., C.I.E., Private Secretary to His Excellency Lord Carmichael.

†Published in Calcutta Gazette of the 20-12-1876 at pages 1516 and 1517.

that 11 locations within the Darjeeling Municipality were required for public purposes, viz.

> Sunny Slope, Rose Mary Bank, Strawberry Bank, Birch Hill No. I, Birch Hill No. II, Birch Hill No. III, Fern Hill, Prospect Hill, Sunny Hill, Darjeeling Hotel, and Lockinvar Hill.

All the above locations forming part of what is known as the Trust for the family or children of Samuel Smith represented by the Official Trustee of Bengal.

By a letter dated 5th May, 1877 the official Trustee expressed his willingness to accept a sum of Rs. 30,000/- in full payment of all compensation under all sections and clauses of the Act.

On the 16th July, notices under section 9 of the Act were issued to the said Official Trustee and to Mr. William Lloyd husband to one of the children of Samuel Smith interested in the above Trust. Notices were also posted on the lands calling on all persons interested in the land to appear personally or by Agent on the 1st August to state the amount of their interests and claims.

On this date Mr. William Lloyd who holds a power of attorney from the Official Trustee appeared before me. It appears from his statements that there are no conflicting claims among the parties interested in the Trust; and that the official Trustee acts in all matters on behalf of the children of Samuel Smith. I consider therefore that the award under Section 14 can be legally made. Mr. Lloyd as representative of one of those interested has expressed personally his willingness to agree to the terms accepted by the Official Trustee in his letter of the 5th May.

The amount awarded as market value of the lands under Section 24 is Rs. 26,088/- to which will be added Rs. 3,912/- being 15 per cent. on that amount payable under Section 42 of Act X.

I hereby award the above sum of Rs. 26,088/- on account of the full value of the land described in the notification of the

19th December to the Official Trustee of Bengal on behalf of the Smith's Family Trust.

The total sum of Rs. 30,000/- will be payable to the Official Trustee in Calcutta and will be remitted to him there, on his sending to me the leases and other deeds relating to the Locations referred to in the present award.

(Sd.) J. WARE EDGAR,
Deputy Commissioner.

APPENDIX V.

The Questing Spirit.

In 1883, Kabru (24,015′) had to acknowledge defeat at the hands of Mr. W. W. Graham.

Everest—'Joma Kang Kar,'—or 'Our Lady Of The Snows'—situated about 70 miles within the frontiers of a "forbidden State" (Nepal), and which hitherto has been regarded as beyond the purview of explorers, is now, thanks to the successful negotiations of Mr. C. A. Bell, Political Officer, Sikkim, to be attempted through Tibet. Its towering, snowy dome is an object of veneration and reverence over a vast area, and the visit of white men may cause trouble; indeed, the fate of a part of the late Mr. A. F. Mummery's party near the foot of Nanga Parbat should be kept well to the fore, for they disappeared totally, and though it may be convenient to say that an avalanche caused the disaster, those who know the skill and foresight of the greatest of British mountaineers resent the suggestion.

Kinchenjunga has yielded up some of its secrets to Mr. Freshfield, who succeeded in making a complete contour of this mountain after essaying passes at altitudes varying from 22,000 to 23,000 feet.

The next highest known peak is 'K2' which, having steep slopes and over-hanging precipices, will never succumb to assault by man. In 1909, the Duke of the Abruzzi scaled one of its peaks (24,600′) since known as Mount Godwin-Austen. This intrepid mountaineer reached a height of 25,600′ without quite reaching the summit of Mount Brido.

If the experience of these climbers, and that of Mrs. Fanny Bullock Workman, F.R.S.G.S., M.R.A.S., &c., who was compelled to relinquish her attempt in the Karakoram range, Kashmere, after reaching 23,260′ only (where owing to the extreme cold the thermometer registered *minus* 40° Fahrenheit

---

*This Appendix was written before the attempt to conquer Everest was made in 1921.

and the rarefied atmosphere both her husband and the Swiss guide were compelled to halt at the 23,000′ level) are any criterion then it may safely be asserted in regard to Everest—'Thus far and no further', for "The saints alone around his throne, May walk the heights of God"*

Should Everest succumb, what great things will there be left for man to accomplish?

The North and South Poles have been visited. The maps of all countries bear witness to the work of explorers. No notable stretch of land remains that has not been surveyed. This is not only a depressing idea, but also an incorrect one. If the Map of the World will be carefully examined it will be found that about two-thirds of its surface has not been trodden by man. These areas, as well as the vast ocean-beds, invite exploration. The floor of the seven seas are still virgin territory.

Man who has mastered the clouds has not been able to plunge lower than 300 feet below the surface of the sea, lest the cockle-shell crunch in. And staring us in the face are depths of 12,000 feet!

There are, too, great pits bearing the same relation to the average level as mountains do to the surface of the exposed land. There is the Kei Trench in the Malay Sea, 21,342 feet deep. In the Indian Ocean the Sunda Trench has a depth of 22,968. And in the Pacific, there is an enormous depression where Mount Everest itself could be submerged nearly 3,000 feet below the surface.

Our only means of probing blindly into these great depths is an apparatus consisting of a leaden weight and a bit of tubing. Deep-sea sounding is carried on to-day by means of a lead weighing 70 lbs. attached to steel piano wire one-thirtieth of an inch in diameter. Affixed to the lead is a tube which, when the bottom is reached, gathers a specimen of the ground on which it rests. Our knowledge of these beds is due to the labours of such men as the Prince of Monaco, and Professor

---

*In the second attempt led by Genl. Bruce, two members of the party succeeded with the aid of oxygen in attaining the record height of 27,300 feet.

Alexander Agassiz. Beyond the facts recorded by these explorers we have little to go upon.

But there are some conjectures which have the force of facts. It is certain, for instance, that ships sunk over the great depths can never reach the bottom. There must come a strata where the terrific compression holds them in crushed, eternal stillness. It is also certain that there must be a depth below which no form of life can exist. And it is reasonable to suppose that at lesser depths than these there are forms of life which could not live to reach the surface if they were brought up, but would perish as the weight of the down-bearing water diminished.

Will man ever explore these hidden places? Who can tell? The only certain thing is that he will make the attempt. For when the earth's surface holds no more challenges for him, his eternally questing spirit will drive him to seek the adventures which wait in the deep waters.

INDEX